COMMUNITY ORGANIZATIONS

YALE STUDIES ON NONPROFIT ORGANIZATIONS

Program on Non-Profit Organizations
Institution for Social and Policy Studies
Yale University

JOHN G. SIMON, CHAIRMAN
PAUL DiMAGGIO, DIRECTOR

PAUL DiMAGGIO
Nonprofit Organizations in the Arts: Studies in Mission and Constraint

DANIEL C. LEVY
Private Education: Studies in Choice and Public Policy

SUSAN ROSE-ACKERMAN
The Economics of Nonprofit Institutions: Studies in Structure and Policy

Other titles to be announced

Community Organizations

Studies in Resource Mobilization and Exchange

Edited by
CARL MILOFSKY

New York · Oxford
OXFORD UNIVERSITY PRESS
1988

Oxford University Press

Oxford   New York   Toronto
Delhi   Bombay   Calcutta   Madras   Karachi
Petaling Jaya   Singapore   Hong Kong   Tokyo
Nairobi   Dar es Salaam   Cape Town
Melbourne   Auckland

and associated companies in
Berlin   Ibadan

Copyright © 1988 by Yale University

Published by Oxford University Press, Inc.,
200 Madison Avenue, New York, New York 10016

Oxford is a registered trademark of Oxford University Press

Library of Congress Cataloging-in-Publication Data

Community organizations.

(Yale studies on nonprofit organizations)
Includes bibliographies and index.
1. Voluntarism—United States.   2. Community
organization—United States.   3. Corporations, Nonprofit—
United States.   I. Milofsky, Carl.   II. Series.
HN90.V64C645   1988   307'.06   87-18499
ISBN 0-19-504680-3

10 9 8 7 6 5 4 3 2 1

Printed in the United States of America
on acid-free paper

Series Foreword

This volume and its siblings, comprising the Yale Studies on Nonprofit Organizations, were produced by an interdisciplinary research enterprise, the Program on Non-Profit Organizations, located within Yale University's Institution for Social and Policy Studies.* The Program had its origins in a series of discussions initiated by the present author in the mid-1970s while serving as President of Yale—discussions that began with a number of Yale colleagues, especially Professor Charles E. Lindblom, Director of the Institution, and Professor John G. Simon of the Law School faculty. We later enlisted a number of other helpful counselors in and out of academic life.

These conversations reflected widespread agreement that there was a serious, and somewhat surprising, gap in American scholarship. The United States relies more heavily than any other country on the voluntary nonprofit sector to conduct that nation's social, cultural, and economic business—to bring us into the world, to educate and entertain us, even to bury us. Indeed, the United States can be distinguished from all other societies by virtue of the work load it assigns to its "third sector," as compared to business firms or government agencies. Yet this nonprofit universe had been the least well studied, the least well understood aspect of our national life. And the nonprofit institutions themselves were lacking any connective theory of their governance and function. As just one result, public and private bodies were forced to make policy and management decisions, large and small, affecting the nonprofit sector from a position of relative ignorance.

To redress this startling imbalance, and with the initial assistance of the late John D. Rockefeller III (soon joined by a few foundation donors), the Program on Non-Profit Organizations was launched in 1977. It seeks to achieve three principal goals:

1. To build a substantial body of information, analysis and theory relating to nonprofit organizations.

---

* The sharp-eyed copy editors at Oxford University Press requested that we explain the presence of an intrusive hyphen in the word "Non-Profit" in the Program's title and suggested that the explanation might be of interest to this volume's readers. The explanation is simple: At the Program's inception, it adopted the convention, in wider currency than it is today but even at that time incorrect, of hyphenating the term "Non-Profit." Since then the Program has mended its ways wherever the term "nonprofit" is not used as part of the Program's title. But in the Program's title, for reasons both sentimental and pragmatic, the hyphen remains, as a kind of trademark.

2. To enlist the energies and enthusiasms of the scholarly community in research and teaching related to the world of nonprofit organizations.
3. To assist decision makers, in and out of the voluntary sector, to address major policy and management dilemmas confronting the sector.

Toward the first and second of these goals the Program has employed a range of strategies: research grants to senior and junior scholars at Yale and at 41 other institutions, provision of space and amenities to visiting scholars pursuing their research in the Program's offices, supervision of graduate and professional students working on topics germane to the Program's mission, a summer graduate fellowship program for students from universities around the country.

The Program's participants represent a wide spectrum of academic disciplines—the social sciences, the humanities, law, medicine, and management. Moreover, they have used a variety of research strategies, ranging from theoretical economic modeling to field studies in African villages. These efforts, supported by 50 foundation, corporate, governmental, and individual donors to the Program, have gradually generated a mountain of research on virtually every nonprofit species: for example, day-care centers and private foundations, symphony orchestras and wildlife advocacy groups—and on voluntary institutions in 20 other countries. At this writing the Program has published 100 Working Papers and has sponsored, in whole or in part, research resulting in no fewer than 175 journal articles and book chapters. Thirty-two books have been either published or accepted for publication. Moreover, as the work has progressed and as Program-affiliated scholars (of whom, by now, there have been approximately 150) establish links to one another and to students of the nonprofit sector not associated with the Program, previously isolated researchers are forging themselves into an impressive and lively international network.

The Program has approached the third goal, that of assisting those who confront policy and management dilemmas, in many ways. Researchers have tried to design their projects in a way that would bring these dilemmas to the fore. Program participants have met with literally hundreds of nonprofit organizations, either individually or at conferences, to present and discuss the implications of research being conducted by the Program. Data and analyses have been presented to federal, state, and local legislative and executive branch officials and to journalists from print and electronic media throughout the United States, to assist them in their efforts to learn more about the third sector and the problems it faces.

Crucial to the accomplishment of all three goals is the wide sharing of the Program's intellectual output not only with academicians but also with nonprofit practitioners and policymakers. This dissemination task has been an increasing preoccupation of the Program in recent years. More vigorous promotion of its Working Paper series, cooperation with a variety of non-academic organizations, the publication of a handbook of research on nonprofit organizations, and the establishment of a newsletter (published with increasing regularity for a broad and predominantly nonacademic list of subscribers) have all helped to disseminate the Program's research results.

These efforts, however, needed supplementation. Thus, the Program's Working Papers, although circulated relatively widely, have been for the most part drafts rather than finished papers, produced in a humble format that renders them unsuitable for the relative immortality of library shelves. Moreover, many of the publications resulting from the Program's work have never found their way into Working Paper form. Indeed, the multidisciplinary products of Program-sponsored research have displayed a disconcerting tendency, upon publication, to fly off to separate disciplinary corners of the scholarly globe, unlikely to be reassembled by any but the most dogged, diligent denizens of the most comprehensive of university libraries.

Sensitive to these problems, the Lilly Endowment, Inc., made a generous grant to the Program to enable it to overcome this tendency toward centrifugality. The Yale Studies on Nonprofit Organizations represents a particularly important part of this endeavor. Each book features the work of scholars from several disciplines. Each contains a variety of papers, many unpublished, others available only in small-circulation specialized periodicals, on a theme of general interest to readers in many regions of the nonprofit universe. Most of these papers are products of Program-sponsored research, although each volume contains a few other contributions selected in the interest of thematic consistency and breadth.

The present volume, edited by Carl Milofsky, Associate Professor of Sociology at Bucknell University and a longtime participant in the work of the Program on Non-Profit Organizations, deals with the roles, functions, governance, and nurturance of nonprofit organizations that work on behalf of the welfare of citizens of specific communities. Such organizations, which often exemplify the participatory values of much of the nonprofit sector, are usually small, often fragile, and, as a group, marked by high rates of initiation and closure. Consequently, they present difficult targets for scholarly inquiry; are often overlooked in favor of larger, more established institutions; and have received much less research attention than their role in our society warrants. In assembling the material included in this volume, Professor Milofsky thus renders an important service.

As the reader will already have observed, I do not write the Foreword as a stranger. I am very much a member of the family as someone who was present at the creation of the Program on Non-Profit Organizations and continues to chair its Advisory Committee, and who also serves Oxford as Master of University College. What this extended family is doing to advance knowledge about the third sector is a source of considerable satisfaction. From its birth at a luncheon chat more than a decade ago, the Program on Non-Profit Organizations has occupied an increasingly important role as the leading academic center for research on voluntary institutions both in America and abroad. And, now, the publication by Oxford

University Press of this volume and the other "Yale Studies on Nonprofit Organizations" enlarges the reach of the Yale Program by making its research more widely available within the scholarly community and to the larger world that lies beyond.

Kingman Brewster

Preface

In recent years organizational theory has more and more moved away from the view of organizations as autonomous, highly structured, rational social machines which prevailed in the early days of administrative science. The more we study organizations, the more impressed we are with the unpredictability of events, with the possibilities for subordinates to challenge the authority of their superiors, and with the permeability of organizational boundaries. Indeed, most of the attributes which defined organizations as attractive objects for study thirty years ago today seem like abstractions which only occasionally fit the organizations we see in real life. In response, organizational theory has sought to grapple with loose coupling within organizations, ambiguity in planning, and the dependence of organizations on their environments.

If this is true of large, complex organizations like corporations, government bureaucracies, or educational institutions, the problem is magnified when we turn our attention to community organizations. In this book, we use the term "community organization" loosely. In some chapters we are referring to large institutions like museums, symphony orchestras, or United Ways. In other chapters we are concerned with community self-help organizations that generally are small, voluntaristic, and loosely structured. In all cases, however, these are organizations which prosper by immersing themselves in local community life and acquiring resources by working in close coordination with other, usually more institutionalized organizations. Sometimes they do this by seeking grants from foundations, corporations, or from the government—as Milofsky and Romo describe in their study of funding arenas. Other times they do this by building networks of supporters, perhaps capitalizing upon preexisting social networks among members of the community elite—as in Galaskiewicz and Rauschenbach's study of community elite networks.

Some of the chapters in this book simply describe in detail how particular community organizations work, such as the chapters on the United Way by Deborah Kaplan Polivy and by Susan Rose-Ackerman and a chapter on child care by Susan Rose-Ackerman. Most of the chapters, however, attempt to create new theoretical frameworks by which concepts from the contemporary literature on complex organizations can be applied to community organizations. This is not a simple act of rewriting what has already been articulated for more "important" organizations. In most cases, community organizations present new challenges because—as Milofsky

observes in his paper on the structure of participatory organizations—the
ambiguity people have observed in larger, more formalized organizations
is generally magnified where community organizations are concerned. Perhaps this is why there is so little theory which usefully examines the structural characteristics of these small, informal organizations. Chapters in this
book thus draw upon a variety of theoretical traditions. Hunter and Staggenborg apply theories of community politics to resource mobilization theory. McPherson extends theories of population ecology in the animal world
to the process of membership recruitment. DiMaggio and Powell use interorganizational theory to examine the tendency for organizations within
institutional fields to become more similar over time. Milofsky uses mass
society theory to suggest that there are two broadly defined but sharply
different types of community organizations. Weiss examines the symbolism of politics and considers how that symbolism shapes actual organizational behavior.

Readers will notice that for the most part there is little explicit attention
given to questions about how nonprofit legal status shapes organizations.
How did these grow out of a research center supposedly concerned only
with nonprofit organizations? Most of the research in this volume was
conducted by sociologists. Sociology as a discipline, in contrast to economics, law, and political science, has not viewed nonprofit organizations as a
useful, distinctive category of organizations. Sociologists traditionally would
argue that there is no reason to think that complex organizations will differ from each other because those who control resources may or may not
appropriate excess income over expenses or because organizations are governmental or private. Rather than frontally challenging this skepticism, those
of us working at the Program on Non-Profit Organizations in its early
years chose instead to focus our attention in areas of sociological research
in which there was a de facto concern for nonprofit organizations.

Community studies is the most important area where this is true, so our
research focused on community power or elite studies and on the dynamics
of voluntary associations at the community level. What we shared and
what was unique about our combined effort was that many of us strove
to translate theories directed at larger social entities—communities, elite
networks, markets, or population ecologies—into propositions about the
structural characteristics of specific, community based organizations and
institutions. What emerges from the pages that follow are diverse views of
how issues of resource mobilization and exchange shape organizations.

While all of the authors who contributed to this volume have been participants in the Program on Non-Profit Organizations, the work represented here is not primarily collaborative. Several of the papers are contributions by people who were in residence at Yale. The papers by McPherson,
by Galaskiewicz and Rauschenbach, and by Hunter and Staggenborg were
originally written for a conference on Survey Approaches to Community
Organization Research funded jointly by the Program on Non-Profit Organizations and the American Sociological Association, which was orga-

nized by Carl Milofsky, Paul DiMaggio, and Barbara Heyns. Papers by Milofsky, Milofsky and Romo, and Hunter and Staggenborg do come out of a collaborative research project which was partly stimulated by the PONPO-ASA conference. Together we have analyzed data collected in consultation with the New World Foundation in its national study of community self-help organizations. A description of that study is contained in the Appendix.

Lewisburg, Pennsylvania   C.M.
October 1987

Contents

Contributors   xv

Introduction
Networks, Markets, Culture, and Contracts: Understanding
Community Organizations   3
Carl Milofsky

1. Scarcity and Community: A Resource Allocation Theory of
    Community and Mass Society Organizations   16
    Carl Milofsky

2. A Theory of Voluntary Organization   42
    J. Miller McPherson

3. The Iron Cage Revisited: Institutional Isomorphism and
    Collective Rationality in Organizational Fields   77
    Paul DiMaggio and Walter W. Powell

4. Substance versus Symbol in Administrative Reform:
    The Case of Human Services Coordination   100
    Janet A. Weiss

5. The Corporation-Culture Connection: A Test of
    Interorganizational Theories   119
    Joseph Galaskiewicz and Barbara Rauschenbach

6. United Charities: An Economic Analysis   136
    Susan Rose-Ackerman

7. The United Way: Understanding How It Works Is the
    First Step to Effecting Change   157
    Deborah Kaplan Polivy

8. The Market for Loving-Kindness: Day-Care Centers and the
    Demand for Child Care   170
    Susan Rose-Ackerman

9. Structure and Process in Community Self-Help
Organizations   183
Carl Milofsky

10. The Structure of Funding Arenas for Neighborhood Based
Organizations   217
Carl Milofsky and Frank P. Romo

11. Local Communities and Organized Action   243
Albert Hunter and Suzanne Staggenborg

Appendix
The New World Survey of Community Self-Help
Organizations   277
Carl Milofsky

Index   285

Contributors

Paul DiMaggio is Associate Professor at Yale University in the Institution for Social and Policy Studies, Department of Sociology, and School of Organization and Management and is Executive Director of Yale's Program on Non-Profit Organizations. He has written widely on complex organizations and the sociology of culture.

Joseph Galaskiewicz is Professor of Sociology at the University of Minnesota. He is author of two books: *Exchange Networks and Community Politics* (Sage, 1979) and *Social Organization of an Urban Grants Economy: A Study of Business Philanthropy and Nonprofit Organizations* (Academic, 1985). He is currently working on a third monograph (with Wolfgang Bielefeld) that looks at both nonprofit organization and community institutional responses to funding cutbacks in the early 1980s.

Albert Hunter is Associate Professor of Sociology at Northwestern University. He is author of *Symbolic Communities* (University of Chicago Press, 1974) and of numerous articles on urban communities. He is Chairman of the Community Section of the American Sociological Association and has been editor of the *Urban Affairs Quarterly*.

J. Miller McPherson is Professor of Sociology, University of South Carolina. He has been working in the area of voluntary associations for several years and has published papers in *Science, American Sociological Review, American Journal of Sociology, Social Forces, Sociological Review,* and other journals. He is currently analyzing the results of a National Science Foundation funded study of the organizations of ten communities in the Midwest.

Carl Milofsky is Associate Professor of Sociology at Bucknell University. He is author of *Special Education: A Sociological Study of California Programs* (Praeger, 1976) and is presently completing a second book on special education, and he is author of various articles on special education. While a faculty member in the Institution for Social and Policy Studies, he was a member of the Program on Non-Profit Organizations as well as a member of the Education Study Group.

Deborah Kaplan Polivy is Executive Director of the Jewish Endowment Foundation of the Springfield (Mass.) Jewish Federation. She received her Ph.D. from the Florence Heller School for Advanced Studies in Social Welfare, Brandeis University. She has worked for a community council (funded by a United Way) and for several Jewish Federations. She has taught at Smith College of Social Work, McGill University School of Social Work, and St. Joseph's College (Hartford, Connecticut). She also served as an Associate Research Scientist at Yale University's Program on Non-Profit Organizations, during which time she completed the study reported in this volume.

Walter W. Powell is Associate Professor in the School of Organization and Management and in the Department of Sociology, Yale University. His most recent book is *Getting into Print: The Decision-Making Process in Scholarly Publishing* (University of Chicago Press, 1985). With Lewis Coser and Charles Kadushin he also is author of *Books: The Culture and Commerce of Publishing* (Basic Books, 1982).

Barbara Rauschenbach is a graduate student in the Department of Sociology, University of Minnesota. The title of her dissertation thesis is "Legislation in the States: A Diffusion Perspective." She recently (1985) co-authored an article in *Social Forces,* entitled "The influence of corporate power, social status and market position on corporate interlocks in a regional network."

Frank P. Romo is Assistant Professor of Sociology at the State University of New York at Stony Brook. Recipient of a Ph.D. from Yale University, he has worked extensively in the areas of social networks and nonprofit organizations.

Susan Rose-Ackerman is Professor of Law and Political Economy and Director of the Center for Law and Economic Studies at Columbia University. She is the editor of *The Economics of Nonprofit Institutions: Studies in Structure and Policy,* also in this series, and the author of *Corruption: A Study in Political Economy* (Academic Press, 1978) and of numerous articles on law and economics, public choice, and domestic social and regulatory policy.

Suzanne Staggenborg is Assistant Professor of Sociology at Indiana University. She received her Ph.D. at Northwestern University, and her dissertation research focused on social movement organizations.

Janet A. Weiss is Associate Professor in the Graduate School of Business Administration and the Institute of Public Policy Studies at the University of Michigan. After receiving a Ph.D. in Psychology at Harvard University, she taught at the Yale School of Organization and Management. While at Yale she participated in the Program on Non-Profit Organizations. Since her move to Michigan, her work has focused on the uses of information in making and implementing public policy, on the ways to manage cooperation among levels of government, and on the dynamics of compliance with government regulation.

COMMUNITY ORGANIZATIONS

Introduction

Networks, Markets, Culture, and Contracts
Understanding Community Organizations

CARL MILOFSKY

Efforts to change social life at the local community level tend to be atheoretical. To the extent social theory has been recruited to attack social problems, the targets have been issues that affect whole societies, large formal institutions, or, at the opposite extreme, individuals. What all of these entities share is that they are bounded systems in which definite norms have been established, some sort of stable social structure can be modeled, and, because the system is crystallized, cause/effect statements can be made about processes within the system. Such theory as exists to explain change at the local level is outmoded and not very useful either to professional social workers or to activists who would attack the local social, political, and economic structure to bring about change.

The reasons social theory is not of much use to local practitioners are partly cultural. Alvin Gouldner points out that American activism has a history of anti-intellectualism[1] and this would prevent theory from being applied even if it existed. We also lack powerful ways of thinking about the primary vehicle of change at the local level, community or neighborhood based organizations. These are generally small, loosely structured, voluntaristic, and heavily democratic organizations that identify themselves with a specific geographic area of a city, town, or rural area. They include everything from block clubs, co-ops, ethnic cultural associations, and women's centers to housing rehabilitation groups, free schools, and disabled rights lobbying groups. These groups are hard to study using methodological and analytic techniques of social science developed since World War II because those techniques emphasize quantitative measurement and a conception of society and its units as strong and determinative. In a society made up of such strong units, one can have real social *science*.

Communities and their organizations are hard to study using such approaches because they exist primarily in the minds of people. Each member perceives a different community, as roles, geographic location, cultural background, occupation, and a host of other factors vary.[2] "Community" also is a background factor in the lives of most people. The collectivities that embody community life have only secondary importance in the lives of nearly everyone who participates.[3] Because of this, we have little case study research that treats community organizations as an independent variable. These organizations are critical for explaining other things like democratic pluralism,[4] economic development,[5] or crime rates.[6] But since they are not the focus of attention, information about how they work or what they do is fragmented and not systematically presented.

The papers that make up this book represent several approaches to studying community organizations in new and more systematic ways. Since this is a collection of papers from the research projects of independent scholars, the presentation you will find here is not systematically coherent. However, because all of the authors in this volume worked together at the Program on Non-Profit Organizations, presentations in the various chapters do speak to each other and address similar issues, if in different ways. In this chapter, I shall suggest that the divergence among these chapters arises in part because different dimensions of community life shape local voluntary associations and different dimensions are the focus of each chapter.

Two variables interact to define the character of voluntary associations: the degree to which exchange is rationalized and the extent to which social structure is crystallized. Money or some other universal method for determining value allows exchange to be rationalized. Then people can translate many different kinds of value into a single form and compare the worth of different activities and products. Exchange is less rationalized in a barter system or when people accept what Titmuss calls a "gift relationship,"[7] an altruistic relationship in which one expects only indirect benefits from doing a favor for another.

One can best understand what constitutes a crystallized social system by contrasting one with an *interactive* social system. In interactive systems, a few general norms set boundaries of behavior but most day-to-day action is creative, based on innovation, calculation, political action, or game playing. Individuals respond to the opportunities they confront in a shifting environment whereas the system as a whole is made up of the sum of these creative individual efforts. Examples of such interactive systems are exchange networks and economic markets.

Crystallized systems, in contrast, are composed of role systems, tied together by an explicit and elaborate division of labor. Occupants of roles confront elaborate role expectations that may specify appropriate behavior in some detail or, more commonly, simply identify an array of inappropriate actions. In addition to behavior norms being clearly identified, crystallized systems have extensive machinery for social control that monitor

Table I.1 Types of Voluntary Associations

Open Systems	"Gift" Exchange	Monetary Exchange
Interactive Systems	Networks 1	Markets 2
Crystallized Systems	3 Cultural communities	4 Formal organizations (contractual systems)

Closed Systems

behavior and correct deviance. Examples of crystallized groups are formal organizations, tightly organized local communities, and legal systems.

Interaction of the two variables, media of exchange and the crystallization of structure, generates the four-cell construct shown in Table I.1. This scheme for describing voluntary associations is similar to one offered by Janowitz[8] and Mitchell[9] in their analyses of community organizations. It is useful because there are sharply different styles of analysis in social science associated with each of the cells. This happens because the object of study in each has such different qualities that assumptions made for organizations in one cell do not hold for those in another.

This is especially true as one moves down the diagonal. In the upper left corner, associations are more like aggregations or what social scientists call "open systems." They lack clear boundaries, norms are not consensually held on many issues, and uncertainty about outcomes abounds.[10] In the lower right corner, systems are more like closed systems. They have sharp boundaries and thus can more easily be separated from their environments and discussed as independent, rationally constructed social systems.

Despite these organizational differences, real organizations overlap these typological categories. Some are mixtures of different organizational forms. Others are parts of organizational systems in which different forms are represented. Hierarchical relationships are often between more and less formal organizations. This analytic scheme, thus, is not intended to tell readers that if only one will sort voluntary associations into one of these four boxes, their dynamics will become clear. The distinctions are useful because they correspond to different analytic styles or tools used by observers of community organizations. As organizations become more or less formal and more or less rational about exchange, certain analytic tools become more powerful. This variation is represented in the chapters that follow. Let us consider these different styles of analysis.

NETWORKS

Networks are social matrices tied together by relationships or "ties" that are directional—that is, person A recognizes a relationship with person B but person B *may* not recognize a reciprocal relationship. The content of a tie is almost infinitely varied. Anything that creates a feeling of loyalty, power, subservience, affection, identification, or obligation (there must be dozens more feelings one could add to the list) can generate a tie and, in turn, a system of ties—a network. Each quality generates a separate kind of network—there are friendship networks, job finding networks, status networks, political networks, and so on. Consequently, every person is simultaneously involved in many different networks. Those networks are to different extents made up of reciprocated (or balanced) ties, and to different extents networks defined by different qualities overlap with each other. The more networks are balanced and overlapping, the denser a social structure will be. As a network becomes denser, it becomes more of a crystallized social system.[11]

What makes network analysis useful for studying voluntary associations is that no assumptions are made about the nature or structure of whole social systems. Systems of interaction are built up from the behaviors and choices of individuals, and structures are made up of aggregations of choices.[12] This contrasts with concepts like "community,"[13] "social facts,"[14] or mass movements,[15] phenomena that are fundamentally collective and cannot be reduced to the level of individual action. Networks may be sparsely populated and "weak"[16] or dense, "multiplex" or multileveled[17] and strong.

This mode of analysis works well in urban areas and other areas where one cannot assume much interconnection among those who live in a residential district. Those working in the "urbanism" tradition of Louis Wirth[18] like Claude Fischer have thus used network techniques effectively.[19]

In this volume, network analysis is primarily used to focus on the relationships between organizations and their environments. Where community organizations are concerned, we may not be able to bound an association, thus making clear distinctions between it and its surroundings. McPherson (Chapter 2) deals with this problem by treating communities as comparable to biological ecologies. Community organizations are the organisms, each filling a functional niche and attracting different kinds of members. Some organizations compete with each other for the same members, while others coexist, feeding off different resource bases. Equating members with animal feed overcomes the problem of how an organization can be a meaningful concept if membership is shifting and overlapping with other entities. To McPherson, an organization is less a structure than a functional position in larger system.

Galaskiewicz and Rauschenbach (Chapter 5) treat the cultural and arts organizations they study as part of an exchange system in which corporations and other sources of money support theaters, symphonies, or art museums in return for an intangible but valuable resource, "legitimacy."

This approach is like McPherson's in that particular organizations are subordinate to an encompassing system, the status system of a community. Galaskiewicz and Rauschenbach are following in the tradition of community power studies that treat certain voluntary associations as vehicles by which community elites enhance their personal prestige and compete for power.[20] They add a twist to those studies, however, by arguing that cultural organizations can also be seen as productive firms, manufacturing and selling a product called legitimacy. This suggests that arts organizations probably belong in the second cell of Table I.1 since they are based on a system of rationalized exchange.

For Hunter and Staggenborg (Chapter 11) the aggregation of humanity that makes up a city tends to disorganization, as the proponents of urbanism assert. But the city also contains powerful forces that encourage or generate a community orientation. They suggest that these forces are economic and communal or cultural. These forces may operate in tandem. But in upper middle class neighborhoods, since people often have little interest in the local community, social problems often are solved when people raise money and hire people to attack local problems. In low income communities, money often is not available, but there may be a surplus of labor, time, and energy from local residents. These local resources are supplemented by extracommunity forces—government agencies mainly— that create community institutions by offering money, establishing mandates, or threatening those localities that fail to organize themselves.

Hunter and Staggenborg locate themselves firmly in cell one and ask how it happens that local organizations become more institutionalized and communities more integrated. This happens, they suggest, to the extent that voluntary associations move toward cells two and three. Communities may move preponderantly in one direction or the other, or they may simultaneously generate both money and local cohesion to solve problems. In any case, community development requires network building. Economic development and communal development demand different kinds of networks not available in every kind of community.

MARKETS

Markets are interactive systems in which members make action decisions by calculating the relative costs and benefits of alternatives with reference to some universal system of currency. The most familiar example, of course, is the economic market, but the underlying *organizational* model has been applied by pluralist political scientists to governmental systems as well.[21] For pluralists, influence and favors take the place of money as being the universal medium of exchange that quickens the system.

Economic analysis provides powerful tools for making sense of individual behavior and for explaining the survival, death, and behavior of different kinds of firms in an organizational system. This analysis can be applied as readily to the services community organizations provide as it can to other commodities as Rose-Ackerman demonstrates in her chapters on the United Way and on day-care services. Individuals create community organizations in response to need, and the success and survival of voluntary associations depend on how well they serve the needs of their constituents. This is easiest to demonstrate when organizations provide services that are specific, stable over time, and easy to analyze in terms of costs and prices. However, as Mancur Olson[22] and Russell Hardin[23] have shown, even economically ambiguous examples like the free rider problem can be analyzed using this methodology.

Where voluntary associations are concerned, the greatest gains from the market model may come not from these orthodox applications of economics but rather from efforts to recognize and apply the underlying organizational theory. For example, fundamental to the market is that no single firm is important. A market is healthy only when the whole system is healthy. That requires that individual firms die off or change dramatically when they are no longer productive. It also requires that as demand for products falls off, producers switch to provide new products. The market model suggests that the dynamics of production and competition may be quite different from product to product so the notion that industries are segregated from each other becomes important.

All of these ideas are familiar from Economics 100, but they run directly counter to the reality that prevails in most social service systems, as Weiss shows in Chapter 4, and to the rationale that informs conventional organizational theory. Both of those emphasize that firms should strive to survive at whatever cost, and they suggest that it is reasonable for established firms to attack new, innovative programs. That is intrinsic to the operating principles of the United Way, for example, as Polivy (Chapter 7) indicates.

Romo and I in Chapter 10 suggest that these monopolistic tendencies also work against the welfare of the community. We have redefined "industry." Rather than emphasizing a system of firms producing similar products, we focus on neighborhood based organizations (NBOs) that draw funds from similar sources. Such similar sources we call funding arenas and, we suggest, NBOs are shaped by the demands of these arenas. NBOs shift arenas no more easily than productive firms shift products. However, when an NBO can no longer support itself and dies out, its members may go on to form new organizations that tap other, more accessible funding sources. Where NBOs are concerned, the particular organization is perhaps not very important. What *is* important is that communities, like markets, have the capacity to generate many small organizations that can address many functions and tap many resource pools.[24] Thus, market analysis provides us with useful ways of conceptualizing "organization" as well as with a methodology for analyzing aggregated choices—the latter are the traditional techniques of economics.

CULTURAL COMMUNITIES

By cultural communities I mean geographically based entities in which local social life is bounded and sufficiently intense that strong norms and
traditions are generated. In such places basic tasks of living like finding
employment or housing, tying into a friendship group, and affiliating with
political organizations all involve the same cast of characters so that the
social life is multi-dimensional, characterized by high interdependence and
directed by intrusive social control mechanisms. We have numerous case
studies describing such communities where the mechanisms of organization are strikingly similar, even though communities are very different in
composition, location, historical period, and origins.[25]

Again and again, observers of these communities have emphasized the
importance of voluntary associations as a central means of mobilizing
members for action, addressing conflict-ridden issues, creating local traditions, providing settings for expressive rituals, and generating the substance of local social life. Yet while these associations serve an important
function, particular associations are not in themselves important. Warner
and Lunt spoke of them as "secondary" organizations, distinguishing them
from the "primary" organizations of the family, economy, polity and so
on.[26] Secondary organizations are placed behind other life commitments
when claims are made on one's time and energy. Because commitments are
shallow, people tend to belong to many such associations—at least so the
theory goes[27]—that vary in the inclusiveness of their members, the speci-
ficity of their activities, and the intensity of involvement they call forth.

As I indicate in Chapter 1, the many associations and their overlappng
memberships knit a community together and link it to the outside world.[28]
People from different class, ethnic, and religious backgrounds meet in some
associations just as they are excluded from others. Status distinctions are
blurred when wealthy or highly educated community members are led in
their associations by people who have more humble jobs. Conflicts are
limited or directed towards constructive ends when the associations with
overlapping social networks include influential people who can convince
combatants to channel their hostility into competitive or symbolic activities that support rather than undermine the community.

The symbiotic relationship between voluntary associations and the community as a whole means that in a tightly structured community, participation in associations may not be instrumental or rational in the economic
sense. Being part of an association is a way of being part of the community
or of doing service to the community. One's immediate activities may be
less important than the contribution one makes or one's involvement in
the whole. Consequently, many of the activities of these associations seem
trivial, flat, and ritualistic. One wonders how they can sustain a membership and why people go out of their way to participate. Participation cannot be understood on its own terms, however. It is based on something

like Titmuss' "gift relationship"[29] and is the opposite of Janowitz' "community of limited liability."[30]

Returning to our typology, communities make indistinct what returns one may gain from participation. Thus, they are sharply different from market-oriented or economic organizations that are so heavily based on rational calculation of benefits. They are also different from network organizations, although here the difference is more one of degree than of kind. Communities are network phenomena. They are networks, however, where the complexity of relationships makes ties static, predictable, bounded, and, hence, crystallized. Thus, the individualistic action that characterizes mere aggregations or the market is absent. In communities, action is social and socially meaningful.

FORMAL ORGANIZATIONS

Formal organizations are social systems that are legally constituted to achieve goals. They do not always achieve their goals, but a task orientation rationalizes drawing explicit membership boundaries, articulating a decision-making structure and hierarchy of power, and defining the participants' activities. Most of what we know about organizations has come from research aimed at making them more efficient at carrying out their tasks, making workers coordinate their work more closely, and restructuring organizations to be more effective. A good review of this literature is provided by DiMaggio and Powell in Chapter 3.

Formal organizations combine types two and three in our typology. There are powerful tendencies for organizations to be communal and culture-creating social systems. They can have most of the attributes of tightly structured residential communities: boundaries, multiplex social networks, frequent and intense social interaction, a high level of interdependency among members, and a rich symbolic life. Analysts like Weiss in Chapter 4, Selznick,[31] Sarason,[32] and Merton,[33] along with numerous case study analysts[34] including Polivy in Chapter 7, have demonstrated these qualities. Members become committed not just to their task but to the very idea of the organization so that organizations often reveal a powerful drive to survive,[35] to grow, and to dominate their environment.[36]

While organizations may have these communal features, they are often also market organizations, existing to carry out tasks efficiently. From an economic perspective, organizational culture is irrelevant. If markets are composed of firms competing to provide equivalent products at the lowest price, one does not need to know much about the internal dynamics of firms to understand how the market works. Markets will work best when workers, suppliers, and consumers all respond straightforwardly to price variation. An organizational culture that values survival at all costs may well be economically inefficient, since the market seeks to eliminate or kill off nonproductive units. Market pressure tends to make organizations per-

meable to outside forces and their members responsive to outside constituencies' legal and economic demands.

Our knowledge about these issues in business, government, and some
non-profit organizations is extensive. The situation is quite different for
community organizations, however, as I suggest in Chapter 9. Being voluntaristic, more committed to the process than the product of organizational action, open in their membership policies, and sometimes vague in
their goal orientations, these organizations do not themselves constitute
communal social systems, nor do they fit well the economic conception of
market firms. We need concepts like those DiMaggio and Powell introduce
to explain how administrative cultures are transmitted from organization
to organization other than by contract or market coercion.

MAKING SENSE OF COMMUNITY ORGANIZATIONS

In offering this typology, I do not mean to suggest that these chapters are
fragmented and unrelated. The core problem they all struggle with is how
to study social systems that are fluid, loosely structured, and ever-changing:
As we seek theoretical purchase on questions like where community organizations come from, how they get work done, how they provide political
and economic power, and so on, we see that the theoretical traditions
associated with each cell are in some way inadequate.

Traditional organizational theory is distorted when the units under study
are loosely bounded, concerned more with process than with products,
heavily democratic, and transient. The effort it would take to do a proper
organizational study of a voluntaristic community organization seems foolish
when no member seems very committed to the enterprise at hand, the
organization does not seem to accomplish anything much, and it is difficult
to figure out who the members are. The organization may be vitally important at certain times—when a disaster strikes the community, for example—but the organization itself—the unit of analysis in organizational
theory—is less important than its relationship to the surrounding community. As a consequence, a theory of community groups that treats each
unit as an autonomous social system encourages a sort of administrative
narcissism that clashes with the pragmatic needs of local activists.

Traditional market analysis is distorted in two ways. First, it often is
difficult to model a process of production in community organizations. It
is hard to determine units of value for members in a community arts council, a women's support group, a local business association, or a block watch
association. It is hard to know how people affix values to alternative ways
they might spend their time and what value the activities of local voluntary
associations have. This is partly because people do not think about such
activities in quantitative ways. It is also because costs and benefits are
collectively shared.

The second problem with economic analysis is that it does not explain altruism well. As Hardin and Olson show, economics is not helpless before the challenge of explaining why people make gifts expecting no return.[37] But as Titmuss argues, "economic man" represents a cultural orientation rather than a fundamental human attribute.[38] If people always thought in cost-benefit terms, certain kinds of institutions would collapse. The survival of certain institutions and practices requires that individuals believe they should act for the good of the community because that action is intrinsically valuable—an attitude basic to many community organizations.

While economic analysis has trouble making sense of local voluntary associations, community theories that are well equipped to explain collectivism are equally limited. While there are important examples of highly structured, crystallized communities in the modern urban world, most of us live in a more cosmopolitan, loosely structured world. Communities do not bind us, and therefore we are reluctant to invest time and energy to be with people we do not particularly like, carrying out activities that seem silly. The "community of limited liability,"[39] in which people are jealous about volunteering time unless they see real personal benefits, is real and brings an economic sensibility to local community organizations.

While neither economic nor community theories quite explain where community organizations come from or how they work, it is wrong to say there is no meaningful local community in today's world. Cell 1 suggests that the modern world is simply an aggregation of individuals, loosely tied together by networks that rarely overlap. Community does exist. There is a market for services that local nonprofit organizations provide. Social cohesion provides important benefits, generating the infrastructure that allows low income communities to develop and the framework for mutual aid that allows people to recognize and solve social problems more sensitively and efficiently than any formal government agency could. It *is* important for our society to learn how local cohesion arises, how voluntarism identifies and attacks social problems, and how indigenous resources can be mobilized to promote social betterment. A social theory that assumes atomism misses all of this.

Each of the four theoretical approaches is limited and yet each contributes important insights to understanding local voluntary organizations. The chapters in this volume attempt to capitalize upon those insights and to overcome the limitations. Doing so, we are trying to devise analytic tools that are at once powerful and consistent with the common-sense understanding that local activists have about the work they do.

NOTES

1. Alvin Gouldner, *The Coming Crisis of Western Sociology* (New York: Avon Books, 1971), pp. 4–9.

2. Albert Hunter, "Imprecated Social Organization," Working paper, Center for Urban Affairs and Policy Research, Northwestern University (Evanston, Ill.: Northwestern University, 1986).

3. This has long been recognized by observers of communities. William Lloyd Warner, J. O. Low, Paul S. Lunt, and Leo Srole in *Yankee City* (New Haven: Yale University Press, 1963), p. 118, spoke of community organizations as secondary institutions, distinguished from primary ones, such as the school, the family, or the economy. Allen H. Barton in *Communities in Disaster: A Sociological Analysis of Collective Stress Situations* (Garden City, N.Y.: Doubleday, 1969) operationalized a measure of this secondary status when he studied communities in disaster. In a disaster, individuals often are torn between obligations to families and work and commitments to voluntary associations. The group people choose to support provides a measure of the relative importance of these different associations. When community organizations are the last chosen, as they often are, then disaster relief work suffers. Peter L. Berger and Richard Neuhaus in *To Empower People: The Role of Mediating Structures in Public Policy* (Washington, D.C.: American Enterprise Institute, 1977) take a more upbeat approach. They see these organizations not as unimportant groups but rather as linking institutions, mediating between local and nonlocal primary institutions.

4. See Robert Dahl, *Who Governs?* (New Haven: Yale University Press, 1961) and Edward C. Banfield, *Political Influence* (Glencoe, Ill.: Free Press, 1961).

5. Ken Auletta, *The Underclass* (New York: Vintage, 1983), Morris Janowitz, *The Community Press in an Urban Setting* (Chicago: University of Chicago Press, 1967), and Neil S. Mayer and Jennifer Blake, *Keys to the Growth of Neighborhood Development Organizations* (Washington, D.C.: Urban Institute Press, 1981).

6. Jane Jacobs, *The Death and Life of Great American Cities* (New York: Vintage, 1961), pp. 29–73 and Oscar Newman, *Defensible Space* (New York: Collier, 1973), pp. 78–101.

7. Richard M. Titmuss, *The Gift Relationship: From Human Blood to Social Policy* (New York: Vintage, 1972).

8. Janowitz, in *The Community Press in an Urban Setting*, suggests that there are three organizational dimensions to urban life, the economic, the political or geographic, and the social or neighborhood. These distinctions can also be found in Max Weber, *The City*, trans. Don Martindale and Gertrud Neuwirth (New York: Free Press, 1958) and in T. H. Marshall, "Citizenship and Social Class," in *Class, Citizenship and Social Development* (Chicago: The University of Chicago Press, 1964), pp. 71–134, although these two authors present the ideas as macrosociological concepts rather than as concepts relevant to understanding the social organization of local communities. Each aspect presented by Janowitz fosters a different sort of social organization with different norms of formality, rationality, and so on. The similarity to my framework is his recognition that these different qualities of social organization coexist, overlaying each other, and that they foster sharply different sorts of social organization. I have added a type and recast the independent variables.

9. J. Clyde Mitchell, "The Concept and Use of Social Networks," pp. 1–50 in J. Clyde Mitchell (ed.), *Social Networks in Urban Situations: Analyses of Personal Relationships in Central African Towns* (Manchester: University of Manchester Press, 1969), p. 44.

10. An early but important discussion of differences between closed and open organizational systems is in James D. Thompson, *Organizations in Action* (New York: McGraw-Hill, 1967), pp. 84–93.

11. Mitchell in "The Concept and Use of Social Networks" explains this crystallization process. Elizabeth Bott in *Family and Social Network* (New York: The Free Press, 1957) discusses the distinction between crystallized social networks and open family systems as a major distinction between the family styles of the working and middle classes. Georg Simmel in "The Web of Group Affiliations," trans. Reinhard Bendix, in *Conflict and the Web of Group-Affiliations* (New York: The Free Press, 1955), pp. 125–195, provides one of the most important treatments of this process.

12. Raymond Boudon in *The Logic of Social Action* (London: Routledge and Kegan Paul, 1979) argues the advantages of "methodological individualism" in building up social explanations compared to collectivist theories.

13. "Community" is one of those terms with dozens of definitions. Here I call attention to those who focus on community as a normative and expressive entity into which participants submerge their egos. One thinks of Emile Durkheim's concept of mechanical solidarity,

in *The Division of Labor in Society*, trans. George Simpson (New York: The Free Press, 1933), pp. 70–110. This is expressed with special clarity in studies of utopian communities such as those of Rosabeth Kanter, *Commitment and Community: Communes and Utopias in Sociological Perspective* (Cambridge, Mass.: Harvard University Press, 1972) or Benjamin Zablocki, *The Joyful Community* (Chicago: The University of Chicago Press, 1980).

14. Emile Durkheim, *Suicide*, trans. John A. Spaulding and George Simpson (New York: Free Press, 1951), pp. 309–310.

15. José Ortega y Gasset, *The Revolt of the Masses* (New York: Mentor, 1932).

16. Mark Granovetter, "The Strength of Weak Ties," *American Journal of Sociology* 78:1360–1380 (May 1973).

17. J. Clyde Mitchell, "The Concept and Use of Social Networks," p. 15.

18. Louis Wirth, "Urbanism as a Way of Life," *American Journal of Sociology* 44 (1938), 3–24.

19. Claude S. Fischer, *Networks and Places: Social Relations in the Urban Setting* (New York: Free Press, 1977) and *To Dwell among Friends: Personal Networks in Town and City* (Chicago: The University of Chicago Press, 1982).

20. See, for example, Floyd Hunter, *Community Power Structure* (Garden City, N.Y.: Anchor, 1963) or Edward Laumann and Franz Pappi, *Networks of Collective Action* (New York: Academic Press, 1976).

21. See Banfield, *Political Influence*, pp. 307–323.

22. Mancur Olson, *The Logic of Collective Action* (New York: Schocken Books, 1971).

23. Russell Hardin, *Collective Action* (Baltimore: Johns Hopkins University Press for Resources for the Future, 1982).

24. This idea is developed more fully in Carl Milofsky, "Neighborhood Based Organizations: A Market Analogy" in Walter W. Powell (ed.), *Between Public and Private: The Nonprofit Sector* (New Haven, Conn.: Yale University Press, 1987).

25. See, for example, Patricia Wheeldon, "The Operation of Voluntary Associations and Personal Networks in the Political Processes of an Inter-ethnic Community" in J. Clyde Mitchell (ed.), *Social Networks in Urban Situations*, Benjamin Zablocki, *The Joyful Community*, William Lloyd Warner and Leo Srole, *The Social Systems of American Ethnic Groups* (New Haven: Yale University Press, 1945), and Jennie Keith, *Old People: New Lives* (Chicago: The University of Chicago Press, 1982).

26. Warner et al., *Yankee City*.

27. Pluralist political theory tracing its roots to Alexis de Tocqueville's *Democracy in America*, trans. Philips Bradley (New York: Knopf, 1945), argued that democracy is rooted in the inclination of Americans to belong to many associations. When survey research tools became available, sociologists examined the empirical basis of this proposition and found that relatively few Americans belong to voluntary associations. See H. H. Hyman and C. R. Wright, "Trends in Voluntary Association Memberships of American Adults," *American Sociological Review* 36 (1971), 191–206, and Stephen L. Cutler, "Voluntary Association Membership and the Theory of Mass Society," pp. 133–159 in Edward O. Laumann (ed.), *Bonds of Pluralism: The Forces and Substance of Urban Social Networks* (New York: Wiley Interscience, 1973).

28. In addition to Peter L. Berger and Richard Neuhaus, *To Empower People*, S. N. Eisenstadt, "The Social Conditions of the Development of Voluntary Associations: A Case Study of Israel," *Scripta Hierosolymitana* 3 (1956), 104–124, discusses this issue.

29. Richard Titmuss, *The Gift Relationship*.

30. Morris Janowitz, *The Community Press in an Urban Setting*.

31. Philip Selznick, *Leadership in Administration* (New York: Harper and Row, 1957).

32. Seymour Sarason, *The Culture of the School and the Problem of Change* (Boston: Allyn and Bacon, 1971).

33. Robert K. Merton, *Sociological Ambivalence and Other Essays* (New York: Free Press, 1976).

34. Charles Perrow, *Complex Organizations: A Critical Essay* (Glenview, Ill.: Scott,

Foresman and Company, 1972), pp. 177–204, calls this approach institutional analysis and gives a good overview of this tradition in sociology.

35. A famous case study illustrating this point is David Sills, *The Volunteers: Means and Ends in a National Organization* (Glencoe, Ill.: The Free Press, 1957). He describes the struggle of the March of Dimes to find a new function once polio had been cured.

36. James D. Thompson, in *Organizations in Action*, discusses the need by organizations to reach out and control their environments.

37. Russell Hardin, *Collective Action*, and Mancur Olson, *The Logic of Collective Action*.

38. Richard Titmuss, *The Gift Relationship*.

39. Morris Janowitz, *The Community Press in an Urban Setting*.

1

Scarcity and Community
A Resource Allocation Theory of Community and Mass Society Organizations

CARL MILOFSKY

Mankind's old greatness was created in scarcity.
But what can we expect from plenitude?
Saul Bellow, *Humboldt's Gift*

In the twenty-five years since the Ford Grey Areas Program and the President's Committee on Juvenile Delinquency ushered in an era of citizen participation sponsored and mandated by the federal government, community oriented nonprofit organizations have been granted major responsibility for helping to resolve our urban social problems. Many new organizations have been created. Others, moribund during prior years, have sprung back to life, broadened their activities, and revitalized their organizational missions. Soured by the rapid centralization of social services and of government funding which occurred during the 1950s and 1960s, many cities, counties, and states have begun contracting out responsibility for providing basic social services.

Peculiarly, at the same time that there has been a wholesale adoption of small, local nonprofits as the vehicles for all manner of social programs recent years have seen widespread criticism of and dissatisfaction with community organizations as agents of social change and social action. Because activists and policymakers treat these organizations so harshly, there seems to be little recognition of what changes have occurred, the reasons behind those changes, and the scenario for the future. This chapter offers a revision of conventional wisdom about the role played by community organizations in democratic society. I wish to place the large scale changes which have occurred among community organizations in a broader context.

One of the reasons they are so widely misunderstood has to do with the organizational mechanisms by which people believe that community organizations get things done. They involve the sense of solidarity, mutual support, identification with a locale or a group of people, and warm feelings which we believe accompany "community." We are cynical about the utility of community organizations because there is widespread feeling—and considerable academic research suggesting—that in a modern urban industrial society like the United States there are a variety of forces at work which atomize locality based social groups such as ethnic groups, extended families, and neighborhoods. Further, it is believed that once community is destroyed in a society it is nearly impossible to regenerate it on a large scale. The dominance of self-interest in action, professional career orientations, and political oppression so discourages communal feelings that community organizations are helpless to bring about important social changes or to represent the interests of disenfranchised groups.[1]

I shall argue that while solidarity is an important quality of communities, the growth of community service and action organizations has an origin separate from it. What we have seen in the past four decades is a profound, societywide change in the means by which state resources are distributed to the public through civic organizations. Today, as in the past, community organizations remain essential for the distribution of collective goods to groups and to localities which have never succeeded in accumulating much political capital for themselves.

The conventional argument is that prior to about 1960, public goods were primarily distributed through a system of interlinked, hierarchically organized political and social organizations. Political scientists have talked about these collections of organizations as influence systems presided over by professional politicians who trade in and bank influence.[2] Policy changes are achieved as politicians use their accumulated influence to build coalitions in support of particular proposals. Essentially the same arrangements of community organizations have been described as aggregations of voluntary associations by sociologists[3] and anthropologists doing research on communities.[4] To them these organizations are essential to maintaining social integration and to preserving order within communities.

Since about 1960, few sociologists have analyzed communities and their constituent voluntary associations as central organizational features of society in the way earlier analysts like Warner or Toennies[5] had. The neglect of research on communities in mainline sociology did not happen without precedents, however. For several decades one of the major reasons sociologists studied localities was to show how community and communalism were declining as central processes in modern society.[6] Political sociologists especially focused on the decline of community in an effort to explain the rise of totalitarian political systems in Germany and in the Soviet Union.[7] They argued that communities have become progressively less influential as mechanisms of socialization and political control as the Western world has progressively become a mass society. In a mass society, people are atomized, self-interested, geographically and socially mobile, and strongly influenced in their political views by the mass media. This promotes a volatile, single issue oriented polity in which dogmatism and charismatic political leaders easily hold sway.[8] This contrasts with a more conservative style of politics which holds sway in societies where communities are strong. In the latter, the social controls built into local social life act both as instruments of political control, limiting the extremism of political movements, and as vehicles by which political interests of the people are expressed in a pluralistic, representative system.[9]

One reason sociological interest in communities seems to have died out is that this theory of community decline and of the emergence of mass society is implicitly evolutionary. In its view, once the forces of massification take over, communities are systematically undercut. Once undone, communities are not easily rebuilt, the theory argues. Consequently, one must expect that the period of strong community influence on American life is largely past. Community research may remain a topic of interest to specialists in urban sociology or in social welfare planning, but it has little to contribute to basic sociological theory, the mass society theory suggests.

Following work by Moynihan[10] and Eisenstadt,[11] I shall argue a contrary position in this chapter. During the period when social scientists were describing the disintegration of various communities in the United States, I believe they were documenting a broad scale change in the way that public resources were being distributed in American society. Moynihan argued that for the first time there was a surplus of resources in centers of government and commerce. Eisenstadt suggests that the decline of community reflected the fact that the central distributional problems of society no longer had to do with how local collectivities should distribute scarce resources among members. Rather, questions of equal access to and equal distribution of the surplus of resources and of personal opportunities at the level of the state came to the fore.

The growing importance of the national state and of large bureaucracies and corporations as centers of resource distribution in our society over the past century has indeed brought about profound changes in the mechanisms of political representation and of moral commitment to society. However, in my view this change does not reflect an unraveling of the moral fiber of society and a descent into an impersonal, irresponsible, permanently incorrigible society, as mass society theorists suggest.

When the major distributional problems of society change, as they seem to be doing again with a world economic slowdown and a political climate in which social programs are unpopular, the forces of community decline can also be expected to slow down. As retrenchment and distribution of scarce resources become more and more frequent problems for institutions, governments, and communities in our society, I would suggest that tradition and communalism will become more and more important. This is because these are social mechanisms which are especially effective at managing and legitimating the outcomes of conflicts of interest in which combatants must have continuing relationships with each other.

If it is correct that our society is entering a new age of scarcity, one consequence ought to be that local communities and the variety of voluntary associations which undergird them will reemerge as an important force in American life. However, as the community decline researchers have shown, local organizations are fragile creatures. Communities become meaningful when local residents begin interacting with each other in many different contexts—at work, in schools, at church, in the neighborhood, in politics, and in family gatherings. Relationships in these many contexts are woven together as people create small, voluntaristic organizations which link different institutions. This density of interaction and the variety of little, informal organizations which supports it are hard to create from scratch. It is difficult to interest people in the PTA or a union or a church social club or a block watch when such organizations are not supported by a richer community social life. However, that richer community life depends on a web of social affiliations to pull people in and convince them to identify strongly with the other people who live in their neighborhood. The evolutionary view of the community decline theorists is justified in part by the difficulty of reestablishing social density in a community once it has become unraveled.

These problems of reconstruction are discouraging, however, only if one believes that solidarity, shared values, and adherence to tradition are the main social mechanisms which produce community. Once solidarity is broken and traditions are lost it is hard in a mass society to recapture the consensus which allowed community to happen in the first place, community decline theorists suggest. They imply that these moral virtues are not routinely created but rather that they represent an inheritance from a primordial village society.

I will challenge this discouraging perspective by arguing that one of the main functions community organizations traditionally performed in the old, solidary communities was the management and resolution of conflicts over how scarce collective resources should be distributed. In my view, value consensus is the product of efforts to resolve such local disputes. Communities and the voluntary associations which hold them together have been on the decline over the past three to five decades. This has happened, however, because in a growth economy there are fewer local disputes over how scarce resources should be distributed among permanent community members. Losers can leave and thus, to follow Hirschman's[12] usage, there is less need for voice or loyalty.

Accepting that communities in the traditional mode have been in decline is not to say that over the past several decades there has been no important presence of community organizations. The contrary has been the case. Creation of the War on Poverty and of numerous categorical grants programs has transferred more and more of the formal social service functions of society to small, local nonprofit organizations. Sociologists have done very little systematic research on these organizations, however, because they do not play an important role in our theories of society.

One of the major purposes of this paper is to offer an interpretation of why small social organizations have an important function in American life. From a resource allocation point of view, they are logical descendants of the voluntary associations which earlier sociologists described in their community studies. They have a sharply different organizational form and perform different functions in the communities they serve, however. This is because their main task is to locate resources available in the broader society and attract them to the locality. They rarely are involved in the kinds of local, zero-sum conflicts which give life to voluntary associations in socially dense communities. Rather, they are entrepreneurial and outward looking.

This causes sharp differences in the structure of the community organizations which predominate today compared to those which existed fifty years ago. However, the structural differences between them can largely be accounted for by the different problems of resource location and distribution organizational leaders confront.

The following pages are devoted to making this contrast explicit. The chapter has two major sections. In the first, I shall review the literature on community structure and on mass society from a resource allocation point of view. Since most research projects in these two areas have as their central concern problems of political representation and social order, this review is necessary to show that resource allocation issues have been discussed in some detail in these studies. They have been largely overlooked because the allocation issues have not been considered central. In the second section I shall discuss how some common organizational patterns we find in the two kinds of community organizations—those voluntary associations that occur in socially dense communities and the small social service nonprofits which predominate today—are related to resource allocation issues. From this detailed organizational discussion I hope to make clear the process by which more participatory community organizations might reemerge as an important force in local community life.

THE DISTRIBUTIONAL STRUCTURE OF COMMUNAL LIFE

"Community" and "mass society" are summary terms which, among other things, distinguish between open and closed social systems. Communities are closed when their extensiveness is sharply bounded in some manner—by ethnicity, race, geography, special training or experience, ideology, religion, and so on. While all boundaries are to some extent permeable, our theories treat communities as small, self-contained, and quite self-sufficient. They are whole social systems in which most members either know each other or are likely to interact in many different contexts. Communities are closed in the sense that they can be treated as finite social matrices. Mass systems are so large that, although they are theoretically finite, we lack the technology to analyze them systematically as matrices. As individuals we face cognitive mapping problems trying to find our way around them and we have trouble comprehending the variety and the array of elements within them.

In the mass society theory (which posits their decline) communities help people to find meaning in life and to find value either in activities which are routine or simply in interaction with other members. Communities are value creating entities. They define appropriate behavior as well as the kinds of personal goals people "like us" ought to have. Being somewhat cut off from the outside, the members create a reality that is distinctive to them. That reality gains credence in part because it explains everyday events.[13] It also is supported because people in communities are protected from others who have radically different views so they do not have to confront the fact that their views are parochial. Communities also contain mechanisms of social control which are directed at disruptive behavior, some of which is heretical and some of which involves simple interest conflicts among community members. This social control creates pressure for members to accept the local ideology.[14]

The theory of community emphasizes closedness not because there are objective standards which define what are boundaries in one or another situation. Rather, the theory requires that relationships be stable since for values to be created and maintained claims must be made on members. Open communities do not encourage people to know each other in many different contexts. Rather, an open system encourages them to move spatially when they have new opportunities. Such a system encourages people to have contacts with others who come from different cultural backgrounds and who have had sharply different personal experiences.[15] It also provides ways for people to escape collectivities they find punitive, distasteful, coercive, or restrictive. This makes it hard for people to agree on proper behavior, and it undermines the creation of parochial values. Mobility encourages people to support values which emphasize democracy, universalistic evaluation, and freedom of taste and of choice.[16]

These open society values are sharply different from those that predominate in closed communities, and this is one reason the metaphor of closedness is used. Beyond the fact of contrast is the notion that open societies erode the boundaries of closed ones. Open societies provide opportunities in far-flung locations to people dissatisfied with conditions in a locality. That is a central organizing principle of the market today. Such opportunities are dangerous to the integrity of closed communities.

The richness in the social life of closed communities derives from members' having to tolerate unpleasant things about the people they live with and about the conditions of life within their locality. Participatory—as opposed to productive or output oriented—activities are important because they encourage people to interact even though they may have specific, substantive grievances with each other. That members face limited opportunities is a critical factor in the creation of a stable social hierarchy which members accept as legitimate.

As Weber[17] argues in his essay *The City*, provision of opportunities via economic markets has historically created dissatisfaction with the existing hierarchy and with the system for distributing resources and privileges. Conversely, much of the symbolic complexity in closed communities derives from the need to explain and to come to terms with bad luck or personal disasters in which friends and relations benefit.

We cannot say exactly what boundaries are or what degree of containment is needed for closed communities to form. But theory tells us that if an elaborate symbolic world, strong informal social controls, and multidimensional social relationship hold sway among members of a group, then the group is bounded. One of the main reasons the community decline theory is an evolutionary one is that criteria for measuring boundaries are lacking. We assume that boundaries exist and we outline them when describing particular cases. But we have failed to describe their characteristics in ways which are both inclusive of known cases and meaningful in terms of the theory of value creation and social process.

The evolutionary suggestion is mistaken because it implies that boundaries are real rather than symbolic. It is not important that a group is situated on an island from which its members cannot escape or that it represents an ethnic tradition or a racial combination which others in a society oppress. Rather, it is important that people *feel* that opportunities are restricted, that they have extended periods of living near or interacting with a group of definite membership, that they submit to making personal sacrifices at the demand of the collectivity or of its leaders, and that they come to identify with a tradition and a history which they accept as emblematic or representative of the experience of people "like us."

Physical boundaries, social stigmata, and shared histories are important reasons people develop feelings of community, but they are not the only ones. Symbolism; ritual, multidimensional, or "multiplex"[18] relationships; and subordination of individual tastes, desires, and inclinations to the needs of the collectivity are all product of certain kinds of organizational processes. If people interact in many different contexts together, one would hypothesize, they begin to look for points of communality such as common ethnic background or shared geographic identification.

As Lasker and Strodtbeck[19] show, they also are likely to be aware that aggressive actions toward others—including frank evaluations of their behavior—have consequences in other parts of their social lives. This is less true in an urban, cosmopolitan society where networks are open ended. Lasker and Strodtbeck argue that this lack of feedback is essential if people are to develop universalitic attitudes about how to judge others.

Shifting our focus from boundaries to organizational mechanisms as causes of community, the availability of resources and the way that they are allocated are critical causal factors. Resources are referred to here in a noneconomic sense and include more than commodities. As the Lasker and Strodtbeck study shows, social goods such as friendship, respect, and neighborliness are valued qualities which may be lost and which people take great care to protect.

Especially important resources are opportunities for personal advancement. Imagine that any society and any economy possesses a variety of career tracks which individuals may pursue. Many of these careers are organized around employment. However, there are important other careers in areas such as politics, philanthropy, art, or crime in which people need not be employed to move along a career track. Some careers allow people to accumulate wealth or social status and respect or personal power or all of these. Careers are made up of a series of distinct phases or steps. People progress from one step to the next by accepting or having imposed upon them a position in an organization or a social system which could go to someone else and which changes his or her status within society.[20]

A defining characteristic of open systems is that there are large numbers of alternative positions open to individuals at each stage of their careers. They may have difficulty finding those positions, and choosing a given one at some stage of a career may disqualify a person for other positions later on. Nonetheless, if people are willing to consider a wide enough range of possibilities and if they are good at generating information about positions, most people will have more than one choice.[21]

In a closed community there is a scarcity of choices. This means two things. First, qualified candidates for advancement pile up at choice points. Let us consider this scarcity in the university context. More people with Ph.D.s are graduated each year than there are appropriate jobs for them. As years pass, the surplus is increased because people from past years remain in the job market, increasing the imbalance between opportunities and candidates. A consequence of such bottlenecks is that community members seek orderly ways for others to wait in line which give those in queue support and some assurance that those waiting longest will get special consideration when openings occur.[22]

Postdoctoral fellowships in the social sciences do this by giving recent Ph.D.s a way of appropriately upgrading their credentials while they remain in the job market. A similar process of queuing and waiting occurs when young people in a residential community wait for older people to retire from preferred jobs or when they prepare to take over positions as community spokesmen[23] They are likely to remain in a holding pattern within the community longer than they would were they living in an open community. While career progress may be slow in an open community, people are likely to move from location to location rather than to wait in line.

The second consequence of a scarcity of choices is that even with arrangements which allow people to wait in line there comes a time when some people are passed over for career advancement. At critical points in careers, failures to advance close off later chances for equivalent gains. If failed and successful people must continue to deal with each other, as they must in closed communities, it becomes important to develop mechanisms that manage the hostilities competitors are likely to feel. Participatory rituals, symbolic events, subordination to community elders, and acceptance of values about appropriate behavior and proper expectations all work to control interpersonal rivalries.

Research on small group processes suggests that if people remain together as a group for a long enough time, if they cannot escape a setting, and if they must interact with each other, rituals, norms of etiquette, status relationships, and collective means of controlling conflicts will evolve.[24] On a larger and more complex scale these are the qualities which make for communities. The richness of community social life is a product of continuous interaction and of a collective need to solve problems, like that of conflict between individuals, which threaten to be disruptive to the collectivity. If those people who fail cannot manage to escape they pose a problem for the community. They are likely to be angry with decision makers and with the victors in competition.

This means that it is not so much the closedness of communities which leads to complex, richly symbolic organizational arrangements. Rather, the unwillingness or inability of people who fail in their careers to leave and the necessity of those people who are successful to face those who must suffer as a consequence of their victories demand richness if a social order is to survive.

In closed community systems voluntary associations and community organizations gain their importance by providing opportunities and settings for resident participation. Participation is important for its own sake, regardless of whether or not an organization generates useful, concrete outputs. The community is made up of overlapping and embedded networks of relations. Community organizations provide a framework on which these relationships can be built. They are not important in and of themselves but rather to the extent they are part of a broader social system.

Participation in these organizations is especially valued for its own sake in closed communities because it helps to solve internal allocation problems and to control conflict. As the boundaries which maintain the closedness of communities decay participatory organizations tend to be casualties. This is partly because public interest in them declines. It also is because different issues of equity in allocation of collective resources become important. The result is that as opportunities for participation die out, people become more alienated from the locality because conflicts are not resolved well. Rather than being patient and tolerant, losers and young people eager for opportunities to work are quick to leave. Gradually community declines.

THE DISTRIBUTIONAL STRUCTURE OF MASS SOCIETY

Mass society is an open rather than a closed system. It is so large that the results of action are often unpredictable. The problem of obtaining information about the location of resources, opportunities, services, or products is often greater than the mechanics of a particular task. Granovetter's[25] discussion of the "strength of weak ties," although applied only to the problem of finding a job, describes a general solution to a vast array of social tasks people face.

As a system becomes larger, the probability declines that using the influence of friends to obtain a job—or an apartment or a spouse—will actually help you get one. At some point, it becomes more efficient to invest energy that might have been used to create and to maintain strong friendships or "ties" in which there would be strong loyalty—as in closed communities—in making many shallow acquaintances.

This is because as a system gets larger, impersonal qualities such as credentials become important as signs or signals decision makers such as employers use to evaluate the quality of candidates and to form the basis of a decision which seems to them rational. The records and the public personal history one builds up by going to school, being trained, holding jobs, or publishing qualify one or disqualify one for work independently of personal contacts. Contacts and personal appearance, of course, continue to play a role. But as a system becomes larger the relative causal contribution of impersonal characteristics compared to those related to influence becomes large.

At some tipping point it no longer is strategic to try to get a job by relying on one's sponsors. One is better advised to invest energy in collecting information about openings—what I am calling opportunities. If one can learn of those jobs for which one is qualified, personal qualities such as credentials and experience which require no investment in building relationships will eventually get one a job. If learning about the availability of jobs is the main problem, one is better off having many acquaintances, each of whom may hear gossip about possibilities, than a few close personal friends who, though they might promote one for jobs they know about, are not likely to know about many. The same logic applies to any number of other problems of living in a complex society: finding an apartment, finding dates, finding an abortionist in the old days,[26] finding restaurants,[27] or finding a foundation or a government agency likely to be interested in one's research or one's social service program.[28]

The converse of this information problem is that of how to select among candidates for favors. In an open system it is likely that many qualified individuals will learn of those opportunities that exist. Think of the excess of well qualified applicants to top law schools or the number of interesting papers that must be rejected by top academic journals. Inevitably, there is a certain arbitrariness in the selection processes used for distributing favors.[29] A variety of shorthand methods are produced by those responsible for making decisions.

Commonly, market signals such as reputations or the credentials of applicants[30] are used as ways of selecting among substantively equivalent candidates. Neither of these provides complete information to decision makers, and often they do not tell much about how an applicant for a job, for example, will perform when carrying out the actual functions required. Use of literacy tests to select workers for manual jobs has been attacked legally for producing signals irrelevant to the tasks workers are being selected for.[31] Still, such devices are important to employers and other decision makers who suffer from inadequate information about candidates. Tests, old school ties, and quantitative measures of performance, flawed though they may be, provide rationales for selection that can be defined and that reduce uncertainty for decision makers.

Because there are these problems of information and choice in a mass society, there is persistent pressure for the credentials of applicants and the rules which govern decision making to be standardized. Public and private organizations increasingly are required to follow procedures of due process in making decisions which would deprive people of opportunities or of deserved rewards. Classification decisions in schools and in business organizations are structured so that staff members can avoid accepting responsibility for evaluative decisions. Rather, standardized tests have been used, which are believed to be more legitimate because they are blind to color, personalities, and conflicts. With impersonal record keeping, people can build official biographies and these can be compared with those of other candidates for opportunities in a manner which allows review of the decision making process. It is as though once people have overcome the problem of finding opportunities suited to their credentials the decision making process should be automatic and predictable. In many respects it is.

The mass system rewards an ability to accumulate information and to find opportunities in which the entry requirements match one's biographical qualities. Granovetter's[32] paper suggests that this information gathering is a process of mechanically spreading a net to capture as many acquaintances and as many bits of information as possible. More accurately, creativity, knowledge of the dynamics of a system, and an understanding of its history and a sense of where new opportunities will break are all important. This knowledge guides one's network-building efforts. These characteristics, the skill and the energy to search, make up a quality I shall call entrepreneurship.

Rewarding entrepreneurship and individual effort, the mass system also encourages a commitment to self-interest and to self-indulgence. This atomizes the population. Atomization happens less in societies that are built on overlapping communities. The integration of people at the local level makes it possible for communities to work as effective power blocs. Because leaders can influence and discipline followers, politicians must court them if they are to accumulate sufficient influence to gain office and to push through political decisions. This breaks down in a mass society. As it does, it becomes possible for more and more individuals to accumulate sufficient wealth to make important unilateral political and economic decisions.[33]

The centralization of the state and of the economy also causes institutions and corporations to form larger units. They too become insulated from outside social influences and become more capable of making unilateral decisions based on their internal organization and on the influence of those few people who have accumulated large amounts of economic, social, or political influence.

Finally, the breakdown of community integration removes an important source of opinion formation at the local level. In closed communities leaders interpret events in broader society for residents. Political attitudes, consequently, are conditioned by the stabilizing social forces that operate in local communities.[34] In mass society, the media play this role, and they are the major forces of opinion formation. Since the media include no mechanism for making the public accountable, mass opinion becomes volatile. The public mood is easily controlled by charismatic leaders who are freed of the requirements for accountability built into a community based, or pluralistic, political system.[35]

The distributional structures of closed system communities and of open system mass societies are different from each other. Societal change from a community system of organization to a mass system is discontinuous because the two forms of organization are mutually exclusive. Stability is maintained in closed communities in direct proportion to how effective members are at disciplining peers who act against collective interests or whose personal interests conflict with those of the group. If individuals remain free to act in ways that are destructive to the community or, when their interests are violated, if they are free to leave the community to seek their fortunes elsewhere, many distinctive features of community life dissolve. Participatory aspects, the richness of community rituals and symbolic life, and belief that one cannot live differently than one lives in the community all turn on the collective need to manage deviance and conflicts internally. These are turned toward the creation of values and an ideology.

In the mass system, it is precisely the capacity to escape the encumbrances of strong ties to family, neighbors, and friends which drives the motivations and commitments of individuals. The mass of individuals succeed in their personal careers in proportion to how good they are at locating opportunities they are well suited for *and* opportunities that other people with equal qualifications have not discovered. While individuals in closed communities find opportunities and build careers based on resources and opportunities gathered from within their immediate social system, people in a mass system look outward for these. They prosper because of the uncertainty, complexity, and indeterminateness of their world.

THE DECLINE OF COMMUNITY AND
THE GROWTH OF MASS INSTITUTIONS

When they are juxtaposed, community tends to be eroded by mass society forces. Meanwhile, mass institutions are indifferent to the existence of communities. It is this proposition which makes the theory of community decline and mass society an evolutionary theory. Communities break down in the face of mass pressures and as long as those pressures persist, communities remain difficult to reconstruct. Several reasons are given for this.

As noted previously, one reason community is hard to reconstruct is that conflict and deviance management require that individuals subordinate their dissatisfaction, their discomfort, and their tastes to community values. People do not always make these sacrifices willingly, but they submit in communities because the structure gives them few choices. The collectivity controls distribution of many opportunities, and it has certain coercive powers to bring recalcitrants into line. Once outside opportunities appear and beckon, however, dissidents have alternatives which they may choose rather than accepting discipline. It may be expected in response to necessary community efforts at social control that there will be a steady flow of desertions as people capable of doing so enter the mass entrepreneurial system.

A second reason communities are hard to reconstruct once they decline is that the fabric of cross-cutting relationships and affiliations which makes community life vital only works when the system is complete and complex. When the same people encounter each other in many different settings— at work, at church, in school, on the street, in ethnic gatherings, and at family events—the general experience of participating in community life becomes larger than the particular issues and activities which motivate involvement in the individual institutions or settings. Fraternal conflicts or personal involvements in any of these institutions tend to be subordinated to the requirements of participation in the broader community. When neighborhood life becomes less mulitidimensional, the experience of community is lost. People develop specialized interests and try to avoid local entanglements which might require that they put time into activities they have no special interest in. In Janowitz's[36] terms, people who live in non-communal neighborhoods try to form "communities of limited liability" which allow them to be involved only in those local affairs in which they have a particular interest. Their involvement in any of these local activities is conditioned on their being able to refuse to become involved in irrelevant social events or in political battles in which they have little personal stake.

Communities are hard to reconstruct because it is difficult to overcome the desire of residents to form local relationships which minimize their liability to invest time and energy in community organizations. In fully developed communities the reverse is true. People seek out community organizations and voluntary associations. This is partly because they want to socialize with their neighbors and they are intrinsically interested in community affairs. They also become involved in voluntary organizations, however, because there often arise issues which affect several local institutions simultaneously. The major representatives of particular institutions may not be able to legitimately try to affect the practices of the other major institutions.

Without residents who participate together in many different institutions and without voluntary associations or "secondary organizations"[37] which link the major institutions, issues tend to become sectarian and dominated by the professionals who run those institutions. When ethnic groups compete for ascendancy in a union, conflict between the groups might erupt into open ethnic war if there were no other common local involvements to mediate and channel the conflicts. When competing ethnic groups live close by in a neighborhood, however, hostilities are channeled into such things as soccer leagues, in which different parishes or ethnic social clubs compete; people see each other on the street or in local bars; and children attend the same schools.[38]

These many involvements force the union competitors to see each other as whole, complex human beings rather than as two-dimensional enemies. The voluntary associations allow people to know each other in this more complex way. They also provide a stage on which competition and hostility can be played out. After an intense soccer match is played, some of the hostility of ethnic competition in the union is dissipated and a certain camaraderie between groups grows up. In this way, feelings of community smother the hostilities which create factionalism. However, when there is no full-blown community life to minimize the importance of factional disputes, the mediating voluntary associations which glue the community together tend to seem silly and trivial. It is hard to get people involved in them. Without the associations it is difficult for people to feel community.

A third reason mass society forces erode community is that large, complex organizations which dominate mass society have built-in biases toward growth and decision making independence. Over the past century large for-profit corporations have used their ability to create and to sell to a mass clientele in order to undercut small manufacturing concerns around which communities like those described by Warner and Gouldner[39] were organized.[40] This has not happened in some industries such as steel, where the production process gives primary groups of workers autonomy and power. Thus, as Kornblum[41] shows, work can become the center of local community organization. In most industries, however, economies of scale have made large, centralized productive units more efficient than small town factories and have helped tear away the social fabric which in the past encouraged many in the working class to create closed communities.[42]

Meanwhile, there has been persistent growth, centralization, and elimination of competing forms of service provision among public sector organizations. Warren[43] points out that there exists a small set of governmental or quasi-governmental (e.g., United Ways and so-called community foundations) institutions which make funding and program decisions for their cities within their areas of specialization and dominance. Warren calls these "community decision organizations," or CDOs.

Most CDOs are monopolies and have a guaranteed mandate to function. It is difficult to force CDOs such as the schools, the police, the welfare department, the housing authorities, the hospitals, and the social case work agencies to change practices in response to social needs defined by outsiders or to demands made by their clients. These institutions sometimes directly undercut community life through their standard operating procedures as Gans[44] shows for urban renewal and Valentine[45] and Labov[46] show for schools. Being monopolistic, however, they also interfere with the grass-roots creation of service alternatives. By interfering with local self-help efforts, social service institutions keep people from forming local communities of concern.

The citizen participation programs of the 1960s were partly inspired by a desire to change these monolithic institutions, as the histories of Marris and Rein,[47] Moynihan,[48] and Rose[49] indicate. The small, local nonprofit organizations which were created to challenge existing institutions were soon overwhelmed by the system of established social welfare institutions.

This leads to a fourth reason that it is hard for communities to recover once their structure has decayed and has lost its power to bind and to control members. Community organizations are the key to holding communities together. But in the absence of a well integrated local social system these organizations either die out or become more professional and bureaucratic to allow survival in the mass social welfare institutional system. Adapting to the demands of this system is an organizational necessity. Within highly structured communities voluntary associations are by design insipid, nonintense, and permeable to diverse community influences. However, in an environment in which other organizations aggressively seek out and attempt to control available resources, passive organizations which are not independently wealthy are soon starved out.

Rather than starve, many community organizations have taken on organizational characteristics which allow them to compete better in the mass social system. They narrow the activities they undertake in an effort to claim to be sole providers in some part of the service system. They expand those services for which it is easy to show efficient functioning in hopes of convincing distant resource providers that theirs are well run and accountable programs. Recognizing their survival problems, boards of directors count themselves fortunate to be able to hand control of their organizations to aggressive, entrepreneurial directors who are able to build contacts to new sources of funding and who may radically restructure the organization.[50] The staff members of such organizations, no longer wishing to be confused with lay volunteers, seek recognition by creating specialized professions in hopes that they will be paid in keeping with such status and that recognition of their skills will give them greater autonomy, responsibility, and respect in their world.[51]

All of these changes often make small local nonprofits unsuited to community building because they no longer encourage and reward participation. Their decision making processes no longer are forums in which interpersonal disputes with origins outside the organization are worked out. They no longer are free to shift goals to meet immediate community needs. By giving employees adequate pay and by recognizing their skills, in the recruitment of workers they no longer depend on the capacity of an organization to tie into local influence and network structures. These changes in local nonprofits make them easier to finance and run than voluntary associations. They also solve many organizing problems endemic to participatory organizations. But they also allow people to escape making commitments to their neighbors, to avoid intervening on destructive behavior, and to avoid being strongly controlled by other locals.

THE DECLINE OF MASS SOCIETY

Although these arguments about why communities are fragile in the face of challenges from mass society forces are compelling, it is important to remember that the decline of community as a general phenomenon does not mean that there do not remain many examples of robust, densely organized local communities in the United States. When we speak of the decline of community we are speaking in probabilistic terms and we are talking about the lessening impact of communal styles of local organization on politics and on the social lives of citizens. In this section I shall argue that the institutions of mass society, like those of community, also are fragile when they are confronted with unfriendly social and economic conditions. I shall argue that as the economy slows down, it is likely that the social dynamics which have stimulated individuals to participate in the mass system will be undermined. At the level of community organizations one might have expected wholesale organizational death in the early 1980s. This does not mean that the major institutions which have caused the growth of mass society—large corporations or centralized government—will be much reduced. However, there may be a striking change in the way local social and political life is structured.

To make this argument, it is necessary to explore how the general organizational qualities I have attributed to life in mass society are translated into the system of local social service nonprofits which make up the most visible group of community organizations today. I shall focus on the way that these organizations as a group attract resources to their communities and how as a group they contribute to the distribution of excess public resources that might accumulate at the federal level or in other centers of concentrated political and economic power. By seeing how individual organizations adapt to achieve success in this broader system, we can see what direction their decline might follow.

There are many ways to attract resources to a locale. Community organizations are generally less important than business firms or political influentials at doing so. After the War on Poverty in the United States conducted by the Office of Economic Opportunity (OEO) through its Community Action Program (CAP), however, there emerged a special role for community organizations. Increasingly they have come to allow public resources to be distributed in a way which does not favor large, centralized economic, service, and political organizations. The federal government and increasingly national foundations, state governments, and some corporate foundations have funded programs which are narrowly defined and conceived as attempts to solve particular social problems. These regional or national programs give funds to local ones which fit narrowly circumscribed sets of criteria and which promise to carry out specific kinds of work. They are called categorical grants programs.

With resources from categorical grants programs, community organizations have gained new power. Between the two of them resources can be channeled to areas and populations that are political weak. Community organizations have become an important vehicle for bypassing those political jurisdictions that lie between the federal government and localities in distributing resources. If funds are passed through these intervening jurisdictions, it has been argued by some social scientists and policy makers, a large portion will be channeled into powerful, bureaucratic organizations. Granting money to community organizations directly as they respond to narrowly phrased requests for proposals (RFPs) allows federal policymakers to distribute money on the basis of respondents' expertise and in response to extensive specialized networks of acquaintances local organizational leaders develop.

Categorical grants programs have revised the federal funding allocation process. A system of funding sources has been created which is so large, complex, and decentralized that it is difficult for a few community decision making organizations representing a particular geographic area to monopolize or control all of them. When most of the federal funds for a particular area come from a small number of funding programs, it is possible for powerful politicians and representatives of large jurisdictions to bring enough pressure to bear on granting agencies to influence the direction of the funding flow. It then is difficult to avoid having federal grant money become a part of local patronage systems or part of the budget base of local CDOs. When this happens, funds intended to bring about social change may contribute to the maintenance of organizations and elite social groups which partially caused the problems that are supposedly being solved.

The growth of categorical grants programs occurred as a result of a self-conscious federal policy to create programs which attack social problems directly without having policy decisions mediated by several intervening layers of government at the state and local levels. The first effort to do this was through creation of the OEO and its system of CAPs in the early 1960s. Much has been written about the demise of this program at the hands of local political influentials who did not want federal funds to be used to sponsor political groups opposed to them within their communities.[52]

I would argue, however, that the attacks on OEO had relatively minor consequences for community social action programs. It is a mistake to see the formal mission of OEO—the federal initiative to attack powerful local institutions and to fight poverty through a grass-roots strategy aimed at simultaneously attacking many causes of poverty—as the major contribution of that program to American society. OEO was more important as the first draft of a federal policy of funding social programs through categorical grants. The OEO experience taught the architects of such programs that they cannot deny local politicians a voice in determining which local agencies may receive funding. At the same time, whether this was recognized consciously or not by policymakers, as categorical grants programs proliferated the control of local political influentials became less and less relevant to the shape taken by service programs. Politics has relatively little relation to the way grants and other resources are distributed, the kinds of programs that are created, and the ability of politically powerful jurisdictions to claim more than their share of the resources from politically insignificant communities. This is true for two reasons.

First, categorical grants programs, by emphasizing the importance of technical expertise in grant writing, make it difficult for nonexperts to criticize policymakers' plans or practices. Nonexperts are not likely to be intimately familiar with the problems at hand or with state-of-the-art solutions as are those writing proposals so it is hard for them to suggest meaningful revisions to proposals. This makes it relatively easy for grantsmen to coopt community leaders very much in the way that Selznick[53] describes the leaders of the then new Tennessee Valley Authority coopting local community leaders.

Second, categorical grants programs give community organizations new influence because there are many granting programs and their criteria for grant making are so particularistic and complex that it is difficult for a small number of community decision organizations or a set of political actors to control how money will be distributed.[54] What OEO did was to create new principles and mechanisms for distributing national resources to localities.

The previous system was one based on a model of decision making in a democracy in which political units are built upon the strong ties of influence relations. Funding allocations serve as a variety of patronage. The flaw in this distributional model was its hypothesis, following de Tocqueville,[55] that citizens in the United States belong to many voluntary associations and that they are represented in pluralist politics through these associations.

The 1950s and 1960s saw growing public recognition that in fact most Americans belong to few voluntary associations and that they are poorly represented through informal linkages to the political system. This impression was borne out in studies by Hyman and Wright.[56] Democratic theorists in the Banfield[57] and Dahl[58] tradition had what Wrong[59] calls "an oversocialized conception of man." Most Americans, rather than being part of a tightly organized system of political influence like that Laumann and Pappi[60] describe for a German city or that Banfield and Dahl describe for American ones, are only loosely tied into political systems.

Categorical grants programs allow national resources to be distributed in a more equitable manner given the looseness with which most Americans are tied into centralized political and social institutions. They reward the ability to fit a set of narrowly defined program criteria to local conditions and to write proposals which provide a convincing rationale for allocating funds to these narrow local programs. The detail, particularism, number, and variety of categorical grants programs create an information glut which is hard to manage in a centralized way. Successful grant writing requires entrepreneurship. However, because entrepreneurship is a creative, eclectic activity its practitioners[61] are hard to control through rules or through the explicit controls of a political influence system based on strong ties between leaders. This means that any community or any special population group or even any ambitious individual has about as good a chance of raising substantial amounts of grant money as does a large city or an important political jurisdiction.

Despite federal capitulation to local government demands for fiscal control in the aftermath of the OEO experiment, the number and variety of categorical programs has grown steadily since 1960. Many local programs' applications are only taken seriously by granting agencies if they first receive approval from local government officials. In a survey conducted by the New World Foundation and HUD of community self-help groups around the nation, federal grant income was generally accompanied by substantial state and local grant income as well.[62] This suggests that community self-help groups cannot easily go off and apply for federal money simply because their leaders may be able to write competent proposals. Implicitly, to receive local funding these organizations usually must receive local government approval.

Yet even with the right to license grantees of categorical programs city halls have minimal control. The small nonprofit organizations which receive grants are relatively autonomous. The large number of potential grant sources makes it difficult for one actor or set of actors to know about and to have well developed contacts with all potential sources of money. In addition each granting program has complex and constantly changing priorities. Not only must those contemplating applications have a catalog of sources that might address local needs. They must also have ways of learning what the priorities of grantors are and how local needs or desired local programs can be presented so that they appear to fit those priorities.

These information problems can be overcome by allowing entrepreneurs in the nonprofit sector who have extensive networks of friends and acquaintances in different specialized areas to screen possible funding sources and to write grant applications as they choose. In exchange, these entrepreneurs are allowed to establish their own organizations. Local governments may use their licensing power to discipline organizational leaders and to prevent the creation of other nonprofits which compete with those that are licensed and which have claimed a particular domain. Since the kinds of entrepreneurs that are available in a particular region is somewhat a matter of chance, local governments are likely to supplement programs provided through small nonprofits with some in-house programs which also seek nonlocal grants. Where this happens, however, the public programs may look more like the other autonomous community self-help organizations than like departments in a bureaucracy.

Combining these in-house efforts and those of local entrepreneurs one can imagine that some local governments will intentionally build up a substantial base of externally funded programs. Because the funding for these programs depends upon a type of expertise rather than on wealth or influence, a large base could be built up in areas where local politicians are not very well organized or where they are not influential within the local or national political culture. Areas can attract people with specialized networks of acquaintances, and if leaders can encourage these people to create organizations, substantial program resources can be accumulated with little obvious local investment. For small cities, minority communities, and those interested in serving specialized clienteles, this is a way of providing a rich variety of programs without having to compete for funds with locally powerful community decision organizations which monopolize municipal budgets and United Way allocations. They do not have to compete for a part of a fixed pot of local money.

ECONOMIC CONTRACTION

The discussion I have presented thus far is reminiscent of an argument Eisenstadt[63] offered to explain a massive and sudden change in the character of community organizations in Israel following statehood. Like Moynihan[64] in his discussion of OEO, Eisenstadt saw the change as a shift in the major allocational problems of the society. Where prior to independence, communities were sharply bounded, autonomous, and self-sufficient, afterward they compared with other communities for societal resources. The same people who had previously been the social leaders of the communities now had to leave the communities to compete in the national arena. The new availability of resources at the state level required, just as it later would in the United States, evolution of a new political system which would legitimately and equitably solve the distributional problems.

If closed, mutually reinforcing community organizations break down and change their orientation in response to the sudden growth of state resources we must ask what will happen when there is a decline in public resources as there appears to be today in the United States. The organizational argument suggests there will be a return to more community-based allocation. There are several reasons for this.

First, as the national resource pool dries up, it will become increasingly expensive for entrepreneurs in local nonprofits to seek funding. For small nonprofits to support entrepreneurship, it is necessary for them to accumulate or borrow sufficient resources to support grantsmen who look for money and who are not productive in the short run. For grantsmanship to be profitable, it is essential that some stable rate of grant approval be achieved. If a grantsman's batting average is too low, the cash reserve available to pay his or her salary during a resource search will run out and the person will either have to do work which is productive in the short run or be laid off.

The scarcer resources become nationally, the more small, poor, entrepreneurial nonprofit organizations will be cut out of the resource distribution system. Since these are the organizations most likely to route resources into underserved communities, their decline would cause the system to become more concentrated. Large research and social service organizations which can support extensive grant seeking efforts should eventually be the only ones left. These organizations, being both dominated by experts and bureaucratic, are more closed to public criticism, accountability, and review than are either political machines or smaller nonprofits. They may be vulnerable to political attack as older political arrangements are reenacted. Whether or not they are, the concentration of the nonprofit sector would substantially change the decentralized distribution pattern which has evolved from the programmatic descendants of the War on Poverty.

Second, nonprofit entrepreneurship depends on individuals being mobile both occupationally and geographically. A key element of the system is that individuals develop personalized weak tie networks focused on a particular service and granting sector. They may take risks in a particular organization because their value is based on personal knowledge, contacts, and expertise. If it turns out that they fail to obtain grants within the period of time necessary for a particular nonprofit to maintain its minimum rate of cash flow, they can move to or create a new organization which can use their skills. In this they are like other professionals who advance personally by jumping from one organization to another. If they are to be effective entrepreneurs, grantsmen ought to be no more bound to stay with an organization that no longer can afford their services than is a doctor required to remain with a clinic that has gone bankrupt.

Mobility is important to maintaining the independence of the grantsman. As mobility is reduced, it becomes more dangerous for entrepreneurs to take risks. One sort of risk is the investment of resources in projects with uncertain payoffs. It is important to spend time writing proposals if one wants to live on soft money. But the returns to proposal writing are uncertain compared to other activities with more concrete or more certain short run payoffs. It also is risky to propose big expensive programs since, though they may produce a large payoff, big grants also are harder to get and thus it is more risky to invest time in seeking them.

A different sort of risk is the possibility of a program failing. Grantsmen live by pyramiding different kinds of programs to pay for continued exploration of the funding world and by trying out new kinds of programs whose results are uncertain. Grantsmen can get into legal trouble by overextending themselves and using funds from one program to pay for the activities of another or for continued entrepreneurship. They also may get into trouble by agreeing to undertake a program they are not equipped to carry out or which fails because it is experimental. Their adventures can destroy an organization, and such failures can make it difficult for them to find new jobs. If entrepreneurs cannot move on easily, they are likely to become risk averse and less effective at searching out new resources. This too would tend to concentrate resources in larger organizations which can better afford systematic resource searches.

Third, as opportunities for mobility are reduced and as people are forced to compete with the same people within a community for a limited number of chances for advancement, the social mechanisms which make voluntary associations strong in closed communities may again come into play. People may not be able to leave communities and may become increasingly dependent on other community members for help and support. The health and survival of the community as a corporate entity may become increasingly important to all members. As this happens, it may become more important for the community to be able to control conflicts and competition in a legitimate way and to maintain discipline and control over members. Voluntary associations, communal rituals, clearly defined and well established values and traditions all come more strongly into play. All of these depend on strong relationships between individuals and on an elaborated, crystallized social structure. All of these social needs may create pressure for legitimate community leaders to take over established local organizations. They may gradually replace the pool of entrepreneurs as leaders, which in turn would make community organizations less effective in seeking out and competing for grant money.

CONCLUSION

With the budget cuts of the Reagan administration there is nothing startling in my suggestion that the next few years will see a sharp reduction in the funding available to small social-service nonprofits in communities. However, the liberal public debate focuses only on the possibility that in withdrawing funds from social service programs the framework of welfare programs erected since the New Deal will be eliminated, leaving less privileged members of the population with little protection from hardship.

No doubt it is true that the sharp reduction in social program funding from the federal government will cause serious gaps in the service available to poor people. However, in addition to seeing services reduced in response to the efforts of a conservative president we probably also are witnessing a sea change in the allocational problems of our society and in the structure of institutional arrangements which help to resolve them. The death of many small nonprofits is not just a sign of the casualties of conservative public policy. This also is a reflection of the reemergence of institutional forms which govern the distribution of public resources in times of scarcity. Thus, after a period of confusion and decline of social services, we should begin to see new kinds of organizations and service programs emerge which can survive despite reduced federal funding.

One might expect that a decline in the institutions of mass society would lead to a simple resurgence of the old style community institutions. This seems unlikely on a broad scale, however. The decline of mass society forms of community organizations does not mean the other institutions of mass society will suffer nearly as steep a decline and that the trends of one hundred years will be reversed. Rather, what we should expect is that new kinds of funding and indirect resources will become progressively important in the coming years. State governments and corporate foundations appear today to be the most important new source of funds for community organizations. We should expect community organizations which are effective at locating and obtaining resources from these new sources to emerge.

With the emphasis on private sector funding, community organizations may seek funding from more diverse sources than they have in recent years. Such a development will probably be slow in coming. Not only will it take time for new actors in the private sector to make resources available to community groups. If my discussion of the relationship between resource mobilization problems and the organizational structure of community organizations in the past is correct, small nonprofits have to become structurally specialized in order to seek and compete for resources in new private sector arenas. For example, a different sort of organization is likely to be required to raise funds from a local United Way than from a local church. The former organization will have to be profession and service oriented, whereas the latter may be more project oriented—churches have sponsored many housing developments in the past.

Presumably there are a variety of funding arenas which are relatively distinct from each other and which make different structural demands on the community organizations which they fund. I have explored the variety and structure of some of them in other papers. Over time it seems that different arenas provide the largest portion of funding to community organizations. The ascendancy of one arena and the organizational styles required to successfully raise funds mean that certain forms dominate our awareness. Fifty years ago, most resources for social services were provided locally, often informally. Consequently, the dominant form of community organization in the eyes of social scientists were the small, participatory voluntary associations described by the authors of community studies. The War on Poverty and the growth of categorical grants programs caused more professional social service organizations to become the predominant form of community organization. As social service agencies decline with the falloff in federal funding, new organizational forms will predominate.

NOTES

1. See David Kirp, "Has Organizing Survived the 1960's?" *Social Policy* 3 (4) (1972–1973), 44–49.
2. Edward C. Banfield, *Political Influence* (New York: Free Press, 1961).
3. See William Lloyd Warner et al., *Yankee City* (New Haven, Conn.: Yale University Press, 1963).

4. See Kenneth L. Little, *West African Urbanization: A Study of Voluntary Associations in Social Change* (New York: Cambridge University Press, 1965).

5. Ferdinand Toennies, *Community and Society (Gemeinschaft und Gesellschaaft)*, ed. and trans. Charles P. Loomis (New York: Harper and Row, 1963).

6. See Robert A. Nisbet, *The Quest for Community* (Oxford: Oxford University Press, 1953) and Maurice R. Stein, *The Eclipse of Community: An Interpretation of American Studies* (Princeton: Princeton University Press, 1960).

7. See Irving Howe and Lewis A. Coser, *The American Communist Party* (New York:; Praeger, 1962) and Philip Selznick, *The Organizational Weapon: A Study of Bolshevist Strategy and Tactics* (Glencoe, Ill.: The Free Press, 1960).

8. William Kornhauser, *The Politics of Mass Society* (Glencoe, Ill.: The Free Press, 1959).

9. See Daniel P. Moynihan, *Maximum Feasible Misunderstanding* (New York: Free Press, 1969).

10. Moynihan, *Maximum Feasible Misunderstanding.*

11. S. N. Eisenstadt, "The Social Conditions of the Development of Voluntary Associations—A Case Study of Israel," *Scripta Hierosolymitana* 3 (1956), 104–125.

12. Albert O. Hirschman, *Exit, Voice and Loyalty: Responses to Decline in Firms, Organizations and States* (Cambridge, Mass.: Harvard University Press, 1970).

13. See William Lloyd Warner, *The Living and the Dead: A Study of the Symbolic Life of Americans* (New Haven, Conn.: Yale University Press, 1959).

14. See T. A. Barnes, "Class Committees in a Norwegian Island Parish," *Human Relations* 7 (1954), 39–58, and J. Clyde Mitchell, *Social Networks in Urban Situations* (Manchester: University of Manchester Press, 1969).

15. See Louis Wirth, "Urbanism as a Way of Life," *American Journal of Sociology* 44 (July 1938), 3–24, and Lyn H. Lofland, *A World of Strangers: Order and Action in Urban Public Space* (New York: Basic Books, 1973).

16. See T. H. Marshall, "Citizenship and Social Class," in *Class, Citizenship and Social Development* (Cambridge: Cambridge University Press, 1950), pp. 71–134. See also Karl R. Popper, *The Open Society and Its Enemies* (New York: Harper, 1962).

17. Max Weber, *The City*, ed. and trans. Don Martindale and Gertrud Neuwirth (New York: The Free Press, 1958).

18. Mitchell, *Social Networks in Urban Situations.*

19. Harry M. Lasker and Fred L. Strodtbeck, "Self-Protectiveness in an Insular Society," Prepared for the 14th Seminar of the Committee on Family Research, Curaçao, 1975.

20. See James E. Rosenbaum, *Making Inequality: The Hidden Curriculum of High School Tracking* (New York: John Wiley & Sons, 1976).

21. Mark Granovetter, "The Strength of Weak Ties," *American Journal of Sociology* 78, 6 (May 1973), 1360–1380, and Granovetter, *Getting a Job: A Study of Contacts and Careers* (Cambridge, Mass.: Harvard University Press, 1974).

22. See Barry Schwartz, *Queuing and Waiting: Studies in the Social Organization of Access and Delay* (Chicago: University of Chicago Press, 1975).

23. See William Kornblum, *Blue Collar Community* (Chicago: University of Chicago Press, 1974) and Patricia D. Wheeldon, "The Operation of Voluntary Associations and Personal Networks in the Political Processes of an Inter-Ethnic Community," in *Social Networks in Urban Situations*, ed. J. Clyde Mitchell (Manchester: University of Manchester Press, 1969), pp. 128–180.

24. See Robert Fred Bales, *Personality and Interpersonal Behavior* (New York: Holt, Rinehart and Winston, 1970).

25. Granovetter, "The Strength of Weak Ties," and Granovetter, *Getting a Job: A Study of Contacts and Careers.* See also Scott A. Boorman, "A Combinational Optimization Model for Transmission of Job Information through Contact Networks," *The Bell Journal of Economics* 6, 1 (1975), 216–249.

26. See N. H. Lee, *The Search for an Abortionist* (Chicago: University of Chicago Press, 1969).

27. See Lofland, *A World of Strangers: Order and Action in Urban Public Space.*

28. See Neil S. Mayer and Jennifer Blake, "Keys to the Growth of Neighborhood Development Organizations" (Washington, D.C.: Working Paper 1330-2. The Urban Institute, 1980) and New World Foundation, *Initiatives for Community Self-Help: Efforts to Increase Recognition and Support* (New York: New World Foundation, 1980).

29. See Stephen Cole, Jonathan Cole and Gary A. Simon, "Change and Consensus in Peer Review," *Science,* 214, 20 (20 November 1981), 881–886.

30. See A. Michael Spence, *Market Signaling: Informational Transfer in Hiring and Related Screening Processes* (Cambridge, Mass.: Harvard University Press, 1974).

31. See David Kirp and Mark G. Yudoff, *Educational Policy and the Law* (Berkeley, Calif.: McCutcheon, 1974).

32. Granovetter, "The Strength of Weak Ties."

33. See Weber, *The City.*

34. See Eisenstadt, "The Social Conditions of the Development of Voluntary Associations—a Case Study of Israel."

35. See Kornhauser, *The Politics of Mass Society.*

36. Morris Janowitz, *The Community Press in an Urban Setting* (Chicago: University of Chicago Press, 1967).

37. William Lloyd Warner and P. G. Lunt, *The Status System of a Modern Community* (New Haven, Conn.: Yale University Press, 1942).

38. Kornblum, *Blue Collar Community.*

39. Alvin W. Gouldner, *Wildcat Strike: A Study of an Unofficial Strike* (London: Routledge and Kegan Paul, 1955).

40. See Maurice R. Stein, *The Eclipse of Community: An Interpretation of American Studies* (Princeton: Princeton University Press, 1960).

41. Kornblum, *Blue Collar Community.*

42. Bennett M. Berger, *Working Class Suburb* (Berkeley: University of California Press, 1960).

43. Roland L. Warren, "The Interorganizational Field as a Focus for Investigation," *Administrative Science Quarterly* 12, 3 (December 1967), 396–419. See also R. L. Warren, Stephen M. Rose and Ann F. Bergunder, *Structure of Urban Reform: Community Design, Organization and Stability and Change* (Lexington, Mass.: Lexington Books, 1974).

44. Herbert F. Gans, *The Urban Villagers: Group and Class in the Life of Italian Americans* (New York: Free Press, 1962).

45. Charles A. Valentine, "Deficit, Difference and Bi-Cultural Models of Afro-American Behavior," *Harvard Educational Review,* 41, 2 (1971), 137–1957.

46. William Labov, *Language in the Inner City* (Philadelphia: University of Pennsylvania Press, 1972).

47. Peter Marris and Martin Rein, *The Dilemmas of Social Reform* (New York: Atherton, 1967).

48. Moynihan, *Maximum Feasible Misunderstanding.*

49. Stephen M. Rose, *The Betrayal of the Poor: The Transformation of Community Action* (Cambridge, Mass.: Schenkman Publishing Company, 1972).

50. See Dennis Young, "Motives, Models and Men: An Exploration of Entrepreneurship in the Non-Profit Sector," Program on Non-Profit Organizations Working Paper no. 4 (New Haven, Conn.: Yale University, Institution for Social and Policy Studies, June 1978).

51. See John Case and Rosemary Taylor (eds.), *Coops, Communes and Collectives: Experiments in Social Change in the 1960s and the 1970s* (New York: Pantheon, 1979).

52. See Moynihan, *Maximum Feasible Misunderstanding* and Rose, *The Betrayal of the Poor: The Transformation of Community Action.* See also Warren, Rose, and Bergunder, *Structure of Urban Reform: Community Design, Organization and Stability and Change.*

53. Philip Selznick, *TVA and the Grassroots: A Study on the Sociology of Formal Organization.* (New York: Harper and Row, 1966).

54. In his 1982 State of the Union Address, President Reagan stated that there were approximately 500 federal grants-in-aid programs (categorical grants programs) when he took office. He stated:

A maze of interlocking jurisdictions and levels of government confronts the average citizens in trying to solve even the simplest of problems. They do not know where to turn for answers, who to hold accountable, who to praise, who to blame, who to vote for or against.

The main reason for this is the overpowering growth of Federal grants-in-aid programs during the last few decades.

In 1960, the Federal Government had 132 categorical grants programs, costing $7 billion. When I took office there were approximately 500, costing nearly $100 billion—13 programs for energy conservation, 36 for pollution control, 66 for social services and 90 for education. The list goes on and on. Here in the Congress, it takes at least 166 committees just to try to keep track of them.

You know and I know that neither the President nor the Congress can properly oversee this jungle of grants-in-aid; indeed, the growth of these grants has led to a distortion in the vital functions of Government. As one Democratic Governor put it recently: "The national government should be worrying about 'arms control not pot-holes.' " *The New York Times* 27 January 1982, p. A16.

55. Alexis de Tocqueville, *Democracy in America,* vol. 2, trans. Philips Bradley (New York: Alfred A. Knopf, 1945). Also A. de Tocqueville, "Associations in American Life," in *Perspectives on the American Community,* ed. Roland L. Warren (Chicago: Rand McNally, 1966), pp. 444–447.

56. C. R. Wright and Herbert H. Hyman, "Voluntary Association Memberships of American Adults: Evidence from National Sample Surveys," *American Sociological Review,* 23 (1958), 284–294, and Herbert H. Hyman and C. R. Wright, "Trends in Voluntary Association Memberships of American Adults," *American Sociological Review,* 36 (April 1971), 191–206.

57. Banfield, *Political Influence.*

58. Robert A. Dahl, *Who Governs? Democracy and Power in an American City* (New Haven, Conn.: Yale University Press, 1961).

59. Dennis Wrong, "The Oversocialized Conception of Man in Modern Society," *American Sociological Review,* 26 (1961), 183–193.

60. Edward O. Laumann and Fran U. Pappi, *Networks of Collective Action: A Perspective on Community Influence Systems* (New York: Academic Press, 1976).

61. See Young, "Motives, Models and Men: An Exploration of Entrepreneurship in the Non-Profit Sector."

62. See Carl Milofsky and Frank Romo, "Funding Arenas and the Structure of Community Organizations," chapter 10 in this volume.

63. Eisenstadt, "The Social Condition of the Development of Voluntary Associations—a Case Study of Israel."

64. Moynihan, *Maximum Feasible Misunderstanding.*

2

A Theory of Voluntary Organization[1]

J. MILLER McPHERSON

Social theorists have used the biological metaphor for social life since before sociology was a discipline. Herbert Spencer[2] was an early advocate of a biological paradigm for the study of society, although the anology between social and organic forms goes back at least as far as Aristotle.[3] The organic analogy has been used to greatest effect in human ecology and social evolutionary theory, exemplified by the work of Amos Hawley[4] and Gerhard Lenski,[5] respectively.

An image borrowed from this work has been the basis for a minirevolution in the field of complex organizations.[6] The result has been a dynamic picture of the births and deaths of organizations in a population. Only organizations which match the requirements of the environment will survive. The basic principle which shapes the characteristics of organizations is selection. Organizational forms which are successful spread through growth and imitation, whereas unsuccessful forms disappear into history (or are absorbed into other organizations). Natural variability in the form of new organizations ensures a constant supply of variation for the selection process.

One problem with the population ecology model is that the theory is very difficult to test without experimental evidence. As it applies to observations at a single point in time, the argument is tautological: organisms are fit because they have survived, and they have survived because they are fit.[7] In contrast to organizational researchers, animal and plant ecologists have recourse to the laboratory; organizational ecologists fall back on the strategy of observing ongoing systems, which was used with great success by Hannan and Freeman and their associates, who have been able to show that selection plays a role in determining the composition of communities of organizations.[8]

A second problem with applying the population ecology model to organizations is that they are not self-contained units as plants and animals are. Organizations are constantly losing, sharing, and competing for members. Organizations often grow at each other's expense; there is a constant flow of individuals from organization to organization. In addition, it is possible for a single organization to grow large enough to monopolize all the resources available, even in a time of great growth in the resource.[9] There is seldom an internally determined absolute limit to the size of an organization; neither is there a limit to the ability of organizations to cannibalize one another for members. Animal organisms, on the other hand, reach a genetically determined maximum size when the environment supplies enough food.

Another problem is that the same people may be involved in various organizations. The analysis of individuals' multiple affiliations is a major theme of research on a variety of organizations, from voluntary associations[10] to interlocking corporate directorates,[11] to the military-industrial complex.[12] What we see when we look at a population of organizations, then, is not a set of discrete creatures who must mate with each other to reproduce, but a froth of bubbles, constantly sharing or exchanging members, growing and dying, forming and being absorbed in response to changing conditions.

Yet, like animals, organizations must compete with each other for resources. An extremely important resource for which organizations compete is their members.[13] For organizations to grow in size they must acquire them somewhere. That somewhere, in urban society, is other organizations. This paper is about the competition of organizations for members. To understand this competition, we must first understand the niche.

THE NICHE

In his classic text, *Human Ecology,* Hawley equates the niche with the functional role of the organism—what the organism does in the habitat.[14] With a slight change of emphasis, Hannan and Freeman define the niche as "those combinations of resource levels at which the population can survive and reproduce itself."[15] Hannan and Freeman then go on to discuss fitness functions for different types of organizations, without giving empirical examples of important resources.[16] This paper will show that the concept of the niche can be clearly and accurately measured in a way that places it squarely in the mainstream of current sociological theory and ties together geography, time, and social space into a coherent picture of human organization.

In animal ecology, the niche is a location in a multidimensional property space defined by the resources in the environment. These dimensions usually fall into three general categories, describing what the animal eats, where it eats, and when it eats. The measured dimensions of the niche depend on the species being studied. For instance, in a study of desert lizards, ecologists have used time of most activity, habitat preference, and type of prey as the niche dimensions for different species of lizards.[17] Species A may have similar habitat preference and prey, but different hours of activity from species B, and species C may differ from both A and B on habitat but have similar prey. Thus, each species occupies a unique location in multidimensional space, even though each may have identical values on one or more of the dimensions.

It is important to realize that each species' niche has evolved through interaction with other species. The presence or absence of given competitors will affect the location of the niche in the multidimensional space. Thus, there is no absolute species-specific niche in a real community; the ecological literature is replete with examples of the expansion or contraction of niches in response to exogenous events.[18] The entire system of niches for the species in the community is interdependent; the details of species location may well be unique in each community.[19]

Niche dimensions are very difficult to measure in animal ecology. For instance, ecologists often use very indirect indicators such as beak size to measure type of prey.[20] In fact, field observation alone is usually not sufficient to establish niche characteristics with much certainty. Much of the work done on niches focuses on partial description and fragmentary measures, rather than a complete analysis of community niche organization.[21] Not only are the dimensions hard to measure, but an infinite number of dimensions could be relevant to the structure of the community.[22] Ecologists, then, resort to the same sort of ceteris paribus assumptions about the omitted dimensions that sociologists do when they are engaged in causal modeling.[23]

However, we can measure directly many of the important resources for human organizations. Entire disciplines such as history and geography have grown up around the questions of the spatial and temporal patterns in human activity. The most important resource dimensions in purely social terms are defined by the characteristics of the individuals who make up the organizations. Organizations almost always recruit from a limited segment of the community. The characteristics of these individuals define dimensions of the niche for the organization. In terms of our discussion of animal ecology, this set of dimensions is analogous to the prey of the species—what the organization "eats." Characteristics of individuals which are nearly universal in their impact on social life are the basic sociodemographic variables such as age and sex. An example of age as a niche dimension for two types of voluntary organizations is presented in Figure 2.1.[24]

As the figure illustrates, the niches of voluntary organizations serving youth and the elderly have very little overlap on the age dimension. This unremarkable finding illustrates an extreme example of niche differentiation along a single resource dimension. This example is a bit unusual, in that the two niches show almost no overlap on a single resource dimension.[25] Ordinarily, we would expect two different types of organizations to be completely differentiated only in a multidimensional property space, with many resource continua.

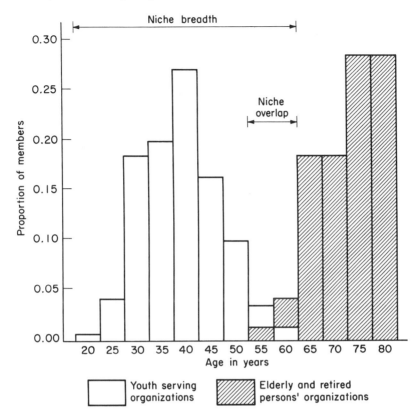

Figure 2.1   Age as a Niche Dimension.

A more typical example of niche differentiation is given in Figure 2.2, which contrasts veterans groups with professional organizations in the education dimension. Two important features of the model which this paper will develop are illustrated in Figure 2.1. The niche breadth is the space along the resource dimension which the organization occupies. The organization uses this space just as the animal species may select from a range along a prey size dimension. The niche overlap between two organizations is part of the dimension where the two organizations occupy common ground. The two organizations are feeding in the same social space.

One of the most critical dimensions for human organizations is the time dimension. Clearly, organizations compete in time. Also, organizations may be linked to one another sequentially in time through common members, just as two animal species may frequent the same areas at different times of the day. For human organizations, the time scale involved may vary from hours to a matter of years.[26]

Occupational activity tends to peak at the midmorning and midafternoon, whereas voluntary organization activity has a major peak around

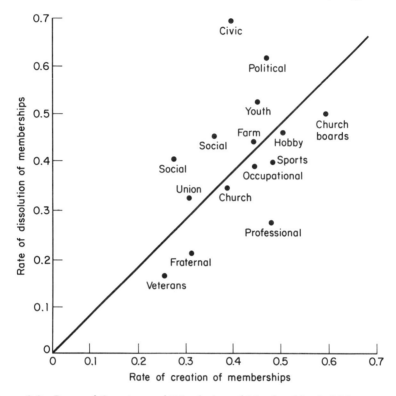

Figure 2.2 Rates of Creation and Dissolution of Memberships in Voluntary Associations.

eight o'clock at night, after most people have completed their work for the day. Voluntary organizations tend to meet during times when sustenance activity is light. Thus, voluntary and sustenance organizations may occupy identical niches except for the time dimension; members of sustenance organizations flow from these organizations into voluntary organizations, and vice versa, over the course of time.

The physical location of organizations will dictate where the members come from. A number of factors will affect the distribution of organizations, including the size of the community. Table 2.1 gives estimates for the number of face to face voluntary organizations in towns of varying size in a midwestern state. As the table shows, the number of organizations increases dramatically with the city size. Yet, the number of organizations per person actually declines with city size. This counterintuitive result is due to the fact that the average organization is larger in larger communities.[27] Thus, the increased number of people available in larger communities supports not only more organizations, but larger ones. The relationship between the number of potential members of the organization and the observed members will loom large in later discussion.

Table 2.1   The Distribution of Voluntary Organizations in Communities of
Varying Size

Community Size	380,000	160,000	30,000	7,500	500
Number of Organizations	10,000	5,000	1,000	380	30
Organizations per Person	.026	.031	.033	.051	.060

SOURCE: Data are estimates adapted from J. Miller McPherson, "Hypernetwork Sampling: Duality and Differentiation among Voluntary Organizations," *Social Networks* 3 (1982), 225–250, based on the Nebraska Annual Social Indicators Survey described by David R. Johnson in *Nebraska Annual Social Indicators Survey 1977*, Report 5, "Designs, Procedures, Instruments and Forms for the 1977 NASIS" (Lincoln, Nebr.: Bureau of Sociological Research, University of Nebraska-Lincoln, 1977).

The essential point about the geography of organizations is that niche similarity depends on the location of the individuals which the organization recruits. Organizations recruiting from the same geographical area are more likely to compete for members. On the other hand, two organizations can be in competition for members, even if separated by considerable distances, if their niche similarity is high enough on other dimensions. Boards of directors of large corporations are a good example of this phenomenon. Directors are often flown into meetings from great distances at times when the scheduling of a meeting does not conflict with other organizational responsibilities. The tremendous similarity of these boards on the social composition dimensions is well known; almost all studies of boards of directors emphasize the great similarity in background and experience of the members.[28] These organizations will have extremely narrow niches with respect to composition, but very wide niches geographically. This pattern is often characteristic of elite organizational niches.

At the other end of the continuum, organizations which have narrow geographical niches will be very limited in size or will recruit from a much broader subset of the population—their social composition will be much more heterogeneous. Local community clubs must be less choosy about who will be a member, or be very small.

To illustrate these ideas, let us consider a simple example of the concept of niche volume. The two hypothetical organizations Acme Steel and the Centerville Bowling League occupy niches which are close but do not overlap in time; the bowlers will meet from seven until nine at night, and Acme's doors are open from eight to five weekdays. The bowling league has members from a number of locations, some of which are farther from the center of town than Acme. Acme has a number of bowling employees and some nonbowlers, including professional and managerial personnel with higher levels of education.[29]

For this contrived example, the niche volume of Acme Steel is the product of its niche breadths on the three resource dimensions, 5 years of education × 1 unit of distance × 9 hours per day = 45 units of volume. The bowling league has 4 years × 2 hours × 1 distance = 8 units. Thus, the niche volume of Acme is over five times the volume of the bowling league, because of the fact that Acme's greater niche breadths in education and time outweigh the bowling league's larger geographical base.[30]

The key insight of this conception is that organizations which have overlapping niches are recruiting from the same pool of potential members, at the same time. Acme Steel does not compete with the Centerville Bowlers because the two organizations have disjoint niches in the time dimension. The Centerville Bowlers will, on the other hand, compete with the Crosstown Pin Punchers, who are located close enough to attract some of the members from Centerville's geographic area. Since the two niches overlap, they are recruiting similar individuals for overlapping times.

THE DYNAMICS OF COMPETITION

Let us imagine, for a moment, an organization in an infinitely rich environment, where there are no environmental limits on organizational growth. In such a case we expect the organization to grow. Of course, different types of organizations may still grow at different rates under such circumstances, because of different recruitment mechanisms, and so forth.[31] Let us define the rate at which the ith organization grows under these ideal conditions as r_i. This unrestricted growth rate is analogous to the interest offered by a bank; at each period, the growth rate of the organization is applied to its current size. This hypothetical situation leads to a simple differential equation describing the growth of the ith organization:

$$dM_i/dt = r_iM_i \tag{1}$$

where M_i is the size of the ith organization and r_i is the rate of unrestricted growth described previously. Now, this simple equation cannot possibly describe a real organization, because there is a finite limit to the number of potential members.

Define the carrying capacity of the community for the ith organization as K_i. This carrying capacity is simply the number of people in the community who are similar to the actual members in the organization, in the sense discussed previously. The number of actual members of organization i is M_i. Now, the rage of growth in organization i will be a function of the number of actual members, the carrying capacity, and the unrestricted growth potential:

$$dM_i/dt = r_iM_i(1 - M_i) \tag{2}$$

Equation (2) is a form of the Lotka-Yolterra equation,[32] in which the growth rate of an organization depends on the remaining proportion of the carrying capacity of the community. As the actual membership approaches the maximum (M_i approaches K_i), the rate slows. When the actual membership equals the carrying capacity, the term in parentheses equals zero, the growth rate is zero, and the system is in equilibrium. Should the carrying capacity decline at some time when the system is in equilibrium, the term in parentheses will become negative, and the growth rate will become a rate of decline until the system once more reaches equilibrium.

Equation (2) makes no reference to competition between organizations for members. We can take competition into account by modifying (1) to reflect the proportion of the carrying capacity of organization i that is used by organization j:

$$dM_i/dt = r_iM_i(1 - M_i/K_i - a_{ij}(M_j/Ki)$$

and
$$dM_j/dt = r_jM_j(1 - M_j/K_j - a_{ij}(M_i/K_j)) \qquad (3)$$

where a_{ij} and a_{ji} are the coefficients of competition between i and j. These coefficients will be equal to 1.0 when i and j occupy identical niches (that is, when they recruit from exactly the same subset of the community and have activities at competing times). In this case the carrying capacity for organization i is reduced one member for each member of j. As the second equation shows, the system is now composed of two organizations, which affect each other's sizes through competition. The second equation is simply a mirror image of the first. The a_{ij} coefficient will be zero when the two organizations occupy completely different niches, and the carrying capacity of i is unaffected by j. The a_{ij} coefficient may be thought of as the proportional effect of each membership in j upon the effective carrying capacity of the community for i. If $a_{ij} > 0$, then each membership in j reduces by fraction a_{ij} the effective pool of potential members for i. This latter interpretation is clear in the equilibrium solution for (2), in which the membership sizes of organizations i and j are maximum:

$$M^*u = K_i - a_{ij}(M^*j)$$

and
$$M^*j = K_j - a_{ji}(M^*i) \qquad (4)$$

Equation (3) is obtained from (2) by setting dM_i/d (and dM_j/dt) equal to zero and solving for the resulting value of Mi (and Mj), which are M^*i (and M^*j).[33] Equation (3) makes explicit that, in equilibrium, the carrying capacity of i is reduced a_{ij} times the number of members in organization j.[34]

The nature of the ecological competition in the model needs clarification. First, we need to understand that competition need not be conscious. Organizations competing for members may not bear any relationships to one another in the minds of members. What is required for competition is that the organizations recruit from the same pool of potential members at the same time. If organizations A, B, and C recruit from exactly the same segment of the community at the same time, then they are in competition, even though they may be totally unaware of each other's existence.

Second, we need to realize that competition does not depend on the activities taking place inside the organizations. A voluntary organization can compete with a factory, if the two have members from identical segments of the community and if they meet at the same time. In fact, this is precisely what happens in the case of unions and factories. Strikes are obvious examples of the union's obtaining a temporary edge in the competition for members. But this example is not a typical one. A more typical instance would be the worker who takes a leave of absence or quits his job to work for a political candidate or the secretary who takes off the afternoon to go on a church retreat. When the Governor calls out the National Guard, local businesses temporarily lose some members.

Third, we must be clear that the competition is ecological, not economic. There is not necessarily any bidding process for members involving rational calculation of costs or benefits. The regions of the niche space in which organizations overlap could possibly define a market in which economic competition for members occurs (as might be the case for sustenance organizations), but economic competition does not always occur.

Finally, competition occurs in time. Only when organiational activities overlap in time do organizations compete directly with each other. Of course, indirect competition may occur because time is not an expandable resource. Organizations which increase their time domain may do so at the expense of others who may not be directly linked in time but are crowded with other activities. When businesses require more overtime before Christmas, voluntary organizations may suffer a temporary drop in attendance because of time pressure on members, even though the overtime does not directly conflict.[35]

The a_{ij} coefficients could be estimated for a community directly if data were available on all organizations and their members. In particular, assuming statistical equilibrium for equations (3), we could use equations (4) to express the competition coefficients for the entire system of organizations. Rewriting (4) in terms of the Ks, we have:

$$K_i = M^*i + a_{ij}(M^*j)$$
and
$$K_j = M^*j + a_{ji}(M^*i) \tag{5}$$

Generalizing the equations to describe r different organizations:

$$
\begin{bmatrix} K_1 \\ K_2 \\ K_3 \\ . \\ . \\ . \\ K_r \end{bmatrix} =
\begin{bmatrix}
1 & a_{12} & a_{13} & \ldots & a_{1r} \\
a_{21} & 1 & a_{23} & \ldots & a_{2r} \\
a_{31} & a_{32} & 1 & \ldots & a_{3r} \\
. & . & & \ldots & . \\
. & . & & \ldots & . \\
. & . & & \ldots & . \\
a_{r1} & a_{r2} & a_{r3} & \ldots & 1
\end{bmatrix}
\begin{bmatrix} M^*1 \\ M^*2 \\ M^*3 \\ . \\ . \\ . \\ M^*r \end{bmatrix} \tag{6}
$$

which may be written in matrix form as $K = AM^*$. This equation expresses the carrying capacities (K_i) of the r organizations in the system in terms of the competition coefficients (a_{ij}) and the equilibrium sizes (M^*i) of the organizations.

We must keep in mind that the carrying capacities for the different organizations have quite clear sociological interpretations: they are simply the number of people in the niche for that organization.[36] What equation (6) forces us to see is that the observed size of an organization will never equal the carrying capacity unless it has no competitors in its niche. In this sense, equation (6) explains why everyone in the niche will not ordinarily be a member of the organization. Usually, an organization will have many competitors who overlap in the niche, consuming many of the potential members of the organization.

The coefficients in the A matrix give us a powerful description of social structure; they are measures of the extent to which two organizations inhabit the same social space. Coefficient a_{ij} measures the proportion of j's niche volume overlapping with organization i. Thus, j will compete with i to the extent that they recruit from the same part of town, from members with the same social characteristics, at the same time.[37]

Notice that membership in j exerts a smaller proportional effect on i if j occupies a larger niche volume. In this case, their overlap will be a greater part of i's niche than j's, and a greater proportion of the people in i will have been recruited from j's niche. If i were completely subsumed by j, then each i member reduces by one person the available carrying capacity for j. The volume of each organization in social and geographic space, exclusive of the time dimension, we will call the niche base. Organizations with large niche bases are generalists; those with smaller bases are specialists. Organizational specialists, as Hannan and Freeman[38] point out, accept the risk of focusing on a narrow band of resources to exploit that resource intensively. The risk, of course, is that the resource will disappear or that some other competitor may monopolize the resource.

The time dimension presents a special case. Increasing time demands on members will increase coordination problems with other organizations, decreasing the proportion of people in the niche base that will participate. Since each individual in a community is affiliated with many organizations, increased time demands of one will tend to make scheduling connections with other organizations problematic.

On the other hand, if the core technology of the organization permits sequential flow of individuals through the organization, then expanding the time niche breadth may increase the pool of potential members. Examples of this strategy are flextime in the business sector and community centers in the voluntary sector.

It may well be that the case that the niche volume, including time, is the domain in which the much researched relationship between system size and structural differentiation[39] actually occurs. That is, groups which are extremely large can sustain what would be impossibly simple structures (in the sense of minimal role differentiation, very simple communication flows, and so forth) for short periods of time; witness large lectures, sports events, and other ephemeral gatherings. These short term phenomena are dramatically undifferentiated because their niche volumes are quite small because of their short duration of activity, even though their sizes, measured conventionally, are tremendous. On the other hand, groups which remain in existence for very long periods of time may become quite differentiated even though they are relatively small in size. The family is probably the prototypical example of this case.[40]

Equation (6) would allow us to test the model by generating predictions for the relationships between the observed organizations and the populations of individuals, if we had complete data. If the model fit well, we could interpret the a_{ij} coefficients as describing the competitive structure of the community. Unfortunately, no such data set exist for any community.[41] Therefore, in order to apply the model, we have to follow a slightly different strategy for the analysis, as the next section will show.

ESTIMATING COMPETITION

Most data sets on organizations either have information on only the larger, well established organizations or are focused only on narrowly defined organizational types.[42] Since variety among organizations is a necessary precondition for this type of model, we need to study a sample of a wide variety of organizational types, rather than attempt a total census of one type (a strategy followed by Nielsen and Hannan[43] and Carroll,[44] who test some explicitly dynamic hypotheses about the population ecology of organizations).

Since the model attends to interorganizational competition for members, the ideal arena to test the model is one in which members are most free to move from organization to organization. This arena is, of course, the voluntary sector. The best data set available on voluntary associations for our purposes is from the Nebraska Annual Social Indicators Survey.[45] These data are best suited because they (1) are part of a long series of studies of voluntary affiliation in that geographical region, (2) are based on a probability sample of individuals from a well-defined geographical area, (3) have a number of measures of organizational characteristics unavailable in other probability samples such as organization size, and (4) are part of a two wave panel study, which allows us to test the assumption of equilibrium.

The Nebraska Annual Social Indicators Survey is a statewide probability sample of noninstitutionalized adults. The respondents in 1977 were chosen through a combination of random digit dialing and a multistage stratified area probability sample of households. Respondents within households were chosen through a random process, which produces a sample which can be weighted to produce a representative sample of individuals. The organizations with which the respondents were affiliated were elicited through aided recall; very detailed information on the sampling design of the study, the questionnaire, coding information, and all other relevant aspects of the study are documented in Johnson.[46] The community with the most complete data is the city of Omaha, in which 521 people were sampled; we use this community for the present study. See McPherson and Smith-Lovin[47] for another example of the use of this data set.

There are some real advantages in studying voluntary organizations. First, they are much more diverse in many ways than business organizations. Businesses are primarily profit-driven; voluntary organizations carry out a much wider range of activities. Second, voluntary organizations are free to choose among individuals without regard to government regulation or other formalized external control.

In addition, voluntary organizations are appropriate for an illustration of the model becasue their memberships are less ambiguous than those of some other types of organizations. We may find it difficult, for instance, to decide whether customers of a business are actually members of the organization, under the model.[48] Finally, voluntary organizations are likely to be subjected to great selective pressures, since they must compete with other discretionary activities for time.

The hypothetical example we presented earlier treated each organization as the species for which the niche is to be established. Actually, Hannan and Freeman make a powerful argument for treating classes or types of organizations as the species analogue.[49] We will use this strategy, which has both positive and negative aspects. On the negative side, we lose the ability to use geographic and temporal data, since we will be averaging across a number of organizations within a type. On the positive side, classes of organizations are conceptually more defensible as species in a number of ways. For example, one sports team may not be expected to grow without limit in the presence of an expanded pool of potential members, but the class of sports organizations may well respond with virtually unlimited growth.

In terms of sampling organizations, there is an advantage in allowing many examples of a type to be used in the analysis, rather than using each occurrence as a unique instance, since historically unique factors which may affect a single organization are averaged out. With any typology or classification scheme, questions arise about the validity of the categories. As will be seen, the typology captures a great deal of the differentiation along the various resource dimensions.[50]

Before we can estimate the structure of competition in the community, we must examine the question of equilibrium. The derivation of the expression for the a_{ij} coefficients in equations (5) and (6) assumes that the process is equilibrium. Equilibrium implies that no systematic changes in the sizes of organizations (or types, in our analysis) is under way. Equilib-

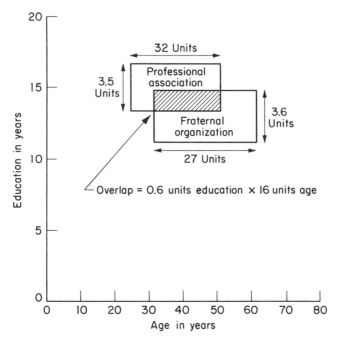

Figure 2.3   The Niches of Two Organizations in Two Dimensions.

rium does not mean that no flow of individuals into or out of organizations is taking place. Rather, it entails a balance between inflow and outflow over time.

The equilibrium assumption is examined for 12 types of voluntary organizations in Figure 2.2. As the figure shows, all types of organizations appear to be in rough equilibrium, with a balance of creation and dissolution of memberships over a two-year period. The single exception to this picture is civic organizations, which seem to be losing memberships at a greater rate than the gains over the period. Overall, however, we are satisfied that the assumption of equilibrium is met fairly well for these data.

As we know, the carrying capacity K_i for the ith type of organization is the number of potential members of the organization—the quantity fitting into its niche base. Since a niche consists of a volume in n- dimensional space, the niche base will be a function of each of the niche breadths. The simplest such function is based on the assumption that niches are rectangular, as in Figure 2.3. Rectangular niche shapes greatly simplify the calculation of the volumes of the niches and their overlaps, since the volume of a rectangular shape is the simple product of the breadth on each dimension. When the niches are rectangular, their overlaps are rectangular.

The niche breadth for each organizational type is formed by constructing a 1.5 standard deviation "window" for each dimension, centered on the mean.[51] Experiments with a variety of window widths suggested that this window produced a maximum discrimination between organizations, while retaining a reasonable degree of overlap. It is interesting that this empirically derived window agrees closely with the results of animal ecologists, who find that the optimum distance between niche centers is slightly more than 1.4 standard deviations.[52] The niche breadths of 12 types of organizations are presented in Table 2.2.

The two types with the narrowest age niche breadths are organizations serving youth and the elderly, both with a niche breadth of 12 years of age. The broadest age breadth is for civic organizations, with a breadth of 28 years. The broadest niche in occupational status is for hobby organizations, with a breadth of 35 socioeconomic index points. The narrowest niche breadth on education is for professional organizations; the broadest is for organizations for the elderly. As is clear from the table, the largest niche bases are for hobby groups; these organizations are the most socially heterogeneous. The organization type with the smallest niche base is youth serving, primarily because of its restricted age and education range.

The niche overlaps for the 12 types of organizations are off the diagonal in Table 2.3. The most obvious fact about Table 2.3 is the total lack of overlap between organizations for the elderly and all others. This lack of overlap is due to the fact that elderly organizations occupy a range on the age dimension overlapping with no other organizational types; the nearest types on the age dimension are fraternal and veterans, with an upper limit of 61 years, as Table 2.2 shows. Thus, organizations for the elderly occupy a distinctive niche in social space, since their overlap with other organizations is at a minimum.[53] The other nonoverlapping pair of organizational types is the union-professional pair (fifth row and third column of Table 2.3). This instance is due, of course, to the fact that professional and union

Table 2.2 Niche Breadths for Twelve Types of Organizations

	Age	Occupation	Sex	Education
Church related	35–59	35–67	.49–1.0	11.7–15.6
Church boards	32–54	34–68	.26–.99	11.7–16.3
Professional	28–50	55–79	.01–.82	14.5–18.0
Civic	31–59	49–75	.06–.83	12.1–16.9
Union	28–48	22–53	.00–.51	11.1–14.1
Sports	25–46	38–68	.14–.89	12.2–15.5
Social	35–59	38–66	.28–1.0	12.2–15.5
Fraternal	34–61	32–65	.08–.83	11.5–15.1
Veterans	41–61	27–60	.00–.73	10.6–15.4
Youth	32–44	37–65	.32–1.0	12.0–15.7
Elderly	65–77	29–65	.43–1.0	9.8–16.7
Hobby	30–55	30–65	.20–.95	12.0–15.8

SOURCE: Data are from the Omaha subsample of the Nebraska Social Indicators Survey 1977, described exhaustively in Johnson, "Designs, Procedures, Instruments and Forms for the 1977 NASIS." Each breadth is formed by establishing a 1.5 standard deviation window about the mean for each variable, for each type of organization. See text for additional details.

organizations are disjoint in the education dimension (rows three and five of column four in Table 2.2).

The absence of overlap for elderly organizations in Table 2.3 produces zero coefficients of competition for this organizational type in Table 2.4. Since there is no overlap, the proportion of the niche base shared with other organizational types is zero, and elderly organizations compete only minimally for members with any other types. In terms of our earlier discussion of fundamental and realized niches (note 2), the elderly organizations have reached the limits of their fundamental niche and have no major (measured) competitors in the community.

It is interesting to note that almost all types compete heavily with hobby and church board organizations (rows 2 and 12). This result occurs because these organizations occupy very large niche bases (2653 and 2489) and have substantial overlaps with more specialized organizations. For instance, youth serving organizations are almost entirely inside the volume occupied by church boards (0.98); 895 of 916 youth servings units fall inside the 2653 units of church boards' volume. Thus, 98% of memberships in youth serving organizations come from the same social space as church board memberships.

On the other hand, only about 34% of the church board memberships come from the social space occupied by youth serving organizations. Church

Table 2.3 Niche Overlaps for Twelve Types of Organizations (Niche Bases on Diagonal)

	Ch	Cb	Pr	Ci	Un	Sp	So	Fr	Ve	Yo	El	Ho
Church related	1496											
Church boards	1187	2653										
Professional	60	244	1247									
Civic	489	1024	672	2644								
Union	9	193	0	67	957							
Sports	399	859	158	644	197	1505						
Social	1131	1319	94	744	92	622	1625					
Fraternal	823	1208	76	881	331	625	1041	2401				
Veterans	400	596	26	428	263	188	564	1325	2252			
Youth	481	895	81	380	87	656	606	449	99	916		
Elderly	0	0	0	0	0	0	0	0	0	0	1661	
Hobby	970	1618	162	904	275	962	1232	1343	757	829	0	2489

NOTE: The niche base is a volume in four-dimensional hyperspace which is formed by taking the products of the niche breadths from Table 2.2 for each type. For example, the niche base for church related organizations is

$$(59-35)(67-35)(1.0-.49)(15.6-11.7) = 1496$$

(not exact because of rounding error; more significant digits are carried in the actual calculations than can be presented in the table). The overlap coefficients are formed by calculating the volume of the hyperbox in the four-dimensional space which represents the intersection of the volumes of each organizational type in the four-dimensional space. This volume is the product of the niche breadth overlap on each dimension for each type of organization. For instance, the overlap between church related groups and church boards is

$$(54-35)(67-35)(.99-.49)(15.6-11.7) = 1187$$

(not exact because of rounding).

Table 2.4 Competition Coefficients (*A*-matrix) among Twelve
Types of Organizations

	Ch	Cb	Pr	Ci	Un	Sp	So	Fr	Ve	Yo	El	Ho
Church related	1.00	.45	.05	.19	.01	.27	.70	.34	.18	.52	.00	.39
Church board	.79	1.00	.20	.39	.20	.57	.81	.50	.26	.98	.00	.73
Professional	.04	.09	1.00	.25	.00	.10	.06	.03	.01	.09	.00	.07
Civic	.33	.39	.54	1.00	.07	.43	.46	.37	.19	.42	.00	.36
Union	.01	.07	.00	.03	1.00	.13	.06	.14	.12	.10	.00	.11
Sports	.27	.32	.13	.24	.21	1.00	.38	.26	.08	.72	.00	.39
Social	.76	.50	.07	.28	.10	.41	1.00	.43	.25	.66	.00	.49
Fraternal	.55	.46	.06	.33	.35	.42	.64	1.00	.59	.49	.00	.54
Veterans	.27	.22	.02	.16	.27	.12	.35	.55	1.00	.11	.00	.30
Youth serving	.32	.34	.06	.14	.09	.44	.37	.19	.04	1.00	.00	.33
Elderly	.00	.00	.00	.00	.00	.00	.00	.00	.00	.00	1.00	.00
Hobby	.65	.69	.13	.34	.29	.64	.76	.56	.34	.91	.00	1.00

NOTE: The competition coefficients are the ratio of the volume of overlap between two types of organizations and the volume of the niche base for the type under examination. For example, the ratio 1187/1496 = .79 (from the first and second rows of Table 2.3) is the proportion of the church related type's volume which is shared with the church boards type.

boards are far more generalist organizations; they have a much larger volume. Since most youth serving memberships come from the church board domain, each such youth membership will reduce the available pool for church boards by nearly one unit. Conversely, since most church board memberships come from outside youth's domain, each church board membership does not, on the average, reduce the available pool for youth serving organizations so much. Thus, the generalist organizations compete moderately over a wide range, whereas the specialists compete intensively in their narrower niche.

When specialists and generalists compete, the competition coefficients are asymmetric; the specialist competes more intensively with the generalist than vice versa. On the other hand, when generalists compete with other generalists, the coefficients are more symmetric. For instance, observe that social organizations compete more or less equally with church related organizations (0.70 and 0.76). Both types are generalists and have relatively high overlap.

Specialists don't compete intensely with one another, since they occupy small regions in social space where they presumably are well adapted to monopolize resources. For example, the three most specialized types—union, professional, and youth serving—have a mean coefficient of less than 0.06 among them. Compare this result to the mean of 0.48 for the most generalist types civic, hobby, and church boards. Of course, the really high coefficients tend to occur only when a specialist competes heavily with a generalist: youth serving with church boards = 0.98; youth serving with hobby = 0.91, and so forth.

Overall characteristics of the *A* matrix contain useful information. The overall mean of the coefficients in the matrix tells us how closely packed the organization types are in the niche space. Extremely high means would suggest that the organizations are very similar to one another in composition and that the occupied part of the niche space is densely filled with competing organizations. Very low means would suggest that the organizations are dissimilar in composition and that the space is not densely packed. The overall mean for our matrix in Table 2.4 is 0.26, suggesting that the orgranizations are fairly loosely packed in the community. Of course, the overall mean is a function of the window chosen; using three standard deviations for the niche breadth would fill the A matrix with ones.

The variance of the coefficients gives information about clustering in the resource space of the community. Very high variability in the a's would suggest that the organizations were clustered into sectors, with high competition among some organizations and low cross-sector competition. The standard deviation of our coefficients is 0.24, which suggests a fairly high amount of variability around the mean of 0.26. One obvious cluster is the church related–church board–social group cluster, with mean intracluster a's of 0.67. Clearly, more sophisticated quantitative analysis of the A matrix could give insight into the social dimensions of the organizational types. Possible approaches include cluster analysis, block modeling, and multidimensional scaling.

These extensions are beyond the scope of this paper. Also beyond the scope of this paper are more explicitly dynamic analyses of the system, such as the mathematical analysis of stability conditions for the community. Our preliminary analysis of the determinant of the matrix and its subdeterminants suggest that the system meets the basic prerequisites for stability.[54] An extended analysis of the question of the dynamics of the community, given our cross-sectional data, would be premature.[55]

TESTING THE MODEL

As we have suggested, one of the problems of the population ecology model is that it is very difficult to test, even in biology. One reason for this difficulty is that the carrying capacity for a species remains an inferred quantity. However, organizations are composed of people, so our carrying capacities can be estimated from the number of people with the characteristics observed in actual members of the organization. Thus, we can test the model in cross section using equation (6), which expresses the carrying capacities for the organizational types in terms of the A matrix and the observed memberships in the organizations.[56]

To illustrate how the equations work, we will focus on civic organizations, represented by the third row and column in the competition matrix of Table 2.4. The entries across the row indicate the proportional effect of an average membership in each of the other types of organizations upon the number of members available for civic groups. The value of 0.54 in

Table 2.5 The Number of Memberships in the Community, Number of People Occupying Niche Base, and Predicted Number of People in the Niche Base for Twelve Types of Organizations

	Number of Memberships (M^*)	Individuals in Niche Base (K)	Predicted Number in Niche Base (predicted K)
Church related	52,647	59,808	120,306
Church boards	16,265	91,900	166,541
Professional	32,198	35,009	48,418
Civic	5,643	67,102	106,125
Union	12,282	53,244	30,035
Sports	58,090	62,726	123,651
Social	22,904	59,808	133,415
Fraternal	18,921	62,726	125,656
Veterans	8,962	36,468	62,592
Youth	29,543	37,927	96,069
Elderly	5,643	16,775	5,643
Hobby	6,971	76,583	156,693

NOTE: The number of memberships is extrapolated from Nebraska Annual Social Indicators Survey 1977 sample results following McPherson (1982), and the number of people in the niche is estimated from data on the community contained in Nebraska Annual Social Indicators Survey 1978 (Johnson 1978). The predicted number of people in the niche comes from equation (6) in the text (see the example calculation in the text). Pearson product-moment correlations are $r(M^*, K) = .056$; $r(M^*, \text{predicted } K) = .228$; $r(K, \text{predicted } K) = .866$.

the fourth row and third column of the matrix indicates that each professional organization membership, on the average, reduces the total number of memberships available to civic organizations by 0.54 memberships.

Table 2.5 presents the number of memberships in the different types of organizations in the community estimated from our sample data *(M)*, the number of people in the community who have the characteristics of members of that type *(K)*, and the number of such people who are predicted to have those characteristics by the model (predicted *K*). Inclusion of an individual in the niche base depends upon the intersection of all criteria; that is, falling outside the niche breadth on any resource dimension excludes an individual from the niche base. Since *K* and *M* are estimated from different samples, they are independently determined quantities.[57]

In order to illustrate how the model produces the predicted values of *K*, we will show how the observed memberships are translated into the predicted carrying capacity for a single type of organization. Focusing our attention on civic organizations again (the fourth row of Table 2.5), we see that the number of observed memberships is approximately 5600, and the number in the niche base is approximately 67,000. The discrepancy, according to the theory, is the interference of the other types, described by the matrix of competition coefficients. Equation (6) allows us to calculate the number of people who should be in the niche base, given the number of observed memberships and the competition matrix.

For civic organizations, the predicted number of people in the niche base

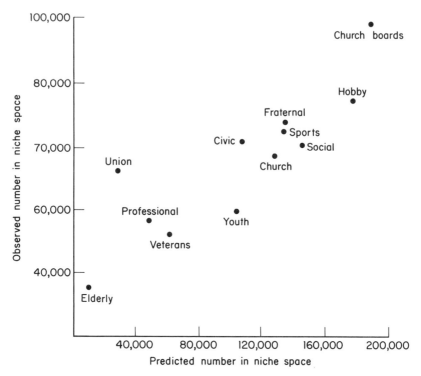

Figure 2.4 Testing the Model.

is the product of the fourth row of the competition matrix *(A)* with the vector of observed memberships *(M):*

$$.33(52,647) + .39(16,265) + .54(32,198) + 1.0(5643) + .07(12,282)$$
$$+ .43(58,090) + .46(22,904) + .37(18,921) + .19(8962) + .42(29,543)$$
$$+ .00(5643) + .36(6,666,971) = 106,125. \textit{ (not exact due to rounding)}$$

The predicted number of people in the niche base, then, is approximately 106,000 (the fourth row of column three in Table 2.5), which is consid- erably greater than the observed number of approximately 67,000. Clearly, there are omitted competitors which we do not have explicitly in the model. However, the evidence that the model captures a great deal of the process is presented in Figure 2.4, which correlates the observed and predicted quantities for all types of organizations.

As the figure shows, there is an extremely strong correlation between the observed and predicted carrying capacities across the 12 types of or- ganizations. The correlation of 0.87 demonstrates that the competition coefficient matrix translates the human resources of the community into the observed organizational resources, with a startling degree of accuracy. The negligible correlation between the observed number of members and the number of people in the niche base has been transformed by the competition matrix into a substantial relationship. Thus, the interorganizational competition for members explains the negligible relationship between the potential and actual membership volumes in the community. The fact that organizations tend to "feed" in the same areas of social space shows why not all similar individuals belong to similar organizations.

The skeptical reader may still be arguing mentally that the strong association is mostly definitional, since we are correlating two closely related quantities, the number of individuals found in a region of social space and the number we expect to find there, given the numbers of members in organizations with known composition.

This argument is plausible, but not supported by the data. If the correlation in Figure 2.4 were simply definitional, we would observe a very strong correlation between the number of members in the different types of organizations and the number in the corresponding organizational niches. In fact, this correlation between the number of actual members and the number of individuals in the niche volumes, ignoring competition, is less than 0.06, as we have seen. Thus, the transformation of niche inhabitants into organizational members by the A matrix of equation (6) not only is extremely powerful, but results in predicted carrying capacities which are strongly related to the observed values.[58]

Figure 2.4, although giving excellent results, is far from a perfect test of the theory. We only have rudimentary measures of our dimensions: none at all for geography and only four social composition dimensions. Nor have we exhausted all the types of organizations in the community; omitted competitors in the A matrix will produce distortions in the translation of observed memberships into predicted carrying capacity.

The reader will have noticed that the model, with only two exceptions, overestimates the number of individuals in the niche base. This result is due to the fact that we have significant numbers of omitted competitors— we have not taken into account all organizations in the community. Because these omitted competitors (families and businesses come readily to mind) exist for most people, the model tends to predict more people in the niche base than are actually there. The extent of overestimation is a measure of the influence of the omitted competitors in the system. With more complete data on a wider variety of organizations, the absolute scales of the two variables would converge. Notice, however, that there is quite a strong relationship between the variables even with these limited data. The omitted competitors are apparently averaging out their effects across the organizational types we have measured.

We believe that better data on more organizational types and more dimensions will improve the absolute fit of the model and improve the already strong correlation in Figure 2.4. Given better data on geography and time and a more exhaustive set of organizations, we believe that the model will account for the distribution and variability in human organizations with great precision. Further, the model will generate a large number of quantitative and qualitative hypotheses about human organizations. In order to set the stage for these hypotheses, we have to make several important theoretical connections.

ANOTHER APPROACH

It is important to underscore the differences between our approach and the theoretical line taken by Freeman and Hannan.[59] They are most interested in the dynamic processes governing slices of the entire range of social organizations and have developed unique and extraordinary methods for the temporal analysis of their data. We are interested in the equilibrium distribution of our much more heterogeneous set of organizations, and with the structure of entire communities of organizations.[60] Freeman and Hannan's concern with dynamics of well defined types of organizations enables them to study the factors contributing to the death rates of organizations under different conditions. In particular, they are interested in the different death rates of generalists and specialists facing different levels of environmental uncertainty.

Our approach is different, since we want to deal with a wide array of organizational types, from the Parent-Teacher Association to the local Plumbers Union. Ultimately, we would like to be able to encompass the structure of entire community systems. Since relatively little is known about the broad range of social organizations (particularly voluntary organizations) as they actually exist in community systems, we begin with cross-sectional analysis. This static model is logically prior to the dynamic analysis which will flow naturally from the logic of McPherson.[61] Our conception of specialism-generalism has the advantage of applying to all types of human organization, since individuals make up those organizations. Since Freeman and Hannan[62] study only one type of organization (restaurants), they can narrow their conception of specialism to one form peculiarly appropriate to a sustenance organization in a market economy (menu variety).

One cannot argue for the superiority of either approach; they are two sides of the same coin. We broaden our conception of niche width to embrace a variety or organizations in cross section, and they narrow theirs to study one type over time. We believe that both approaches will merge theoretically as they broaden the scope of their inquiry to include more diversity in organizations (e.g., unions) and as we gather more dynamic data on our organizations.

NICHE SHAPE: THE LOCATION OF INDIVIDUALS IN SOCIAL SPACE

So far, the niche space has been treated as if it were uniformly inhabited by individuals. Of course, this is not so. Many dimensions will have non-rectangular univariate distributions, and their multivariate distributions will be at least as complicated. In fact, most of the dimensions will probably be correlated; dimensions such as age, education, and occupation have been targets of correlation studies since survey analysis was invented.

We must distinguish between two different kinds of distributional phenomena: intraorganizational distributions and community level distributions. When we speak of the distribution of a social resource such as years of education in the community, we are in a domain well explored by conventional survey research. Literally thousands of univariate and correlational studies have mapped their way through the distributions of education, occupation, income, and so forth. Less well mapped, but beginning to draw some serious attention, is the distribution of social resources inside organizations. For instance, Kaufman and Spilerman[63] analyze the age distribution across a variety of occupations, uncovering a distinctive set of "shapes" in the age patterns. They distinguish among occupations with peaks at young, middle, or elderly ranges; occupations with U-shaped distributions; and uniformly distributed occupations. Related analyses are beginning to appear under the rubric of organizational demography.[64] This work studies the distribution of social characteristics within organizations.

The model in this paper connects the interorganizational distribution and community level distribution of social resources. The composition of the organization defines a key aspect of its niche in the community. From inside the organization, however, the composition of the organization is its demography. The distribution of the social attributes of members, such as sex and race, define the domain of demographic models for organizational structure.[65] Organizational demography, then, is the link between the interorganizational community which our model analyses and the internal dynamics of single organizations. As Pfeffer[66] notes, organizational demography has an impact on internal processes such as administrative succession, innovation, adaptability, turnover, power, and a host of other variables.

The ecological model and the demographic model complement each other in several key respects. First the ecological model makes sense of the environment for organizational demography. The members who enter and leave the organization are givens for the demographic model; for the ecological model they are the phenomenon to be explained. The ecological model locates the organization in an interorganizational field defined by the characteristics of members. The demographic model describes the consequences of that location for an organization and its members. Thus, organizational demography and the ecological model are conceptual duals of each other; what is internal to one is external to the other.

Second, the ecological model supplies an unambiguous theoretical context for the internal demography of organizations. Members of the organizations define the interorganizational field in the community. It is easy to envision straightforward extensions of our model which predict the intensity of competition for different types of organizational members, thus supplying theoretically rooted supply and demand functions. Clearly, there can be variation in the strength of competition in different zones of an organization's niche volume. For instance, an organization may have multiple competitors for members in certain zones of education (e.g., M.B.A.s or lawyers), while having little competition for others (e.g., high school graduates).

We suspect that these variations will be intimately tied to internal structure in the organization. The model at its current stage of development treats the organization as something of a "black box" in multidimensional space; this black box is the domain of the demography of organizations. One ecological concept which could prove to be very useful here is the notion of polymorphism. A polymorphic organization is one which can be thought of as a combination of specialized forms. Heterogeneity in the composition of the polymorphic organizations signals the presence of specialized functions in the organization, rather than simply stochastic variability in the resource dimension.

CORRELATED NICHE DIMENSIONS

The multivariate distribution of individuals in the niche space will affect the nature of the organizations in the community. If the niche dimensions are correlated with each other, then individuals' location on one dimension will be related to their location on the other dimensions. This issue has been treated most recently by Peter Blau,[67] who derives a number of propositions about the effects of "consolidated parameters" (correlated niche dimensions) on system structure.

Correlated resource dimensions imply that individuals will not be evenly distributed through the niche space. If education and income are correlated, then individuals will cluster in the high education–high income, and low education–low income areas of the space. The more densely occupied areas of the niche space will be richer in resources for the organizations which are located there. Thus, the correlated resource dimensions contract and simplify the niche space. If two dimensions are perfectly correlated, then one can substitute for the other; no additional information is contained in the redundant dimension.

In animal ecology, the correlation of resource dimensions has the effect of decreasing the number of species which can inhabit the community.[68] This reduction occurs because the effective resource volume of the community is decreased by the redundancy in the resource dimensions. A statistical analogy to this effect is multicolinearity, in which the effects of correlated predictor variables cannot be separated.

The broad macrostructural constraints on the community produced by correlated parameters, then, set the stage for competition among organizations for members. Systems with low correlations among resource dimensions will accommodate a wider variety of organizational types than systems with high correlations, since the effective niche space will be much greater in a system with lower correlations.

As a simple example, consider a system in which income and education are weakly correlated. In such a system, there will be substantial numbers of people with high disposable income and little education. Organizations which would flourish in that niche base may include snowmobile and motorcycling clubs, hunting and shooting organizations, and the like. Organizations focusing on the high education, low income niche base would include book clubs, chess clubs, and so forth. Systems with more strongly correlated resource dimensions will tend to stratify the population of individuals, so that most people with high income will tend to have high education. The decrease in diversity among individuals will then be reflected in a decrease in diversity among organizations.

In general, correlations among resource dimensions will define upper limits to the potential diversity among organizations. Strongly correlated dimensions will mean that organizations with restricted variance in one resource characteristic will have similarly restricted variance in other characteristics. Organizations will thus have the opportunity to exercise tremendous selectivity with respect to social characteristics, since there will exist a relatively large number of socially homogeneous potential members. This fact will increase the competition among organizations, since individuals will be concentrated in restricted regions of the niche space. The narrowing of the available niche space will pack organizations into smaller volumes, decrease diversity, and encourage organizations to specialize. Organizations which select on one characteristic (e.g., education) are forced to select on others (e.g., minority status). The stronger the correlations, the greater the number of resource dimensions in which organizations will overlap, if they overlap at all.

On the other hand, when correlations are low, then an organization can specialize in one dimension without being forced to specialize in others as a result. If sex is not strongly correlated with education and income, then an organization can contain only females without necessarily having low status as well. The correlations among dimensions, then, either mitigate or magnify the effects of selectivity on the part of the organizations. We know that a black organization in South Africa will be composed of primarily low status people, because of income and educational discrimination in that country. In contrast, a black organization in a major urban area in the United States could be composed exclusively of high status professionals, low status workers, or members having tremendous diversity in status. All of these hypotheses will become testable when good comparative data across a number of systems are available.

SOME ILLUSTRATIVE HYPOTHESES

Hypotheses About Niche Volumes (Specialism versus Generalism)

Hypothesis A: Organizational Size Is Positively Related to Niche Volume and Inversely Related to Competition

In order to grasp the proposition of the relationship of organizational size to niche volume and competition, it is necessary to remember that the carrying capacity is the number of person-time units potentially available to the organization in the community, ignoring competition. The niche volume is the area in social, geographical, and temporal space "occupied" by the organization. Although niche volume and carrying capacity will be strongly correlated, they are neither identical nor even in the same units. Now, equation (6) shows that the carrying capacity of each organization is decomposable into r components, where the size of the ith organization is the ith component. Each of the other r components consists of two terms, a competition coefficient and the observed size of one of the other organizations. For instance, for the first organization,

$$K_{21} = M^*_{21} + a_{12}(M^*_{22}) + a_{13}(M^*_{23}) + \ldots + a_{1r}(M^*_{2r}) \qquad (7)$$

where K_{21} is the carrying capacity of the first organization, M^*_{21} is the size of that organization, and the $r-1$ subsequent terms are the sizes of the remaining organizations, reduced by the competition coefficients. Now, if an organization has no competition, it will tend to reach its carrying capacity in size. Conversely, when it has many strong competitors, it will reach an equilibrium point far below its carrying capacity. Since, in general, greater niche volume will entail a larger carrying capacity, it follows from equation (7) that size (M^*_{21}) will be directly related to niche volume and inversely related to competition (the $[r-1]$ remaining terms of [7]).

On the conceptual level, the first part of hypothesis A asserts that organizations with a large niche volume (that is, heterogeneous organizations, or organizations covering large amounts of space and time) can recruit from a larger pool of resources. The second part is analogous to the principle of competitive exclusion,[69] in which two species' occupying the same niche produces an unstable dynamic condition, leading to the exclusion of one of the species.

Hypothesis B: Larger Communities Will Have More Specialized Organizations

In a very general sense, the hypothesis that large communities have more specialized organizations has its roots in the size-differentiation principle so much researched in the complex organization literature.[70] The basic idea is that the components of a system will increase both in size and in number with increases in system size. With increase in number of organizations, the principle of competitive exclusion mentioned previously will generate specialization over time. The equilibrium distribution of organizations in large systems will contain a large number of specialized organizations, which find enough people in their small niche to survive. The connection between this proposition and the Durkheimian theories of division of labor[71] and theories of the other founding fathers of sociology is clear.

This idea, like all of our illustrative hypotheses, is actually a bundle of hypotheses about a general topic. For instance, one implication of this line of reasoning is that as communities grow, their niche structure simply becomes more elaborate. An obvious corollary question is whether these competitive structures are similar for different communities. That is, are there fundamental niches for organizational types, which are more or less invariant across systems, or does historical accident determine location in the niche space?

*Hypothesis C: Organizational Formalization Is Positively Related to
Niche Volume, ceteris paribus*
The proposition that organization formalization is positively related to niche volume, all else being equal, comes from the basic idea that internal heterogeneity in the members of an organization (large niche volume produced by variation in the social composition of the members, or larger geographical or temporal spread) will increase the difficulties of coordination. Clearly, the effects of niche volume must be evaluated with awareness of the well documented correlation of organization size and formalization.[72] In fact, one important problem for study is whether niche volume, instead of size, is actually the fundamental variable affecting specialization, centralization, hierarchy, and so forth.

*Hypothesis D: Friendship Network Density within Organizations Is
Inversely Related to Niche Volume Arising from Social and
Spatial Diversity and Directly Related to Temporal Dispersion*
Hypothesis D is rooted in the homophily principle.[73] Organizations with large niche volumes in the social domain will be socially heterogeneous. The homophily hypothesis argues that like individuals will tend to associate with higher frequency.[74] The spatial part of the hypothesis comes from the well documented finding that friendship links are inversely related to geographic distance. The temporal part of the argument is rooted in the basic social fact that the longer a system is in existence, the higher the probability of contact between members.

Hypotheses about Competition

Hypothesis A: Intraclass Competition Will Exceed Interclass Competition
Hypothesis A comes directly from bioecology, where it is virtually axiomatic that intraspecies competition exceeds interspecies competition.[75] The logic here is that each member of a species uses one unit's worth of the resources which are characteristic of that species. Competitors, which will

not ordinarily occupy exactly the same niche, will use, on the average, less of the resource than a member of the same species will. Analogously, each member of one bowling team will reduce by one the possible members for another team which bowls at the same time. Teams which play at different times will not be affected so absolutely, and the Parent-Teachers Association may not be affected at all. Thus, organizations forming a class will have higher rates of competition with one another than organizations from different classes.

Data on the geographic dispersion of members will be a very crucial part of the test of this and related hypotheses, since many organizations will be geographically localized. For instance, religious organizations of the same denomination tend to have territorial domains as a result of their affiliation with a church, which tend to limit their direct competition for members. Similarly, neighborhood groups may be similar to each other in composition and yet have no overlap in space.

The geographic dispersion of members will assume greater importance in direct proportion to the compositional similarity of the other organizations. Organizations recruiting from very disparate social categories or at dramatically different times will be able to overlap geographically to a much greater degree than highly similar organizations. A similar hypothesis is found in the ecological literature,[76] where it is argued that similar competing species will tend toward geographic exclusively.

Hypothesis B: Competition Will Be More Intense in Systems with Correlated Resource Dimensions

There are two major sources for hypothesis B. The first link is to that of Blau,[77] who has devoted major effort to the study of what he calls "correlated parameters." His parameters are none other than our resource dimension—the basic sociodemographic characteristics which affect social interaction. Our argument is that correlations among these resource dimensions have the effect of concentrating individuals in localized areas of the niche space. These concentrations will force the organizations to congregate in the high density areas for members. Thus, correlated resource dimensions contract and simplify the niche space, pushing the organizations to narrower regions.

There is a similar discussion in the ecological literature. MacArthur[78] discusses the effect of correlated n dimensions on coexistence of species in the community, concluding that correlated dimensions have the effect of reducing the net resources in the niche space, and thus the number of species. Thus, there are a number of subhypotheses for this proposition, including predictions about the diversity of types of organizations and the extent of competition among the ones which are in the community.

Hypothesis C: Competition Will Be More Intense at Higher Ranges of Status and Other Valued Resources

Hypothesis C is a first approximation toward breaking down the niche space into constituent regions. Certain regions of the niche space will be more contested because they contain resources which are useful to many organizations. Regions with individuals having large amounts of disposable income or time are obvious candidates for substantial competition.

There is indirect evidence for this idea in the voluntary association literature. It is probably one of the most replicated findings in sociology that people with higher education, income, and occupational prestige belong to more voluntary organizations.[79] The conceptual dual of this finding is, of course, that organizations focusing on these people will be competing for their time and other resources. We think that our new perspective on this old problem may go a long way toward releasing this literature from the mire of low level empirical generalization it has occupied for decades.

Hypothesis D: The Competition Equations Can Account for the Diversity and Location of Organizations in Communities
Hypothesis D is obviously not developed formally yet. However, it summarizes the main direction in which the theory should go. Equation (2) is stated in terms of the translation of observed sizes of organizations into community level carrying capacities. By far the more interesting form of the equation would be its inverse—accounting for the sizes of the organizations given the resources in the community. However, in any application of (2) to an observed community, an error term representing the disparity between observed and theoretical carrying capacities must be added. This error term complicates the inversion of (2) to predict organizational size, since it, like most error terms, is unobserved, and obtained empirically by subtraction during estimation.

Thus, we regard this hypothesis as a direction for further development, which can be addressed by the data when the theory is worked out in greater detail. We are currently working on adaptations of logic used by geographical ecologists[80] and results from general ecology.[81]

SUMMARY AND DISCUSSION

We have outlined what we believe is a new and powerful way of thinking about organizations. In a sense, this model is the logical extension of the germ of an idea from Aristotle, through Hawley and Duncan[82] via Darwin and Spencer, to the current organizational ecologists. The basic idea has been in the literature for some time; however, we believe that this application is novel.

Our empirical results are for voluntary organizations, but we have given examples which are relevant to other types of organizations. Obviously, many compromises have been made in estimation and analysis. However, the power of the model shows itself not least in the fact that even with available data, the model produces interesting and plausible results. We are not surprised that hobby organizations are generalist organizations; we feel comfortable that church boards are so similar to church related organizations; it makes sense to us that organizations for the elderly should be somewhat isolated from the rest of the system.

The methods we have developed for operationalizing the concept of niche are at once quite simple, yet extremely general. A reader has pointed out that any characteristic which varies among individuals could be incorporated into the model, including (such epiphenomena as) attitudes, values, and the like. These characteristics should be very interesting to organizational researchers who would like to explain how organizations with similar social composition may still engage in observably different activities, as in the case of two social influence groups, one proabortion, and the other antiabortion. Once the major dimensions of sociodemographic characteristics had been taken into account, then the explanatory power of social psychological characteristics could be tested. We will leave such exercises to future researchers.

We have emphasized voluntary organizations because they provide a purer case for the competition model, and because the variability in social composition for voluntary organizations is great enough to show strong results. We do not, however, believe that the model is in any way limited to voluntary organizations. It is true that the growth of money-driven organization is responsive to economic conditions; however, when the organization does expand, the members must come from somewhere. We believe that this model will ultimately give us a powerful way of understanding where these new members will come from (and when), and what will be the implications for other organizations in the system.

NOTES

1. Portions of this paper appeared in the *American Sociological Review*, 48 (1983), 519–532, © American Sociological Association, and are reprinted by permission. Work on this paper was supported in part by National Science Foundation Grants SES-8120666 and SES-8319899. Many people have given helpful comments on versions of this paper. In alphabetical order, they are Howard Aldrich, Nicholas Babchuk, Glenn Carroll, O. D. Duncan, Omar Galle, Amos Hawley, David Knoke, Gerhard Lenski, Rachel Rosenfeld, Moshe Semyonov, and Seymour Spilerman. I would also like to thank the members of the structuralist seminar at the University of South Carolina for their comments and suggestions: Professors Charles Brody, Peter Mariolis, Bruce Mayhew, Patrick Nolan, Theresa Robinson, Eui-Hang Shin, John Skvoretz, Lynn Smith-Lovin, and Lala Steelman. The data were provided by the Nebraska Annual Social Indicators Survey, Bureau of Sociological Research, University of Nebraska, Lincoln, Nebraska. The author bears full responsibility for data analysis and interpretation.

2. *The Study of Sociology* (New York: Appleton and Company, 1874).

3. Kenneth Bock, "Theories of Progress, Development, Evolution," chapter 2 in *A History of Sociological Analysis* ed. Tom Bottomore and Robert Nisbet (New York: Basic Books, 1978).

4. Amos Hawley, *Human Ecology* (New York: The Ronald Press, 1950).

5. Gerhard Lenski, *Power and Privilege: A Theory of Social Stratification* (New York: McGraw-Hill, 1966).

6. Michael T. Hannan and John T. Freeman, "The Population Ecology of Organizations,"

American Journal of Sociology 82 5 (March 1977), 929–964, and Howard Aldrich, *Organizations and Environments* (Englewood Cliffs, N.J.: Prentice-Hall, 1979).

7. G. Hardin, "The Competitive Exclusion Principle," *Science* 131 (1960), 1292–1297, and R. H. Peters, "Tautology in Evolution and Ecology," *American Naturalist* 110 (1976), 1–12.

8. Michael T. Hannan and John H. Freeman, "The Population Ecology of Organizations," "Internal Politics of Growth and Decline," in *Environments and Organizations: Theoretical and Empirical Perspectives* ed. Marshall W. Meyer and Associates (Ed.) (San Francisco: Jossey-Bass, 1981), and "Niche Width and the Dynamics of Organizational Populations," Technical Report no. 2, Organizational Studies Section, Institute for Mathematical Studies in the Social Sciences, Stanford University.

9. Hannan and Freeman, "The Population Ecology of Organizations."

10. Cf. Constance Smith and Anne Freedman, *Voluntary Associations: Perspectives on the Literature* (Cambridge, Mass.: Harvard University Press, 1972).

11. P. Mariolis, "Interlocking Directorates and Control of Corporations: The Theory of Bank Control," *Social Science Quarterly* 56 (1975), 425–439.

12. Charles C. Moskos, "The Military," in Alex Inkeles, James Coleman and Neil Smelser, eds., *Annual Review of Sociology,* 2 (1976), 55–77.

13. There are two pervasive themes in the organizational literature which argue that this is so. First, there is very substantial evidence that organizational size is a dominant force in determining organizational outcomes, whether through direct political influence in the mobilization of votes or the threat of doing so (cf. J. D. McCarthy and M. Zald, "Resource Mobilization and Social Movements: A Partial Theory," *American Journal of Sociology* 82 [1977], 1212–1241, or through the increased ability of larger organizations to influence their environments directly (cf. Aldrich, *Environments and Organizations*). For instance, larger organizations can generate publicity for activities, are more newsworthy, tend to have larger geographic bases, and so forth. Second, there are powerful internal processes which tend toward increases in organizational size (and thus increased competition for members): a wide range of studies shows that those who control organizations benefit from increasing the number of people under their authority (cf. Herbert A. Simon, "The Compensation of Executives," *Sociometry* 20 [1957] 32–35), and Peter M. Blau, "A Macrosociological Theory of Social Structure," *American Journal of Sociology* 83 [1977] 26–54). The benefits of increased size apply not only to superordinates, but to all members; in "Bringing the Boss Back in: Employer Size Employee Schooling and Socioeconomic Achievement," *American Sociological Review* 43 (1977) 813–828, Ross Stelzenberg reviews a wide body of literature which links size to increased worker earnings, profitability, decreased economic competition, and so forth. Given the powerful strains toward increases in size and the sheer number of organizations in industrial society, it is obvious that members are a critical resource for organizations.

14. Hawley, *Human Ecology,* 44.

15. Hannan and Freeman, "The Population Ecology of Organizations," 947.

16. But see Michael T. Hannan and John H. Freeman, "Niche Width and the Dynamics of Organizational Populations," Technical Report no. 2, Organizational Studies Section, Institute for Mathematical Studies in the Social Sciences, Stanford University.

17. E. R. Pianka, "The Structure of Lizard Communities," *Annual Review of Ecological Systems* 4 (1973), 53–74.

18. Cf. W. A. Cameron, "Mammals of the Islands in the Gulf of St. Lawrence." *Bulletin of the Natural Museum of Canada,* vol. 154 and R. MacArthur and E. Pianka, "On Optimal Use of a Patchy Environment," *American Naturalist* 100 (1966), 603–609.

19. Ecologists sometimes distinguish between fundamental and realized niches, which refer to niches formed in noncompetitive and competitive situations, respectively. See D. H. Morse, *Behavioral Mechanisms in Ecology* (Cambridge, Mass.: Harvard University Press, 1980). The fundamental niche is the niche which could be exploited by the species if there were no competitors—a situation unlikely to occur anywhere outside the laboratory. The fundamental niche can only be changed through genetic change in the species—a process occurring over quite long periods of time. The realized niche, however, can change simply with the presence

or absence of a given competitor. See D. H. Morse, "Ecological Aspects of Some Mixed Species Foraging Flocks of Birds," *Ecological Monographs*, 40 (1970), 119–168.

20. M. L. Cody, "Optimization in Ecology," *Science* 183 (1974), 1156–1164.

21. Robert E. Ricklefs, *Ecology* (New York: Chiron Press, 1979).

22. R. MacArthur, "The Theory of the Niche," in *Population Biology and Evolution*, ed. R. C. Lewontin (Syracuse, N.Y.: Syracuse University Press, 1968), chapter 11.

23. Hubert M. Blalock, *Theory Construction: From Verbal to Mathematical Formulations* (Englewood Cliffs, N.J.: Prentice-Hall, 1969).

24. The question of which resource dimensions are important is a critical issue. In animal ecology, the assumption is often implicitly made that any resource dimension which differentiates species is either a dimension which is functionally important to the relations among species or a dimension which has been so in the past. See, for example, Ricklefs, *Ecology*, 742. Here we will concentrate on basic sociodemographic dimensions which are nearly universally recognized as important in the social distinctions among people.

25. The example appears to be trivial because the names contain information on the age characteristics of the organizations. However, the differences we show can be critical for a variety of reasons. When organizations are differentiated in this fashion, each is embedded in a totally different interorganizational context. Organizations for the elderly will be connected through their members to entirely different sectors of the federal government (Social Security, Medicare) than youth organizations (Department of Education, Department of Defense), and to different sectors of the economy (job entry versus pension), and so forth. Thus, apparently trivial differences in composition on even a single dimension may have broad consequences for the relationships among organizations.

26. The detail with which we decide to measure time as a dimension will dictate whether we have to deal with the issue of multiple memberships for individuals. Ovbiously, people have multiple jobs, although they don't often work at them at exactly the same time. People can belong to several voluntary organizations, but they do not often meet with more than one at a given instant. If we don't have continuous records of individual behavior, then our imperfect measurement of the time dimension will dictate that we observe certain compromises in the measurement of the niche characteristics, as will be seen.

27. This finding is anticipated by Roger G. Barker, *Ecological Psychology* (Stanford, Calif.: Stanford University Press, 1968), who interprets results such as these in terms of "manning effects." Note that the term "community" enters our analysis as a primitive, corresponding roughly to the concept "town" or "city." We believe that this definition is appropriate to the case at hand, since members of organizations generally come from the city in which the organization is located, or from the same general geographical area. If one were interested in studying systems at a higher level of organization such as nations, the methods of our analysis could be easily adapted to these cases.

28. G. W. Domhoff, *The Higher Circles: The Governing Class in America* (New York: Random House, 1970).

29. One might reasonably ask why education could be important to a bowling league. The sense in which a restricted range of variation in education for bowling groups needs to be explained is exactly the same sense in which one may want to analyze a significant coefficient in a structural equation model. See Otis D. Duncan, *Introduction to Structural Equation Models* (New York: Academic Press, 1975). We may pursue several possibilities in the case of the bowling example. Recruitment of the league may be through friendship networks, which tend to be homogeneous with respect to education—the homophily principle which underlies much work in structural analysis, as in Peter M. Blau, "A Macrosociological Theory of Social Structure," *American Journal of Sociology* 83: 1 (1977), 26–54. The point at which we decide to leave a correlation or an observed niche differentiation along a resource dimension unanalyzed depends on our theoretical goals. The converse question—how do we select dimensions which may prove to be important—also has analogues in structural equation modeling. We choose variables for structural equation models which (1) have a plausible theoretical interpretation, (2) have been shown to have effects on the endogenous variables

in the past, or (3) are available and serendipitously have interpretable relationships to the other variables in the model. Notice that we are not claiming that it is somehow necessary for bowling groups to have this sort of restriction on recruitment—only that the observed one does in this community. As we will see in the next section, these restrictions in niche breadth can arise because of accommodations to the presence of competitors in the community.

30. The multiplication of each of the breadths results in a scalar quantity which is sensitive to the measurement units of each of the dimensions. For instance, we could have measured education in semesters or quarters, instead of years. The resulting volumes would have been doubled or quadrupled. Note, however, that our only use of these volumes is in relation to other such volumes, measured in the same scale. Anticipating later results, the original scales of the dimensions will disappear when we form our competition coefficients, since these coefficients are ratios of volumes. These ratios are pure numbers, devoid of unit. Thus, the measurement units of the dimensions are not a problem for our analysis.

31. J. Miller McPherson, "A Dynamic Model of Voluntary Affiliation," *Social Forces* 59, 3 (1981), 705–728, and "The Size of Voluntary Organizations," *Social Forces* 61 (1983), 1044–1064.

32. P. J. Wangersky, "Lotka-Volterra Population Models," *Annual Review of Ecological Systems*, 9 (1978), 189–218.

33. See John Vandermeer, *Elementary Mathematical Ecology* (New York: John Wiley & Sons, 1981).

34. Note that the equations place no intrinsic upper limit to the size of the organization. This logically implies that the organization will grow until it (1) exhausts the carrying capacity (no competitors) or (2) recruits from its niche base until it has acquired all individuals not in a competing organization. The community is in equilibrium when all organizations are relatively stable in size. One reader has argued that some business firms may be inclined to minimize the number of employees to maximize profits. This argument could be true for some constant level of profit, but we believe that the pressures toward organizational growth outlined in note 1 will prevail under ordinary conditions.

35. These comments about expansion (or contraction) or the niche apply to all dimensions within the limits set by the fundamental niche (see note 2). Major changes in structure tend to occur only over long periods of time, barring catastrophic events. Such catastrophes would include the disappearance of a large, formerly dominant organization from the scene or the introduction of a new, highly efficient organization into the community. Analogies to these events in plant or animal ecology include the selective removal of a species through epidemic disease or the introduction of a new competitor with no natural predators as described in R. MacArthur, "The Theory of the Niche," 169ff. In either case, such changes tend to come from exogenous sources.

36. In the most general formulation, the carrying capacity is the number of person-hours (or days, or whatever unit we measure time with) available. When we ignore the time dimension, we will henceforth refer to the niche of an organization as the niche base. The niche base is the volume of the organization in special space, exclusive of the time dimension. The carrying capacity in this instance is the number of people in that volume. If we are ignoring time, the carrying capacity is an integer representing individuals with the appropriate characteristics for potential membership in the organization. If we are explicitly including time, the carrying capacity will be in person-time units.

37. This representation is correct, even if the dimensions are not directly connected to causal processes related to organizational survival. One could imagine, for instance, that eye color might be a dimension which could distinguish one organization from another. This result is similar to a spurious correlation in survey analysis, where the relationship between two variables is due to the action of a third unspecified variable. The unspecified variable in the example is likely to be race or ethnicity. Eye color can stand as a proxy if race is not explicitly considered as a dimension, even if we are not acute enough to discover its true (indirect) relationship to the functioning of the system through race. This discussion parallels

the line of argument in G. E. Hutchinson, "When Are Species Necessary?", in *Population Biology and Evolution*, ed. R. C. Lewontin (Syracuse, N.Y.: Syracuse University Press, 1968), chapter 12.

38. Hannan and Freeman, "The Population Ecology of Organizations."

39. See Peter M. Blau, "A Formal Theory of Differentiation in Organizations," *American Sociological Review* 35 (1970), 201–218.

40. See J. Miller and H. H. Garrison, "Sex Roles: The Division of Labor at Home and in the Workplace," in *Annual Review of Sociology*, ed. R. H. Turner and J. H. Short, 8 (1982), 237–262.

41. Some alternative data sets are those of Joseph Galaskiewicz, "The Structure of Community Organizational Networks," *Social Forces* 57 (1979), 1346–1364, and David Knoke and James R. Wood, *Organized for Action: Commitment in Voluntary Associations* (New Brunswick, N.J.: Rutgers University Press, 1981). Each of these has significant limitations for our purposes. The early community studies undoubtedly had the information we need, but not, of course, in accessible form.

42. J. Miller McPherson, "Ephemera and Periphera in Social Organization: Studying Voluntary Organizations with Survey Methods." Paper presented at the Conference on Survey Approaches to Community Organizational Research, Yale University, May 1981.

43. F. Nielsen and M. T. Hannan, "The Expansion of National Educational Systems: Test of a Population Ecology Model," *American Sociological Review* 42 (1977), 479–490.

44. G. R. Carroll, "Dynamics of Organizational Expansion in Systems of Higher Education," *American Sociological Review* 46 (1981), 585–599.

45. D. R. Johnson, *Nebraska Annual Social Indicators Survey 1978* (Lincoln, Nebr.: Bureau of Sociological Research, 1978).

46. Johnson, *Nebraska Annual Social Indicators Survey 1978*.

47. J. Miller McPherson and Lynn Smith-Lovin, "Women and Weak Ties: Differences by Sex in the Size of Voluntary Associations," *American Journal of Sociology* 87 (1982), 883–904.

48. We are indebted to Professor Amos Hawley (personal communication) for this insight, which has several subtle but important implications for applying the model to more general types of organizations than our data allow at present.

49. Hannan and Freeman, "The Population Ecology of Organizations": 934–936.

50. When the analysis rests upon types or classes of organizations, as in this paper, the observed variability in the resource dimension (the niche breadth) is a function of differences both within and between organizations. If the differences are large between organizations part of the observed variability for the class, then the typology producing the classes has low validity. In this sense, the strong results for the model found in the next section serve as a reassuring check on the validity of the typology.

51. This operationalization is very simple. More sophisticated methods, allowing more complex shapes in the (hyper) spaces of niches, will undoubtedly yield more powerful results. Some ideas for such approaches will be discussed in the final section of the paper. We ask the reader to suspend judgment on the issue until the section on testing the model. We believe that our results are surprisingly strong, even with these heuristic methods.

52. R. Levins, *Evolution in Changing Environments: Some Theoretical Explorations* (Princeton, N.J.: Princeton University Press, 1968) and Robert H. MacArthur, *Geographical Ecology: Patterns in the Distribution of Species* (New York: Harper and Row, 1972).

53. These zero overlaps do not imply that no elderly people belong to any other type of organization. This interpretation would be correct only if the niche breadth were defined by the total range along the resource dimension. If this definition were used, a single deviant case would arbitrarily expand the niche breadth to any value. Likewise, the zero values do not prove that there are literally no competitors in this region of the niche space. It seems very likely that there are significant ommitted competitors for elderly individuals, such as hospitals, other institutions, the extended family, and so forth. It is significant that increasing the window width only slightly produces nonzero overlaps for veterans and fraternal groups

with organizations for the elderly (see Table 2.2). The decision to display the given niche was made on the grounds that these values gave the best fit to the observed data for Figure 2.5.

54. R. Levins, *Evolution in Changing Environments*.

55. The basic conditions for a community to be stable are that the determinant of the *A* matrix be positive, and that the determinant of the symmetrized matrix whose elements are $(a_{ij} + a_{ji})/2$ must be positive. In addition, subdeterminants formed by striking out a row and the corresponding columns must be positive. See R. Levins, *Evolution in Changing Environments: Some Theoretical Explorations*, chapter 3. Vandermeer, *Elementary Mathematical Ecology*, states essentially the same conditions in terms of the eigenvalues of the Jacobian matrix formed from the *A* matrix (Chapter 9). See also the discussion in Carroll, "Dynamics of Organizational Expansion in Systems of Higher Education."

56. The carrying capacity in equation (6) is the realized carrying capacity, defined by the realized niche referred to in note 2. A test of the model based on estimating the carrying capacities of each type of organization across a wide range of different communities (thus allowing the niches to vary across different communities, with different histories, sizes, and so forth) produced strikingly similar results. The correlation between expected and observed carrying capacities for this parallel analysis was 0.79—close to the 0.87 correlation of Figure 2.2 and Table 2.5.

57. The Nebraska Annual Social Indicators Survey 1978, the source for the observed numbers, is the trend study corresponding to the off-year for the panel study described in David R. Johnson, *Nebraska Annual Social Indicators Survey 1977*, Report no. 5, "Designs, Procedures, Instruments and Forms for the 1977 NASIS (Lincoln, Nebr.: Bureau of Sociological Research, University of Nebraska, 1977). Details on the 1978 study can be found in Johnson, *Nebraska Annual Social Indicators Survey 1978*.

58. The importance of each different dimension can be tested empirically, using equation (6). The procedures is conceptually similar to stepwise regression analysis. A dimension is dropped from the analysis and the competition matrix is reconstructed. The predicted and observed carrying capacities are correlated, as in Table 2.5 the most important dimension by this criterion is age, whose omission reduces the correlation between predicted and observed capacities to less than 0.4. Ranked in decreasing order of their importance by this criterion are occupation, education, and sex. Additional dimensions could be evaluated similarly.

59. John Freeman and Michael T. Hannan, "Niche Width and the Dynamics of Organizational Populations," *American Journal of Sociology* 88, 6 (May 1983), 1116–1145.

60. For an interesting look at the ongoing debate about equilibrium competitive analysis in bioecology see Roger Lewin, "Santa Rosalia Was a Goat," *Science* 221 (1983a), 636–639 and "Predators and Hurricanes Change Ecology," *Science* 221 (1983b), 737–740.

61. J. Miller McPherson, "The Size of Voluntary Organizations," *Social Forces* 61 (1983), 1044–1064.

62. John Freeman and Michael T. Hannan, "Niche Width and the Dynamics of Organizational Populations," *American Journal of Sociology* 88, 6 (May 1983), 1116–1145.

63. R. L. Kaufman and S. Spilerman, "The Age Structures of Occupations and Jobs," *American Journal of Sociology* 87 (1982), 827–851.

64. Jeffrey Pfeffer, "Organizational Demography," in *Research in Organizational Behavior*, ed. L. L. Cummings and B. M. Staw, vol. 5 (Greenwich, Conn.: JAI Press, 1983).

65. Nathan Keyfitz, *Applied Mathematical Demography* (New York: John Wiley & Sons, 1977).

66. Pfeffer, "Organizational Demography."

67. Peter M. Blau, *Inequality and Heterogeneity: A Primitive Theory of Social Structure* (New York: Free Press, 1977).

68. Ricklefs, *Ecology*.

69. Ricklefs, *Ecology*.

70. P. M. Blau and R. A. Schoenherr, *The Structure of Organizations* (New York: Basic Books, 1971), P. M. Blau, "A Formal Theory of Differentiation in Organizations," *American Sociological Review* 35 (1970), 201–218, and so on.

71. Durkheim, Emile, *The Division of Labor in Society*, trans. George Simpson (New York: Free Press, 1964).

72. For example, John Child, "Strategies of Control and Organizational Behavior," *Administrative Science Quarterly* 18 (March 1973), 1–17.

73. Paul F. Lazarsfeld and Robert K. Merton, "Friendship as Social Process: A Substantive and Methodological Analysis," in *Freedom and Control in Modern Society*, ed. Morroe Berger, Theodore Abel, and Charles H. Page (New York: D. Van Nostrand Company, Inc., 1954), chapter 2.

74. For example, Blau, "A Macrosociological Theory of Social Structure."

75. For example, Ricklefs, *Ecology*, 567.

76. For example, Robert H. MacArthur, *Geographical Ecology: Patterns in the Distribution of Species* (New York: Harper and Row, 1972).

77. Blau, *Inequality and Heterogeneity.*

78. MacArthur, "The Theory of the Niche."

79. For example, Smith and Freedman, *Voluntary Associations.*

80. For example, Robert H. MacArthur, *Geographical Ecology: Patterns in the Distribution of Species* (New York: Harper and Row, 1972).

81. Ricklefs, *Ecology.*

82. Otis D. Duncan and Leo F. Schnore, "Cultural, Behavioral and Ecological Perspectives in the Study of Social Organization," *The American Journal of Sociology* 65 (1959), 132–146.

3

The Iron Cage Revisited

Institutional Isomorphism and Collective Rationality in Organizational Fields[1]

PAUL DIMAGGIO and WALTER W. POWELL

In *The Protestant Ethic and the Spirit of Capitalism*, Max Weber warned that the rationalist spirit ushered in by asceticism had achieved a momentum of its own and that, under capitalism, the rationalist order had become an iron cage in which humanity was, save for the possibility of prophetic revival, imprisoned "perhaps until the last ton of fossilized coal is burnt."[2] In his essay on bureaucracy, Weber returned to this theme, contending that bureaucracy, the rational spirit's organizational manifestation, was so efficient and powerful a means of controlling men and women that, once established, the momentum of bureaucratization was irreversible.[3]

The imagery of the iron cage has haunted students of society as the tempo of bureaucratization has quickened. But while bureaucracy has spread continuously in the eighty years since Weber wrote, we suggest that the engine of organizational rationalization has shifted. For Weber, bureaucratization resulted from three related causes: competition among capitalist firms in the marketplace; competition among states, increasing rulers' need to control their staff and citizenry; and bourgeois demands for equal protection under the law. Of these three, the most important was the competitive marketplace. "Today," Weber wrote,

it is primarily the capitalist market economy which demands that the official business of administration be discharged precisely, unambiguously, continuously, and with as much speed as possible. Normally, the very large, modern capitalist enterprises are themselves unequalled models of strict bureaucratic organization.[4]

We argue that the causes of bureaucratization and rationalization have changed. The bureaucratization of the corporation and the state have been

achieved. Organizations are still becoming more homogeneous, and bureaucracy remains the common organizational form. Today, however,
structural change in organizations seems less and less driven by competition or by the need for efficiency. Instead, we will contend, bureaucratization and other forms of organizational change occur as the result of
processes that make organizations more similar without necessarily making them more efficient. Bureaucratization and other forms of homogenization emerge, we argue, out of the structuration[5] of organizational fields.
This process, in turn, is effected largely by the state and the professions,
which have become the great rationalizers of the second half of the twentieth century. For reasons that we will explain, highly structured organizational fields provide a context in which individual efforts to deal rationally with uncertainty and constraint often lead, in the aggregate, to
homogeneity in structure, culture, and output.

ORGANIZATIONAL THEORY AND ORGANIZATIONAL DIVERSITY

Much of modern organizational theory posits a diverse and differentiated
world of organizations and seeks to explain variation among organizations
in structure and behavior.[6] Hannan and Freeman begin a major theoretical
paper[7] with the question, "Why are there so many kinds of organizations?" Even our investigatory technologies (for example, those based on
least-squares techniques) are geared toward explaining variation rather than
its absence.

We ask, instead, why there is such startling homogeneity of organizational forms and practices; and we seek to explain homogeneity, not variation. In the initial stages of their life cycle, organizational fields display
considerable diversity in approach and form. Once a field becomes well
established, however, there is an inexorable push toward homogenization.

Coser, Kadushin, and Powell[8] describe the evolution of American college textbook publishing from a period of initial diversity to the current
hegemony of only two models, the large bureaucratic generalist and the
small specialist. Rothman[9] describes the winnowing of several competing
models of legal education into two dominant approaches. Starr[10] provides
evidence of mimicry in the development of the hospital field; Tyack[11] and
Katz[12] show a similar process in public schools; Barnouw[13] describes the
development of dominant forms in the radio industry; and DiMaggio[14]
depicts the emergence of dominant organizational models for the provision
of high culture in the late nineteenth century.

What we see in each of these cases is the emergence and structuration
of an organizational field as a result of the activities of a diverse set of
organizations, and, second, the homogenization of these organizations, and
of new entrants as well, once the field is established.

By organizational field, we mean those organizations that, in the aggregate, constitute a recognized area of institutional life: key suppliers, re-

source and product consumers, regulatory agencies, and other organizations that produce similar services or products. The virtue of this unit of analysis is that it directs our attention not simply to competing firms, as does the population approach of Hannan and Freeman,[15] or to networks of organizations that actually interact, as does the interorganizational network approach of Laumann et al.,[16] but to the totality of relevant actors. In doing this, the field idea comprehends the importance of both *connectedness*[17] and *structural equivalence*.[18,19]

The structure of an organizational field cannot be determined a priori but must be defined on the basis of empirical investigation. Fields only exist to the extent that they are institutionally defined. The process of institutional definition, or "structuration," consists of four parts: an increase in the extent of interaction among organizations in the field, the emergence of sharply defined interorganizational structures of domination and patterns of coalition, an increase in the information load with which organizations in a field must contend, and the development of a mutual awareness among participants in a set of organizations that they are involved in a common enterprise.[20]

Once disparate organizations in the same line of business are structured into an actual field (as we shall argue, by competition, the state, or the professions), powerful forces emerge that lead them to become more similar to one another. Organizations may change their goals or develop new practices, and new organizations enter the field. But, in the long run, organizational actors making rational decisions construct around themselves an environment that constrains their ability to change further in later years. Early adopters of organizational innovations are commonly driven by a desire to improve performance. But new practices can become, in Selznick's works, "infused with value beyond the technical requirements of the task at hand."[21] As an innovation spreads, a threshold is reached beyond which adoption provides legitimacy rather than improves performance.[22] Strategies that are rational for individual organizations may not be rational if adopted by large numbers. Yet the very fact that they are normatively sanctioned increases the likelihood of their adoption. Thus organizations may try to change constantly, but, after a certain point in the structuration of an organizational field, the aggregate effect of individual change is to lessen the extent of diversity within the field.[23] Organizations in a structured field, to paraphrase Schelling,[24] respond to an environment that consists of other organizations responding to their environment, which consists of organizations responding to an environment of organizations' responses.

Zucker and Tolbert's[25] work on the adoption of civil service reform in the United States illustrates this process. Early adoption of civil service reforms was related to internal governmental needs and strongly predicted by such city characteristics as the size of immigrant population, political reform movements, socioeconomic composition, and city size. Later adoption, however, is not predicted by city characteristics, but is related to institutional definitions of the legitimate structural form for municipal administration.[26] Marshall Meyer's[27] study of the bureaucratization of urban fiscal agencies has yielded similar findings: strong relationships between city characteristics and organizational attributes at the turn of the century, null relationships in recent years. Carroll and Delacroix's[28] findings on the birth and death rates of newspapers support the view that selection acts with great force only in the early years of an industry's existence.[29] Freeman[30] suggests that older, larger organizations reach a point where they can dominate their environment rather than adjust to it.

The concept that best captures the process of homogenization is *isomorphism.* In Hawley's[31] description, isomorphism is a constraining process that forces one unit in a population to resemble other units that face the same set of environmental conditions. At the population level, such an approach suggests that organizational characteristics are modified in the direction of increasing compatibility with environmental characteristics; the number of organizations in a population is a function of environmental carrying capacity; and the diversity of organizational forms is isomorphic to environmental diversity. Hannan and Freeman[32] have significantly extended Hawley's ideas. They argue that isomorphism can result because nonoptimal forms are selected out of a population of organizations or because organizational decision makers learn appropriate responses and adjust their behavior accordingly. Hannan and Freeman's focus is almost solely on the first process: selection.[33]

Following Meyer[34] and Fennell,[35] we maintain that there are two types of isomorphism: competitive and institutional. Hannan and Freeman's classic paper,[36] and much of their recent work, deals with competitive isomorphism, assuming a system rationality that emphasizes market competition, niche change, and fitness measures. Such a view, we suggest, is most relevant for those fields in which free and open competition exists. It explains parts of the process of bureaucratization that Weber observed and may apply to early adoption of innovation, but it does not present a fully adequate picture of the modern world of organizations. For this purpose it must be supplemented by an institutional view of isomorphism of the sort introduced by Kanter[37] in her discussion of the forces pressing communes toward accommodation with the outside world. As Aldrich[38] has argued, "the major factors that organizations must take into account are other organizations." Organizations compete not just for resources and customers, but for political power and institutional legitimacy, for social as well as economic fitness.[39] The concept of institutional isomorphism is a useful tool for understanding the politics and ceremony that pervade much modern organizational life.

Three Mechanisms of Institutional Isomorphic Change

We identify three mechanisms through which institutional isomorphic change occurs, each with its own antecedents: (1) *coercive isomorphism* that stems from political influence and the problem of legitimacy, (2) *mimetic iso-morphism* resulting from standard responses to uncertainty, and (3) *normative isomorphism*, associated with professionalization. This typology is an analytic one; the types are not always empirically distinct. For example, external actors may induce an organization to conform to its peers by requiring it to perform a particular task and specifying the profession responsible for its performance. Or mimetic change may reflect environmentally constructed uncertainties.[40] Yet, although the three types intermingle in empirical setting, they tend to derive from different conditions and may lead to different outcomes.

Coercive Isomorphism
Coercive isomorphism results from both formal and informal pressures exerted on organizations by other organizations upon which they are dependent and by cultural expectations in the society within which organizations function. Such pressures may be felt as force, as persuasion, or as invitations to join in collusion. In some circumstances, organizational change is a direct response to government mandate: manufacturers adopt new pollution control technologies to conform to environmental regulations; nonprofits maintain accounts and hire accountants in order to meet tax law requirements; and organizations employ affirmative action officers to fend off allegations of discrimination. Schools mainstream special students and hire special education teachers, cultivate PTAs and administrators who get along with them, and promulgate curricula that conform with state standards.[41] The fact that these changes may be largely ceremonial does not mean that they are inconsequential. As Ritti and Goldner[42] have argued, staff become involved in advocacy for their functions that can alter power relations within organizations over the long run.

The existence of a common legal environment affects many aspects of an organization's behavior and structure. Weber pointed out the profound impact of a complex, rationalized system of contract law that requires the necessary organizational controls to honor legal commitments. Other legal and technical requirements of the state—the vicissitudes of the budget cycle, the ubiquity of certain fiscal years, annual reports, and financial reporting requirements that ensure eligibility for the receipt of federal contracts or funds—also shape organizations in similar ways. Pfeffer and Salancik[43] have discussed how organizations faced with unmanageable interdependence seek to use the greater power of the larger social system and its government to eliminate difficulties or provide for needs. They observe that politically constructed environments have two characteristic features: political decision makers often do not experience directly the consequences of their actions; and political decisions are applied across the board to entire classes of organizations, thus making such decisions less adaptive and less flexible.

Meyer and Rowan[44] have argued persuasively that as rationalized states and other large rational organizations expand their dominance over more

arenas of social life, organizational structures increasingly come to reflect
rules institutionalized and legitimated by and within the state.[45]
    As a result, organizations are increasingly homogeneous within given
domains and increasingly organized around rituals of conformity to wider
institutions. At the same time, they are decreasingly structurally determined by the constraints posed by technical activities and decreasingly held
together by output controls. Under such circumstances, organizations employ ritualized controls of credentials and group solidarity.
    Direct imposition of standard operating procedures and legitimated rules
and structures also occurs outside the government arena. Michael Sedlak[46]
has documented the ways that United Charities in the 1930s altered and
homogenized the structures, methods, and philosophies of the social service agencies that depended upon them for support. As conglomerate corporations increase in size and scope, standard performance criteria are not
necessarily imposed on subsidiaries, but it is common for subsidiaries to
be subject to standardized reporting mechanisms.[47]
    Subsidiaries must adopt accounting practices, performance evaluations,
and budgetary plans that are compatible with the policies of the parent
corporation. A variety of service infrastructures, often provided by monopolistic firms—for example, telecommunications and transportation—exert
common pressures over the organizations that use them. Thus, the expansion of the central state, the centralization of capital, and the coordination
of philanthropy all support the homogenization of organizational models
through direct authority relationships.
    We have so far referred only to the direct and explicit imposition of
organizational models on dependent organizations. Coercive isomorphism,
however, may be more subtle and less explicit than these examples suggest.
Milofsky[48] has described the ways in which neighborhood organizations
in urban communities, many of which are committed to participatory democracy, are driven to developing organizational hierarchies in order to
gain support from more hierarchically organized donor organizations.
Similarly, Swidler[49] describes the tensions created in the free schools she
studied by the need to have a "principal" to negotiate with the district
superintendent and to represent the school to outside agencies. In general,
the need to lodge responsibility and managerial authority at least ceremo-
nially in a formally defined role in order to interact with hierarchical organizations is a constant obstacle to the maintenance of egalitarian or collectivist organizational forms.[50]

Mimetic Processes
Not all institutional isomorphism, however, derives from coercive authority. Uncertainty is also a powerful force that encourages imitation. When
organizational technologies are poorly understood,[51] when goals are ambiguous, or when the environment creates symbolic uncertainty, organizations may model themselves on other organizations. The advantages of
mimetic behavior in the economy of human action are considerable; when

an organization faces a problem with ambiguous causes or unclear solutions, problemistic search may yield a viable solution with little expense.[52]

Modeling, as we use the term, is a response to uncertainty. The modeled organization may be unaware of the modeling or may have no desire to be copied; it merely serves as a convenient source of practices that the borrowing organization may use. Models may be diffused unintentionally, indirectly through employee transfer or turnover, or explicitly by organizations such as consulting firms or industry trade associations. Even innovation can be accounted for by organizational modeling. As Alchian[53] has observed:

While there certainly are those who consciously innovate, there are those who, in their imperfect attempts to imitate others, unconsciously innovate by unwittingly acquiring some unexpected or unsought attributes which under the prevailing circumstances prove partly responsible for the success. Others, in turn, will attempt to copy the uniqueness, and the innovation-imitation process continues.

One of the most dramatic instances of modeling was the effort of Japan's modernizers in the late nineteenth century to model new governmental initiatives on apparently successful Western prototypes. Thus, the imperial government sent its officers to study the courts, army, and police in France; the navy and postal system in Great Britain; and banking and art education in the United States.[54] American corporations are now returning the compliment by implementing (their perceptions of) Japanese models to cope with thorny productivity and personnel problems in their own firms. The rapid proliferation of quality circles and quality-of-work-life issues in American firms is, at least in part, an attempt to model Japanese and European successes. These developments also have a ritual aspect; companies adopt these "innovations" to enhance their legitimacy, to demonstrate they are at least trying to improve working conditions. More generally, the wider the population of personnel employed by, or customers served by, an organization, the stronger the pressure felt by the organization to provide the programs and services offered by other organizations. Thus, either a skilled labor force or a broad customer base may encourage mimetic isomorphism.

Much homogeneity in organizational structures stems from the fact that despite considerable search for diversity there is relatively little variation to be selected from. New organizations are modeled upon old ones throughout the economy, and managers actively seek models upon which to build.[55] Thus, in the arts one can find textbooks on how to organize a community arts council or how to start a symphony women's guild. Large organizations choose from a relatively small set of major consulting firms, which, like Johnny Appleseeds, spread a few organizational models throughout the land. Such models are powerful because structural changes are observable, whereas changes in policy and strategy are less conspicuous. With the advice of a major consulting firm, a large metropolitan public television station switched from a functional design to a multidivisional structure. The stations' executives were skeptical that the new structure was more efficient; in fact, some services were now duplicated across divisions. But they were convinced that the new design would carry a powerful message to the for-profit firms with whom the station regularly dealt. These firms, whether in the role of corporate underwriters or as potential partners in joint ventures, would view the reorganization as a sign that "the sleepy nonprofit station was becoming more business-minded."[56] The history of management reform in American government agencies, which are noted for their goal ambiguity, is almost a textbook case of isomorphic modeling, from the PPBS (Programs Planning and Budget System) of the McNamara era to the zero-based budgeting of the Carter administration.

Organizations tend to model themselves after similar organizations in their field that they perceive to be more legitimate or successful. The ubiquity of certain kinds of structural arrangements can more likely be credited to the universality of mimetic processes than to any concrete evidence that the adopted models enhance efficiency. John Meyer[57] contends that it is easy to predict the organization of a newly emerging nation's administration without knowing anything about the nation itself, since "peripheral nations are far more isomorphic—in administrative form and economic pattern—than any theory of the world system of economic division of labor would lead one to expect."

Normative Pressures
A third source of isomorphic organizational change is normative and stems primarily from professionalization. Following Larson[58] and Collins,[59] we interpret professionalization as the collective struggle of members of an occupation to define the conditions and methods of their work, to control "the production of producers,"[60] and to establish a cognitive base and legitimation for their occupational autonomy. As Larson points out, the professional project is rarely achieved with complete success. Professionals must compromise with nonprofessional clients, bosses, or regulators. The major recent growth in the professions has been among organizational professionals, particularly managers and specialized staff of large organizations. The increased professionalization of workers whose futures are inextricably bound up with the fortunes of the organizations that employ them has rendered obsolescent (if not obsolete) the dichotomy between organizational commitment and professional allegiance that characterized traditional professionals in earlier organizations.[61] Professions are subject to the same coercive and mimetic pressures as are organizations. Moreover, while various kinds of professionals within an organization may differ from one another, they exhibit much similarity to their professional counterparts in other organizations. In addition, in many cases, professional power is as much assigned by the state as it is created by the activities of the professions.

Two aspects of professionalization are important sources of isomorphism. One is the resting of formal education and of legitimation in a cognitive base produced by university specialists; the second is the growth and elaboration of professional networks that span organizations and across which new models diffuse rapidly. Universities and professional training institutions are important centers for the development of organizational norms among professional managers and their staff. Professional and trade associations are other vehicles for defining and promulgating normative rules about organizational and professional behavior. Such mechanisms create a pool of almost interchangeable individuals who occupy similar positions across a range of organizations and possess similar orientations and dispositions, which may override variations in tradition and control that might otherwise shape their actions.[62]

One important mechanism for encouraging normative isomorphism is the filtering of personnel. Within many organizational fields filtering occurs through the hiring of individuals from firms within the same industry; through the recruitment of fast-track staff from a narrow range of training institutions; through common promotion practices; such as always hiring top executives from financial or legal departments; and from skill level requirements for particular jobs. Many professional career tracks are so closely guarded, both at the entry level and throughout the career progression, that individuals who make it to the top are virtually indistinguishable. March and March[63] found that individuals who attained the position of school superintendent in Wisconsin were so alike in background and orientation as to make further career advancement random and unpredictable. Hirsch and Whisler[64] find a similar absence of variation among *Fortune* 500 board members. In addition, individuals in an organizational field undergo anticipatory socialization to common expectations about their personal behavior, appropriate style of dress, organizational vocabularies,[65] and standard methods of speaking, joking, or addressing others.[66] Particularly in industries with a service or financial orientation (Collins[67] argues that the importance of credentials is strongest in these areas), the filtering of personnel approaches what Kanter[68] refers to as the "homosexual reproduction of management." To the extent managers and key staff are drawn from the same universities and filtered on a common set of attributes, they will tend to view problems in a similar fashion; see the same policies, procedures and structures as normatively sanctioned and legitimated; and approach decisions in much the same way.

Entrants to professional career tracks who somehow escape the filtering process—for example, Jewish naval officers, woman stockbrokers, or black insurance executives—are likely to be subjected to pervasive on-the-job socialization. To the extent that organizations in a field differ and primary socialization occurs on the job, socialization could reinforce, not erode, differences among organizations. But when organizations in a field are similar and occupational socialization is carried out in trade association workshops, in-service educational programs, consultant arrangements, employer-professional school networks, and the pages of trade magazines, socialization acts as an isomorphic force.

The professionalization of management tends to proceed in tandem with the structuration of organizational fields. The exchange of information among professionals helps contribute to a commonly recognized hierarchy of status, of center and periphery, that becomes a matrix for information flows and personnel movement across organizations. This status ordering occurs through both formal and informal means. The designation of a few large firms in an industry as key bargaining agents in union-management negotiations may make these cultural firms pivotal in other respects as well. Government recognition of key firms or organizations through the grant or contract process may give these organizations legitimacy and visibility and lead competing firms to copy aspects of their structure or operating procedures in hope of obtaining similar rewards. Professional and trade associations provide other arenas in which center organizations are recognized and their personnel given positions of substantive or ceremonial influence. Managers in highly visible organizations may in turn have their stature reinforced by representation on the boards of other organizations, participation in industrywide or interindustry councils, and consultation by agencies of government.[69] In the nonprofit sector, where legal barriers to collusion do not exist, structuration may proceed even more rapidly. Thus executive producers or artistic directors of leading theaters head trade or professional association committees, sit on government and foundation grant award panels, consult as government- or foundation-financed management advisers to smaller theaters, or sit on smaller organizations' boards, even as their stature is reinforced and enlarged by the grants their theaters receive from government, corporate, and foundation funding sources.[70]

Such central organizations serve as both active and passive models; their policies and structures will be copied throughout their fields. Their centrality is reinforced as upwardly mobile managers and staff seek to secure positions in these central organizations in order to further their own careers. Aspiring managers may undergo anticipatory socialization into the norms and mores of the organizations they hope to join. Career paths may also involve movement from entry positions in the center organizations to middle management positions in peripheral organizations. Personnel flows within an organizational field are further encouraged by structural homogenization, for example the existence of common career titles and paths (such as assistant, associate, and full professor) with meanings that are commonly understood.

It is important to note that each of the institutional isomorphic processes can be expected to proceed in the absence of evidence that they increase internal organizational efficiency. To the extent that organizational effectiveness is enhanced, the reason will often be that organizations are rewarded for being similar to others in their fields. This similarity can make it easier for them to transact with other organizations, to attract career minded staff, to be acknowledged as legitimate and reputable, and to fit into administrative categories that define eligibility for public and private grants and contracts. None of this, however, ensures that conformist organizations do what they do more efficiently than do their more deviant peers.

Pressures for competitive efficiency are also mitigated in many fields because the number of organizations is limited and there are strong fiscal and legal barriers to entry and exit. Lee[71] maintains this is why hospital administrators are less concerned with the efficient use of resources and more concerned with status competition and parity in prestige. Fennell[72] notes that hospitals are a poor market system because patients lack the needed knowledge of potential exchange partners and prices. She argues that physicians and hospital administrators are the actual consumers. Competition among hospitals is based on "attracting physicians, who, in turn, bring their patients to the hospital." Fennell[73] concludes that

Hospitals operate according to a norm of social legitimation that frequently conflicts with market considerations of efficiency and system rationality. Apparently, hospitals can increase their range of services not because there is an actual need for a particular service or facility within the patient population, but because they will be defined as fit only if they can offer everything other hospitals in the area offer.

These results suggest a more general pattern. Organizational fields that include a large professionally trained labor force will be driven primarily by status competition. Organizational prestige and resources are key elements in attracting professionals. This process encourages homogenization as organizations seek to ensure that they can provide the same benefits and services as their competitors.

PREDICTORS OF ISOMORPHIC CHANGE

It follows from our discussion of the mechanism by which isomorphic change occurs that we should be able to predict empirically which organizational fields will be most homogeneous in structure, process, and behavior. Although an empirical test of such predictions is beyond the scope of this paper, the ultimate value of our perspective will lie in its predictive utility. The hypotheses discussed below are not meant to exhaust the universe of predictors, but merely to suggest several hypotheses that may be pursued using data on the characteristics of organizations in a field, either cross-sectionally or, preferably, over time. The hypotheses are implicitly governed by *ceteris paribus* assumptions, particularly with regard to size, technology, and centralization of external resources.

Hypothesis A: Organizational Level Predictors

There is variability in the extent to and rate at which organizations in a field change to become more like their peers. Some organizations respond to external pressures quickly; others change only after a long period of resistance. The first two hypotheses derive from our discussion of coercive isomorphism and constraint.

Hypothesis A-1: The Greater an Organization's Dependence on Another, the More Similar It Will Become in Structure, Climate, and Behavioral Focus

Following Thompson,[74] and Pfeffer and Salancik,[75] the proposition of Hypothesis A recognizes the greater ability of organizations to resist the demands of organizations on whom they are not dependent. A position of dependence leads to isomorphic change. Coercive pressures are built into exchange relationships. As Williamson[76] has shown, exchanges are characterized by transaction-specific investments in both knowledge and equipment. Once an organization chooses a specific supplier or distributer for particular parts or services, the supplier or distributor develops expertise in the performance of the task as well as idiosyncratic knowledge about the exchange relationship. The organization comes to rely on the supplier or distributor, and such transaction-specific investments give the supplier or distributor considerable advantages in any subsequent competition with other suppliers or distributors.

Hypothesis A-2: The Greater the Centralization of Organization A's Resource Supply, the More Organization A Will Change Isomorphically to Resemble the Organizations on Which It Depends for Resources

As Thompson[77] notes, organizations that depend on the same sources for funding, personnel, and legitimacy will be more subject to the whims of resource suppliers than will those that can play one source of support off against another. In cases where alternative sources are either not readily available or require effort to locate, the stronger party to the transaction can coerce the weaker party to adopt its practices in order to accommodate the stronger party's needs.[78]

The third and fourth hypotheses derive from our discussion of mimetic isomorphism, modeling, and uncertainty.

Hypothesis A-3: The More Uncertain the Relationship between Means and Ends, the More an Organization Will Model Itself after Organizations It Perceives to Be Successful

The mimetic thought process involved in the search for models is characteristic of change in organizations in which key technologies are only poorly understood.[79] Here our prediction diverges somewhat from Meyer and Rowan,[80] who argue, as we do, that organizations which lack well defined technologies will import institutionalized rules and practices. Meyer and Rowan posit a loose coupling between legitimated external practices and internal organizational behavior. From an ecologist's point of view, loosely coupled organizations are more likely to vary internally. In contrast, we expect substantive internal changes in tandem with more ceremonial practices, thus greater homogeneity and less variation and change. Internal consistency of this sort is an important means of interorganizational coordination. It also increases organizational stability.

Hypothesis A-4: The More Ambiguous the Goals of an Organization, the More It Will Model Itself after Organizations It Perceives to Be Successful

There are two reasons for the relationship postulated in Hypothesis A-4. First, organizations with ambiguous or disputed goals are likely to be highly dependent upon appearances for legitimacy. Such organizations may find it to their advantage to meet the expectations of important constituencies about how they should be designed and run. In contrast to our view, ecologists would argue that organizations that copy other organizations usually have no competitive advantage. We contend that, in most situations, reliance on established, legitimated procedures enhances organizational legitimacy and survival characteristics. A second reason for modeling behavior is found in situations where conflict over organizational goals is repressed in the interest of harmony; thus participants find it easier to mimic other organizations than to make decisions on the basis of systematic analyses of goals since such analyses would prove painful or disruptive.

The fifth and sixth hypotheses are based on our discussion of normative processes found in professional organizations.

Hypothesis A-5: The Greater the Reliance on Academic Credentials in Choosing Managerial and Staff Personnel, the More an Organization Will Become Like Other Organizations in Its Field

Applicants with academic credentials have already undergone a socialization process in university programs and are thus more likely than others to have internalized reigning norms and dominant organizational models.

Hypothesis A-6: The Greater the Participation of Organizational Managers in Trade and Professional Associations, the More Likely the Organization Is to Become Like Others in Its Field

Hypothesis A-6 is parallel to the institutional view that the more elaborate the relational networks among organizations and their members, the greater the collective organization of the environment.[81]

Hypothesis B: Field Level Predictors

The following six hypotheses describe the expected effects of several characteristics of organizational fields on the extent of isomorphism in a particular field. Since the effect of institutional isomorphism is homogenization, the best indicator of isomorphic change is a decrease in variation and diversity, which could be measured by lower standard deviations of the values of selected indicators in a set of organizations. The key indicators would vary with the nature of the field and the interests of the investigator. In all cases, however, field level measures are expected to affect organizations in a field regardless of each organization's scores on related organizational level measures.

Hypothesis B-1: The Greater the Extent to Which an Organizational Field Depends upon a Single Source of Support for Vital Resources (or Several Similar Sources), the Higher the Level of Isomorphism
The centralization of resources within a field both directly causes homogenization by placing organizations under similar pressures from resource suppliers and interacts with uncertainty and goal ambiguity to increase their impact. This hypothesis is congruent with the ecologists' argument that the number of organizational forms is determined by the distribution of resources in the environment and the terms on which resources are available.

Hypothesis B-2: The More the Organizations in a Field Transact with Agencies of the State, the Greater the Extent of Isomorphism in the Field as a Whole
Hypothesis B-2 follows not just from the previous hypothesis, but from two elements of state/private sector transactions; their rule-boundedness and formal rationality, and the emphasis of government actors on institutional rules. Moreover, the federal government routinely designates industry standards for an entire field which require adoption by all competing firms. John Meyer[82] argues convincingly that the aspects of an organization which are affected by state transactions differ to the extent that state participation is unitary or fragmented among several public agencies.

The third and fourth hypotheses follow from our discussion of isomorphic change resulting from uncertainty and modeling.

Hypothesis B-3: The Fewer the Number of Visible Alternative Organizational Models in a Field, the Faster the Rate of Isomorphism in that Field
The predictions of Hypothesis B-3 are less specific than those of others and require further refinement, but our argument is that for any relevant dimension of organizational strategies or structures in an organizational field there will be a threshold level, or a tipping point, beyond which adoption of the dominant form will proceed with increasing speed.[83]

Hypothesis B-4: The Greater the Extent to Which Technologies Are Uncertain or Goals Are Ambiguous within a Field, the Greater the Rate of Isomorphic Change
Somewhat counterintuitively, abrupt increases in uncertainty and ambiguity should, after brief periods of ideologically motivated experimentation, lead to rapid isomorphic change. As in the case of A-4, ambiguity and uncertainty may be a function of environmental definition, and, in any

case, interact both with centralization of resources (A-1, A-2, B-1, B-2) and with professionalization and structuration (A-5, A-6, B-5, B-6). Moreover, in fields characterized by a high degree of uncertainty, new entrants, which could serve as sources of innovation and variation, will seek to overcome the liability of newness by imitating established practices within the field.

The two final hypotheses in this section follow from our discussion of professional filtering, socialization, and structuration.

Hypothesis B-5: The Greater the Extent of Professionalization in a Field, the Greater the Amount of Institutional Isomorphic Change
Professionalization may be measured by the universality of credential requirements, the robustness of graduate training programs, or the vitality of professional and trade associations.

Hypothesis B-6: The Greater the Extent of Structuration of a Field, the Greater the Degree of Isomorphics
Fields that have stable and broadly acknowledged centers, peripheries, and status orders will be more homogeneous both because the diffusion structure for new models and norms is more routine and because the level of interaction among organizations in the field is higher. Although structuration may not lend itself to easy measurement, it may be tapped crudely with the use of such familiar measures as concentration ratios, reputational interview studies, or data on network characteristics.

This rather schematic exposition of a dozen hypotheses relating the extent of isomorphism to selected attributes of organizations and of organizational fields does not constitute a complete agenda for empirical assessment of our perspective. We have not discussed the expected nonlinearities and ceiling effects in the relationships that we have posited. Nor have we addressed the issue of the indicators that one must use to measure homogeneity. Organizations in a field may be highly diverse on some dimensions, yet extremely homogeneous on others. Although we suspect, in general, that the rate at which the standard deviations of structural or behavioral indicators approach zero will vary with the nature of an organizational field's technology and environment, we will not develop these ideas here. The point of this section is to suggest that the theoretical discussion is susceptible to empirical test and to lay out a few testable propositions that may guide future analyses.

IMPLICATIONS FOR SOCIAL THEORY

A comparison of macrosocial theories of functionalist or Marxist orientation with theoretical and empirical work in the study of organizations yields a paradoxical conclusion. Societies (or elites), so it seems, are smart and organizations are dumb. Societies comprise institutions that mesh together comfortably in the interests of efficiency,[84] the dominant value system,[85] or, in the Marxist version, capitalists.[86] Organizations, by contrast, are either anarchies,[87] federations of loosely coupled parts,[88] or autonomy seeking agents[89] laboring under such formidable constraints as bounded rationality,[90] uncertain or contested goals,[91] and unclear technologies.[92]

Despite the findings of organizational research, the image of society as consisting of tightly and rationally coupled institutions persists throughout much of modern social theory. Rational administration pushes out no bureaucratic forms, schools assume the structure of the workplace, hospital and university administrations come to resemble the management of for-profit firms, and the modernization of the world economy proceeds unabated. Weberians point to the continued homogenization of organizational structures as the formal rationality of bureaucracy extends to the limits of contemporary organizational life. Functionalists describe the rational adaptation of the structure of firms, schools, and states to the values and needs of modern society.[93] Marxists attribute changes in such organizations as welfare agencies[94] and schools[95] to the logic of the accumulation process.

We find it difficult to square the extant literature on organizations with these macrosocial views. How can it be that the confused contentious bumblers that populate the pages of organizational case studies and theory combine to construct the elaborate and reproportioned social edifice that macrotheorists describe?

The conventional answer to this paradox has been that some version of natural selection occurs in which mechanisms operate to weed out those organizational forms that are less fit. Such arguments, as we have contended, are difficult to mesh with organizational realities. Less efficient organizational forms do persist. In some contexts efficiency or productivity cannot even be measured. In government agencies or in faltering corporations selection may occur on political rather than economic grounds. In other contexts, for example the Metropolitan Opera or the Bohemian Grove, supporters are far more concerned with noneconomic values such as aesthetic quality or social status than with efficiency per se. Even in the for-profit sector, where competitive arguments would promise to bear the greatest fruit, Nelson and Winter's work[96] demonstrates that the invisible hand operates with, at best, a light touch.

A second approach to the paradox that we have identified comes from Marxists and theorists who assert that key elites guide and control the social system through their command of crucial positions in major organizations (e.g., the financial institutions that dominate monopoly capitalism). In this view, whereas organizational actors ordinarily proceed undisturbed through mazes of standard operating procedures, at key turning points capitalist elites get their way by intervening in decisions that set the course of an institution for years to come.[97]

While evidence suggests that this is, in fact, sometimes the case—Barnouw's account of the early days of broadcasting or Weinstein's[98] work on the Progressives are good examples—other historians have been less successful in their search for class-conscious elites. In such cases as the development of the New Deal programs[99] or the expansion of the Vietnamese conflict,[100] the capitalist class appears to have been muddled and disunited.

Moreover, without constant monitoring, individuals pursuing parochial organizational or subunit interests can quickly undo the work that even the most prescient elites have accomplished. Perrow[101] has noted that despite superior resources and sanctioning power, organizational elites are often unable to maximize their preferences because "the complexity of modern organizations makes control difficult." Moreover, organizations have increasingly become the vehicle for numerous "gratifications, necessities, and preferences so that many groups within and without the organization seek to use it for ends that restrict the return to masters."

We reject neither the natural selection nor the elite control arguments out of hand. Elites do exercise considerable influence over modern life, and aberrant or inefficient organizations sometimes do expire. But we contend that neither of these processes is sufficient to explain the extent to which organizations have become structurally more similar. We argue that a theory of institutional isomorphism may help explain the observations that organizations are becoming more homogeneous and elites often get their way, while also enabling us to understand the irrationality, the frustration of power, and the lack of innovation that are so commonplace in organizational life. What is more, our approach is more consonant with the ethnographic and theoretical literature on how organizations work than are either functionalist or elite theories of organizational change.

A focus on institutional isomorphism can also add a much needed perspective on the political struggle for organizational power and survival that is missing from much of population ecology. The institutionalization approach associated with John Meyer and his students posits the importance of myths and ceremony but does not ask how these models arise and whose interests they initially serve. Explicit attention to the genesis of legitimated models and to the definition and elaboration of organizational fields should answer this question. Examination of the diffusion of similar organizational strategies and structures should be a productive means for assessing the influence of elite interests. A consideration of isomorphic processes also leads us to a bifocal view of power and its application in modern politics. To the extent that organizational change is unplanned and goes on largely behind the backs of groups that wish to influence it, our attention should be directed to two forms of power. The first, as March and Simon[102] and Simon[103] pointed out years ago, is the power to set premises, to define the norms and standards which shape and channel behavior. The second is the point of critical intervention[104] of which elites can define appropriate models of organizational structure and policy which then go unquestioned for years to come.[105] Such a view is consonant with some of the best recent work on power.[106] Research on the structuration of organizational fields and on isomorphic processes may help give it more empirical flesh.

Finally, a more developed theory of organizational isomorphism may have important implications for social policy in those fields in which the state works through private organizations. To the extent that pluralism is a guiding value in public policy deliberations, we need to discover new forms of intersectoral coordination that will encourage diversification rather than hastening homogenization. An understanding of the manner in which fields become more homogeneous would prevent policymakers and analysts from confusing the disappearance of an organizational form with its substantive failure. Current efforts to encourage diversity tend to be conducted in an organizational vacuum. Policymakers concerned with pluralism should consider the impact of their programs on the structure of organizational fields as a whole, and not simply on the programs of individual organizations.

We believe there is much to be gained by attending to similarity as well as to variation among organizations and, in particular, to change in the degree of homogeneity or variation over time. Our approach seeks to study incremental change as well as selection. We take seriously the observations of organizational theorists about the role of change, ambiguity, and constraint and point to the implications of these organizational characteristics for the social structure as a whole. The foci and motive forces of bureaucratization (and, more broadly, homogenization in general) have, as we argued, changed since Weber's time. But the importance of understanding the trends to which he called attention has never been more immediate.

NOTES

1. This article first appeared in the *American Sociological Review* 48 (1983), 147–160, © 1983. Reprinted by permission.

A preliminary version of this paper was presented by Powell at the American Sociological Association meetings in Toronto, August 1981. We have benefited considerably from careful readings of earlier drafts by Dan Chambliss, Randall Collins, Lewis Coser, Rebecca Friedkin, Connie Gersick, Albert Hunter, Rosabeth Moss Kanter, Charles E. Lindblom, John Meyer, David Morgan, Susan Olzak, Charles Perrow, Richard A. Peterson, Arthur Stinchcombe, Blair Wheaton, and two anonymous *ASR* reviewers. The authors' names are listed in alphabetical order for convenience. This was a fully collaborative effort.

2. Max Weber, *The Protestant Ethic and the Spirit of Capitalism* (New York: Scribners, 1952), pp. 181–182.

3. Max Weber, *Economy and Society: An Outline of Interpretive Sociology,* 3 vols. (New York: Bedminster, 1968).

4. Weber, *Economy and Society,* p. 974.

5. Anthony Giddens, *Central Problems in Social Theory: Action, Structure, and Contradiction in Social Analysis* (Berkeley: University of California Press, 1979).

6. Joan Woodward, *Industrial Organization, Theory and Practice* (London: Oxford University Press, 1965). See also John Child and Alfred Kieser, "Development of Organizations Over Time," in *Handbook of Organizational Design,* ed. Paul C. Nystrom and William H. Starbuck (New York: Oxford University Press, 1981).

7. Michael T. Hannan and John H. Freeman, "The Population Ecology of Org/ American Journal of Sociology, 82 (1977), 929–964.

8. Lewis Coser, Charles Kadushin and Walter W. Powell, Books:The Culture and Commerce of Book Publishing (New York: Basic Books, 1982).

9. Mitchell Rothman, "The Evolution of Forms of Legal Education," unpublished manuscript, Department of Sociology, Yale University, New Haven, Conn., 1980.

10. Paul Starr, "Medical Care and the Boundaries of Capitalist Organization," unpublished manuscript, Program on Non-Profit Organizations, Yale University, New Haven, Conn., 1980.

11. David Tyack, The One Best System: A History of American Urban Education (Cambridge, Mass.: Harvard University Press, 1974).

12. Michael B. Katz, Class, Bureaucracy, and Schools: The Illusion of Educational Change in America (New York: Praeger, 1975).

13. Erik Barnouw, A History of Broadcasting in the United States, Three Volumes (New York: Oxford University Press, 1966–1968).

14. Paul DiMaggio, "Cultural Entrepreneurship in Nineteenth-Century Boston, Part 1: The Creation of an Organizational Base for High Culture in America," Media, Culture and Society, 4 (1981), 33–50.

15. Hannan and Freeman, "The Population Ecology of Organizations."

16. Edward O. Laumann, Joseph Galaskiewicz and Peter Marsden, "Community Structure as Interorganizational Linkage," Annual Review of Sociology, 4 (1978), 455–484.

17. Laumann et al., "Community Structure as Interorganizational Linkage."

18. Harrison C. White, Scott A. Boorman and Ronald L. Breiger, "Social Structure from Multiple Networks: I—Block Models of Roles and Positions," American Journal of Sociology 81 (1976), 730–780.

19. By connectedness we mean the existence of transactions tying organizations to one another: such transactions might include formal contractural relationships; participation of personnel in common enterprises such as professional associations, labor unions, or boards of directors; or informal organizational level ties such as personnel flows. A set of organizations that are strongly connected to one another and only weakly connected to other organizations constitutes a clique. By structural equivalence we refer to similarity of position in a network structure: for example, two organizations are structurally equivalent if they have ties of the same kind to the same set of other organizations, even if they themselves are not connected: here the key structure is the role or block.

20. Paul DiMaggio, "The Structure of Organizational Fields: An Analytical Approach and Policy Implications," paper prepared for SUNY–Albany Conference on Organizational Theory and Public Policy, 1–2 April 1982.

21. Philip Selznick, Leadership in Administration (New York: Harper and Row, 1957).

22. John Meyer and Brian Rowan, "Institutionalized Organizations: Formal Structure as Myth and Ceremony," American Journal of Sociology, 83 (1977), 340–363.

23. By organizational change, we refer to change in formal structure, organizational culture, and goals, program, or mission. Organizational change varies in its responsiveness to technical conditions. In this paper we are most interested in processes that affect organizations in a given field: in most cases these organizations employ similar technical bases; thus we do not attempt to partial out the relative importance of technically functional versus other forms of organizational change. While we shall cite many examples of organizational change as we go along, our purpose here is to identify a widespread class of organizational processes relevant to a broad range of substantive problems, rather than to identify deterministically the causes of specific organizational arrangements.

24. Thomas Schelling, Micromotives and Macrobehavior (New York: W. W. Norton, 1978), p. 14.

25. Lynne G. Zucker and Pamela S. Tolbert, "Institutional Sources of Change in the Formal Structure of Organizations: The Diffusion of Civil Service Reform, 1880–1935," paper presented at American Sociological Association annual meeting, Toronto, Canada, 1981.

26. Knoke (1982), in a careful event-history analysis of the spread of municipal reform,

refutes the conventional explanations of culture clash or hierarchal diffusion and finds but modest support for modernization theory. His major finding is that regional differences in municipal reform adoption arise not from social compositional differences, "but from some type of imitation or contagion effects as represented by the level of neighboring regional cities previously adopting reform government" (p. 1337).

27. Marshall Meyer, "Persistence and Change in Bureaucratic Structures," paper presented at American Sociological Association annual meeting, Toronto, Canada, 1981.

28. Glenn R. Carroll and Jacques Delacroix, "Organizational Mortality in the Newspaper Industries of Argentina and Ireland: An Ecological Approach," *Administrative Science Quarterly*, 27 (1982), 169–198.

29. A wide range of factors—interorganizational commitments, elite sponsorship, and government support in form of open-ended contracts, subsidy, tariff barriers and import quotas, or favorable tax laws—reduce selection pressures even in competitive organizational fields. An expanding or a stable, protected market can also mitigate the forces of selection.

30. John H. Freeman, "Organizational Life Cycles and Natural Selection Processes," in *Research in Organizational Behavior*, vol. 4, ed. Barry Staw and Larry Cummings (Greenwich, Conn.: JAI Press, 1982), p. 14.

31. Amos Hawley, "Human Ecology," in *International Encyclopedia of the Social Sciences*, ed. David L. Sills (New York: Macmillan Publishing Company, 1968).

32. Hannan and Freeman, "The Population Ecology of Organizations."

33. In contrast to Hannan and Freeman, we emphasize adaptation, but we are not suggesting that managers' actions are necessarily strategic in a long-range sense. Indeed, two of the three forms of isomorphism described later—mimetic and normative—involve managerial behaviors at the level of taken for granted assumptions rather than consciously strategic choices. In general, we question the utility of arguments about the motivations of actors that suggest a polarity between rational and nonrational. Goal oriented behavior may be reflexive or prerational in the sense that it reflects deeply embedded predispositions, scripts, schema, or classifications; and behavior oriented to a goal may be reinforced without contributing to the accomplishment of that goal. While isomorphic change may often be mediated by the desires of managers to increase the effectiveness of their organizations, we are more concerned with the menu of possible options that managers consider than with their motives for choosing particular alternatives. In other words, we freely concede that actors' understandings of their own behaviors are interpretable in rational terms. The theory of isomorphism addresses not the psychological states of actors but the structural determinants of the range of choices that actors perceive as rational or prudent.

34. John W. Meyer, "The Impact of the Centralization of Educational Funding and Control on State and Local Organizational Governance" (Stanford, Calif.: Institute for Research on Educational Finance and Governance, Stanford University, Program Report No. 79-B20, 1979).

35. Mary L. Fennell, "The Effects of Environmental Characteristics on the Structure of Hospital Clusters," *Administrative Science Quarterly*, 25 (1980), 484–510.

36. Hannan and Freeman, "The Population Ecology of Organizations."

37. Rosabeth Moss Kanter, *Commitment and Community* (Cambridge, Mass.: Harvard University Press, 1972), pp. 152–154.

38. Howard Aldrich, *Organizations and Environments* (Englewood Cliffs, N.J.: Prentice-Hall, 1979), p. 265.

39. Carroll and Delacroix (1982) clearly recognize this and include political and institutional legitimacy as a major resource. Aldrich (1979) has argued that the population perspective must attend to historical trends and changes in legal and political institutions.

40. This point was suggested by John Meyer.

41. John W. Meyer, W. Richard Scott and Terence C. Deal, "Institutional and Technical Sources of Organizational Structure Explaining the Structure of Educational Organizations," in *Organizations and the Human Services: Cross-Disciplinary Reflections*, ed. Herman Stein (Philadelphia, Pa.: Temple University Press, 1981).

42. R. R. Ritti and Fred H. Goldner, "Professional Pluralism in an Industrial Organization," *Management Science* 16 (1979), 233–246.

43. Jeffrey Pfeffer and Gerald Salancik, *The External Control of Organizations: A Resource Dependence Perspective* (New York: Harper and Row, 1978), pp. 188–224.

44. Meyer and Rowan, "Institutionalized Organizations: Formal Structure as Myth and Ceremony."

45. Also see John W. Meyer and Michael Hannan, *National Development and the World System: Educational, Economic, and Political Change* (Chicago: University of Chicago Press, 1979).

46. Michael W. Sedlak, "Youth Policy and Young Women, 1950–1972: The Impact of Private Sector Programs for Pregnant and Wayward Girls on Public Policy," Paper presented at National Institute for Education Youth Policy Research Conference, Washington, D.C., 1981.

47. Lewis Coser et al., *Books: The Culture and Commerce of Book Publishing.*

48. Carl Milofsky, "Structure and Process in Community Self-Help Organizations," chapter 9 in this volume.

49. Ann Swidler, *Organization Without Authority: Dilemmas of Social Control of Free Schools* (Cambridge, Mass.: Harvard University Press, 1979).

50. See Kanter, *Commitment and Community.* Also see Joyce Rothschild-Whitt, "The Collectivist Organization: An Alternative to Rational Bureaucratic Models," *American Sociological Review* 44 (1979), 509–527.

51. See James G. March and Johan P. Olsen, *Ambiguity and Choice in Organizations* (Bergen, Norway: Universitetsforlaget, 1976).

52. See Richard M. Cyert and James G. March, *A Behavioral Theory of the Firm* (Englewood Cliffs, N.J.: Prentice-Hall, 1963).

53. Arman Alchian, "Uncertainty, Evolution, and Economic Theory," *Journal of Political Economy,* 58 (1950), 211–221.

54. See D. Eleanor Westney, *Organizational Development and Social Change in Mejii, Japan* (forthcoming).

55. See John Kimberly, "Initiation, Innovation and Institutionalization in the Creation Process," in *The Organizational Life Cycle,* ed. John Kimberly and Robert B. Miles (San Francisco: Jossey-Bass, 1980).

56. Walter W. Powell, "The Political Economy of Public Television," Program on Non-Profit Organizations, Yale University, 1987.

57. John W. Meyer, Remarks at ASA session on "The Present Crisis and the Decline in World Hegemony" (Toronto, Canada, 1980).

58. Magali Sarfatti Larson, *The Rise of Professionalism: A Sociological Analysis* (Berkeley: University of California Press, 1977).

59. Randall Collins, *The Credential Society* (New York: Academic Press, 1979).

60. See Larson, *The Rise of Professionalism: A Sociological Analysis,* pp. 49–52.

61. See Richard Hall, "Professionalization and Bureaucratization," *American Sociological Review,* 33 (1968), 92–104.

62. See Charles Perrow, "Is Business Really Changing?" *Organizational Dynamics* (Summer 1974), 31–44.

63. James C. March and James G. March, "Almost Random Careers: The Wisconsin School Superintendency, 1940–72," *Administrative Science Quarterly* 23 (1977), 3378–3409.

64. Paul Hirsch and Thomas Whisler, "The View From the Boardroom," paper presented at Academy of Management Meetings, New York, 1982.

65. See Aaron Cicourel, "The Acquisition of Social Structure: Toward a Developmental Sociology of Language," in *Understanding Everyday Life,* ed. Jack D. Douglas (Chicago: Aldine, 1970), pp. 136–168. See also Oliver E. Williamson, *Markets and Hierarchies, Analysis and Antitrust Implications: A Study of the Economics of Internal Organization* (New York: Free Press, 1975).

66. See William G. Ouchi, "Markets, Bureaucracies and Class," *Administrative Science Quarterly* 25 (1980), 129–141.

67. Collins, *The Credential Society.*

68. Rosabeth Moss Kanter, *Men and Women of the Corporation* (New York: Basic Books, 1977).

69. See Michael Useem, "The Social Organization of the American Business Elite and Participation of Corporation Directors in the Governance of American Institutions," *American Sociological Review*, 44 (1979), 553–572.

70. See DiMaggio, "The Structure of Organizational Fields: An Analytical Approach and Policy Implications."

71. M. L. Lee, "A Conspicuous Production Theory of Hospital Behavior," *Southern Economic Journal*, 38 (1971), 51.

72. Fennell, "The Effects of Environmental Characteristics on the Structure of Hospital Clusters."

73. Fennell, "The Effects of Environmental Characteristics," p. 505.

74. James Thompson, *Organizations in Action* (New York: McGraw-Hill, 1967).

75. Pfeffer and Salancik, *The External Control of Organizations: A Resource Dependence Perspective*.

76. Oliver E. Williamson, "Transaction-Cost Economics: The Governance of Contractual Relations," *Journal of Law and Economics*, 22 (1979), 233–261.

77. Thompson, *Organizations in Action*.

78. See Walter W. Powell, "New Solutions to Perennial Problems of Bookselling: Whither the Local Bookstore?" *Daedalus* 112 (1983), 51–64.

79. James G. March and Michael Cohen, *Leadership and Ambiguity: The American College President* (New York: McGraw-Hill, 1974).

80. Meyer and Rowan, "Institutionalized Organizations."

81. Meyer and Rowan, "Institutionalized Organizations."

82. John Meyer, "The Impact of the Centralization of Educational Funding and Control on State and Local Organizational Governance."

83. See Mark Granovetter, "Threshold Models of Collective Behavior," *American Journal of Sociology* 83 (1978), 1420–1443. See also Scott A. Boorman and Paul R. Levitt, "The Cascade Principal for General Disequilibrium Dynamics" (Cambridge, Mass./New Haven, Conn.: Harvard-Yale Preprints in Mathematical Sociology, Number 15, 1979).

84. See Burton R. Clark, *Educating the Expert Society* (San Francisco: Chandler, 1962).

85. See Talcott Parsons, *The Social System* (Glencoe, Ill.: Free Press, 1951).

86. See J. William Domhaff, *Who Rules America?* (Englewood Cliffs, N.J.: Prentice-Hall, 1967). See also Louis Althusser, *For Marx* (London: Allan Lane, 1969).

87. See Michael D. Cohen, James G. March and Johan P. Olsen, "A Garbage Can Model of Organizational Choice," *Administrative Science Quarterly*, 17 (1972), 1–25.

88. See Karl Weick, "Educational Organizations as Loosely Coupled Systems," *Administrative Science Quarterly*, 21 (1976), 1–19.

89. See Alvin W. Gouldner, *Patterns of Industrial Bureaucracy* (Glencoe, Ill.: Free Press, 1954).

90. James G. March and Herbert A. Simon, *Organizations* (New York: John Wiley & Sons, 1958).

91. See David L. Sills, *The Volunteers: Means and Ends in a National Organization* (Glencoe, Ill.: Free Press, 1957).

92. March and Cohen, *Leadership and Ambiguity: The American College President*.

93. See Alfred D. Chandler, *The Visible Hand: The Managerial Revolution in American Business* (Cambridge, Mass.: Harvard University Press, 1977). See also Talcott Parsons, *The Evolution of Societies* (Englewood Cliffs, NJ: Prentice-Hall, 1977).

94. See Frances Fox Piven and Richard A. Cloward, *Regulating the Poor: The Functions of Public Welfare* (New York: Pantheon, 1971).

95. See Samuel Bowles and Herbert Gintis, *Schooling in Capitalist America* (New York: Basic Books, 1976).

96. See Sidney G. Winter, "Economic 'Natural Selection' and the Theory of the Firm," Yale Economic Essays, 4 (1964), 224–272. Winter, Optimization and Evolution in the Theory of the Firm," in *Adaptive Economic Models*, ed. Richard H. Day and Theodore Graves (New York: Academic Press, 1975), pp. 73–118. See also Richard R. Nelson and Sidney Winter, *An Evolutionary Theory of Economic Change* (Cambridge, Mass.: Harvard University Press, 1982).

97. Katz, *Class Bureaucracy and Schools: The Illusion of Educational Change in America.*

98. James Weinstein, *The Corporate Ideal in the Liberal State 1900–1918.* (Boston: Beacon Press, 1968). Barnouw, *A History of Broadcasting in the United States.*

99. See Ellis W. Hawley, *The New Deal and the Problem of Monopoly: A Study in Economic Ambivalence* (Princeton, N.J.: Princeton University Press, 1966).

100. Mortin H. Halperin, *Bureaucratic Politics and Foreign Policy* (Washington, D.C.: The Brookings Institution, 1974).

101. Charles Perrow, "Control in Organizations," paper presented at American Sociological Association annual meeting, New York, 1976, p. 21.

102. March and Simon, *Organizations.*

103. Herbert A. Simon, *Administrative Behavior* (New York: Free Press, 1957).

104. William J. Domhoff, *The Powers That Be: Processes of Ruling Class Domination in America* (New York: Random House, 1979).

105. See Katz, *Class, Bureaucracy and Schools: The Illusion of Educational Change in America.*

106. See Steven Lukes, *Power: A Radical View* (London: Macmillan, 1974).

4

Substance versus Symbol in Administrative Reform

The Case of Human Services Coordination[1]

JANET A. WEISS

Some policy debates appear to be impervious to evidence, to the frustration and puzzlement of analysts with evidence to the point. Policy actors may close their eyes to data on the performance of policies and programs for a number of reasons, some of them purposeful, others accidental, sometimes justifiable, other times inexplicable. Some quintessential examples of such refusals may be found in the debate over the coordination of human services. Policymakers in human services have paid little attention to seemingly pertinent research and evaluation data about the performance of programs to coordinate the delivery of human services. In this chapter I suggest that decision makers have continued to advocate coordination reforms in the face of consistently discouraging evidence, because they have been seduced by the symbolic and expressive content of the coordination message. Because so much attention has been captured by the symbolic issues, little has been left for such mundane concerns as the poor performance of operating programs. Thus the coordination story offers another in a long series of instructive lessons about the obstacles to using research and analysis to improve the quality of public policy.

The contrast between policy on the symbolic level and policy as translated into real, operating programs is particularly vivid in the human services, dealing with the diverse needs of those who are too old, too young, physically handicapped, mentally retarded or disturbed, hungry, sick, addicted, homeless, troubled, or abused—in short, too dependent. Our impulses to help have historically conflicted with the limited resources we have been willing to devote to helping. Thus our system of human services has developed in fits and starts, responding to the needs of one group here, another group there, sharing the load among public, private, and voluntary organizations. In the past decade or so, we have discovered ourselves enmeshed in a vast, complex system characterized by enormous budgets (billions of dollars a year in federal Title XX funds alone), dispersed responsibility, fragmented funding and structure of service agencies, and inaccessible, unresponsive, discontinuous service delivery. For example, in 1971 in New York City, 6000 public, quasi-public, and voluntary agencies served 4 million clients with no central source of information and no overall mechanism for coordination among agencies. Nationwide, fewer than half of those multiproblem clients referred by one agency to another ever received the help they needed.[2]

There are many possible policy responses to these problems, but the current rhetoric of reform in human services leans heavily on coordination as the path to efficient, improved service delivery.[3] But "coordination" means many things. My use of the term here is intended to reflect the wide variety of programs at federal, state, and local levels that call themselves coordination programs because they aim to enhance the effectiveness and/ or efficiency of human service delivery through changes in organizational or administrative arrangements. These programs work by establishing linkages among various administrative, financial, and service delivery functions, either within or across levels of government or between public and private agencies. Some of the more popular examples are information sharing, joint planning or programming, centralized budgeting, collocation of service delivery sites, centralized support services, multiproblem case coordinators, and joint record keeping. Sometimes these efforts are called "services integration," but the overlap is so substantial that services integration can be seen as a species of coordination program.

Programs labeled either way may take a number of similar forms, including efforts to foster voluntary cooperation, coordination by formal or informal bargaining to a consensus on priorities or programs, legally mandated coordination, consolidation of related programs under a single leadership, creation of new service organizations, or establishment of new administrative relationships among service delivery organizations. Some programs call for coordination of all services to specific client groups, others for coordination of all service delivery within limited geographic areas, others for various strategies of coordination on various administrative levels.[4]

In the following discussion, I first review the experience with this array of coordination programs. The theme here is the frequent frustration, conflict, and disappointment associated with these programs, as recorded in anecdotes, case studies, and systematic evaluations. I discuss some of the reasons for these experiences, then turn to the puzzle of the enduring appeal of coordination remedies in the face of such evidence. Finally, I examine the confusion associated with a policy that has such enormous symbolic and expressive value but such a poor record of substantive accomplishment and offer some suggestions toward constructive clarification.

THE OPERATING REALITIES OF COORDINATION

The activity of coordination is itself fraught with peril. Amid all the attempts and all the species of coordinating mechanisms, this message is clear. Many devices are tried, but few human service programs designed to do so ever result in more coordination. For example, one survey reported that "twenty per cent of the [seventy coordination/service integrational] projects contacted had no fiscal, personnel, locational, organization, or other administrative link that we could detect."[5] Another survey of thirty-five programs found that "no project had fully developed a majority of linkages. . . . [Many] were focusing primarily on service delivery and not coordination."[6] In recognition of the problem, Henton's review of coordination projects sponsored by the U.S. Department of Health, Education, and Welfare (HEW) investigated whether each project had adopted one or more direct service linkages (including central intake, joint case management, collection, or shared management information systems), regardless of how well the linkage worked. Over half of the projects in his sample of thirty-three had instituted none of these linkages.[7]

The roots of this implementation failure lie in the ways that social service organizations deal with their clients, their staff, their sources of income, and each other. Intrinsic, deep-seated organizational processes have turned out to be formidable impediments to creating interorganizational ties. Acknowledging the intractability of these obstacles may give us pause in our headlong rush to salvation through coordination.

Conceptual Conflict

Although the basic idea of improving coordination among service providers is perfectly straightforward, there is a great deal of ambiguity in translating the idea into administrative and professional practice. In developing specific procedures, and attempting to operationalize program objectives, program designers may confront the underlying ambiguity of those objectives.

Some advocate coordination that operates to the benefit of clients, making it easier for them to get the help they deserve. Others advocate coordination that operates to the advantage of the professional providers, making it easier for them to do their jobs as they see fit. Still others advocate coordination that works to please administrators and funding authorities by cutting costs, eliminating waste, and increasing efficiency and financial accountability.

While all these are worthy goals, they are by no means the same. Different objectives may well imply contradictory courses of action in any given instance. Setting up a coordination program to eliminate duplication of services in no way guarantees a coordination program that improves the comprehensiveness of services provided to clients. When a coordination program is launched, the vague sense that coordination will be effective often camouflages the multiple, conflicting hopes that clients, politicians, administrators, professional service providers, and interest groups each cherish independently. Since the coordinators may not even recognize these conflicts, they may see no need to reconcile them. The result is a persistent lack of both consensus and clarity over what the program should do and thus what it can be expected to accomplish.

Even in those cases in which all the groups involved happen to agree upon goals, a second type of conceptual or ideological conflict often occurs. While it may be easy to agree about the need for more coordination, it may be difficult to agree about just what needs to be coordinated (information? procedures? programs? planning? resources?) and impossible to agree about who should do the coordinating (clients? professional service providers? administrators? legislators?) Eliminating fragmentation and discontinuity may be a desirable goal, but there are many possible ways to attack it and no very good way to know which one is most likely to work. This is illustrated in a number of cases in which coordinators of mental retardation programs knew just what they wanted but made serious errors in trying to achieve it. The description by Aiken and others reveals a general lack of knowledge about how best to bring about coordination and the pitfalls encountered in attempting to coordinate information or planning when the problems lie in programs or procedures or in attempting to focus on providers when the problems are experienced by clients.[8]

Sometimes the choice of ineffective means is deliberate in that a reorganization is used as an excuse to consolidate power or to implement change for other purposes (see the discussion on politics that follows). More often such errors are due to the complexities of organizational change or to the absence of some necessary ingredient for success. The most common planning mistake seems to be underestimating the inertia in the system, expecting relatively small changes to have large impact.

Lack of clarity about means and conflict over ends have consequences for the eventual success of a coordination program. Coordination reforms must be implemented in complex settings with the participation of a number of interested parties with stakes in the outcomes of the reforms. To the extent that the parties disagree explicitly or implicitly over means or ends, they may fail to participate effectively, be angry at having their expectations violated, or end up working at cross-purposes. In any case, effective reform will be more difficult to achieve.

Professional Resistance

In many cases professionals have resisted being integrated or coordinated. This is due in large part to their roles, training, and objectives.

The professional service providers, as the ones who deal with clients, are the people who must change their daily work behavior if the service delivery system is to be changed in any meaningful way. They bear the brunt of systemwide reform. This role in the frontline gives professionals the sense that they are, by training and experience, the guardians of quality in the management and delivery of services; it makes them suspicious of change imposed on them by those without similar experience.[9]

This suspicion tends to be particularly severe in the case of service coordination and integration projects. Professionals may perceive such projects as techniques to increase management control rather than as genuine reform. Coordination programs seem to them to threaten professional control over allocations of time and resources without much connection to improvements in service delivery. Most professionals see their objective as the delivery of high quality services and thus resist programs that interfere with their ability to do their job as they see fit. For example, Laurence Lynn describes the response of mental health professionals in Florida to a proposed reorganization of service delivery:

Many saw the prospect that deprofessionalization and politicization would be pushed to their ultimate limits. . . . The red tape, undertainty, and nonprofessional scrutiny of division [of mental health] activities was regarded as a clear procedural setback. . . . Some mental health officials also worried that reorganization would discourage highly qualified professionals from joining Florida's system. . . . In short, the mental health community saw the reorganization as a distinct threat to the delivery of quality mental health care.[10]

Another source of professional resistance grows out of conflicts among professionals rather than between professionals and administrators or politicians. The system of social services employs many different kinds of professionals—physicians, social workers, physical therapists, teachers, psychologists, counselors, family therapists, ad infinitum. Each professional group has been trained to understand and treat problems in its own way, and each specializes in certain kinds of clients and certain kinds of problems. Calls for generalist coordinators or for closer cooperation among groups of different professionals directly threaten the structure of specialization and indirectly threaten professional expertise within each area of specialization.[11]

Because training and socialization vary, different professionals define the same set of client or community problems in different ways and therefore see the need for different sorts of treatment. Each group operates under somewhat different assumptions. Each profession thinks that it should be the core of any comprehensive treatment program; each is unwilling to subordinate itself to alternative philosophies of treatment. In spite of obvious overlap, such differences among professions make close cooperation difficult. Forcing service providers to coordinate across professional lines may be in the best interests of the clients and the service organization and indirectly threaten professional expertise within each area of specialization.

Those coordination projects that provoke the least resistance seem to accomplish that feat by setting up appropriate incentives for the professional service providers. Coordination and integration programs may offer increased funding, various types of comprehensive information systems, availability of more and more varied professional expertise, increased planning or analytical capability, or physical facilities such as multiservice centers.[12] Thus coordination reform sweetened with incentives seems most likely to appeal to professional tastes. To the extent that professionals feel helped and supported by the reorganization they are likely to work toward its success. To the extent that they feel threatened and undermined by it, they are likely to resist.

Bureaucratic Constraints

Coordination programs attempt to change not simply the behavior of individuals, but also that of ongoing organizations of service providers. It is a truism that organizations resist change. It is obvious that organizations develop standard operating procedures, patterns by which the daily tasks of the organization are carried out. Everyone knows that these patterns become entrenched because of habit and because they are sustained by organizational incentives. But the force of these simple truths is overlooked by many would-be coordinators. The incentive systems that sustain current service delivery networks are not trivial considerations. Change in and of itself has costs. At least in the short term it creates uncertainty; it threatens the positions of key members of the organization; it disrupts organizational functioning. Organizations are unwilling to change unless people believe that the benefits of a proposed change will outweigh the costs. Change will not occur unless the system of incentives is revised so that new operating procedures are seen as more effective, more convenient, more efficient, or more rewarding to staff (although not necessarily to clients) than the old.[13] Coordination reformers cannot simply point out more rational ways for organizations to behave and expect change to result.

The same principle holds for relationships between organizations. Organizations are unlikely to take up cooperation with one another simply because someone says it would be a good idea for them to do so. Changes in interorganizational systems are also costly in time, effort, and morale. For interorganizational relations, like intraorganizational ones, benefits must compensate for the costs in time, energy, and other resources of establishing new linkages or revising old ones.[14]

Indeed, the importance of incentives is especially strong in interorganizational coordination. Coordination programs may require individual agencies to surrender some of their income, clients, staff, power, or autonomy to other organizations or to a coordinator. This constitutes a cost in the usual sense of a loss of resources. But it is also costly in that it threatens an organization's basic maintenance and survival. One of an organization's most important objectives is to perpetuate itself. When coordination programs seem to jeopardize survival, either through the immediate or the long term prospect of absorbing the organization or by forcing it to give up some of its autonomy, resistance is inevitable.

For that very reason, coordination programs organized at the state or federal level in the United States often have little impact at the local level. The local organizations seek to maintain their autonomy. Although they are dependent for funds on higher levels of government, they exchange as little autonomy as possible for state and federal dollars. By maintaining some independence, they try to safeguard their own survival in the face of inevitable changes in policy and organization at other levels. And, to some extent, they have been successful in these efforts. In cases of state level reorganization to promote coordination, it is common to find few changes at the service delivery level.[15]

These two tendencies—to resist change and to maximize autonomy and survival—are characteristic of organizations of all types, as they are characteristic of social service organizations. But these fundamental organizational processes make coordination (like other kinds of change) difficult to implement. Sometimes cooperation can be coerced, but when it cannot, programs must take account of these processes in order to have some hope of producing the desired changes.[16]

Political Contexts

Social service systems are created and paid for by governments as embodiments of political and social purposes. Although I have been discussing the human service system and its problems as if they just happened to be as they are, the system has been shaped over the decades by numerous incremental government decisions about what to do with people in need of various kinds of help. Existing fragmentation, overlapping categorical programs, and the like are the unanticipated side effects of these intermittent political responses to demands for professional assistance and social control. The inherent partisan context of publicly funded social services has important consequences for attempts to coordinate these services.

The most obvious consequence is that attempts to reform the system through coordination become embroiled in political controversy on several levels. Coordination programs (like other kinds of reorganization) become tools in straightforward power struggles over control, priorities, or resources within the social service system. Naturally, each group with a stake in how social services are organized is interested in coordination linkages that operate to its own relative advantage. Naturally, what is advantageous to one group is not advantageous to another. Conflicts between legislators and professionals or between administrators and clients or among any combination of interested parties over control of the system may be acted out in the arena of coordination reform, each group trying to impose its vision of a better-run system on all other groups. Thus coordination, like other political issues, must be the product of compromise, bargaining, and negotiation among power centers.[17] No one group, no matter how noble its motives, can expect to have coordination its own way. The politicization of social service issues makes compliance improbable.

The political division of responsibility among federal, state, and local government throws up more literal barriers to coordinating efforts. A central problem is that almost all federal funds for human services are channeled directly to individual provider agencies; there are few provisions for moving funds from one program to another in response to local needs.[18] But earmarking funds is only one manifestation of Congress's reluctance to bestow unrestricted largess on local governments. A survey of planners and administrators for HEW programs turned up an astonishing assortment of strings attached to federal monies that, in effect, make coordination more difficult: widely variable client eligibility restrictions, conflicting geographical distributing requirements, requirements for advisory and community groups, sign-off regulations, out-of-sequence funding application schedules, difficulties in anticipating levels of federal funding, difficulties in locating federal responsibility, inconsistent requirements for agency structure and organization.[19] State and local administrators live with the justifiable fear that coordinating several programs, each with its own web of regulations and restrictions, will lead rapidly to knots.

Another set of consequences stems from the political context of the social services. As I noted previously, social services are the expression of diverse political purposes and values that must compete for scarce resources. Under such circumstances attempts at coordination may actually be dysfunctional. As Landau has shown, the elimination of duplication and overlap may serve to remove safeguards and redundancies that increase the likelihood of successful system performance.[20] Streamlining may also mean the elimination of diversity, the homogenization of services. For example, central intake and referral systems may provide clients with increased access to services but eliminate their freedom of choice among treatment types or philosophies. Overlap may permit experimentation with alternative methods of treatment, because professionals, administrators, and clients all know that traditional help is available elsewhere. Discouraging waste may thus unfortunately discourage innovation. As expressions of our political purposes, social services reflect the pluralistic character of those purposes. Rationalizing the system through coordination may destroy some of this pluralistic character.[21]

But our political purposes are not simply diverse; they are often inconsistent and contradictory. We want to foster family well-being by having welfare mothers care for their own children, and we also want welfare mothers to work so that their families can be self-supporting. We want mentally handicapped children to receive the best possible education by mainstreaming them into regular classrooms, and we do not want the learning of normal children to be adversely affected by the presence in classrooms of the mentally handicapped. In a fragmented system these contradictions are not directly confronted and thus do not have to be resolved. Attempts to coordinate may lead to the surfacing of may such inconsistencies and contradictions in our values.[22]

There is some advantage to knowing the contradictory messages that our social policies convey. But there is some social danger in making these conflicts explicit in ways that provoke confrontation, sharpen divisions, or pose irreconcilable dilemmas.[23] The more comprehensive the coordination, the more likely it is to require direct and explicit decisions about trade-offs in allocation of resources to various disadvantaged groups and the more likely, perhaps, that socially destructive comparisons may be made.

So, in several ways, coordination is likely to become the focus of political conflict. The political setting puts constraints on possible strategies of coordination, and coordination in turn feeds back unanticipated dilemmas for political resolution. For both reasons, coordination efforts that fail to accommodate the political setting are likely to find political obstacles littering the path to reform.

THE OUTCOMES OF COORDINATION

The array of obstacles is daunting. Experience teaches us caution about our ability to implement coordinating linkages. If we cannot expect our program to achieve intended coordination, still less should we expect to reap the benefits of efficiency and effectiveness that coordination is purported to sow. Failure to create coordination leads quite naturally to failure of coordination efforts to produce outcomes. Even in those cases of successful implementation, the effects on service delivery have been uncertain.

One common goal of coordination is to eliminate waste, duplication, and overlap, thereby reducing costs. According to data from existing programs, those who expect cost reduction are engaging in delusionary fantasies. In many cases efforts to implement changes result in increased rather than decreased costs. Morrill summarizes HEW's experience: "Services integration seldom reduces costs . . . [and] most often requires shared information systems that are often expensive."[24] Gans and Horton conclude their analysis of thirty-five coordination projects: "although there are some cost savings resulting from economies of scale and reduction of duplication, they do not appear (at least in the first run) to equal the input costs of administrative and core service staff required to support integrative efforts."[25] Analyses over the longer run of programs in mental retardation and child care have shown no significant improvements in efficiency and no cost savings.[26] thus there is little evidence that short- or long-term financial benefits do materialize and some evidence that they do not.

The cost-cutters also ignore the fact that most coordination projects aim, at least in part, at service objectives incompatible with reduced costs. Successful attempts to increase accessibility, to centralize intake, to identify and refer multiproblem clients, or to improve comprehensiveness of available services all eventually result in increased caseloads. Even if such successful programs also succeeded in eliminating duplication and increasing administrative efficiency it is far from clear that the net result would be lower budgets.

The second important objective of coordinators is usually an improvement in quality and effectiveness of services provided to clients. Unfortunately there are few adequate ways to evaluate the impact of coordination programs on the quality of service delivery. Client reports of satisfaction with services are generally agreed to be less than reliable; O'Donnell and Sullivan reviewed data showing that many clients of neighborhood service centers reported feeling "better off" because of the centers but also reported that the centers had done nothing specific for them or their families.[27] But other indicators are equally weak. A study of Model Cities' City Demonstration Agencies used the agencies' ability to spend their appropriation as a measure of quality of their services, on the questionable assumption that cities that spent their money did so by providing more services. The degree of intracity coordination did not affect this indicator of the quality of service delivery.[28] Many evaluations have not even attempted to link coordination reform with changes in effectiveness or quality. A host of researchers have noted that, because of data problems, they were unable to test the hypothesis that coordinated systems are better than uncoordinated ones.[29]

A careful evaluation of statewide services integration in Florida concluded that "evidence and testimony . . . both supports and opposes the view that service quality has been maintained. Both views appear to be partly true." Different techniques of measuring quality led to different conclusions. Furthermore, the evaluators report, "It is impossible to apply any one measure to the quality of each and all of the large and varied array of services. . . . We sought many objective measures of the status of, and trends in client services, staffing, and expenditures; we found gross or spotty data of little usefulness. . . . [The available data] add little to our understanding of trends in the quality of client services or our ability to distinguish the effects of the reorganization from the many other local, state, and national factors affecting service."[30] For example, professional judgments of the quality of services may or may not correspond with judgments of the kindness or dignity with which clients are treated, although both can be considered to be measures of service quality. Other analyses have grappled with the same measurement problems and often have reached similarly equivocal conclusions.[31] Note that the appropriate conclusion is that no evidence exists to show whether coordinated service delivery systems provide better service than uncoordinated ones. We can safely conclude only that coordination projects tend to be expensive and difficult to implement and have unknown consequences for the quality of services delivered to clients.

In some cases, however, coordination linkages are clearly feasible and desirable. Brewer and Kakalik describe fruitful efforts to coordinate the delivery of diverse services to a narrowly defined target population, handicapped children and their parents.[32] Several cases of successful interagency cooperation on a city- or county-wide basis are reviewed by Anderson, Frieden, and Murphy.[33] On a small scale, in a response to a specific crisis, with an easily bounded target group, or on an informal basis, coordination efforts have been implemented and may even have produced desired results.

It is nevertheless the case that our reach frequently exceeds our grasp; nearly all participants in coordination projects find the impact on service delivery to be negligible. In light of the elusiveness of effective implementation, such a conclusion is hardly surprising.

THE SYMBOLIC VALUE OF COORDINATION

The failures of coordination programs have not interfered with the popularity of the coordination message. Given the evidence of the past, how can we sustain such high expectations for the future? In this section I analyze the siren call of coordination remedies, concluding with some speculation about the invulnerability of the appeal on the symbolic level to attack from the substantive level.

The first step in understanding the widespread attraction to coordination is to understand the problems for which coordination is invoked as a solution. Thousands of independent human service programs are funded by local, state, and federal governments. After a sustained period of exponential growth in spending, budgets for most of these programs have leveled off or even declined. Public expectations, however, have continued to rise. Clients, professionals, administrators, and politicians have raised questions about the effectiveness of current modes of treatment and about the efficiency with which treatment is delivered. Worries about size, cost complexity, accountability, and uncertain efficacy have prompted widespread calls for reform.

In Edelman's terms, this situation lends itself to symbolic political debate.[34] The problems in the human service arena are poorly defined, poorly understood, and emotionally laden. Worse yet, they are almost intolerably complex—a stew of philanthropic, professional, bureaucratic, financial, and political factors. Under such circumstances, people "respond chiefly to symbols that oversimplify and distort," rather than to arguments that attempt to confront the full complexity.[35] When symbols that simplify are also capable of generating emotional commitment, their political persuasiveness can be irresistible.

The blend of emotional and objective content in the call for "coordination" has made it an apt symbol for human services policy. The very word is somehow reassuring. As Wildavsky writes, it is one of the golden words of our time; given a choice, no one would prefer to be uncoordinated.[36] Whereas reforms advocating more services or fewer have been easy to brand as profligate, bleeding-heart liberalism or as heartless, callous stinginess, coordinators have a symbol that allows them to support both improved services and lower costs. The symbol epitomizes widely shared social values of rationality, comprehensiveness, and efficiency, thus reinforcing public confidence in the role of reason in policy-making. By simply invoking coordination, public officials may share in this heady mixture of political benefits.

In practice, the intangibility of human service coordination as a strategy can take many concrete manifestations. Programs billed as coordination or integration of services have attempted to accomplish not only better coordination among service providers but also comprehensiveness, accountability to clients, accountability to government, accessibility, administrative efficiency, improved participation by clients, communication among providers, and innumerable other worthy objectives.[37] The concepts of coordination and services integration have attached to so many purposes that their meaning has been blurred. In many ways they have evolved into generic terms for change and reform of the service system. Thus complaints that some system of services isn't coordinated often boil down to no more than complaints about what the system is doing; a grievance over results is not the same as a charge that a system is not doing what it is doing efficiently. Often a vague sense that somehow a system could be doing better turns into the proposition that the system should be better coordinated. With or without responsible analysis, with or without reliable evidence, it is safe to assume that a complex interorganizational network could be better coordinated. Thus coordination only continues to grow more popular as a convenient political device that legitimates calls for change.

Of course, change is often good, and many changes masquerading as coordination are desirable improvements on existing systems. But to confuse them with coordination is to sacrifice clarity for expedience. Use of "coordination" as synonym for "reform" explains some of its attractiveness and some of its resistance to evidence of poor performance. The social service system will always cause dissatisfaction, will always need reform. If reform equals coordination, we will always need more coordination. No data are necessary to sustain the logic of that progression. In part because we permit it to have so many diverse and contrary meanings, coordination flourishes as a continuing refrain in policy-making in human services.

Another ingredient in the emotional appeal of coordination is the tidy way in which it structures and simplifies our human services problems. A system is, in theory, perfectly coordinated when the actions of different individuals or agencies are tuned to each other such that production of any one output cannot be increased without an increase in costs or decrease in production elsewhere in the system. By contrast, the actual operation of the social service system is extremely complex, with multiple layers of authority and influence, numerous interest groups, many sorts of output, and many inadequacies. Devising systematic strategies to correct all the deficiencies would be an impossible undertaking even if we knew what would be "correct." Coordination programs are promoted to make it seem as though simple solutions, easily understood, can resolve these Byzantine difficulties.

Moreover, coordination relates to managerial arrangements by which output is produced and ignores the professional technology of production.

Thus public officials and managers feel competent to advocate this type of reform in spite of their total ignorance of how a professional talks to a family in disarray, helps the elderly stay out of institutions, deals with an abused child, or gets an alcoholic into treatment. From the public point of view, coordination simplifies the problems in human services by implying that the worst problems are merely administrative and that improvements in service quality will follow automatically once the organizational questions are resolved. As one federal official explained his support for service integration, "administrative efficiency should raise the quality, scope, and variety of service offerings . . . [through] the assignment of functions to jurisdictions that have the management expertise, scope of functional responsibility, geographic scale, and legal authority to perform a service in an authoritative and technically proficient manner."[38] Where the technical proficiency would come from was clearly not his concern.

In addition to its conveniently ambiguous definition and its ability to simplify complicated problems, coordination has still another essential source of appeal. It retains its preeminent political position because it evokes shared social values and expressed commitments that all can support.

The first of the shared commitments is to rationality. Coordination strategies carry an authoritative ring of technical competence and planning. They are not helter-skelter. They are reasonable. They seem to be focused on objective, systematic analyses of resources and capabilities. "The most obvious point is that integration of human services makes sense," declares the Connecticut Human Services Reorganization Commission.[39] This rationality is particularly seductive given the diffuse nature of policymaking about social services. The hodgepodge of diverse services, clients, and regulations makes it difficult to understand what is happening beyond the bounds of any one agency or one level of government. A reform strategy that claims to bring order out of chaos becomes very appealing. There is, according to Smith, "a deep and pervasive vein of current conventional wisdom, namely that all things should be unified, quantified, ordered, consolidated, and computerized. . . . Unification is good, duplication is bad; . . . official order is safe, pluralistic disorder is less than safe."[40] Coordination appeals to this predisposition. When public officials or planners try to make sense of their options, needs, and resources on a jurisdictionwide basis, they are understandably drawn to strategies that unite, order, consolidate, and rationalize. Indeed, all parties to the human service system are drawn to reforms that suggest possibilities for containing such refractory problems.

A second shared value is cooperation. "Inherent in the very concept of social services integration is the recognition of the desirability of cooperation," writes Parr.[41] In human service networks, interorganizational relationships are often characterized by both mutual dependence and competitive conflicts of interest. Coordination highlights the former, deemphasizes the latter. By relegating the selfish pursuit of agency self-interest to the shadows, coordinators position themselves in the glow of disinterested commitment to the common good.

Third, coordination taps into two shared objectives in a system characterized by conflict over values and priorities. Although social services are the expression of diverse social and political purposes that compete for support and attention, all groups agree that services should be administered more efficiently with less waste and that, insofar as it is possible, the service system should provide a comprehensive, holistic approach to clients with multiple problems. Coordination is alleged to make progress on both fronts, thus working toward two of the few service objectives that can boast board based support. In an arena in which few groups agree about anything, a reform based on two consensual values becomes particularly attractive.

For these reasons coordination continues to enjoy unusually high prestige. The valuable symbolic function that it serves is the affirmation of our hopes for change, rationality, efficiency, and comprehensiveness. Ideally we would prefer to retain this expressive function without permitting our enchantment with our own rhetoric to interfere with the design and implementation of effective operating programs. Unfortunately we do not seem to have managed this feat.

The Clash of Symbol and Substance

As a result of its symbolic potency, coordination reform in its many manifestations has dominated policy debates over human services for the last decade. As a result of its substantive difficulty, coordination programs have been difficult and expensive to achieve and have seldom produced much in the way of desired results. The popularity has been undimmed by the negative evidence. In spite of what we know, we continue to seek more and better coordination.

To the extent that we conceive the policies about coordination as the rational pursuit of a defined set of objectives, our attachment to a course of action that has not in the past accomplished its stated objectives seems unfortunate. If we think of coordination reform as a vehicle for the expression of social commitments to rationality, comprehensiveness, simplicity, and efficiency, this stubborn persistence comes to seem less perverse. Continued advocacy may depend not at all on payoffs of substantive effectiveness or efficiency, but rather on continued social commitment. Thus the payoffs on the symbolic and political levels effectively obscure the indifferent success, the costs, and the conflict surrounding real world programs. However, we pay a price for our comfortable ignorance of evidence that our values do not translate neatly or directly into effective service delivery. Operating under a policy that embodies such contradictory messages has pernicious consequences.

In this section I discuss two components to the clash. First, some of the very characteristics that make coordination such a compelling symbol have made constructing workable programs difficult. Second, the emotional power of the coordination movement has served to distract us from pursuing other, potentially more useful policies and made it difficult to pay attention to research and analysis about the substantive accomplishments of the programs coordination has spawned.

The definitional ambiguity which makes coordination a handy political device has led to a chasm between rhetoric and operations. Coordination is discussed in the political arena as though everyone knows precisely what it means, when in fact it means many inconsistent things, and occasionally means nothing at all. So the symbolism and the rhetoric, even when codified into legislation, often proceed on their merry ways, devoid of operational guidance for those attempting to provide services for clients. Under these circumstances, little said during the policy-making process may have direct implications for the day-to-day lives of people in operating agencies.

When policies addressed to "coordination" or "service integration" fail to be concrete about what is intended, the lack of guidance undercuts well intentioned attempts at reform. When different special interests in the social service system want change and each party can legitimately call its set of changes coordination, people will find themselves working in theory for the goals, but in effect at cross-purposes. When a variety of changes are packaged and sold as coordination reform, false expectations are encouraged. Participants in the service system are led to believe that coordination linkages will be established when, in reality, other objectives are being implemented. When a program billed as a coordination effort is subjected to evaluation, evaluators looking for evidence of coordination will evaluate on inappropriate criteria and inappropriately find programs wanting. Presumably some of the unfortunate consequences of misspecified calls for reform can be averted by defining "coordination" and "services integration" much more precisely at the outset and then designing programs that promote just those sorts of linkages. Truth in advertising will not guarantee results, but it can avoid these sorts of unproductive confusion.

The simplistic emphasis on a few widely shared values has also interfered with the ability to achieve real change in the ways in which services are delivered to clients. Bemused by the cooperative meanings of coordination, we tend to ignore critical realities of conflict, competition, and mutual adjustment. In the grip of the search for efficiency, planners are wont to neglect the need for organizational, professional, and political expertise. Coordination to rationalize delivery of services or use of resources may result in high priced, technical planning for new programs. But without attention to professional, managerial, and political factors, planning remains incomplete, and resulting programs falter.

Wholesale advocacy of coordination grows in part out of widespread agreement about the need for more efficient, more comprehensive service delivery. But emphasis on these potential benefits of coordinated service delivery has often overshadowed analysis of potential costs. As the literature so poignantly reveals, in many cases costs far outweigh benefits.[42] Although it is not possible to be certain about such cases before the fact, much more attention could be paid to a priori assessment of when, where, and under what circumstances coordination can be implemented at all; thoughtful judgments about potential costs during and after implementation would contribute to discriminating use of coordination as a strategy of reform.

Beyond the problems with making coordination work are the questions of the merit of the entire enterprise. Administrative tinkering may restore the productivity of a system beset by administrative problems alone. But the problems in social service delivery run deeper than the administrative, down to questions of resources, and all the way down to the basic technologies of the service professions. In most cases, resources are inadequate. In others, all the social service treatment at society's command cannot provide the sought-for solutions. At best, changes in organizational arrangements can make better use of existing resources—a desirable, but limited outcome. Coordination cannot generate new resources, cannot devise new treatment methods, cannot solve problems of alienation or mistrust, cannot transmute ineffective service systems into effective ones. Current federal, state, and local provisions for service delivery are flawed in many ways, and multiple problems require multiple treatments. Pouring all our reform energies into coordination channels will usually result in minimal change.

The allure of coordination has distracted us from diligent exploration of all possible paths to higher quality service delivery, and from attempting nonservice strategies to help those in need. While so much attention is absorbed by pulling and hauling over coordination, we have insufficient energy to argue about such central questions as the effectiveness of services provided to those in need, the level of benefits available, the fairness or equity with which benefits are assigned, and effective methods for involving clients in decisions and policies about service priorities. Our focus on some important issues around organizational arrangements—for that is what coordination boils down to—has led to the neglect of other, arguably more important questions about the type, value, amount, and equity of help available to the public. This continuing concentration of reform energy is perhaps the most damaging consequence of the combination of attractive values and flawed performances.

The potency of the coordination message distracts us not only from considering alternative policies but also from appreciating the realities of the current policy. Cautionary research and analyses have not been heeded. Part of this is probably due to the reluctance of policymakers to open up their prized programs to doubts, criticisms, or qualifications. Part of it is probably due to research that understandably mistook the symbolic message of coordination for the reality. Research directed primarily at the substance of reform could not take account of the importance of the symbolic commitments represented by these programs. Thus the research became irrelevant to policymakers and administrators who valued just these symbolic factors.

It is paradoxical. By vigorously pursuing rationality through coordination, we have made it difficult to achieve rationality in policy-making by using the results of research and analysis.

But research need not be irrelevant simply because a policy issue has a dominant symbolic component. There are unique opportunities for influence when analysts reconceive their role and explicitly tackle the job of exploring connections between symbol and substance. For example, researchers can evaluate the internal and external political outcomes of a program in addition to the financial or professional results. Documentation of accomplishments such as reassurance or justification may be valuable for program administrators trying to keep their agencies afloat, as well as for high level policy makers trying to make sensible choices about resource allocation.

Research can examine the ways in which a project's larger objectives (for example, holistic, comprehensive care) can and cannot be effectively translated into organizational practice. As well as evaluating whether a given program succeeded in bringing about more coordination, researchers might also evaluate the extent to which the program's activities led to the achievement of basic goals—more clients receiving multiple (comprehensive) services, lower per-client costs, higher staff morale, easier client access to services, or whatever. Sensitivity to these larger goals of the human service system may also enhance the value of research to decision makers operating in this policy arena.

In a less conventional mode, thoughtful research can remind practitioners, administrators, clients, and the public about the goals and values we express and can perhaps reinforce such symbolic commitments even in the face of the frustration of the moment. In a variety of ways, research has helped us to understand the distance between what we hope for and what we do. In part it allows us to discover when and sometimes why we do not achieve our goals; in part it helps us to make explicit the nature of our values and commitments to each other.

Understanding the symbol and the substance may dispel some of the muddled thinking about coordination. Clarity about the values embedded in coordination programs may help to keep alive our hopes for comprehensive, compassionate, cost-effective treatment, even when the coordination star eventually fades. Clarity about the role of political and organizational factors; attention to professional, administrative, and political costs of coordination; and consideration of when benefits are likely to outweigh costs all may help to keep the value implications of coordination from confusing the planning and management of substantive programs. It is useful to keep the two untangled or at least to have some sense of the trade-offs between them. Regardless of the evidence, and for some excellent reasons, we continue to seek more and better coordination. But for the time being it seems sensible to be realistic about what our pursuit of coordination can and cannot accomplish.

NOTES

1. This paper first appeared in *Policy Analysis* 7, 2, (1981), 21–45, © 1981 by the Association for Public Policy Analysis and Management, Reprinted by permission of John Wiley & Sons, Inc.

2. Wayne Anderson, Bernard Frieden, and Michael Murphy, eds. *Managing Human Services*, Municipal Management Series (Washington, D.C.: International City Management Association, 1977).

3. For a few of many examples, see American Society for Public Administration, *Human Services Integration* (Washington, D.C.: The Society, (1974); William A. Morrill, "Services Integration and the Department of Health, Education, and Welfare," *Evaluation* 3 (1976), 52–57; National Academy of Public Administration, *Reorganization in Florida: How Is Services Integrating Working?* (Washington, D.C.: The Academy, 1977); and Connecticut, Human Services Reorganization Commission, *State of Connecticut Human Services Plan* (Hartford, Conn.: The Commission, 1978).

4. Advocacy of coordination of services to a specific client group is illustrated by Garry D. Brewer and James K. Kakalik, *Handicapped Children: Strategies for Improving Services* (New York: McGraw-Hill, 1979). Edward J. Kelty discusses the model of community mental health centers that serve the population of their catchment area in "Is Services Integration Dangerous to Your Mental Health?" *Evaluation* 3 (1976), 139–142. The strategy of agency consolidation on the state level is discussed in Kathleen G. Heintz, "State Organizations for Human Services," *Evaluation* 3 (1976), 106–110.

5. William A. Lucas, Karen Heald, and Mary Vogel, *Census of Local Services Integration: 1975* (Santa Monica, Calif.: Rand Corporation, 1975).

6. Sheldon P. Gans and Gerald T. Horton, *Integration of Human Services* (New York: Praeger, 1975).

7. Douglas Henton, "The Feasibility of Services Integration," mimeographed report to Interagency Services Integration R&D Task Force (Washington, D.C.: U.S. Department of Health, Education, and Welfare, 1975).

8. Michael Aiken, Robert Dewar, Nancy DiTomaso, Jerald Hage, and Gerald Zeitz, *Coordinating Human Services* (San Francisco: Jossey-Bass, 1975).

9. Alfred J. Kahn, "Service Delivery at the Neighborhood Level: Experience, Theory, and Fads," *Social Service Review* 50 (March 1976), 22–56.

10. Laurence E. Lynn, Jr., "Organizing Human Services in Florida," *Evaluation* 3 (March 1976), 58–78. See also Sidney Gardner, "Roles for General Purpose Governments in Services Integration," *Human Services Monograph Series*, no. 2 (Washington, D.C.: Project SHARE, 1976).

11. National Academy of Public Administration, *Reorganization in Florida*.

12. See Robert E. Quinn, "The Impacts of a Computerized Information System on the Integration and Coordination of Human Services," *Public Administration Review* 36 (March/April 1976), 166–174; Douglas G. Montgomery, "Strengthening a National Network on Aging to Serve the Elderly," *Human Resources Administration* (Washington, D.C.: American Society for Public Administration, 1976); and American Society for Public Administration, *Human Services Integration.*

13. Robert K. Yin, with Suzanne Quick, Peter Bateman, and Ellen Marks, *Changing Urban Bureaucracies: How New Practices Become Routinized* (Santa Monica, Calif.: Rand Corporation, 1978).

14. Good discussions of interorganizational ties may be found in Anant Neghandi, ed., *Interorganizational Theory* (Kent, Ohio: Kent State University Press, 1975); and William M. Evan, ed., *Interorganizational Relations* (Philadelphia: University of Pennsylvania Press, 1978).

15. For discussion of local resistance, see Heintz, "State Organizations for Human Services"; American Society for Public Administration, *Human Services Integration;* and Neil Gilbert, "Assessing Service Delivery Methods: Some Unsettled Questions," *Welfare in Review* 10 (May/June 1972), 25–33. Discussions of the same phenomenon in the European experience are found in Kenneth Hanf and Fritz W. Sharpf, eds., *Interorganizational Policymaking* (Beverly Hills, Calif.: Sage Publications, 1978).

16. The same difficulties arise in other sorts of administrative reform. Donald P. Warwick *(A Theory of Public Bureaucracy* [Cambridge, Mass.: Harvard University Press, 1975]) discusses similar resistance in the U.S. State Department to a reorganization plan designed to streamline the bureaucracy.

17. Harold Seidman, *Politics, Position and Power* (New York: Oxford University Press,

1970) offers an insightful discussion of the inevitable political component in coordination. Henton ("The Feasibility of Services Integration") provides evidence that programs created by bargaining are more likely to survive than programs created by planning.

18. Gardner, "Roles for the General Purpose Governments."

19. U.S. Department of Health, Education, and Welfare, *Ties that Bind: HEW National Management Planning Study* (Seattle, Wash.: HEW Region X, 1976). See also T. Field Benton, and R. Millar, *Social Services: Federal Legislation vs. State Implementation* (Washington, D.C.: Urban Institute, 1978).

20. Martin Landau, "Redundancy, Rationality, and the Problem of Duplication and Overlap," *Public Administration Review* 29 (July/August 1969), 346–358.

21. See discussions of this point in Roland L. Warren, "Alternative Strategies of Interagency Planning," in *Interorganizational Research in Health*, ed. P. White (Washington, D.C.: National Center for Health Services, 1970). See also Martin Rein, "Decentralization and Citizen Participation in Social Services," *Public Administration Review* 32 (October 1972), 687–700.

22. For examples of just such conflicts see Gilbert, "Assessing Service Delivery Methods" (the case of the British Local Authority Social Services Departments) and the case study on child care services in Massachusetts in Selma Mushkin, *Services to People: State and National Urban Strategies* (Washington, D.C.: U.S. Department of Health, Education, and Welfare, 1973).

23. This idea has been developed by Charles E. Lindblom, *The Intelligence of Democracy* (New York: Free Press, 1965).

24. Morrill, "Services Integration."

25. Gans and Horton, *Integration of Human Services.*

26. See Aiken et al., *Coordinating Human Services;* and Gilbert Y. Steiner, with Pauline H. Milius, *The Children's Cause* (Washington, D.C.: The Brookings Institution, 1976).

27. Edward J. O'Donnell and Marilyn M. Sullivan in *A Handbook of Human Service Organizations,* ed. H. W. Demone and D. Harshbarger (New York: Behavioral Publications, 1974).

28. Neil Gilbert and Harry Specht, *Coordinating Social Services* (New York: Praeger, 1977).

29. Lucas, Heald, and Vogel, *Census of Local Services Integration;* Henton, "Feasibility of Services Integration"; Gans and Horton, *Integration of Human Services;* Stephen D. Mittenthal, "A System Approach to Services Integration," *Evaluation* 3 (1976), 142–148.

30. National Academy of Public Administration, *Reorganization in Florida.*

31. See the array of evaluations collected in American Society for Public Administration, *Human Services Integration,* or Adrian L. Webb, "Coordination between Health and Personal Social Services," *Eurosocial Reports* 4 (1975), 103–120.

32. Brewer and Kakalik, *Handicapped Children.*

33. Anderson, Frieden, and Murphy, *Managing Human Services.*

34. Murray Edelman, *The Symbolic Uses of Politics* (Urbana: University of Illinois Press, 1964).

35. Edelman, *The Symbolic Uses of Politics,* p. 31.

36. Aaron Wildavsky, *Speaking Truth to Power* (Boston: Little, Brown, 1979).

37. Murray Meld, "Human Services Integration: Toward a Humanistic Approach," *The Social Welfare Forum, 1976, Proceedings of the National Conference on Social Welfare* (New York: Columbia University Press, 1976).

38. In American Society for Public Administration, *Human Services Integration.*

39. *State of Connecticut Human Services Plan.*

40. Robert Smith, "Reflections on the New Federalism," Human Resource Administration (Washington, D.C.: American Society for Public Administration, 1976).

41. In American Society for Public Administration, *Human Services Integration,* p. 76.

42. For an example, see Roland L. Warren, Stephen M. Rose, and Ann F. Bergunder, *The Structure of Urban Reform* (Lexington, Mass.: Lexington Books, 1974).

5

The Corporation-Culture Connection
A Test of Interorganizational Theories[1]

JOSEPH GALASKIEWICZ and BARBARA RAUSCHENBACH

Patronage has undergone a steady change over the years. Slowly publicly held corporations have joined individuals, families, and private foundations as the benefactors of art museums, theaters, opera companies, colleges, zoological gardens, history museums, public broadcasting, and so forth. If we take the estimate that corporations gave approximately $3.8 billion to charity in 1984[2] and that roughly 10.7% of this was given to culture and the arts,[3] then the total amount contributed by business to culture and the arts was approximately $406.6 million. Furthermore, the Council for Financial Aid to Education[4] estimated that corporate support for education rose to $1.70 billion in 1984.

Our understanding of the relationship between the business donor and the cultural organization is still incomplete at best. Insider accounts of the fashionable world of "high culture" and "big business" pique our curiosity, and these accounts are not to be dismissed lightly. Still, as social scientists, we would like to explore the interface between these two institutional giants in a more systematic way—guided by theory and utilizing data on a sample of business and cultural organizations. Our research questions are simple. What are the terms of the transactions between corporations and cultural organizations? And what sorts of benefits can each actor expect to realize?

For some theoretical direction we turn to the literature in sociology on interorganizational relations. We first look to exchange theory. We view the transactions between corporations and cultural organizations as narrowly instrumental and very specific. For example, corporations may make cash contributions in exchange for a position on the board of directors and shared control over the cultural organization. Alternatively, we turn to institutional theory. Here corporations and cultural organizations strive to enhance their own legitimacy in the broader community by association with actors in the other sector. Thus, corporations may give money to high prestige cultural organizations to lead others to believe that they are very influential in the community; or cultural organizations may put executives of very influential companies on their board to lead others to believe that they are very prestigious. Of course, exchange and legitimation processes may both be at work. If so, then ideally we could sort this out.

We will test several hypotheses derived from each theory, using data from a 1978 survey of 39 nonprofit cultural organizations in the Minneapolis–St. Paul metro area. We will specifically look at board interlocks between Twin Cities corporations and these cultural organizations and cash contributions from these corporations to the nonprofit organizations.

THE EXCHANGE PERSPECTIVE

Exchange theory has been a popular framework within which to study interorganizational transactions.[5] Exchange theory assumes that the acquisition of scarce resources is of primary importance to organizations. Although organizations may prefer to remain autonomous, as open systems they need to secure resources from actors in their environment and will engage in exchange transactions to do so.[6]

One type of exchange is for a corporate actor to offer a position on its board of directors to another corporate actor in exchange for needed resources. This would be attractive to the latter, because it provides an opportunity for the donor or investor to exert some control over how its resources would be used if it provided its partner with the resources it needs. While the few studies on cultural organizations' boards have not addressed the issue of how board linkages can be used to secure resources from the environment,[7] studies of hospital boards[8] and welfare agencies[9] have demonstrated the linkage between board interlocking and the procurement of needed resources.

What resources do cultural organizations need which could be secured from business firms in their community? There is little doubt that money is important. Galaskiewicz,[10] Benson,[11] and Aldrich[12] discuss how all organizations must have access to money and must work out strategies to secure funds from their environment. The Ford Foundation report[13] on financing of the arts and various reports of the Carnegie Foundation on the financing of colleges describe the acute need for money among cultural organizations. Revenues from tuition or "the gate" cannot possibly support these organizations, and revenues from investments and endowments have not been adequate to meet rising costs. As Baumol and Bowen[14] argue, the technology of an arts or education institution cannot be changed to keep pace with costs. As a consequence, more and more business organizations have been solicited for money to make up the income gap, and all evidence indicates that business will be called upon more and more in the future.[15]

Exchange theory would lead us to hypothesize that corporations would provide cash in exchange for a position on the board of the cultural organization. First, corporate executives may see their position on the board as an opportunity to improve the community environment for their employees. When asked in a study by the Business Committee on the Arts[16] why their firms supported cultural organizations, business executives said that they saw this as a practical opportunity to help maintain the "quality of life" for their "quality employees." A second motive might be to ensure that values, beliefs, theories, and symbolic forms that are critical of the free enterprise system and/or traditional values are censored. It may well be that when the managers of business corporations become the governors of the community's cultural organizations, values of efficiency and accountability prevail. "Slack" within the organization, which might allow for more controversial or experimental theater, research or music, is minimized.[17]

If indeed the relationship between cultural and business organizations is basically an exchange of contributions for board membership, realistically the costs or consequences would not be that great for either actor. On the one hand, corporate money for philanthropy is readily available. Under the 1935 Internal Revenue Act, which was in effect at the time of our study, business firms could contribute up to 5% of their total pretax net income to nonprofit organizations and deduct the amount from their earnings. The American Association of Fund Raising Counsel[18] estimated that corporate contributions in 1984 were about 1.61% of corporate pretax net income.

On the other hand, cultural administrators can give away slots on their board and "authoritative control" over their organization to outsiders without any real worry that they or their program will be coopted. In almost all cases there are no set limits to the number of people who may sit on the board of a museum or college. In fact, the more outsiders there are, the less influence any one of them is likely to have. Furthermore, a strong tradition of professionalism among artists, performers, and professors insulates, to some degree, the creativity that takes place within the organization. The administration and board only provide facilities that enable the professional to develop his or her talents or deliver services. The cross-cutting, extraorganizational loyalties of these professionals is a further barrier which prevents administrators and boards from infringing too much on art and/or scholarship.[19]

THE INSTITUTIONAL PERSPECTIVE

The organizational literature has begun to turn its attention away from the narrow, highly calculable exchanges between organizations to the more

nebulous, open-ended transactions between organizations and their institutional environments.[20] Attention has been given to the legitimation of
myths which organizations create about themselves,[21] the manipulation of
external referents of prestige by organizational elites,[22] and the attempts
by organizations to legitimate themselves by identifying with cultural symbols and/or legitimate power figures,[23] or by imitating other organizations
in the environment.[24]

Given the onerous prospects of someday being perceived as illegitimate,
it is to be expected that organizations will pursue interorganizational strategies to enhance organizational legitimacy. For example, a nonprofit may
put an executive of a firm on its board, not so much to secure a donation
from the company as to be identified with the company.[25] The purpose of
the transaction is to enhance the image of the nonprofit organization in
the eyes of some third party. This third party could be the elite of the
community, the foundation community, or even funders in the public sector. It could also be performers, critics, and elites within the cultural community. In other words, getting representatives of influential companies on
the board could have little or nothing to do with securing a particular
donation, contribution, or grant. The purpose may be to establish organizational legitimacy. The strategy is to associate with others who are already seen as prominent in the community.

Similarly the corporations may make a cash contribution not to secure
a board slot and gain control over the curriculum, exhibitions, or the theater season. Rather its purpose may also be to enhance its image in the eyes
of some third party. By associating with the institutions that provide collective goods related to the central value system of the community, corporations can improve their own status in the community. They can be
identified as the guardian and providers of cultural to the community.

Much of the empirical work done on corporate contributions espouses
the institutional model. For example, Miles[26] showed how the tobacco
industry, when challenged by the Sloan-Kettering Commission and the
Surgeon General's Report on smoking's health hazards, immediately responded by funneling millions of dollars to universities and research insti-
tutes which did research on cancer related topics. Indeed, this put them in
touch with research which was of immediate interest to them, but the contributions also gave the public a signal that the industry wanted to do all
it could to support research on cigarettes' "killer-effects."[27]

Ermann[28] also viewed contributions as a strategy to win favorable public opinion. He studied contributions to the Public Broadcasting System
(PBS) between 1972 and 1976 and interpreted them as efforts of upwardly
mobile companies to produce goodwill for themselves among the national
elite and the general public. He cited PBS literature which suggested repeatedly that a gift to PBS was an "investment" that could produce important public opinion gains. Although his research design did not allow
him to see whether elites felt more positively toward firms which donated

to PBS, he did find that many oil companies and firms which had recently increased their profits were among the biggest contributors.

HYPOTHESES

It is always difficult to test propositions derived from either exchange theory or institutional theory. In the first case one faces the problem of tautology. In the second case the analyst encounters many variables which are extremely difficult to measure. Recognizing the pitfalls, still we offer some exploratory hypotheses derived from each theory.

Hypothesis 1: Corporations Are More Likely to Sit on the
Boards of Cultural Organizations to which They Contribute
Hypothesis 1 simply states that companies will gain access to cultural boards if they make a cash contribution. It is a simple exchange: control for money. Although confirmation of this hypothesis would certainly be consistent with exchange theory, we should be aware that there are other possible explanations for the correlation that have nothing to do with interorganizational exchange. For example, nonprofits will often indicate to their board members that they are expected to "hit up" their employer for a corporate contribution. This is a good way to raise money, because companies should be more responsive to the request which an employee makes on behalf of a nonprofit than to the request of a stranger. Besides, a contribution would enhance employee relations. There may be a correlation between board memberships and company contributions, but the causal direction would be just the opposite of what our variant of exchange theory would lead us to believe. Instead of corporate board affiliation's following the corporate contribution, the corporate contribution follows the board affiliation of individual corporate employees. In this case, the corporate contribution is part of the director's "dues" which his/her company pays.

Hypothesis 2: The Greater the Reputed Influence of a
Corporation among the Cultural Elite, the More Cultural Boards
It Will Be Represented on
Hypothesis 2 is derived from institutional theory. On the one hand, it says something about the type of corporation that cultural organizations want on their board. If the goal is to enhance its image, then the cultural organization will try to secure representation of companies which others in the cultural community view as influential in community affairs. On the other hand, it says something about corporations. Firms will be viewed as more influential in community affairs, if they serve on local boards. Given that we have cross-sectional data, both interpretations are equally tenable.

Hypothesis 3: The More Prestigious or the Larger the Cultural
Organization, the Greater Its Number of Corporate Donors

Hypothesis 4: The More Prestigious and *the Larger the Cultural*
Organization, the Greater Its Number of Corporate Donors
Hypotheses 3 and 4 are also derived from institutional theory. On the one
hand, they argue that corporations will target their giving dollar on cultural organizations which are large and/or are viewed as more prestigious
by the cultural community. Just as the cultural organization strives to enhance its prestige through association with the "high flyers" in the business
community, business organizations will seek to associate with the high flyers
in the cultural community.

On the other hand, large and prestigious cultural organizations may be
large and prestigious because they receive corporate contributions and not
vice versa. The size of one budget may be larger than another or the reputation may be that much better than another, because corporate dollars
are going to the former but not to the latter. In other words, the size and
status of the nonprofit are functions of the corporate donation.

Hypothesis 5: The Greater the Number of Corporate Gifts
to Prestigious Cultural Organizations, the Greater the Reputed
Influence of a Corporation among the Cultural Elite

Hypothesis 6: The Greater the Number of Influential Corporations
Represented on a Cultural Board, the Greater the Prestige
of a Cultural Organization among the Cultural Elite
The final two hypotheses suggest that the organizations which are successful at establishing linkages, either through interlocking or a cash contribution, with a more influential firm or more prestigious cultural organization in the other sector will be perceived by members of the cultural
community as more influential/prestigious in their own sphere of activities.
Corporations will be perceived as more influential in community affairs
and cultural organizations will be perceived as more presitigious.

Needless to say, we are again limited by our cross-sectional data. It could
also be that cultural organizations are viewed as more prestigious because
they receive funds from very influential companies; or it could be that
corporations are viewed as more influential because they sit on the boards
of very prestigious corporations. However, since both interpretations are
reflective of institutional theory, we need not be overly concerned here
with establishing the true causal order.

METHODOLOGY

Our first task was to identify all the cultural organizations that were active
in the Minneapolis–St. Paul area in 1976. Since there was no comprehensive listing of local cultural organizations with attendance and budget figures, we had to identify different categories of cultural organizations and
consult the directories appropriate for each. We chose to look at public

and private nonprofit colleges, historical societies, zoos, libraries, public radio and television stations, art and history museums, theatres, orchestras, opera companies, and service organizations. For each category of activity we compiled a list of organizations and tried to obtain information on enrollment, membership, attendance, and budget. The largest organizations were identified and are listed in Table 5.1.[29]

Table 5.1   List of Minneapolis-St. Paul Cultural Organizations and Corporations Included in the Study

Cultural Organizations	Corporations
American Swedish Institute	American Hoist and Derrick
Anoka-Ramsey Community College	American National Bank and Trust of
Augsburg College	St. Paul
Bethel College	Bemis
Children's Theatre Co.	Burlington Northern Railroad
College of St. Catherine	Control Data
College of St. Thomas	Dayton Hudson
Como Zoo	Economics Laboratory
Cricket Theatre Corp.	Farmers and Mechanics Savings Bank
Guthrie Theatre	First Bank System
Hamline University	First National Bank of Minneapolis
Hennepin County Historical Society	First National Bank of St. Paul
Inver Hills Community College	General Mills
James Jerome Hill Reference Library	Hoerner Waldorf
Jewish Community Center	Honeywell
KTCA/KTCI	International Multifoods
Lakeshore Players	Investors Diversified Service
Lakewood Community College	Land O'Lakes
Macalaster College	Midland National Bank of Minneapolis
Metropolitan Community College	Minnesota Mutual Life Insurance Co.
Minneapolis Public Library	National City Bank of Minneapolis
Minneapolis Society of Fine Arts	North Central Airline
Minnesota Artists' Association	Northern States Power
Minnesota Historical Society	Northwest Airling
Minnesota Museum of Art	Northwest BANCO
Minnesota Opera Company.	Northwestern National Bank of
Minnesota Orchestral Society	Minneapolis
Minnesota Private College Fund	Northwestern National Bank of St. Paul
Minnesota Public Radio	Northwestern National Life Insurance
Minnetonka Community Theatre	Company
Normandale Community College	Peavey
North Hennepin Community College	Pillsbury
Ramsey County and St. Paul Historical	St. Paul Cos.
Society	Soo Line Railroad
St. Paul Chamber Orchestra	3M
St. Paul Public Library	
St. Paul Ramsey Arts and Science Council	
The Schubert Club	
Theatre in the Round	
Walker Art Center	

Our goal was to interview representatives of all 39 cultural organizations on our list. We interviewed the top administrator (or his designated representative) of 37 organizations. The manager of the public television station refused to participate in the study, and we could not locate the artists' association. The interviews took place between March 1978 and May 1978. Of the 37 organizations, we subsequently excluded 6 of the 13 public organizations and 2 of the 24 private organizations. These organizations did not solicit the business community, and we felt that our hypotheses really only applied to organizations that sought donations from the private sector. Thus our final N was 29.

The business firms chosen for this study were similarly selected on the basis of size. From *Fortune*'s[30] lists of the 500 largest U.S. industrials, 50 largest financial institutions, 50 largest retailers, 50 largest transportations, and 50 largest utilities for 1976 we identified the largest publicly owned corporations in the metro area. To this list we added the largest banks in the vicinity. Data on bank size were obtained from *Polk's World Bank Directory*.[31] The 32 corporations included in our study are listed in the appendix as well.

We first needed to gather information on the board members of the cultural organizations in fiscal year 1976–77. Their names and business affiliations were obtained from the organizations' annual reports, programs, bulletins, interviews with administrators, *Who's Who in the Midwest,* and the city directories for Minneapolis, St. Paul, and their suburbs. Because of the limited scope of this paper we will pay attention only to board linkages to the 32 corporations we identified. A 29 by 32, cultural organization by corporation, binary array was constructed where the entry was set equal to one if the corporation had a representative on the cultural organization's board and to zero if it did not (BOARD). We were able to gather board data for all 29 of the cultural organizations.

We asked the administrator of each cultural organization to tell us the amount of money that each of the 32 corporations on our list gave to his/ her organization in fiscal year 1976–77. Although respondents gave us dollar categories, we treated the contribution data as binary. A second 29 by 32 binary matrix was constructed where the entry was set equal to one if the corporation had contributed money to the cultural organization and to zero if it had not (MONEY). Although we thought that these data might be difficult to obtain, we received information from 28 of the 29 cultural organizations.

Measuring the size and prestige of the cultural organization was equally straightforward. The budget of the organization for fiscal year 1976–77 was used as a measure of size. We recognize that this is a rather crude measure; however, it does tap the scale of operations of the cultural organizations. For the two organizations that did not report budgets, we used their total income for fiscal year 1976–77 as a measure of their size. For the sake of analyses we dichotomized this variable at its median (SIZE).

For our measure of prestige each administrator was given a list of the cultural organizations in our study and asked to check off the organizations which she or he considered "very prestigious." A prestige score was computed for each organization by simply summing the total number of times it was checked as being prestigious. The most votes than an organization received was 37, and every organization received at least 1 vote. The median number of votes was 14. This variable was also dichotomized at its median (PRESTIGE).

The influence measure for corporations was constructed in a similar way. The cultural administrator was given a list of the corporations in our study and asked to check the corporations she or he considered "very influential" in community affairs. To be sure, this is a crude measure of community power, and there is evidence that reputation scores such as this are not always correlated with actors' success on actual community issues.[32] Also, we recognize that respondents associated with the arts and education may have identified a corporation as influential in community affairs only if it was active in the cultural community. Recognizing this, we still treated this measure as an indicator of the relative community power of the corporations. A score for each corporation was computed by summing the responses of the administrators. The most votes a corporation received was 36, and every firm received at least 1 vote. The median number of votes was 17. This variable was also dichotomized at its median (INFLUENCE).

ANALYSIS

At this point we should remind the reader that our units of analysis were the 928 pairwise relationships between our 29 cultural organizations and 32 business firms less the 32 dyads where we lacked information on donations to one of our cultural organizations. The data to be analyzed are presented in the cross-classification in Table 5.2.

Table 5.3 presents the zero-order correlations (GAMMA) for selected pairs of variables. For example, there was a strong association between MONEY and BOARD (GAMMA = .607). If a company gave money to a cultural organization, it tended to sit on its board as well. Furthermore, cultural organizations which were more prestigious (PRESTIGE) tended to receive contributions from more corporations (MONEY) (GAMMA = .879) and to have more corporations represented on their board (BOARD) (GAMMA = .592). We also see that corporations tended to give money (MONEY) to larger organizations (SIZE) (GAMMA = .411). Finally, we see that corporations which were perceived to be more influential in community affairs (INFLUENCE) tended to be represented on more boards (BOARDS) (GAMMA = .533) and to give money to more cultural organizations (MONEY) (GAMMA = .207).[33]

The partial correlations for these variables and possible higher order effects can be described by using loglinear models for cross-classified cat-

Table 5.2 Five-Variable Crosstabulation of BOARD (B), MONEY (M), PRESTIGE (P), INFLUENCE (I), and SIZE (S). ($N = 896$.)

SIZE (n)	Small								Large							
INFLUENCE (l)	LOW				HIGH				LOW				HIGH			
PRESTIGE (k)	LOW		HIGH		LOW		HIGH		LOW		HIGH		LOW		HIGH	
MONEY (j)	NO	YES	NO	YES	NO	YES	NO	YES	NO	YES	NO	YES	NO	YES	NO	YES
BOARD (i) NO	121	5	44	28	103	8	28	30	92	3	67	62	79	12	41	61
YES	1	1	3	5	15	2	13	9	1	0	1	14	4	1	7	35

The Corporation-Culture Connection

Table 5.3 Zero Order Correlations (GAMMA) between Linkage and Organizational Attribute Variables

	Board	Money	Frequencies				Missing Data
BOARD	—		YES:	115	NO:	813	0
MONEY	.607***	—	YES:	276	NO:	620	32
PRESTIGE	.592***	.879***	HIGH:	480	LOW:	448	0
INFLUENCE	.599***	.207**	HIGH:	464	LOW:	464	0
SIZE	.069	.411***	LARGE:	480	SMALL:	448	0

*** Pearson Chisquare significant at .001 (or less) level
** Pearson Chisquare significant at .01 level
* Pearson Chisquare significant at .05 level

egorical data.[34] Since the three organizational attribute variables define the organizational conditions under which interorganizational relations are formed, they should be treated as having fixed marginal distributions.[35] Thus we control for their joint effects in the following analysis.

The six hypotheses offered earlier can be translated into loglinear models and tested sequentially. For example, hypothesis 1 can be written as follows:

$$\log m_{ijkl} = u + u_{B(i)} + u_{M(j)} + u_{P(k)} + u_{I(l)} + u_{S(n)} + u_{BM(ij)} + u_{PI(kl)} + u_{PS(kn)} + u_{IS(ln)}$$

and the more complicated hypothesis H$_4$ as:

$$\log m_{ijkln} = u + u_{B(i)} + u_{M(j)} + u_{P(k)} + u_{I(l)} + u_{S(n)} + u_{BI(il)} + u_{BM(ij)} + u_{PI(kl)} + U_{PS(kn)} + u_{IS(ln)} + u_{MPS(jkn)}$$

where u represents the grand mean, u_B the marginal effects of BOARD, u_M the marginal effects of MONEY, u_P the marginal effects of PRESTIGE, u_I the marginal effects of INFLUENCE, u_S the marginal effects of SIZE, u_{PI} the fixed marginal effects of PRESTIGE and INFLUENCE, u_{PS} the fixed marginal effects of PRESTIGE and SIZE, u_{IS} the fixed marginal effects of INFLUENCE and SIZE, u_{BM} the two-way interaction effect of BOARD and MONEY, and u_{MPS} the three-way interaction effect among MONEY, PRESTIGE, and SIZE. Because we are unsure of the causal direction among our variables, we forgo logit analysis and instead simply test models for how well they fit the data (i.e., goodness of fit tests) and evaluate the relative strength of each effect parameter in the models.

In Table 5.4 we have translated each of the six hypotheses into Fienberg notation.[36] For example, the first hypothesis suggests that there is a partial correlation between having a director on a nonprofit board and giving the organization a cash contribution *(BM)* controlling for fixed marginal effects *(PI, PS, and IS)* and volume effects. Hypothesis 2 suggests that there is a partial correlation between the reputed influence of a corporation and the number of boards to which it is recruited *(BI)* controlling for the pre-

Table 5.4 Hierarchical Models for Five-Variable Crosstabulation of
BOARD (B), MONEY (M), PRESTIGE (P), INFLUENCE (I), and SIZE (S)

Hypothesis	Model	G^2	df	p	$G_1^2 - G_2^2$	p
1:	BM, PI, PS, IS	352.32	22	.001		
2:	BI, BM, PI, PS, IS	313.84	21	<.001	38.48	<.001
3:	MP, MS, BI, BM, PI, PS, IS	45.47	19	<.001	268.37	<.001
4:	MPS, BI, BM, PI, PS, IS, BP, BS, MI	24.18	15	.062	21.29	<.001
5 and 6:	BPI, MPI, MPS, BM, IS, BS	20.51	13	.083	3.67	.160

viously identified exchange effect *(BM)*, fixed marginal effects *(PI, PS, and IS)*, and volume effects. Hypotheses 3 and 4 suggest that there is a partial correlation between the prestige of the nonprofit and the number of corporations that give it money *(MP)*, a partial correlation between the size of the nonprofit and the number of corporations that give it money *(MS)*, and a significant interaction between the prestige and size of nonprofit and the number of corporations that give it money *(MPS)* controlling for all previously defined effects. Finally, hypotheses 5 and 6 stipulate significant interactions between the prestige of the nonprofit, the reputed influence of the company, and the presence of a board interlock between the two *(BPI)* and between the prestige of the nonprofit, the reputed influence of the corporation, and a donation of money *(MPI)* controlling for all previously defined effects.

Table 5.3 also presents the likelihood ratio chi-square statistic for each of the models and the corresponding *p*-value. We also assess the relative adequacy of each model by testing the difference in G^2 between models. We note immediately that not until we came to the fourth model did we get a satisfactory fit to our data *(p = .062)*. This model included all possible two-variable effects and one three-variable interaction *(MPS)*. We might note in passing that the addition of the three-variable interaction terms in the last model *(BPI and MPI)* did not significantly improve the fit to the data. From this we conclude that there was insufficient support for hypotheses 5 and 6. Thus we will not discuss them further.

Still we need to examine hypotheses 1, 2, 3, and 4 more closely. To do this we examine the *u*-terms for each of the estimated effect parameters derived from the fitted model, the standardized *u*-term for the parameter estimates, and the corresponding *p*-values. This information is presented in Table 5.5. For the uninitiated reader, the *u*-terms can be interpreted in the same way as standardized regression coefficients, insofar as they indicate the relative strength of the association between variables controlling

Table 5.5 Two- and Three-Variable Effects for the Fitted Model:
MPS, BI, BM, PI, PS, IS, BP, BS, MI

Hypothesis	Model	u-term	Standardized u-term	p
1:	BOARD-MONEY (BM)	.217	3.510	<.001
2:	BOARD-INFLUENCE (BI)	.334	5.521	<.001
3:	MONEY-PRESTIGE (MP)	.646	12.148	<.001
	MONEY-SIZE (MS)	.121	2.301	.01
4:	MONEY-PRESTIGE-SIZE (MPS)	−.038	−.733	—
Other Two-Variable Substantive Effects:				
	BOARD-PRESTIGE (BP)	.269	3.834	<.001
	BOARD-SIZE (BS)	−.070	−1.263	—
	MONEY-INFLUENCE (MI)	.110	2.490	<.05
Fixed Marginal Effects:				
	PRESTIGE-INFLUENCE (PI)	−.095	−2.325	.05
	PRESTIGE-SIZE (PS)	.190	3.595	.001
	INFLUENCE-SIZE (IS)	−.004	−.101	—

for all other effects in the model. The standardized u-terms are simply the u-terms divided by their standard error. We derived the p-values for the u-terms following Bishop, Fienberg, and Holland.[37]

From Table 5.4 we see that for every one of the effects which had u-terms twice their standard error turned out to be statistically significant at the .05-level or better. Substantively, this means that hypothesis 1 was confirmed: companies typically had representation on boards where they had made a contribution (BOARD-MONEY; $p<.001$). Hypothesis 2 was also confirmed: the greater the reputed influence of a corporation, the more cultural boards it was represented on (BOARD-INFLUENCE, $p<.001$). Finally, we confirmed hypothesis 3 as well: the more prestigious cultural organizations had more corporate contributors (MONEY-PRESTIGE; $p<.001$) and the larger cultural organizations had more corporate contributors (MONEY-SIZE; $p<.01$).

There were, however, other hypotheses for which we found no support. For example, hypothesis 4 was shown not to be true. The three-variable interaction—MONEY-PRESTIGE-SIZE—was in the model which fit the data, but it was not statistically significant. Thus larger *and* more prestigious cultural organizations did not receive funds from more corporate donors. The size of a cultural organization's budget and its reported prestige each had an independent effect on corporate donations.

There was no support for hypotheses 5 and 6 either. Corporations which gave money to more prestigious cultural organizations were not regarded by the cultural elite as more influential in community affairs (MONEY-PRESTIGE-INFLUENCE). Furthermore, cultural organizations which had directors from more influential companies were not seen as more prestigious by the cultural elite (BOARD-PRESTIGE-INFLUENCE).

The analysis, however, did unearth some effects which were not antici-pated. For example, more corporations were represented on the boards of the more prestigious cultural organizations (BOARD-PRESTIGE; $p < .001$). Also money tended to come from the more influential corporations (MONEY-INFLUENCE; $p < .05$). In our conclusion we will try to assess the implications of all our findings in light of our earlier theoretical discussion.

CONCLUSION

The research questions to be addressed in this paper were, what are the terms of the transactions between corporations and cultural organizations, and what sorts of benefits can each actor expect to realize from the trans-action? We offered two alternative models, derived from exchange theory and institutional theory, and found support for both.

Our results provided support for the thesis that there was an exchange between corporations and cultural organizations: monetary support in ex-change for a position on the board of directors. Yet we must be careful not to overinterpret this result in light of our earlier observation that the company contribution might come after an employee finds himself or her-self on the board of the organization and under pressure to secure a do-nation from his or her employer. Although our results are consistent with the argument that companies buy their way onto cultural boards, we must have better data and do longitudinal analyses before we can draw a firm conclusion.

We also found support for the thesis that contributions and board inter-locking have some relation to organizational legitimacy. We found that more influential companies tended to sit on more boards and to support monetarily more cultural organizations. Whether we think that cultural organizations try to recruit the more influential firms to their board or to secure funding from more influential firms in order to enhance their legit-imacy, or we think that a firm's reputation for being influential is a func-tion of its service to local cultural organizations, our interpretation is con-sistent with institutional theory. In the first case, the cultural organization is striving to enhance its prestige through association with the more influ-ential corporations. In the second case, the company has already enhanced its reputation as being influential through its past association with cultural organizations. It may also be that cultural organizations try to associate with very influential corporations, which have, in turn, gained a reputation for being influential in community affairs because of their association with cultural organizations.

We also found that corporations tended to give money to more presti-gious cultural organizations and to sit on their boards. We may think that corporations were striving to link up with more prestigious nonprofits to enhance their reputed influence, or that a nonprofit's prestige in the community may be a function of it receiving corporate support. Regardless, our findings are again consistent with institutional theory. Either the corporation is striving to enhance its reputation as being influential or the nonprofit has already become prestigious through its association with corporations. Putting the two together, corporations may try to associate with the more prestigious cultural organizations which have, in turn, become very prestigious because of their association with corporations.

Before we get too heady over these results we should remember that companies which gave money to more prestigious cultural organizations were not viewed as more influential and that nonprofits which had more influential firms on their boards were not viewed as more prestigious. However, these findings need not contradict our other results.

It may be that to gain a reputation as a prestigious cultural organization, it is only necessary to receive corporate support—it is not necessary to link up with the more influential corporations in town. Similarly to gain a reputation as a very influential corporation, it may only be necessary to support cultural organizations—it may not be necessary to associate with the most prestigious cultural organizations. In other words, it may only be necessary to reach out into the other sector to win recognition. The prestige or reputed influence of one's associates is not important in defining one's own prestige or influence.

It could, of course, also be that our results have nothing to do with legitimacy whatsoever. Companies may simply want to "do good" and will try to donate their money and employee time to cultural organizations which have a reputation for "doing good things." The donor is not interested in any public relations benefits for itself; it just strives to invest its charitable dollars wisely. Similarly, nonprofits may be simply looking for board members who are bright and have a good working knowledge of community affairs. Thus it would be sensible to secure the services of those whose companies have a reputation for being very influential in the community. Although this interpretation may seen naive, it is consistent with our findings and thus must be considered as well.

Obviously before we can give a definitive answer to our two research questions, longitudinal analyses are necessary. The causal ordering among our variables must be sorted out, which can only be done with a panel study. In this light our efforts must be seen as exploratory at best. We hope, however, we have stimulated some interest in the corporation-culture connection and provided a framework for future research.

NOTES

1. This paper was read at the Annual Meeting of the American Sociological Association, August 27–31, 1979, in Boston. Funding for this study was provided by the Center for Urban and Regional Affairs, University of Minnesota. Summer salary support for the senior author was provided by the National Science Foundation (SOC 77-26038). We would like to thank Kathe Marron, Mary Jane Lehnertz, and Audrey Moller for their capable assistance and

Stanley Wasserman, Vera Zolberg, and John Delany for their helpful comments on earlier drafts.

2. American Association of Fund Raising Counsel, *Giving USA* (New York: American Association of Fund Raising Counsel, Inc., 1986), p. 39.

3. The Conference Board, *Annual Survey of Corporate Contributions*, 1984 ed. (New York: The Conference Board, Inc., 1984).

4. Council for Financial Aid to Education, *Corporate Support for Higher Education, 1985* (New York: Council for Financial Aid to Education, Inc., 1986).

5. See Sol Levine and Paul White, "Exchange as a Conceptual Framework for the Study of Interorganizational Relationships." *Administrative Science Quarterly,* 5 (1961), 583–601, Karen Cook, "Exchange and Power in Networks of Interorganizational Relations," *Sociological Quarterly,* 18 (1977), 62–82, and D. Jacobs, "Dependency and Vulnerability: An Exchange Approach to the Control of Organizations," *Administrative Science Quarterly,* 19 (1974), 45–59.

6. See Mayer Zald, *Power in Organizations* (Nashville, Tenn.: Vanderbilt University Press, 1969), J. Kenneth Benson, "The Interorganizational Network as a Political Economy," *Administrative Science Quarterly* 20 (1975), 229–249, and Howard Aldrich and Jeffrey Pfeffer, "Environments of Organizations," *Annual Review of Sociology,* 2 (Palo Alto, Calif.: Annual Reviews, 1976), 79–105.

Exchange theory typically works under the assumption that organizations are relatively free to establish and terminate working relations as they see fit. Of course, this is not always the case. As Aldrich points out in "Resource dependence and interorganizational relations: Relations between local employment service offices and social services sector organizations," *Administration and Society* 7 (1976), 419–454, relations between organizations are often legally mandated. In the case of transactions between cultural and business organizations, however, it seems safe to assume that legal mandates have little if any effect on interaction.

7. For example, Michael Useem, "The Inner Group of American Capitalist Class," *Social Problems* 25 (February 1978), 225–240 and National Endowment for the Arts, *Museums U.S.A.* (Washington, D.C.: U.S. Government Printing Office, 1974).

8. See Jeffrey Pfeffer, "Size, Composition, and Function of Hospital Boards of Directors: A Study of Organizational Environment Linkages," *Administrative Science Quarterly* 18 (1973), 349–364.

9. See Mayer Zald, "Urban Differentiation, Characteristics of Boards of Directors, and Organizational Effectiveness," *American Journal of Sociology* 73 (1967) 261–272.

10. Joseph Galaskiewicz, *Exchange Networks and Community Politics* (Beverly Hills, Calif.: Sage Publications, 1979).

11. Benson, "The Interorganizational Network as a Political Economy."

12. Aldrich, "Resource Dependence and Interorganizational Relations."

13. *The Finance of the Performing Arts* (New York: Ford Foundation, 1974).

14. William Baumol and William Bowen, *Performing Arts: The Economic Dilemma* (New York: The Twentieth Century Fund, 1966).

15. Ford Foundation, *The Finance of the Performing Arts.*

16. Business Committee on the Arts, *Business in the Arts '70* (New York: Paul Eriksson, 1970).

17. See Rosanne Martorella, "The Relationship between Box Office and Repertoire: A Case Study of Opera," *Sociological Quarterly,* 18 (1977), 354–366.

18. American Association of Fund Raising Counsel, *Giving USA,* p. 39.

19. Although we phrase this as an argument, this also is conjecture that begs for empirical verification.

20. See Talcott Parsons, *Structure and Process in Modern Society* (New York: Free Press, 1960).

21. See David Kamens, "Legitimating Myths and Educational Organization: The Relationship between Organizational Ideology and Formal Structure," *American Sociological Review,* 42 (1977), 208–219, and John Meyer and Brian Rowen, "Institutionalized Organizations:

Formal Structure as Myth and Ceremony." *American Journal of Sociology* 83 (1977), 340–363.

22. See Maw Lin Lee, "A Conspicuous Production Theory of Hospital Behavior," *Southern Economic Journal* 38 (1971), 48–59, and Charles Perrow, "Organizational Prestige: Some Functions and Dysfunctions," *American Journal of Sociology* 66 (1961), 335–341.

23. See Robert H. Miles, *Coffin Nails and Corporate Strategies* (Englewood Cliffs, N.J.: Prentice-Hall, 1982) and Jeffrey Pfeffer and Gerald Salancik, *The External Control of Organizations: A Resource Dependence Perspective* (New York: Harper and Row, 1978).

24. See Paul J. DiMaggio and Walter W. Powell, "The Iron Cage Revisited: Institutional Isomorphism and Collective Rationality in Organizational Fields," *American Sociological Review* 48 (1983), 147–160; reprinted in this volume.

25. See Pfeffer and Salancik, *The External Control of Organizations: A Resource Dependence Perspective.*

26. See Miles, *Coffin Nails and Corporate Strategies.*

27. In the work of Burt (1981) and Fry et al. (1982) it is less clear that contributions are a way to legitimate a firm's goals or activities. These authors view contributions more as "advertising dollars" that consumer oriented firms spend to win the goodwill of prospective customers. Of course, one could make the case the "goodwill" is a type of legitimacy, but we choose not to take this position.

28. David M. Ermann, "The Operative Goals of Corporate Philanthropy: Contributions to the Public Broadcasting Service, 1972–1976," *Social Problems*, 25 (June 1980), 504–514.

29. Anyone who is familiar with the Twin Cities will notice that the University of Minnesota is missing from the list. Because of its size and very unusual organizational structure it was omitted from our study.

30. "The Fortune Directory of the 500 largest U.S. industrial corporations, and the fifty largest commercial banking companies, life insurance companies, diversified financial companies, retailing companies, transportation companies and utilities," *Fortune* 95 (May 1977), 364–385, and 96 (July 1977), 160–173.

31. *Polk's World Bank Directory*, North American Section, R. L. Polk and Company.

32. Galaskiewicz, *Exchange Networks and Community Politics.*

33. It is somewhat inappropriate to present chi-square test statistics, since our data deal with a subset not a sample of organizational linkages in the community.

34. See Joseph Galaskiewicz and Peter Marsden, "Interorganizational Resource Networks: Formal Patterns of Overlap," *Social Science Research* 7 (1978), 89–107.

35. See Stephen Fienberg, *The Analysis of Cross-classified Categorical Data.* (Cambridge, Mass.: MIT Press, 1980).

36. Fienberg, *The Analysis of Cross-classified Categorial Data.*

37. Y. M. M. Bishop, Stephen E. Fienberg and P. W. Holland, *Discrete Multivariate Analysis: Theory and Practice.* Following Bishop, Fienberg, Holland ([1975], 148–149), we used the standardized u-terms to identify effects that were likely to be statistically significant. The criterion was that the u-term was twice as large as its standard error. We then rebuilt a model including only these effects and evaluated how well it fit the data. The model was *(BM, BI, MP, MS, BP, MI, PI, PS)*. The likelihood chi-square statistic (G^2) was 26.35 with 18 degrees of freedom and a p-value of .092. Each of the effect parameters was subsequently deleted from this model, G^2 was recomputed, the parameter was replaced, another was removed, and G^2 was recomputed again. The p-value for each term was taken by computing the change in G^2 as each effect was removed and G^2 was computed for the remaining parameters in the model. Thus there are no p-values for *MPS, BS,* or *IS,* because these parameters had u-terms twice their standard error, and none was included in the model used to derive p-values for the other effect parameters.

6
United Charities
An Economic Analysis[1]

SUSAN ROSE-ACKERMAN

INTRODUCTION

Charities cannot coerce. They can only persuade. A religious charity can threaten the stingy with damnation; a secular charity can announce "fair shares" as a function of income, but neither can enlist the police force to compel a donation.[2] The absence of coercion in fund-raising is only one reason why a charity may be an inefficient producer of public goods.[3] If donors are busy people, they may rationally decide not to bother to learn about charities. Moreover, many nonprofit organizations provide services whose ultimate worth is unknown. Not even "experts" may know whether or not neighborhood centers help prevent juvenile delinquency or whether family counseling reduces welfare dependency. Inadequate information means that donors are uncertain about the value of a gift to charity. If donors are averse to risk, this uncertainty alone will deter them from giving.

In the United States, United Funds (UFs) are often founded in response to donors' lack of information.[4] The funds relieve donors of the difficult task of dividing up their gifts among charities and perform auditing and monitoring functions that assure donors that their money is supporting reputable organizations. With a single coordinated fund drive, less money needs to be spent soliciting donations. This paper looks at the UF both as an efficient fund raiser and as an organization subject to criticism from several different directions. I do not reach a final normative judgment "for" or "against" the UF. Instead, the paper tries to go beyond the spate of current criticism to provide a balanced view of the Fund's particular strengths and weaknesses.

The next section analyzes the UF as an efficient response to donors' ignorance and as a cost saving device for charities.[5] The very efficiency of their fund-raising has, however, recently provoked criticism of UFs. First of all, the UF must allocate campaign resources to individual agencies, and the Funds have been attacked for using mechanical and hidebound allocation techniques. The third section assesses these criticisms in light of evidence on actual UF procedures. Second, the UF has been accused of being a cartel. The fourth section explores the sources of its monopoly power and identifies gainers and losers. Finally, the UF has been criticized for failing to develop a strategy that takes account of the government's substantial stake in social services. The final section considers the relationship between UF and government.

THE UNITED FUND AS AN EFFICIENT RESPONSE TO DONORS' UNCERTAINTY

Donors

Consider a stylized UF consisting of the large numbers of charities that agree to limit their own individual fund-raising activity and support an annual coordinated drive. Member agencies can accept unsolicited gifts, but they cannot actively seek individual contributions.[6] At this stage in the analysis I ignore the UF's privileged access to payroll deductions at the workplace in order to concentrate on informational economies.

Donors have poor information about individual charities. In the absence of a UF they must either spend time finding out about charities, rely on charities to provide information as part of their fund-raising efforts, or simply remain uninformed. A UF benefits donors *not* by providing them with more information but by reducing solicitation costs and permitting donors to delegate a difficult resource allocation task to someone else.[7]

In an atomistic charity market, with no UF, a person's own donation to a charity is used in two ways. One portion is spent to provide services. The rest is spent on additional fund-raising efforts that may produce additional contributions. To take a simple example, suppose that $1 spent on fund-raising produces $4 in contributions. A donor would then not object if his money is spent to raise more money so long as the extra $3 generated is worth at least $1 to him. At some point, the marginal productivity to the donor of a dollar spent on fund-raising will fall to $1 either because donors are harder to find or because of a decline in the marginal value of charitable services as their quantity increases.[8] With no UF, however, the marginal value to donors of money spent of fund-raising may be low. The argument is identical to the critique of private firm advertising that views it as socially wasteful competition for market shares.[9] Even if a charity can attract $4 for every $1 spent on fund-raising, donors will not benefit from the entire net increase of $3 if some portion would otherwise have gone to *other* charities that provide services also valued by donors. The more that donors benefit from learning about the services of charities to which they do *not* contribute and the more insensitive total charitable contributions are to fund-raising appeals, the less value donors place on funds used to increase a charity's budget. Thus, if these conditions hold, a UF is beneficial to donors because less money is wasted on persuading a person to donate to one charity rather than another.[10] Donors perceive that most of their money goes toward providing services and toward persuading others to substitute charitable donations for private consumption.[11] The more inclusive the fund, and the stricter the restrictions on the fund-raising activities of individual agencies, the stronger is this advantage. In fact, early supporters of federated fund drives recognized this benefit and supported a Fund as a way to avoid the "frantic competition" between agencies for resources.[12]

A second benefit for donors resides in the UF's monitoring and allocation procedures. Two types of donors gain from this process. On the one hand, many donors have no strong beliefs about how their gifts should be divided among charitable services. The Fund then relieves them of the problem of allocating their gifts and, in addition, audits the agencies' books and assesses their programs, thus providing a kind of quality control that reduces the risk of giving.[13] On the other hand, some donors do have strong opinions about how charitable dollars should be spent but realize that their own gifts are too small to affect the overall mix of services. By supporting a UF and becoming actively involved in the Fund's allocation process, these opinionated donors gain a measure of control over the way others' gifts are spent.

For these reasons, a UF raises the marginal value of some individual contributions, and people may give more. Donors may not find the UF's mix of services optimal, but neither are they likely to approve entirely of the array of activities provided by an atomistic charity "market"—especially when fund-raising costs are high.

Charities

Even if donors want a UF, charities will not join together and establish a fund unless all of them will benefit. Members give up some of their rights to carry out independent appeals. Each agency must expect that the increase in gifts and the reduction in solicitation costs will outweigh the disadvantage of depending upon the Fund's allocation committee for a portion of their financial support. In making this calculation, a charity must consider the possibility that its competitors may be more productive fund-raisers when organized as a group than they are as separate entities.

Some kinds of charities may be less eager than others to be part of the UF. Those that have special informational advantages will be most likely to reject UF membership. On the one hand, some organizations have a specialized, easy to identify group of donors that can receive concentrated fund-raising appeals. Thus colleges and schools that can solicit graduates, and religious or ideological organizations that can identify believers, may not want to be part of a federated fund drive. I argue later that an ideological group is also not likely to be accepted as a member by an ongoing UF. On the other hand, other organizations have a "brand name" that is well known to a broad spectrum of givers and taken as a symbol of quality. The UF thus provides few benefits to the American Cancer Society or the American Heart Association. A UF, however, may believe that its own fund-raising ability will be increased by having this effective fund-raising agency as a member even though the agency initially does not want to join. Since it is always free to break away and carry out its own drive, this kind of agency is in a strong bargaining position in spite of the expense of running an independent campaign. If there is a net gain in surplus from including this nonprofit in the fund, the agency may be able to negotiate a special arrangement with a UF that guarantees it a fixed allocation or a fixed fraction of fund receipts.

For example, the American Cancer Society has partnership agreements with the United Way (UW) in six states.[14] In New York, Baltimore, Chicago, and Detroit, the Red Cross as well as some other agencies obtain fixed fractions of UW's receipts.[15] Local UWs in Dallas, Los Angeles, Honolulu, and Cleveland have reportedly worked out special arrangements with the Heart Association and the Cancer Society "to guarantee them a minimum take, with the understanding that they won't run competing campaigns."[16]

THE UNITED FUND AS A
RESOURCE ALLOCATION ORGANIZATION

The UF has been criticized for the way it allocates the donations raised as a result of its informational economies. I shall argue, however, that some of this criticism is misplaced. The UF's ability to carry out systematic analyses of allocation alternatives is strictly limited both by its complex political position and by the dearth of adequate analytic techniques.

The UF is caught between donors' desire for accountability and member agencies' desire for independence. Agencies' staffs would like to be thought of as running efficient and effective organizations without actually having to change their behavior. In contrast, donors would like agencies to be monitored and evaluated by the UF's staff and volunteers so long as this is not too costly. The UF's ability to monitor agencies and to change allocation formulas depends upon the bargaining power of individual agencies. Agencies have two related sources of bargaining power. On the one hand, some, like the Red Cross, can credibly threaten to leave the United Way and run their own campaigns. The exiting agency may suffer some loss of donations, but it is well known and powerful enough to damage the remaining agencies by its exit. On the other hand, some agencies, even though they are small and not well known to the public, have important alternative sources of funds through fees, government grants, or foundation gifts. Since the UF provides only a fraction of their budget, they can escape most UF attempts at control by rearranging their budget categories. The UF then faces exactly the same problem that the federal government has when it gives grants to state and local governments. Because it provides only a fraction of agency resources, the UF has difficulty measuring the marginal impact of its contributions. Perhaps, like the federal government, the UF should give matching grants to agencies willing to carry out programs thought to be especially worthwhile.

In the past, partly because of the power of member agencies, UFs have seldom been concerned with developing efficient allocation procedures that compared agencies with each other.[17] Instead it was common for UFs to claim that they were providing "deficit financing" for agencies.[18] Since most agencies, however, have enough ideas to generate deficits of any size, requests routinely exceed UF resources and cannot be used as a guide for allocation. Thus these UFs often merely gave each agency a fixed share of campaign resources.

Declining or slowly growing UF resources, however, have recently led some UFs to reexamine their allocation procedures. Agency opposition may be tempered by the hope that the new procedures will increase gifts. UF staff and major donors then must decide what kind of analysis to carry out. UFs, however, now face a serious conceptual problem: No one is very clear about how to evaluate the services provided by many agencies. Counseling, for example, is provided by many UF agencies, yet its benefits are intangible and hard to assess. Cost-benefit techniques are difficult to apply to social services designed to increase people's sense of well-being, especially since even professionals do not always agree about service goals or output measures.

One way in which a substantial minority of UWs have tried to meet the desire for analysis without upsetting the organization's political balance is through a technique called "priority planning" that attempts to rank services.[19] There are many local variations of this technique: UWs differ in the *information* provided to decision makers,[20] in *whom* they ask to make rankings,[21] in *how* they instruct people to make their choices,[22] and in *what* they do with the rankings. Nevertheless, they share certain common features. First, "priority planning" generally makes no attempt to evaluate agency performance.[23] Instead, the process tries to assess community "needs" and set "priorities" without any specific mention of particular agencies. Second, the technique implies that one can take a list of services and rank them from most to least "needed." The ranking is carried out with no explicit consideration given to relative costs or to the marginal benefits of services.[24] Resource allocation is essentially viewed as a problem in social choice where options are discrete and everyone has good information and clear preferences. Unfortunately, services are not discrete, well understood entities that can be easily ranked, even by social service professionals. Third, UWs share a commitment to the heavy involvement of lay volunteers in the formation of priority plans.[25] These volunteers, however, often lack expert knowledge and have a limited amount of time to devote to the problem. It is not obvious that a vote of lay volunteers should help decide the question of whether a community "needs" subsidized transportation for the elderly more than it "needs" a crisis center for battered wives. Yet these are exactly the choices UW volunteers are being asked to make.

Of course, choices must be made somehow, and priority plans do appear to be bargaining tools that can put a UW Allocations Committee in a somewhat stronger bargaining position vis-à-vis powerful agencies. If a priority planning process gives Allocations Committee members better data than they had before, forces them to think a bit more systematically about their decisions, and makes their value judgments explicit,[26] then it will have served a useful purpose. The danger is that the quantified rankings will be given more truth value than they deserve. They are obviously no better than the quality of the committee's judgments, and they may be very sensitive to the particular ranking procedure chosen.[27]

Nevertheless, few UWs appear to take priority planning "too" seriously. In fact, most of them do not use it at all,[28] and even those with plans only make small year-to-year changes in agency budget shares. If they have any effect at all, it is on the distribution of incremental funds.[29]

Information from several UWs indicates that agencies generally obtain about the same percentage of total funds in one year as they did in the previous year. In addition to data from two of the organizations with recent priority plans,[30] I obtained allocation information from four UWs in the metropolitan areas centered in New Haven; Washington, D.C.; Baltimore; and Derby, Connecticut. Washington developed a priority plan in 1973; Baltimore implemented a multiyear plan in the late 1970s; neither New Haven nor Derby had adopted formal procedures at the time that I gathered my data in 1979.[31] The two Connecticut organizations and one in Akron, Ohio, provided information on agency requests as well as on allocations. I regressed one year's allocation to agencies on the previous year's allocations and, if available, on agency requests. Table 6.1 records the results for the UWs. In all cases, last year's allocation to a member organization is an excellent predictor of this year's allocation.[32] The agencies' annual reports were essentially irrelevant,[33] and there are no obvious differences between UWs that use priority planning and those that do not.

Information from the UWs that use priority plans suggests that the allocations process may make a difference on the margin. Therefore, I looked at the increase or decrease in each agency's allocation between 1978 and 1979. The dependent variable, PCTINC(T), is an agency's share of the UW's incremental funds. It is defined as

$$PCTINC(T) = [ALL(T) - ALL(T-1)]/\Delta RES(T),$$

where ALL(T) is the allocation to an agency in year T, and $\Delta RES(T)$ is the United Way funds allocated to all agencies in year T minus funds allocated in $(T-1)$ minus funds in T allocated to new agencies. The independent variables were the agency's allocation in $(T-1)$ divided by the total allocated in $(T-1)$ [PCTTOT$(T-1)$] and, if available, the agency's request as a proportion of its allocation in $T-1$ [REQ(T)/ALL $(T-1)$].

Table 6.1 United Way

Dependent Variable	Washington, D.C. ALL79	Washington, D.C. ALL78	Baltimore, Md. ALL79	Baltimore, Md. ALL78	Akron, Ohio ALL76	New Haven, Conn. ALL79	New Haven, Conn. ALL78	Fargo, N.D. ALL79	Valley (Derby, Conn.) ALL79	Valley (Derby, Conn.) ALL78
Constant	1652	2806	−334	392	−64.41	−2258	−2864	1527	1745	64.35
	(1.82)	(1.90)	(.19)	(.32)	(−0.08)	(1.47)	(0.50)	(2.56)	(0.49)	(0.12)
$ALL(T-1)$[a]	1.10	1.005	1.066	1.043	0.967	1.08	1.01	1.01	1.51	1.02
	(249)	(139)	(196.96)	(269.85)	(53.05)	(20.31)	(4.99)	(58.17)	(2.33)	(43.78)
$REQ(T)$[b]	—	—	—	—	−0.0047	−0.02	−0.04	—	−0.31	—
	—	—	—	—	(0.29)	(0.46)	(0.29)	—	(0.59)	—
R^{-2}	0.998	0.995	0.998	0.999	0.998	0.997	0.957	0.990	0.72	0.988
d.f.[c]	101	102	86	82	38	22	22	32	21	22
Total Allocations in (T)[d] (Thousands of Dollars)	14,657	13,035	13,397	13,120	3,586	2,620	2,492	747	426	411

NOTE: Figures in parentheses are t statistics.

[a] ALL(T) is the allocation to an agency in year T.

[b] REQ(T) is the agency request in year T.

[c] Degrees of freedom.

[d] Total allocations in T is the total allocations to member agencies in year T including allocations to new agencies not included in the statistical analysis. The UW's own expenses are omitted. New agency allocations were $64,555 in New Haven in 1979 and zero in 1978. In Washington, D.C., they were $92,000 in 1979 and $31,500 in 1978. In Baltimore, new agencies received $56,196 in 1979 and $111,776 in 1978. Neither Fargo nor Akron allocated funds to new agencies. The Valley UW data omit one agency that made no request in 1978 and asked for and received a fraction of its original request in 1979.

SOURCE: The data are from UW of Central Maryland, *Allocations for Fiscal Year 1977, 1978, and 1979*, Baltimore, Md.: United Way, mimeo (1977; 1978a; 1979a); UW of Greater New Haven, *Report of the Allocations Committee*, mimeo (1978) and *Report of the Allocations Committee*, mimeo (1979b); UW of the National Capital Area, *Allocations Report, Fiscal Year 1979*, Washington, D.C.: Membership and Allocations Committee (1978a); and Valley UW, *Allocations Committee Recommendations*, Ansonia, Cn.: United Way, mimeo (1979). Baltimore's long-range plans are described in UW of Central Maryland, *Plan of Action*, Baltimore, Md. (1978b) and *Problems and Proposals*, Baltimore, Md. (1978c).

The results of this exercise are recorded in Table 6.2. Here the results are mixed. For the UWs where agency requests are available, an agency appears to gain nothing from requesting more than it received last year. In several cases an agency's share of the budget in the previous year was a good predictor of its share in the UW's incremental funds. In all cases, however, an important part of the variance was left unexplained, and for Derby, Fargo, and Washington, D.C. (in one year studied) past budget shares had no significant explanatory power. Therefore, in some UWs the allocations process seems to have an important impact on the distribution of incremental funds. Of course, incremental funds are only a small fraction of total funds (see Table 6.2). Thus, for example, in Fargo past allocations explain 99% of the variance in present allocations even though the UW's incremental funds are allocated on the basis of a priority plan that ignores past allocations. A priority plan that is actually used by an Allocations Committee lets one see exactly how these marginal shifts are made even if their justification is ultimately rather weak. Without a priority plan, it is generally difficult for an outsider to know what determined the allocations. In all cases, however, the size of an agency's "historic" budget share is left unjustified except when an organization such as the Red Cross has made an explicit deal with the UW.

Obviously, one should be careful in generalizing from the experience of a few UWs to conclusions about national patterns. Nevertheless, it seems reasonable to suppose that a full survey would confirm the basic picture of fairly constant agency budget shares combined with shifts in emphasis that occur slowly over a period of years. It is easy, moreover, to be overly critical of the mechanical allocation methods used by some UWs.[34] Even a person genuinely concerned with effective and efficient service delivery would be stymied by the lack of adequate measures of agency performance. Furthermore, the UW is not alone in using simple rules of thumb. Students of government budgetary processes have also found association between last year's budget allocations and this year's choices.[35] Given the difficulty of measuring the benefits of services and the UW's complex political position, allocation committees may do no worse than most governments. There is little evidence, however, to indicate that they perform systematically better.

THE UNITED FUND AS A CARTEL

A second strand of criticism focuses on the UF's monopoly power.[36] At first glance these claims appear to lack merit since individual UFs are formally independent of each other, together accounting for only 4% of all private philanthropy and providing only about 25% of member agencies' resources.[37] Nevertheless, UFs do have two real sources of monopoly power. One source is the surplus generated by the informational benefits discussed previously. Less money is spent on fund-raising than in an atomistic char-

Table 6.2 United Way

Dependent Variable	Washington, D.C.		Baltimore, Md.		Akron, Ohio	New Haven, Conn.	Fargo, N.D.	Valley[a] (Derby, Conn.)
	PCTINC79	PCTINC78	PCTINC79	PCTINC78	PCTINC76	PCTINC79	PCTINC79	PCTINC79
Constant	0.001	0.008	−0.0033	0.0007	0.0021	−0.007	0.01	0.087
	(1.92)	(1.90)	(0.56)	(0.32)	(0.19)	(0.15)	(2.56)	(0.35)
PCTTOT($T-1$)	0.883	0.175	1.29	0.942	0.953	1.70	0.090	2.60
	(23.4)	(0.66)	(5.36)	(11.06)	(4.95)	(4.87)	(0.43)	(0.83)
REQ(T)/ALL($T-1$)	—	—			−0.0006	−0.016	—	−0.012
	—	—			(0.14)	(0.56)	—	(0.19)
R^{-2}	0.84	0.004	0.24	0.59	0.38	0.54	−0.025	−0.05
d.f.	105	101	86	82	39	22	32	21
Percentage[b] Increase in Total Funds (%)	11.7	2.7	1.7	4.5	−5.2	2.5	8.3	3.6

NOTE: Figures in parentheses are t statistics.

[a] Omits one agency that made no request in 1978, and asked for and received a fraction of its original request in 1979.

[b] Allocations in T minus allocations to new agencies in T, minus allocations in $T-1$ divided by allocations in $T-1$.

SOURCE: The data are from UW of Central Maryland, *Allocations for Fiscal Year 1977, 1978, and 1979*, Baltimore, Md.: United Way, mimeo (1977; 1978a; 1979a); UW of Greater New Haven, *Report of the Allocations Committee*, mimeo (1978) and *Report of the Allocations Committee*, mimeo (1979b); UW of the National Capital Area, *Allocations Report, Fiscal Year 1979*, Washington, D.C.: Membership and Allocations Committee (1978a); and Valley UW, *Allocations Committee Recommendations*, Ansonia, Cn.: United Way, mimeo (1979). Baltimore's long-range plans are described in UW of Central Maryland, *Plan of Action*, Baltimore, Md. (1978b) and *Problems and Proposals*, Baltimore, Md. (1978c).

ity market, and people may give more because of the UF's monitoring and auditing procedures. Thus if a group of agencies sets up a Fund, they will want to keep these benefits for themselves. They are unlikely to agree to admit a new agency unless it produces an increase in the net receipts available to existing agencies. A UF, however, is not controlled by member agencies alone. Instead it is a coalition of agencies and large and small donors. Therefore, a Fund may actually admit numerous small, unkown, but otherwise uncontroversial organizations if donor representatives control the admissions process. The stated admissions practices of many UWs, however, appear to be quite restrictive and leave considerable room for existing members to oppose new admissions.[38]

Although donors are poorly informed about most agencies' operations and would find it difficult to reproduce the Allocations Committee's deliberations, they may have strong feelings about the value of some charities. These beliefs may have little relation to the efficiency of the agencies' operation or the satisfaction of clients. Instead they may depend upon the donors' ideological commitments. Thus UF contributions may be maximized if controversial agencies associated with birth control or minority rights are excluded from membership.[39] New, unconventional agencies that need monitoring to gain credibility may be excluded if their very riskiness casts doubt on the overall effectiveness of UF allocation procedures.

The membership practices of UFs are themselves likely to affect the mixture of services provided by agencies. A person with a new idea about how to provide services may try to work within an established agency rather than begin a new organization. Thus so long as the managers of established charities are not especially resistant to change, these agencies may diversify and innovate more than if the UF had liberal admissions policies. Of course, the overall number of new projects or new techniques tried in the community may be lower under current admissions procedures, but the UF's critics are surely incorrect to assume that an organization is hidebound just because it is *called* the Salvation Army or the Boy Scouts. Since innovators have difficulty obtaining seed money in most communities, their best chance of getting started may be to operate under the supervision of an existing UF organization.[40]

A second source of UF monopoly power is its privileged access to payroll deductions in the workplace. Many well-known organizations would not seek UF membership if they had access to equally effective and low cost solicitation methods. Access to the payroll deduction permits little-known agencies to benefit both from the UF label and from their association with well-known, uncontroversial organizations such as the Red Cross, the YMCA, and the Girl Scouts.[41]

In order for the UF to obtain a monopoly of payroll deductions, it must be in an employer's interest to restrict payroll deductions and matching gifts[42] to UF agencies only. Employers may favor the UF for two reasons. First, the firm may believe that the UF members provide services that yield external benefits to the firm. Thus most UFs concentrate on locally based

charities that aid area residents. An employer may believe that this group
of services helps dampen community unrest and cushions the effects of
business fluctuations. The firm may then donate some of its profits to the
UF as well as try to generate employee gifts. Second, supporting the UF
may isolate the firm from criticism. On the one hand, UF monitoring and
admissions policies lower the probability that money will be collected for
charities that are too closely associated with particular religious or political viewpoints or that turn out to be disreputable. On the other hand, if
anyone does criticize UF policies, the firm can respond by pointing out
that it is not responsible for Fund choices.

These arguments help explain why combined health appeals, especially
if they include local hospitals and clinics, have been able to obtain access
to some employers' payroll deduction systems whereas federations of radical-
or minority-run agencies experience difficulties.[43] The former are groups
of organizations with secure national and local reputations that provide
services to many employees. The latter are frequently of uncertain quality
and hold ideological positions opposed by management or by important
groups of customers.[44]

Therefore, if the UF's estimates of donors' preferences are correct, combined health appeals are likely to be a far greater threat to the UF movement than coalitions of left-wing or ultra-conservative groups. When two
equally respectable groups solicit in the workplace, the original solicitor
can expect some decline in gifts. This means that even if minority controlled or ideologically oriented organizations succeed in breaking the UF's
privileged access to payroll deductions, the main beneficiaries are likely to
be current Fund members, such as the Red Cross, that are well known
enough to the public to be able to mount campaigns independently of the
UF. The main losers will be Fund members that do not have a well recognized "brand name."

In conclusion, I will briefly consider an alternative model of the way the
UF uses its monopoly power. Under this view, developed by Fisher,[45] the
UF is a monopolist making a tie-in sale. Donors are assumed to be unable
to give to charity except through a UF, and they have clear preferences for
the services of member charities. Before people make donations, the Fund
announces how resources will be divided among members. Since the "price"
of contributing to one's chosen charity has increased, total giving may
increase if demand is inelastic. By forcing donors to "consume" charitable
services in fixed proportions, the Fund may induce them to spend more on
charity even though their utility falls. Thus charities may wish to establish
a UF even though donors are made worse off.

This view, however, overstates the monopoly power of the UF. In fact,
people are permitted to give separately to member agencies, and unaf-
filiated charities, providing substitute services, can attract donors who do
not agree'with the UF's allocation formula. The Fund may eventually fail
as other organizations siphon off contributions. Even if this occurs, donors
will not necessarily be better off after the collapse of the UF. Since in

Fisher's example everyone gives less in an atomistic charity market, donors may lose more from the fall in *others'* gifts than they gain from the ability to allocate their *own* gifts as they wish.

THE UNITED FUND AND THE WELFARE STATE

Founded at a time when government involvement in the provision of social services was minimal, UFs are now faced with the problem of allocating private donations to organizations that are heavily dependent on public support.[46] Furthermore, agency dependence on public money varies widely. In the New Haven UW, one agency obtained 90% of its funds from government, while another received nothing. In New York City agencies aiding children received 95% of their resources from government in 1975, while recreation and group work agencies received only 44%.[47] Agencies may qualify for a public program in one year only to have government funds reduced in the next. The same kind of agency operating in different geographical regions may obtain vastly different amounts of public support.[48] Therefore, some of the current dissatisfaction with UWs may stem from the belief that they are poorly equipped to deal with the shifting priorities of public funding.

No easy solution to their allocation problem exists. So long as the marginal value of various services is unknown and so long as donors disagree on the relative usefulness of different services, there is no *single* best way to distribute UF dollars. Nevertheless, one possible goal for a UF would be to seek to maximize the sum of public and private funds available to member agencies. Although government grants and fees are variable over time, their distribution across agencies does not appear to be entirely random from year to year. This suggests that the UF could respond to agencies' varied success in obtaining money by shifting allocations both toward those who obtain few funds and toward those eligible for matching grants.[49] Although this would suffice if government money were allocated by a fixed formula, the money obtained by nonprofits is generally provided on a discretionary basis.[50] Nonprofits must learn about funding sources and apply for grants or qualify for reimbursement. Clearly, the staff's incentive to do this is less if the UF cuts their allocation by a large amount in response to a successful grant. This possibility restrains the UF from cutting an agency's allocation even though the money is used for projects that the UF's donors and staff do not believe are very worthwhile. Nevertheless, if government support is ignored, the UF runs the risk of discouraging contributions. Donors may then believe that the UF is simply duplicating government efforts. One way around this problem is for the UF to convert lump-sum grants into negative matching grants; i.e., for every dollar in grants, the agency's allocation is cut by less than a dollar.[51] Given the objectives of the nonprofits' staffs, the cost to them of applying for grants, and a measure of the impact of the allocation formula on private donations, one could calculate the "optimal" matching rate for the fund that would maximize the total resources of member agencies.[52]

Instead of concentrating only on the allocation process, the United Fund could also take on an active role vis-à-vis government. On the one hand, there may be economies of scale in grantsmanship, and the UF could become a clearinghouse for information and could assist agencies in making out grant applications or qualifying for purchase-of-service contracts.[53] It could even apply for grants to fund projects that would be carried out jointly by several member agencies.[54] On the other hand, the UF could become involved in politics. Organized to raise private money, it could begin to act as an advocate[55] for charities in the political process. Given their geographic base, these organizations may be especially effective because of the geographic basis of representation in state and national legislatures. In representing their diverse membership, they are likely to support general purpose social service money rather than to press for increases in funds for particular categorical programs that would affect only a few member agencies.

For example, the UW of America joined with the Coalition of National Voluntary Organizations in 1978 to push for a bill in the U.S. Congress that would allow all taxpayers to itemize and deduct charitable contributions whether or not they use the standard deduction.[56] It has provided leadership to the "501(c)3 group," which maintains "close and cooperative relationships" with the Joint Committee on Internal Revenue Taxation, the U.S. Treasury Department, and the Internal Revenue Service.[57] The UW of America also tries to advise HEW on regulatory policies that will affect the nonprofit sector.[58]

UWs may advocate laws that benefit UW members at the expense of other charities. Thus in Connecticut, the executive director of the Hartford area Combined Health Appeal complained that UW officials influenced the wording of a state law allowing payroll deductions by state employees for charitable organizations. He claimed that they successfully pushed for a clause requiring that a fund drive represent at least 25 agencies.[59]

Although "grantsmanship" and "advocacy" can be a useful source of information to policymakers, they can also be as socially wasteful as the scramble for funds in an atomistic local charity "market." I argued previously that the fund-raising efforts of individual charities could be wasteful if total private donations were fairly inelastic. The same holds true for some kinds of grantsmanship and advocacy attempted by the UW. If the pool of funds is fixed and if all uses are equally productive, the struggle to obtain funds wastes resources and has only distributive consequences. The impact may be even more perverse if we suppose that agencies differ in service quality, that nonprofits and UWs differ in grantsmanship ability, and that the skills are not highly correlated. Government money then goes to the "hustlers," not to those providing the best or most useful services.

CONCLUSIONS: THE UNITED WAY
AS A SUBSTITUTE FOR GOVERNMENT

A normative analysis of charitable institutions is difficult for an economist trained to justify government action as a response to free rider behavior. Philanthropic activity looks much less efficient than taxing people, keeping them informed about the use of their money, and permitting them to participate in the process of fixing tax rates and allocating funds. There are two difficulties with this view, however, that leave room for the establishment of private charities. The first caveat is the possibility that people benefit from the act of giving itself. Replacing a gift with an equivalent tax used for the same purpose then leads to a loss of satisfaction.[60] The second position is the "imperfect" operation of government. If people benefit from knowing that charitable services are available but gain nothing from the act of giving, they will try to free ride off the donations of others.[61] An idealized government could then make everyone better off. The problem, of course, is that this is not necessarily what a representative government will do. The majority may try to levy high taxes on those who formerly donated freely, or a politically active minority may impose costs on the rest of society. Governments may fail to keep citizens informed and may administer programs ineffectively.[62] A pessimistic view of the conflict between democracy and efficiency then produces a second-best justification for private charities, especially if people also enjoy making donations.

Given the justification for private charity, we may ask whether UFs can have a useful role. To some extent, they act as a "voluntary" government by economizing on fund-raising costs and providing quality control. Unfortunately, the Fund also seems to face some of the same disadvantages government does. Allocations Committees, like legislatures and executive branch personnel, are subject to political pressures from member agencies and influential people. They may also try to make life easy for themselves by failing to reexamine spending priorities frequently. The scope for discretionary behavior is less broad in a UF than in government, however, since agencies withdraw from the UF, the Fund cannot levy taxes, and people are always free to refuse to give.

Just as those with political power in government may try to benefit at the expense of others, UF agencies may try to gain in relation to other charities. They may try to prevent innovative, experimental charities from joining the UF; maintain old organizations that would have failed without UF support; and make it more difficult for donors to spread their contributions across agencies in the way they would like. If donors oppose UF allocation formulas, however, a combined fund drive can survive only if entry into the charity "market" is restricted or if other benefits, such as matching grants, are provided to induce donors to support the UF in preference to competing, independent nonprofits.

In short, the voluntary nature of UF participation for agencies and donors has both benefits and costs. Unlike government, a Fund cannot coerce donations or mandate changes in agency programs. This makes it difficult for them to overcome free rider problems and to use evaluations of agency performance in allocating funds. The voluntary nature of the association, however, also limits the power of agencies or individuals who seek to control allocation and admissions procedures for their own benefit. Thus, the very inefficiency of charitable giving also provides a check on UF behavior.

Sometimes UF officials have argued that the Fund should be a substitute for government in another sense. Some people have recommended that instead of merely allocating voluntary gifts, UFs should help allocate government social service funds. An organization primarily engaged in private fund-raising, however, cannot be an effective monitor of tax supported social service programs. Local UFs frequently are well informed about member agencies' operations, but their role as fund-raising agents *for* these organizations makes it difficult for them to be agents of government policy. They represent private donors or member agency staffs, and neither of these groups necessarily has the same interests as the majority of taxpayers.

NOTES

1. The research for this paper was partially funded by the Yale Program on Non-Profit Organizations. Pamela Farley and Gary Kaplan provided research assistance. I am grateful to the United Way of America, the United Way of Central Maryland, the Greater New Haven United Way, The Velley United Way, and the United Way of the National Capital Area for supplying data and documents from their files. Richard Nelson and John Simon made helpful comments on earlier drafts.

2. Edith Fisch, Doris J. Freed, and Ester R. Schachter, *Charities and Charitable Foundations* (Pomona, N.Y.: Land Publications, 1974).

3. Harold Hochman and James Rodgers, "The Optimal Tax Treatment of Charitable Contributions." *National Tax Journal* 30 (1977), 1–19.

4. In 1970 the United Community Funds and Councils of America changed its name to the United Way (UW) of America and urged local chapters to follow their lead. The change in name was accompanied by a move in the headquarters to Washington, D.C., and a greater involvement in national politics (UW of America). *People and Events: A History of the United Way* (Alexandria, Va.: United Way, 1977).

5. Some committed UW volunteers and staff members would argue that I have taken an overly narrow view of the UW movement. John Seeley, Buford Junker, R. Wallace Jones, Jr., N. C. Jenkins, M. T. Haugh, and I. Miller, *Community Chest: A Case Study in Philanthropy* (Toronto: University of Toronto Press, 1957), pp. 109–110, report the tension between "those who regard the Community Chest primarily as a semi-sacred movement in the realm of 'community organization' [for which money is, incidentally, needed] and those who regard money-raising as the common sense and natural heart of the enterprise." The UW of America stresses the services provided to agencies and emphasizes its role as an organization run on a volunteer basis by a group of community residents (see United Way of America, *People and Events: A History of the United Way.*) Since this paper deals with only one aspect of the United Way role, I have used the older "United Fund" label except when citing information about actual UWs.

6. Most UWs have established guidelines for supplemental fund-raising and capital campaigns. The Greater New Haven UW's *Manual of Policies and Procedures for United Way Agency Relations* (New Haven, Conn.: United Way, 1979) restrictions appear to be typical.

No limits are placed on revenue from "public and private grants, reimbursements, rental fees or fees for service which normally support agency programs." Supplemental fund raising should be conducted so it does not conflict with the UW campaign. It should be based upon support from individuals having a personal and continuing interest in the agency and its programs or should center in a "value-received" philosophy, in which support is received in exchange for something of reasonable value. Samples or descriptions of all printed materials should be submitted to the UW prior to their use. Capital drives are treated separately. The New Haven UW tries to coordinate the timing of capital drives so that not more than one is scheduled per year.

7. See Gordon Tullock, "Information without Profit," *Papers on Non-Market Decision-making* (Public Choice) 1 (1966), 141–159. See also Thomas Ireland, "Charity Budgeting," in *The Economics of Charity*, ed. T. Ireland and D. Johnson (Blacksburg, Va.: Center for the Study of Public Choice, (1970), pp. 11–69. UW publicity stresses this benefit. In a recent interview, William Aramony, head of the UW of America, is quoted as saying, "Giving to the United Way is saying 'I know I don't know enough to be able to commit my money wisely.' It's not a passive decision; it's an active decision to let the allocations process work." Cook, James, "Is charity obsolete?" *Forbes* 5 February 1979; 45–51.

8. Donors, however, are unlikely to know much about the marginal productivity of money spent to raise more money. At most, they will know the proportion of the total budget allocated to fund-raising and must use this as a rough proxy for the marginal productivity of their dollars. The actual amounts vary widely. In one listing of fund-raising expenses as a percentage of income, some charities spent less than 10% and others spent 40%. Cook, James, "Is Charity Obsolete?" (1979). The data are from the National Information Bureau.

9. Richard Schmalensee, *The Economics of Advertising* (Amsterdam: North-Holland, 1972).

10. Susan Rose-Ackerman, "Charitable Giving and 'Excessive' Fundraising," *Quarterly Journal of Economics* 96 (1982), 193–212. Reprinted in S. Rose-Ackerman, ed., *The Economics of Nonprofit Institutions* (New York: Oxford University Press, 1986), 333–346.

11. This is only a relative advantage. The UW does not have a monopoly of fund-raising activity. In 1978 it raised $1.3 billion out of the $9 billion given to charities by the private sector and the $35 billion given to all philanthropic activities including religion, education, culture, and the arts. James Cook, "Is Charity Obsolete?"

12. Lubove, Roy, *The Professional Altruist* (Cambridge, Mass.: Harvard University Press, 1965).

13. For a somewhat more extensive discussion of these points see Thomas Ireland, "Charity Budgeting."

14. "UW, Cancer Society, have pacts in 6 states." *New Haven Register* 12 February 1979.

15. Nova Institute, *Allocating United Way Dollars in New York City* (New York: Nova Institute, 1978).

16. James Cook, "Is Charity Obsolete?", p. 46.

17. In a massive 1957 study of the Indianapolis Community Chest by Seeley et al., *Community Chest: A Case Study in Philanthropy*, only two or three pages are devoted to the question of "budgeting."

18. A statement of "United Way Allocations Policies and Procedures" by UW of Greater New Haven, *Report of the Allocations Committee* (New Haven, Conn.: United Way, mimeographed, 1979).

19. The discussion in the text is based on Donald Custis, *An Analysis of the Services Priority Project as Conducted by the United Way of Summit County* (Akron, Ohio: United Way of Summit County, mimeographed, 1976) and Harold C. Edelston, *The Painful Necessity of Choice: An Analysis of Priorities Plans and Policies in the United Way Movement* (Alexandria, Va.: United Way of America, 1974), and a review of eight recent priority planning or needs assessment projects. Information on these projects is reported in documents prepared by the UW involved and obtained from the library of the UW of America in Washington, D.C. The projects that I reviewed were carried out in Green Bay, Wisc., by the United Way of Brown County, *Program Evaluation Pilot Project* (1978); Boone County, Ky., Northern Human Services Planning Council, *The Boone County Study: An Assessment of Human*

Service Needs and Resources in Boone County, Kentucky. Newport, Ky.: Northern Kentucky HSPC (1978); Fargo, N.D., United Way of Cass-Clay, *Priorities '78: Guidelines for the Future* (1978); Bridgeport, Conn.: United Way of Eastern Fairfield County, *A Report: Assessment of Community Needs and United Way Priorities, 1979–1981,* United Way, Resource Document 26 (1978); Winston-Salem, N.C., United Way of Forsyth County, *Priorities for United Way Funding of Human Care Services* (1978); Seattle, Wash.: United Way of King County, *Planning Report for 1979,* Planning and Allocations Division (1979); Pontiac, Mich.: United Way of Pontiac/North Oakland, *Update Priorities* (1977); and Akron, Ohio: United Way of Summit County, *Priorities Project Report,* mimeo (1978). Priority plans prepared in Chicago in 1967, in Cincinnati in 1972, and in Los Angeles, Washington, D.C., and Minneapolis in 1973 provided the basic framework followed in the more recent efforts. The Los Angeles experience in the 1960s is reviewed in Beatrice Dinerman, *The Dynamics of Priority Planning: A Study of Decision Making in Welfare* (Los Angeles, Calif.: Ford Foundation Research Department and Los Angeles Welfare Planning Council, 1965).

20. The information is of three kinds: general demographic data on the region covered by the UW, information on the services provided by member agencies, and other non-UW sources of funds for these services. It is generally prepared by UW staff, sometimes with the help of agency professionals. In Bridgeport, Connecticut, however, teams of volunteers were asked to vote on what they thought would happen to various demographic measures in their area over the next ten years: United Way of Eastern Fairfield County, pp. 12–20.

21. Two of the UWs I examined (Akron and Winston-Salem) canvassed several hundred people representing agencies, major employers, ordinary citizens, and client groups. The results of these surveys were among the factors considered by a UW priorities committee in ranking services. In other UWs only a committee was used. One UW (Pontiac, Michigan) was careful to keep agency representatives off this committee. Others (Fargo and Akron) were proud that agency representatives were actively involved in priority setting.

22. Participants are sometimes asked to evaluate the overall importance of each listed service to the community as well as the importance of increased voluntary sector or UW support. Frequently, however, this first stage is omitted and people are asked only whether UW support should increase, decrease, or remain constant. In Bridgeport, people were asked to spread a hypothetical $100 of UW money over service areas. In Akron, Fargo, Pontiac, and Winston-Salem participants were asked to place services in four or five broad priority classes. Individual rankings of committee members and outside panels are aggregated in various ways. Obviously the method of aggregation can affect the ultimate ranking of services. Voting, for example, is sensitive to the definitions of service categories and to the weights assigned to the different alternatives. This is shown explicitly in the Bridgeport plan, which produced several different rankings of services under a series of different criteria. For a discussion of the difficulties of voting procedures see R. Niemi and W. Riker, "The Choice of Voting Systems," *Scientific American* 234, 6 (1976), 21–27.

23. A few UWs do, however, attempt to evaluate particular programs, but such evaluations were not part of any of the priority plans that I reviewed. See the listings in UW of America, *Digest of Selected Reports* (Alexandria, Va.: United Way of America, 1979), vols. 7 and 8, and the discussion of the Chicago UW in Nova, Nova Institute, *Allocating United Way Dollars in New York City,* pp. 51–54 (1978). Nevertheless, evaluations are often viewed as threats to agency autonomy. For example, a proposal to carry out program evaluations was presented to the UW Council of Member Agencies in Green Bay. A report of the meeting states that, "It was apparent that the UW's efforts . . . were considered a threat to the balance of autonomy and dependence between agencies and the United Way," United Way of Brown County, *Program Evaluation Pilot Project,* Green Bay, Wisc., pp. 1–2 (1978).

24. In this respect, it is like planning in the U.S. Department of Defense before the McNamara era. Charles J. Hitch, *Decision-Making for Defense* (Berkeley: University of California Press, 1967) reports that before 1960, "military requirements tended to be stated in absolute terms, without reference to their costs."

25. Lay involvement is a basic principle of UW organization. For example, an official UW of America pamphlet states that "the United Way should support the principle that the gov-

ernance of local United Ways and of every agency should be entrusted to bodies with representation from diverse elements of the community": United Way of America, *Standards of
Excellence for Local United Way Organizations* (Alexandria, Va.: United Way of America,
1977).

26. Harold Edelston, *The Painful Necessity of Choice: An Analysis of Priorities Plans and
Policies in the United Way Movement,* p. 3, defines a priority plan as "a method of syste-
matizing value judgments and making them explicit."

27. See Harold C. Edelston, *The Painful Necessity of a Choice: An Analysis of Priorities
Plans and Policies in the United Way Movement* and Russi D. Sumariwalla, *Planning and
Managing Human Services in Local Communities Under Non-Governmental Auspices* (Al-
exandria, Va.: United Way of America, mimeographed, 1973).

28. Harold C. Edelston, *The Painful Necessity of Choice: An Analysis of Priorities Plans
and Policies in the United Way Movement,* pp. 1–2.

29. Compare Dinerman, Beatrice, *The Dynamics of Priority Planning: A Study of Decision Making in Welfare,* who found that priority planning in Los Angeles had no independent
impact on the allocations. A report from the Seattle UW indicates that several high priority
services received very large increases in their allocations between 1978 and 1979: United Way
of King County, *Planning Report for 1979* (1979).

30. Akron, Ohio, and Fargo, North Dakota, are the United Ways with priority plans.

31. The data are from UW of Central Maryland, *Allocations for Fiscal Year 1977, 1978,
and 1979* (Baltimore, Md.: United Way, mimeographed, 1977; 1978a; 1979a), UW of Greater
New Haven, *Report of the Allocations Committee,* mimeo (1978) and *Report of the Alloca-
tions Committee,* mimeo (1979b), UW of the National Capital Area, *Allocations Report,
Fiscal Year 1979* (Washington, D.C.: Membership and Allocations Committee, 1978a), and
Valley UW, *Allocations Committee Recommendations* (Ansonia, Conn.: United Way, mi-
meographed, 1979). Baltimore's long-range plans are described in UW of Central Maryland,
Plan of Action, Baltimore, Md. (1978b) and *Problems and Proposals,* Baltimore, Md. (1978c).

32. These results are consistent with the evidence in David Horton Smith's, "The Role of
the United Way in Philanthropy," in *Research Papers.* (Washington, D.C.: U.S. Department
of the Treasury, Commission on Private Philanthropy and Public Needs, 1977), vol. II, pp.
1353–1382. Smith used data from the national UW and the UW in one large metropolitan
area.

33. The partial correction coefficient between 1979 requests and 1978 allocations in New
Haven is 0.98 and between (REQ78) and (ALL77) is 0.97. Thus little information is being
added by including the request variable. Although there is a great deal of variation in the
relationship between requests and recommendations (in 1978 in New Haven the mean was
7.7%, but the percentages varied from 49 to 100% with a standard deviation of 11%), the
high correlation between last year's allocations and this year's requests suggests that each
agency has established its own conventional relationship between requests and allocations.

34. See Thomas Ireland, "Charity Budgeting," pp. 57–69, for a defense of an allocation
process based on historic budget shares. The Greater New York Fund uses the most explicitly
mechanical procedures of any UW studied. The Red Cross, the Salvation Army, and a group
of hospitals obtain fixed shares of UW resources. Other agencies receive an allocation equal
to one-tenth of their contributions from other sources in the previous year. In the case of
New York, the method can be justified in part by the fact that UW dollars were only 1.6%
of agency receipts in 1975: Nova Institute, *Allocating United Way Dollars in New York City.*

35. Wildavsky, Aaron, *The Politics of the Budgetary Process* (Boston: Little, Brown, 1964).

36. Bothwell, Robert, *Fund Raising at the Workplace: New Options for Nonprofit Groups
Not Members of the United Way* (Washington, D.C.: National Committee for Responsive
Philanthropy, mimeographed, 1979).

37. James Cook, "Is Charity Obsolete?" and David Horton Smith, "The Role of the United
Way in Philanthropy."

38. See for example, UW of Greater New Haven, *Manual of Policies and Procedures for
United Way Agency Relations* (1979a), and UW of the National Capital Area, *Membership
and Allocations Manual* (1978b).

39. Chernow, Ron, "Cornering the Goodness Market: Uncharitable Doings at United Way," *Saturday Review* 28 October 1978, pp. 15–18; James Cook, "Is Charity Obsolete?"; and David Horton Smith, "The Role of the United Way in Philanthropy," pp. 1373–1374. Only 47 of Planned Parenthood's 191 affiliates are UW members. The Gary, Indiana, UW dropped Planned Parenthood from membership after it decided to provide abortion services: James Cook, "Is Charity Obsolete?" p. 47. "I think they costed us out," Ann McFarren, Executive Director of the Gary area Planned Parenthood League, told a reporter. "They felt they would lose more money if they kept us in than if they kicked us out," as quoted by Ron Chernow, "Cornering the Goodness Market: Uncharitable Doings at United Way," p. 161. Wenocur, Stanley, "The adaptability of voluntary organizations: External pressures and United Way organizations (1975) studied UW admissions and allocations policies with respect to minority controlled agencies and related UW behavior to the existence of active pressure groups. UW of America's head, William Aramony, as quoted by Ron Chernow, "Cornering the Goodness Market: Uncharitable Doings at United Way," p. 18, defends the UW by saying, "By its very nature, the UW cannot have extremes left or right. It's a consensus system. And to that degree, you won't get a radical avant-garde position. Even our haircuts are conservative."

40. In New Haven an endowed organization, the New Haven Foundation, does provide "seed" money to help new organizations get started. In 1978 the Greater New Haven UW admitted three new agencies. All of them had originally obtained funds from the New Haven Foundation. The Greater New Haven UW in its manual, UW of Greater New Haven, *Manual of Policies and Procedures for United Way Agency Relations* (1979), states that an organization cannot apply for admittance unless it has been in existence for at least three years.

41. In recent years about 45% of UW funds went to local chapters of eight organizations: the American Red Cross, the Family Service Agency, YMCA, Boy Scouts, the Salvation Army, YWCA, Boy's Clubs, and the Girl Scouts as explained by James Cook, "Is Charity Obsolete?" p. 45.

42. Although a high proportion of UF gifts come from corporate contributions, only a few employers match employees' gifts. In the Greater New Haven area two insurance companies match employee's gifts. Robert Bothwell, *Fund Raising at the Workplace: New Options for Nonprofit Groups Not Members of the United Way*, pp. 35–40, has compiled examples of firms that match employee contributions.

43. In Hartford, New Haven, San Francisco, Omaha, Santa Barbara, Seattle, and Washington, D.C., combined Health Appeals have been given access to payroll deductions by many employers; as explained by Robert Bothwell, *Fund Raising at the Workplace: New Options for Nonprofit Groups Not Members of the United Way*, p. 30, and C. Kochakian, "Health Fund Drive Will Tap Payrolls," *New Haven Register* 13 May 1979b. The federal government permits payroll deductions for employee contributions to a specified list of national voluntary organizations, as explained by James W. Abernathy, *Fundraising and Federal Employees* (Washington, D.C.: National Committee for Responsive Philanthropy, mimeographed, 1979) and George J. McQuoid, *Evaluation of Fall 1977 Combined Federal Campaigns* (Washington, D.C.: U.S. Civil Service Commission, memorandum, 19 June 1978). Robert Bothwell, *Fund Raising at the Workplace: New Options for Nonprofit Groups Not Members of the United Way*, gives many examples of governments and firms that permit payroll deductions for groups other than the UW. Very few, however, appear to have an open-ended system that includes all tax-exempt organizations. Organized groups are also attempting to reduce the UW's dominant position. The National Health Agencies for the Combined Federal Drive are suing the USCC, claiming that too much money not designated for particular charities is going to the UW ("Suit assails payroll deduction monopoly," *New Haven Register* 12 February 1979). In Washington, D.C., the United Black Fund, a coalition of black-run charities, mounted a legal challenge to the UW's monopoly of payroll deductions. The UW agreed out of court to share its funds with the challengers. Similar challenges in 13 states are being coordinated by the National Black United Fund in Los Angeles. In California, the UWs have been sued twice for allegedly obstructing rivals. In Los Angeles, the Associated Ingroup Donors (AID) sued UW. The result was a court-imposed settlement that bars either group from interfering with the other. Nevertheless, AID's contributions have

plummeted in three years to one-third of their original total. In Santa Clara County, the Combined Health Agencies Drive (CHAD) alleged that the UW "used unfair monopolistic practices" to pressure employers to turn down CHAD's request for a payroll deduction. The California Supreme Court rejected the charge of monopoly and found no conspiracy between the UW and employers ("The Charity Battle," *Newsweek* 7 May 1979, p. 34; "California's major charity group is sued as a monopoly by rival," *New York Times* 21 August 1977; "United Way under fire for use of funds," *New Haven Register* 13 May 1979; Bothwell, *Fund Raising*; Chernow, "Cornering the Goodness Market," p. 18; Cook, "Is Charity Obsolete?" p. 46).

44. For example, United Airlines recently was boycotted by antiabortion groups because some of its employees elected to contribute funds to Planned Parenthood. The boycott came about because of a misleading newspaper article that implied a United Airlines endorsement of the gift ("Abortion Foes Target Airline," *New Haven Register* 18 September 1979).

45. Franklin M. Fisher, "On Donor Sovereignty and United Charities," *American Economic Review* 67 (1977), 632–638.

46. In New Haven, over half of non-UW resources came from government. Government funds received by member agencies rose by 93% between 1973 and 1978. At the same time UW funds rose 33% and agency expenditures rose 40%. In 1973, 30% of agency expenditures came from the government and 17.5% from the UW. In 1978, the UW's share had fallen only slightly to 16.7%, while the government's share rose to 42%. In New York City between 1970 and 1975, government support increased 70% and private earnings fell 39% according to Nova Institute, *Allocating United Way Dollars in New York City*, p. 20.

47. Nova Institute, *Allocating United Way Dollars in New York City*, p. 21.

48. See UW of America, *Local United Way Allocations: Book One: Allocations to Agencies* (1978).

49. A document of the New Haven UW states that one funding method it uses is "allocation to an agency to provide necessary matching revenue required by outside sources of funding." They also state that if a government grant is discontinued and no other sources of support can be found, then the "United Way will support the program or service to the extent possible," *Report of the Allocations Committee* (1979). They obviously recognize that this may deter agencies from seeking grants. Thus they offer to help agencies obtain outside support, and in the Allocations Committee Report, United Way of Greater New Haven, *Report of the Allocations Committee* (1978), they frequently suggest that agencies seek outside funding for particular programs.

50. Under Title XX of the Social Security Act, for example, the state government obtains money from the federal government and must then decide how much to allocate to nonprofits and to various state agencies. The relevant law is P.L. 93–647, which includes the 1974 Amendments to the Social Security Act (Title XX).

51. This is essentially what is done in New York City, where a $1.00 increase in grants reduced UF allocations by $0.10. A recent report recommended changing the formula to benefit those who obtain public money, Nova Institute, *Allocating United Way Dollars in New York City*.

52. A model that demonstrates these calculations is available from the author.

53. A report to the Greater New York Fund/United Way (1978, p. 10) suggests that the UW might help small agencies in "proposal preparation and contract negotiation with government." The UW of America has helped this effort by preparing three publications to aid local UWs: (1) a guide to the 1967 Social Security Amendments, (2) *Guide to Government Grants and Contracts*, and (3) a directory of regional HEW personnel (UW of America, 1977, p. 208).

54. This has happened in the New Haven area. In 1977 the UW of Greater New Haven was awarded a two-year $800,000 grant from the Law Enforcement Assistance Administration to administer a demonstration Juvenile Delinquency Prevention Project. The project involved four area UWs and is being carried out by 35 individual agencies, mostly nonprofit UW members, as explained by George Reynolds, "New Areawide Youth Services Approach of Connecticut United Ways," *Community Focus* 2 (1978), 4 6.

55. Under the Tax Reform Act of 1976, public charities can use from 5 to 20% of their expenditures to work for the passage or defeat of legislation. The percentage is inversely related to the size of the charity (IRC § 501[h]4911). All charities that are tax-exempt under Internal Revenue Code § 501(c)(3) lose their exemption if they participate in electoral campaigns, according to John Simon, "Charity and Dynasty under the Federal Tax System," *The Probate Lawyer* 5 (1978), 1–92.

56. Robert Bothwell, *Fund Raising at the Workplace: New Options for Nonprofit Groups Not Members of the United Way.*

57. United Way of America, *People and Events: A History of the United Way,* p. 229 (1977).

58. United Way of America, *People and Events: A History of the United Way,* p. 225 (1977).

59. "Suit assails payroll deduction monopoly," *New Haven Register* 12 February 1979.

60. K. Arrow, "Gifts and Exchanges," *Philosophy and Public Affairs* 1 (1972) 343–362, distinguishes among three reasons for giving: (1) The welfare of an individual depends on his own satisfaction and the satisfaction obtained by others. (2) The welfare of an individual depends on his own satisfaction, the satisfaction of others, and the individual's contribution to others' satisfaction. (3) There is an implicit social contract so that people perform duties that enhance the satisfaction of all. If reason (2) is important, then a person would rather provide a service through a voluntary gift than through a tax payment. If (1) and (3) hold, gifts are not superior to tax payments. In contrast, if we focus on those aided by charity, some have argued that the beneficiaries' self-respect is enhanced if they receive aid as a right from the state rather than as a gift from those more well-to-do, as explained by Kathleen Jones, John Brown, and Jonathan Bradshaw, *Issues in Social Policy* (London: Routledge & Kegan Paul, 1978).

61. Harold Hochman and James Rodgers, "The Optimal Tax Treatment of Charitable Contributions."

62. Susan Rose-Ackerman, "Inefficiency and Reelection," *Kyklos,* 33 (1980) 287–307.

7

The United Way
Understanding How It Works
Is the First Step to Effecting Change

DEBORAH KAPLAN POLIVY

The United Way has been attacked by critics for years. The accusations are neither few in number nor light in their import. The United Way has been charged with maintaining a monopoly over payroll deductions at the work site and denying other charitable groups access to that lucrative source of funds. It has been accused of using strong-arm tactics to pressure people into giving. The United Way's detractors have claimed that it funds agencies that primarily serve the middle class and that the organization's aphorism—"The United Way works for all of us"—is untrue. The United Way has been accused of not admitting new agencies or, when it does, of granting membership to very few organizations that serve minorities, gays, or women, or that provide what have been called nontraditional or controversial services. Moreover, it has been criticized for erecting barriers to admissions by demanding complex accounting procedures, requiring extensive experience in service delivery as a prerequisite of membership, and then taking long periods of time to process admission applications.

Since the United Way plays such a prominent role in the nonprofit arena as a funder and legitimator of health and welfare organizations, these accusations cannot easily be dismissed. Moreover, although any number of the criticisms could be examined for their accuracy, we chose to address the issue of admissions because of the Reagan administration's cutbacks in human service funding.

Membership in the United Way is important to nonprofit social service organizations because it almost always provides stable funding for its member agencies, and as a result, its beneficiaries can be assured of at least a limited degree of financial security. Thus, at a time of government retrenchment in social services and at a time when the administration was calling upon the private sector (both individuals and corporations) to increase its charitable giving, it seemed appropriate to examine how the United

Way—a major recipient of private charitable donations—was operating to help agencies that needed funding. We thus conducted a study of the admissions policies and practices of United Ways in eight cities—Hartford, Connecticut; Syracuse, New York; Providence, Rhode Island; Newark, New Jersey; San Francisco, California; New Orleans, Louisiana; Worcester, Massachusetts; and Portland, Maine.[1] Since data were collected in only eight cities, our conclusions are tentative and pertain only to the United Way organizations that we studied.

In this chapter we shall report some of our findings, and we shall describe how the structure of the United Way limits its funding choices. Finally, we shall discuss how applicant agencies and the donor public can influence United Way policies and practices.[2]

THE STUDY DESIGN

The study of the admissions policies and practices of the United Way addressed the following four questions:

1. Is the United Way opening up membership opportunities to agencies, and if so, how much money is being allocated to them?
2. What kinds of agencies have these local United Ways admitted? What services do the new member agencies provide and to whom?
3. What factors aid or impede the admission of agencies into the United Way?
4. What process is used to determine which agencies are admitted?

Since the research was exploratory, no attempt was made to select cities systematically to achieve a "representative sample." Several criteria, however, were used in choosing the eight cities. The size of the local United Way was one. For the most part the organizations chosen were categorized as intermediate-sized (Metro II) by the United Way of America, although two large (Metro I) and two small (Metro III) organizations were included to determine if the patterns encountered in the medium-sized United Ways were found in the larger and smaller organizations.[3] For the cities on the eastern seaboard, proximity to our study headquarters at Yale University was a criterion in order to minimize travel costs. Finally, no city was chosen that was known to us to have experienced controversy over its admissions policies. This was done to avoid even the appearance of seeking notorious cases.

Two sources of data were used for the study. The first was personal interviews in each city with the following categories of people: United Way staff and volunteers, staff of agencies that had been admitted to the United Way, staff of agencies that had been refused admission to the United Way, staff of United Way member agencies, and a "third party"—someone who was familiar with the operations of the United Way, but who was not a member of the United Way board or staff. Often the executive director of a local community foundation served in this category. A total of 105 personal interviews was conducted in the eight study cities. Many telephone interviews were also conducted, but no formal count of these was kept. The second source of data was written documents primarily provided by the United Way staff, but also by the other individuals who participated in the study.

THE FINDINGS

We found that the United Ways in our study admitted very few agencies between 1970 and 1981, and none of them admitted new agencies every year during that period. We also found that when a new agency was admitted, very little money was allocated to it in the year of admission. The United Ways rarely allocated more than 3%, and more often than not, they allocated 1% of their total annual allocations to agencies admitted in any one year.

On the other hand, the newly admitted agencies, *for the most part,* did serve minorities or women or provided a nontraditional or controversial service. In other words, when admitting new agencies, the United Ways in our study made an effort to respond to newly identified needs or underserved groups in their communities.

We also found that the factors that seemed to influence the United Way admissions policy and practices were very much related to the organizational structure of the United Way. The United Way is a federation of member agencies that agree to abide by certain rules as long as the United Way continues to provide them with funds. The United Way is dependent upon the general public to provide the funds, which are in turn allocated to the member agencies.

We found that the member agencies of the United Way were ambivalent about admitting new agencies and in many cases antagonistic. The admission of new agencies implied that decreased funds would be available for the "old" members, who were not eager "to divide the pie" into additional pieces. The member agencies proved to be a serious force working against the admission of new agencies. Their power resides in the fact that they can threaten to resign from the federation, and thus threaten the very existence of the United Way itself, or can cause negative publicity for the United Way.[4] The United Way prefers to have no controversy surrounding its operations because, in the United Way's point of view, controversy "gives people a reason not to give." Thus, negative publicity raises the specter of a decline in giving and thus an unsuccessful campaign.

On the other hand, the United Way is also dependent upon its donors for its survival, and donors differ in their attitudes toward the United Way. Some are critical of United Way operations. These "malcontents" include individuals; groups; powerful funders, such as corporations; and sometimes the media. These critics often want the United Way to be more responsive to community needs, to change its funding patterns, and to admit new agencies. They are sometimes very vocal. The United Way may be inclined to make changes so as to avoid the kind of negative publicity that the malcontents can inspire, and consequently, they are strong forces for change.

Supporters of the traditional funding patterns of the United Way are usually constituents of some of its larger recipient agencies—Boys Clubs, Boy Scouts, Girls Clubs, YMCAs, and YWCAs. Although sometimes these supporters of tradition are corporate donors, they are more often members of old families who have lived in the respective community for years. Any threat in funding to their "pet agencies" can arouse their wrath and, again, cause the kind of controversy that the United Way prefers to avoid.

To avoid community controversy at all costs and maintain the largest possible pool of donors, the organization works very hard to balance the forces that represent different funding preferences. The United Ways in our study strove to balance the demands of their primary constituencies—their member agencies (whose views were often consistent with those of the more traditional United Way donors) and the donor public—who in the majority were not the malcontents, but who would respond to negative publicity about the United Way by refusing to give. The United Ways thus admitted very few agencies—assuaging the concern of the member agencies—but when admitting new agencies, chose those serving minorities and new community needs, thus meeting the demands of donors looking for change and "responsiveness." The United Ways worked very hard to keep donors not only happy, but with as little as possible to criticize, to ensure the success of their annual fund-raising campaigns.

THE ORGANIZATIONAL STRUCTURE OF THE UNITED WAY

Since the organizational context of the United Way so clearly circumscribes its admissions behavior, it seems important to understand just what the United Way is and how it operates. The United Way is a federation or coordinating agency of other agencies. This coordinating or federated structure determines to a great extent the organizational behavior of the coordinating agency, which is the maintenance of consensus or more importantly the avoidance of conflict in order to ensure that the members find no reason to pull out of the federation.

Roland Warren has described how such federated organizations make decisions. He writes that the "federative context for inclusive decision-making is exemplified by a council of social agencies . . . or by a council of churches." The subunits are the individual social agencies and are referred to as "member organizations"; they are "autonomous," and each member agency has its own "individual goals." However, there is a sharing of inclusive goals among the members, and a formal organization exists to accomplish the inclusive goals. In addition, "there is a formal staff structure" to carry out the inclusive goals.

Decision making is focused in a specific part of the inclusive structure, but it is in effect subject to ratification by the units. Authority remains at the unit (member) level, with the exception of some administrative prerogatives which were delegated by the units to a formal staff. The norms are for moderate commitment of the (member) units to the inclusive subsystem, but considerable unit autonomy is tolerated and expected. A moderate degree of collectivity orientation—consideration of well-being of the inclusive organization—is expected.

Warren describes the behavior of a federation as dependent "ultimately on the continued assent of its autonomous constituent agencies." Warren states that the federation is "under great constraint to operate on a consensus basis. Since innovations and major system changes are likely to threaten this consensus," the federation and member agencies "are under constraint to avoid them."[5]

Litwak and Hylton state that coordinating agencies will develop and continue in existence if three conditions are present: the formal organizations (or what Warren refers to as the autonomous units or member agencies) "are partly interdependent"; the agencies "are aware of this interdependence"; and the interdependence can be "defined in standardized units of action." The standardized units of action or behavior to which all the member agencies agree maintain the consensus that in turn sustains the coordinating organization. Litwak and Hylton use the Community Chest (one of the original names of what are now referred to in most communities as United Ways) as an example of a coordinating agency or federation which illustrates their argument.

The interdependency of organizations is the first variable, and Litwak and Hylton explain that the origins of the Community Chest are based on this concept of interdependency. They state that historically, social and charitable agencies were all drawing on the same, limited sources of communal funds. Further, as some agencies were successful in obtaining funds from individual donors, the chances that other agencies would receive funds were lessened. In a sense, social agencies were all dependent upon a limited amount of communal funds which would be allotted by individual contributors to charity, and the agencies were interdependent in that each needed funds to survive, so that the success of one agency might hurt the chances for survival of another. Therefore, according to Litwak and Hylton, one reason for the development of federations was the conflict, competition, and interdependency of autonomous agencies.

The second condition for a successful coordinating agency is the member agencies' awareness, "as a matter of public policy," that such an interdependence exists. The struggle for financial resources among the agencies is a constant reminder to them of their financial interdependency.

The third condition for the development and maintenance of a coordinating agency is that the behavior of the coordinating agency is carried out in "standardized actions." Standardized actions, according to Litwak and Hylton, can be defined as "behavior which is reliably ascertained and repetitive in character, e.g., requests for funds, information on whether the client is served by another agency, price of goods, etc." In other words, the expected allocations from the United Way to the member agencies serve as a standardized behavior that keeps the federation together. Like Warren, Litwak and Hylton point out that coordinating agencies need staff of their own to "operate efficiently" and "to carry out the standardized actions."[6]

Just as allocations are standardized, so is fund-raising. Community citizens know that the success of the campaign depends upon their gifts, and they also know just how and when the fund-raising campaign will be conducted annually. Citizens know what "standard" techniques will be used to solicit funds from them from year to year. If any of these standard soliciting behaviors were dramatically changed, the success of the fund-raising campaign could be placed in jeopardy, in turn threatening the United Way itself since it depends on satisfying the financial expectations of its member agencies.

Every organization performs some kind of function or activity. According to Thompson, if the function or activity is "rooted on the one hand in desired outcomes and on the other hand in beliefs about cause/effect relationships, . . . we can speak of technology, or technical rationality." The coordinating agency uses the mediating technology which involves "the linking of clients or customers who are or wish to be interdependent." Fundamental to the mediating technology is the standardization of procedures; "standardization makes possible the operation of the mediating technology over time and through space by assuring each segment of the organization that other segments are operating in compatible ways."[7] In the case of the United Way, the mediating technology involves raising funds from individuals in the community and allocating them to member agencies. The mediating technology "links" the givers to the social service agencies.

Dinerman, too, concludes from her empirical work on United Ways that the standardization of operations and the avoidance of conflict are the primary behaviors of the United Way, particularly in its allocations process. Dinerman concludes that the policies of allocation "are usually based upon past experience; therefore, they tend to reflect the status quo and to protect it from substantive change." Dinerman found that there was an awareness that to change the allocations of member agencies "would violate a crucial, though unstated, 'rule of the game' ":

There are certain agencies, characterized by strong community support, whose strength vis-à-vis the Chest is so great as to nullify any efforts toward a truly empirical evaluation of their value in relation to alternative types of services. For example, the (Allocations) Committee inherently knew that any attempts to place the Boy Scouts in a low priority ranking would produce serious repercussions and evoke criticism strong enough to make implementation of such action completely infeasible. Therefore, such a course of action was not even considered.[8]

Like Dinerman, Wenocur concludes in his study, "Confederation Adaptability to External Change Pressures," that the United Way organization operates on the basis of consensus and that conflict is avoided as much as possible; behaviors are formulated in a standardized fashion to avoid disrupting the confederation and to ensure certainty in the confederation's continued interaction with its member units. Wenocur's conclusions are based on his study of responses of United Way organizations to the demands made by indigenous groups in the 1960s for changes in United Way allocations to better reflect the needs of local people living in poverty.

Wenocur's study is based on the premise that the United Way is a complex organization which is very much in balance with its environment in its fund-raising and fund allocation functions and that any "turbulence" within that environment could threaten its equilibrium. Therefore, he assumes that the United Way must manage to do away with or reduce potential turbulence. The demands of the poverty groups in the 1960s were formidable forces which were capable of debilitating the United Way system.

According to Wenocur, if the demands for resources from these poverty groups were too great, the confederation would not have been able to "fulfill its allocative function to a broad enough constituency, potentially damaging its future fund raising abilities." Also, "too great a claim on resources" might have provoked "destructive conflict, interfering with the consensus required for a unified fund raising effort." Against this background, Wenocur measured the effect of the pressures applied to the United Way in the 1960s by militant groups and found that the federation changed only in ways that did not threaten its own viability. He concluded that the "forces for restoration of equilibrium are powerful in a federative, interorganizational system."[9]

The legitimacy of the United Way as a communal fund-raising agency primarily comes from the community leaders who serve as volunteers both as solicitors in its campaigns and as decision makers on its numerous boards and committees. In a sense the United Way can be categorized as a "commonweal" organization (using Blau and Scott's definition)[10] in that the organization exists for the benefit of the public at large. The latter is both the owner (and its representatives serve as decision makers) and beneficiary, in that agencies funded by the United Way contribute to the well-being of the general community. Wenocur has described how the United Way is served by and, in turn, serves community citizens.

As a private, non-profit corporation the legitimate authority for United Fund policy lies with the community as it is represented in the Boards of Trustees or Directors and their various operating committees. The Fund, after all, is the embodiment of the community's will to provide voluntary health and welfare services in an efficient and coordinated matter. The main functions of the confederation are fund raising and fund allocating, the latter task representing a form of priority planning via its distribution outcomes. The legitimation of the confederation is actually intertwined in both functions. The community legitimates the Fund by supporting it with donations and volunteer efforts so long as the Fund allocations support legitimate agencies in the eyes of the community.[11]

Whereas once the community was represented on the United Way's committees primarily by older families of wealth, these have given way in part to new leaders from local corporations or business. Kravitz found in a study done in the early 1960s that the representatives of old families who were "presumed to have both wealth and social position" had already lost some of their predominance in the United Ways and Funds to what he called the "independent, economic elite," the financially successful "entrepreneurs" and "managerial elite" who were salaried managers in the higher echelons of business or industry and whose wealth and/or community position" was "dependent upon a large business enterprise."[12] Kravitz concluded that these managerial elites would play increasingly larger roles in federated funds as the latter relied more and more on corporations for contributions, employee gifts through payroll deductions, and volunteers.

Kravitz made these statements in the 1960s, and there is no doubt that by the 1980s, the United Way has become intricately tied into corporate America. The latter fulfills its community obligations in large part by participating in United Way annual campaigns. Corporate executives serve the United Way as leaders and solicitors; they give it access to their workers; they allow it to publicize its activities at the work site; and, in the majority of cases, only the United Way is allowed to use the mechanism of payroll deduction for fund-raising. Moreover, corporate contributions to organizations in the field of health and welfare are determined by United Ways. It is against this background and with an understanding of how the United Way operates as (1) a federation of agencies dependent upon mutual consensus and standardized operating procedures and thus expectations and (2) as dependent on the goodwill of a community of donors for its legitimacy, volunteer leadership, and funds that the findings of our study of the admissions policies and practices of eight United Ways make sense.

THE DECISION MAKING CONTEXT OF THE UNITED WAY

The federated nature of the United Way explains much of its admissions behavior. First, it was very clear that admissions would occur (unless there were a grand hue and cry from the public) only in "good" campaign years—when the financial commitments to the member agencies could be met with ease. Thus, for example, admissions would always occur when new revenues exceeded the prior year's campaign by 7%; sometimes new admissions occurred when there was a 5% increase.

Since most United Way allocations were historical, base sums for member agencies were increased annually to account for inflation, and annual campaign goals were calculated to incorporate the prior year's allocations plus increases to account for inflation. Usually goals were established to include expenditures for admissions, but for the most part only when campaign goals were met were the new agencies admitted. The long-established commitment to the member agencies was the primary obligation acted upon by the United Ways.

However, it was not only in terms of allocations that admissions touched on the federative notion. One of the primary admissions criteria was "non-duplication of member agency services." In other words, no agencies were considered for membership that delivered a service that a member agency was already providing or could mobilize itself to provide with little difficulty (and added funding). In other words, the United Way served to protect the "domain" of its own member agencies.

Organizational domain, according to Sol Levine and Paul E. White, includes the "claims which an organization stakes out for itself in terms of (1) diseases covered, (2) population served, and (3) services rendered." (Levine and White developed their concepts using work done in the medical field.)[13] Thompson states that if "range of products" is put in place of "diseases covered," then the Levine and White concept of domain would be universal to all organizations, and in the field of social services, the product would obviously be the service delivered. Warren, by the way, expands the concept of domain to include "channels of access to task and maintenance resources."[14] Warren's concept is important because in the area of admissions the United Way protects the channels of resources of its member agencies from competition from other organizations.

Just as the United Way's federative context influenced its admissions, so too did its reliance on donors and its continued need to ensure their goodwill. The United Way admitted new agencies when donors, especially corporate donors, requested it to do so. For example, in Hartford the corporate community had asked for an expansion of the United Way's package of services. As one respondent in Hartford explained, "there had been a certain growing reluctance on the part of the corporate givers just to 'cough up' more money each year. The corporation wanted to see a broader base of recipients of United Way funds."

The United Way also admitted new agencies if there were an actual threat of public controversy if it refused to do so. Thus, the Executive Director of an agency serving gays and lesbians in San Francisco explained that the United Way admitted agencies serving the gay population because their leaders threatened to "take their case to the media" and to establish a boycott of the United Way campaign by gay and lesbian donors. The Executive Director of the United Way did not agree with that explanation. On the other hand, he did state that donor groups are considered in the admissions process, particularly in relation to the geographic distribution of allocations. He explained that when making admissions decisions, the geographic location of an agency was considered because it was incumbent upon the United Way to show donors that funds were returned to their communities. The Executive Director explained that the United Way must constantly address the "people's perception of whether or not they are getting a fair cut of the United Way pie."

Labor agencies—those that were founded and supported by union groups to provide social services at the work site—were admitted because of direct and indirect pressure from labor groups on the United Way. For example, Connecticut United Labor Community services in Hartford and United Labor Agency in Newark were admitted as a result of union requests.

In all of the study cities, the United Ways appeared to be aware of complaints that United Ways in general gave more money to male-serving agencies than female-serving ones, and they made an effort to admit female-serving agencies if only to demonstrate to female donors that the United Ways were responsive to specifically female needs. Rape crisis centers and battered women shelters were admitted in part in response to female critics of United Way's allocations formulas.

Thus, the perceived reaction of specific groups of donors was weighed in admission decisions. The United Ways needed to demonstrate to donors that they were funding agencies that served minority groups, women, and, in the Bay Area, gays and lesbians. Moreover, if the issue of duplication of services came head to head with that of providing a service to a minority community, the minority community would often succeed. In other words, if a legal aid service for Hispanics was requesting admissions and if a legal aid service was already a United Way agency, the United Way was likely to admit the former in order to be able to claim that it was funding services that specifically met the needs of a minority group.

Another criterion—that of a track record or experience in service delivery—was also considered. However, it was interpreted in several different ways. First, an agency that had received funding at one time from a local corporation, civic group, or community foundation was likely to be admitted by the United Ways in our study. We found that the United Ways would fund agencies that had been supported by the National Council of Jewish Women, Junior League, local labor organizations, such community foundations as the Hartford Foundation for Public Giving and the San Francisco Foundation, and local corporations. In these cases, the initial funding source demonstrated local support for the applicant agency, and from the United Way's perspective that local support could be translated into donor support for the United Way campaign. Furthermore, local support provided applicant agencies with local legitimacy and potential donor pressure on the United Way.[15] For example, one staff person responsible for admissions explained that the amount of "political clout" that could be "mustered by an applicant agency" was considered by the Admissions Committee.

The United Ways appeared to be least likely to fund agencies which were supported by the federal government or national foundations. It may have been that the United Ways concluded that agencies funded by these sources had access to alternative funds. However, one explanation for this behavior may be that the United Way is less apt to fund organizations with national support—whether that be from government or foundations—because these funding sources have no immediate linkage to the local community and thus local United Way campaigns. In other words, they do not represent potential donors to the annual United Way fundraising drive.

CONCLUSION: SOME SUGGESTIONS FOR POTENTIAL UNITED WAY APPLICANTS

We concluded from the analysis of our data and our understanding of the organizational structure of the United Way that its admissions policies and practices were very much related to its need to respond to the demands of its two primary constituencies—its member agencies and its donors. Applicant agencies and donors can have a great deal of influence on United Way's admissions policies once they understand how the United Way operates.

Our findings could be helpful to agencies developing strategies to gain entry to the local United Way. First, of course, any agency considering applying for United Way membership should take the time to learn about its local operation or organization since there are differences in how United Ways operate. Once information is obtained from the local United Way, an agency should determine if it is able to complete the application process and if it can meet United Way expectations. The following suggestions which resulted from our study may help.

1. The United Way places a heavy emphasis on the track record of organizations. This means in part that older, more established organizations will tend to be favored over newer ones. However, even new organizations may be successful if they can show in their application that the staff and the administration are competent and will provide services in a professional manner, and if they can demonstrate what their more unusual or controversial programs will look like in practice. They must convince the United Way that donors would support their programs.
2. Since the United Way often serves as a second funder and is particularly concerned with funding agencies that have local support, an important strategy for approaching the United Way is the creation of a network of people who are familiar with the applicant agency and its clientele. This network should include representatives from the initial funders of the program, whether they be corporations, community foundations, local churches, or ethnic groups. These supporters should be able to "tell the story" of the agency to the United Way as members of volunteer committees or through their friends who serve on these committees.
3. Since the United Way attempts to ensure that no controversy about its activities occurs within a community, a local United Way will find it desirable to dampen local criticism of its policies and practices. Some applicant agencies successfully make use of local criticisms of the United Way by pointing out that their inclusion would effectively do away with critics. This is especially true if the United

Way has been criticized for not funding agencies that serve minority groups or women.

There are two kinds of organizations which seek United Way funding that are most likely to enjoy success: organizations with a track record, that meet an obviously identified community need, and that are receiving or have received funding from local corporations and/or community foundations, and organizations that serve a viable, important activist (or potentially activist) community constituency which is ready to pressure the United Way.

Either singly (if the donor is large enough) or in conjunction with others, donors can influence United Ways' policies. However, they must be willing and desirous to serve as an agent of accountability of the United Way. In other words, donors have to be willing to ask "hard questions" and then to follow up on that questioning to convince the United Way that their "gift" is not automatic. This is not an easy role for donors to follow, especially if their social and community status are intertwined with their relationship to the United Way. Most large donors do not want to be criticized in their respective communities for "taking on" the United Way.

However, our study demonstrates that the United Way is sensitive to the will of the donor, and new trends toward the "donor option" underscore a concern for maintaining donor allegiance. Thus, it is the power of the donor and donor groups that in the long run will have the greatest impact on United Way's admissions policies and practices. Although in the short run agencies applying to the United Way might wisely use a number of strategies to help themselves gain admission, in the long run it is agencies that can educate and influence donors that will have the greatest effect on the United Way's policies and practices. Increasingly, it will be donors who are concerned about how their contributions are spent, who view their contributions as community investments, and who assume the responsibility for monitoring their use who will have the most impact on United Ways.[16]

NOTES

1. The findings are described more extensively in Deborah Kaplan Polivy, "A Study of the Admissions Policies and Practices of Eight Local United Way Organizations," Yale University, Program on Non-Profit Organizations Working Paper no. 49, May 1982.

2. The formal titles of the United Way organizations in the eight cities are the following: United Way of the Capital Area (Hartford), United Way of Central New York (Syracuse), United Way of Southeastern New England (Providence), United Way of Essex and West Hudson (Newark), United Way of the Bay Area (San Francisco), United Way for the Greater New Orleans Area, United Way of Greater Portland, and United Way of Central Massachusetts (Worcester).

3. The United Way of America categorizes cities by the amount of money raised by the local agency. When the research design was developed, those in Hartford and New Orleans were categorized as Metro II organizations. They became Metro I organizations in 1981 when they each raised more than $9 million.

4. For example, when the United Ways in Worcester and Providence threatened to change the formula for allocating funds to traditional member agencies, the latter opposed the change and brought the controversy to the media. As a result, both United Ways withdrew their proposed plans.

5. Roland L. Warren, "The Interorganizational Field as a Focus for Investigation," *Administrative Science Quarterly*, 12 (December 1967), 143–144.

6. Eugene Litwak and Lydia F. Hylton, "Interorganizational Analysis: A Hypothesis on Coordinating Agencies," *Administrative Science Quarterly*, 6 (March 1962), 402–415.

7. James D. Thompson, *Organizations in Action* (New York: McGraw-Hill Book Company, 1967), pp. 14–17.

8. Beatrice Dinerman, *The Dynamics of Priority Planning: A Study of Decision Making in Welfare* (Los Angeles: Ford Foundation and Research Department, Welfare Planning Council, 1965), p. 23. Although Dinerman's research was conducted in the 1960s, her findings are not outdated. In our own study, we found United Ways that had unsuccessfully tried to implement priority plans that would have altered the traditional allocation of funds. Priority reports in Worcester (1977) and Providence (1981) proposed taking funds from those agencies which are often described as providing traditional recreation services—Girl Scouts, Boy Scouts, YWCA, and YMCA—and allocating those funds to new agencies and member agencies which were perceived as delivering high priority services. In both Worcester and Providence the traditional agencies and their supporters vigorously disapproved of the reports and their recommendations. As a result, in Worcester the proposed priority plan was never implemented, and in Providence it was revised with participation of representatives of the member agencies that would have received the largest cuts in funding were the priority plans implemented.

9. Stanley Wenocur, "Confederation Adaptability to External Change Pressures," Diss. University of California, 1974.

10. Peter Blau and Richard W. Scott, *Formal Organizations* (San Francisco: Chandler Publishing Co., 1962), p. 55.

11. Wenocur, "Confederation Adaptability," p. 25.

12. Sanford Kravitz, "Sources of Leadership Input for Social Welfare Planning," Diss., Brandeis University, 1963.

13. Sol Levine and Paul E. White, "Exchange as a Conceptual Framework for the Study of Interorganizational Relationships," *Administrative Science Quarterly*, V (March 1961), 586.

14. Roland L. Warren, Stephen Rose and Ann Bergunder, *The Structure of Urban Reform* (Lexington, Mass.: D. C. Heath and Co., 1974), p. 27.

15. In our study, there were two United Ways that did not operate as second funders, but rather provided "seed" money to organizations without track records. These United Ways were located in Portland, Maine, and Worcester, Massachusetts.

Some similarities in the Portland and Worcester United Ways do exist. The communities in which both are located are small. There were few corporations, particularly in Portland, and no local foundation in the case of Portland and a fledgling foundation in the case of Worcester. In these cities the lack of private funding sources which could assume the risks involved in supporting emerging organizations may have led the United Way to take on that function. In other words, the nature of private philanthropy within the communities may have influenced the funding role played by the United Ways.

16. This has occurred in some communities. For example, in one year McDonnell Douglas-West in Long Beach, California, refused to provide two neighboring local United Ways with its annual gift until the United Ways developed a plan for merging one with the other.

8

The Market for Loving-Kindness
Day-Care Centers and the Demand for Child Care[1]

SUSAN ROSE-ACKERMAN

BASIC ISSUES

The organized day care of young children has frequently been studied as if it were a wholly different activity from the organized provision of other kinds of goods and services. Many suppliers are nonprofit firms,[2] and some scholars have argued that such firms will behave very differently from their nonprofit counterparts.[3] An industry dominated by such suppliers could be very unresponsive to increases in demand. Neither prices nor quantities would shift very much if an increase in demand simply allowed suppliers to screen customers better and improve quality. Some writers argue that since private suppliers have failed to respond to the large "need" for organized day care, the public sector should take over the entrepreneurial function.[4] This conclusion only follows, however, if the market is unresponsive to demand conditions. Thus in this paper I seek to discover whether the market reflects interstate differences in demand, or whether there is considerable unmet demand at prevailing prices. My results show that, although firms may be very heterogeneous and operated by people with a wide range of motivations, the industry behaves on the margin much like one which contains only for-profit firms. Demand may exceed supply for some types of day care, but the dissatisfied customers are accommodated in other parts of the market. Overall there does not appear to be a large unmet "need" in the sense of demand exceeding supply at breakeven prices. While some day-care centers may have long waiting lists because they provide high quality care at low prices, other centers take all applicants. The main remaining difference between this industry and one in which all firms are for-profit will not be in responsiveness to overall demand conditions but in the way children are sorted across suppliers.

The paper begins by discussing the underlying demand and supply conditions in the day-care center industry and outlining the empirical work to follow. The next section describes the data, and the final section presents the empirical results.

DEMAND AND SUPPLY

Any study of the day-care center industry must start by recognizing that only a small proportion of young children are cared for in formal organizations providing fee-for-service care. Most children are cared for by parents[5] or relatives, and another large group is tended by baby-sitters and day-care mothers.[6] Within the day-care *center* industry we can distinguish between two types of suppliers: firms managed by child care ideologues subscribing to various theories of child development and firms managed by profit maximizers. Although it may, in practice, be difficult to categorize individual firms, the existence of a substantial number of providers uninterested in profit maximization is well accepted.[7] The principal hypothesis of this paper, however, is that this subset of providers does not prevent the industry from responding to profitable opportunities on the margin. Suppose that child development professionals provide care that is perceived by many parents as being of high quality and that these managers set prices to break even. Many parents prefer the price-quality combinations provided by these centers, but not all can be accommodated. Excess demand exists both because the child development professionals respond to excess demand not by expanding center size but by screening children and because the number of "ideological" entrepreneurs is limited. However, although many such centers have waiting lists, I assume that most of the children on those lists are cared for either in the informal sector of baby-sitters and day-care mothers or in profit maximizing centers. Therefore, if only some suppliers are day-care ideologues, then the total market will clear through price adjustments and the entry of new suppliers.

In addition to the demand of paying customers, public programs subsidize day care.[8] Some of the subsidized children might otherwise have received day care in other forms. Others might not have been in the market at all. Thus the subsidy programs increase the demand for some kinds of day care and may reduce the demand for others. The overall demand for a particular type of day care is the sum of subsidized and unsubsidized demand. However, these two demands are not independent of each other. Parents will not pay for day care if they can receive the same or higher quality for free. The demand for unsubsidized care is a function of the level of subsidized care, and the allocation and level of subsidy funds may depend on some of the same variables which determine unsubsidized demand.

Under this view of the market for day care there is no overall "unmet" demand even though some centers have waiting lists. In contrast, suppose that all organized day care is provided by a fixed number of child development professionals who set breakeven prices and believe that no center should exceed forty children in size. These managers use donated inputs and charitable contributions so that their breakeven prices are low. If this were anything close to the correct model of the organized day-care sector, one would expect that measures of the demand for day care would have almost nothing to do with measures of the quantity of organized care actually purchased.

Empirical Specification

In order to move from the general framework to a testable model I must make a number simplifying assumptions which reflect the limitations of the data. First of all, I have no systematic data on the informal sector, and I have information for only one substitute for day-care centers: free kindergarten services provided by the public schools. Second, it is not possible to separate ideological from nonideological producers. One can discover how many centers are organized as nonprofit corporations and how many are for-profit corporations, but this is likely to be an imperfect measure of the differences I am trying to capture. Therefore, data limitations require that I study the day-care center industry as a whole. Since this total includes producers who are providing high quality bargains, my statistical results should underpredict the size of the formal day-care sector in states with many relatively inexpensive, high quality producers and overpredict the sector's size in states with few of this type. This is so because, although a reduction in the quantity supplied by day-care ideologues will lead some customers to shift to profit oriented centers, others will go to the informal sector. Third, data on subsidized children only permit one to distinguish those in centers from those cared for by other types of providers. Fourth, data on both the costs and prices of center care are relatively poor. For day-care centers as a group, however, I have measures of average prices and of salaries and regulatory requirements. Data are only available on a state-by-state basis. Thus since I assume that each state forms an independent market, I am looking at average conditions in each state. Effective market areas are, of course, much smaller, but unfortunately, the data do not permit a finer breakdown. To avoid heteroscedastic errors in the actual estimating equations I divide those dependent and independent variables which are correlated with the overall number of children by the number of children in the state.

Since I have data on receipts as well as enrollments and since I am not sure which is more accurate, I estimate both an enrollment and a revenue equation.[9] Since I hypothesize that prices will mirror costs,[10] an expression of the same general form as the quantity regression should explain revenues.

My specification leaves open the possibility that the overall size of the day-care center industry is determined simultaneously with the number of subsidized children. Thus I will first test for simultaneity by estimating the number of subsidized children in day-care centers. This analysis is, however, interesting in its own right since it may shed light on the states' budgetary processes.

In short, after considering the determinants of subsidized care, I will estimate linear reduced form relationships for the number of children in day-care centers and the receipts of the day-care center industry. If I find that basic measures of demand do influence the quantity of day-care center services, this will be consistent with my hypothesis that providers respond to profitable opportunities. Even if there is excess demand for some price-quality combinations, other types of care expand to take up the slack. If demand variables are unimportant, this will suggest that economic incentives are weak determinants of output because child development professionals are the dominant force in the industry. The data also permit me to examine the cost-increasing impact of regulation. I can consider whether states with more stringent regulations have a smaller day-care center sector.

THE DATA

Table 8.1 summarizes the state-by-state data used in the empirical analysis. Readers who want more detailed information on sources and definitions should consult the author's working paper.[11]

In the empirical specification the demand relationship includes several measures of the strength of overall demand. The first is a measure of the strength of job opportunities for women. One can argue that if jobs for women are plentiful, the demand for day care will be high. Unfortunately, one can also make the opposite argument: the existence of plentiful day care encourages women to work.[12] However, since I am looking at an option chosen in 1977 by less than 15% of working women with preschool children, the bias may not be very serious. Nevertheless, as a partial way around the remaining problem of simultaneity, I have used EMPPR, the employment rate of *all* women in the population (i.e., the labor force participation rate times the employment rate of those in the labor force), to measure the availability of jobs to mothers of young children.[13]

One group that is particularly likely to use day-care services is single parent families. Since data are not available for preschool children, I have used a variable which measures the proportion of children under eighteen from single parent families (KIDSP2).

Income has a complicated role because it can affect the quality of care chosen. Thus, I use the employment rate to capture labor market conditions for mothers and family income (INCOME) to determine quality of care chosen by parents.[14] Population density could also affect the demand for organized care. The less dense the population, the less the demand for organized care because higher transportation costs are likely. The variable *URBAN* is a rough proxy for this effect.

Table 8.1 Variables[a]

Variable Name	Units	Sources	Definitions
DCKIDS2	Children in Day Care per 1000 Children under 18[b]	Abt Associates	Children in Day-care Centers Relative to All Children under 18
RCTS2	Dollars per child under 18[a]	Census Bureau	Day-care Center Receipts per Child under 18
DPR2	Dollars per Child under 18	Census Bureau Adjusted by HEW Data	Sum of Day-care Center Receipts from Census plus Direct Provision by Government per Child under 18
PPDPR2	Dollars per Child under 18	Census Bureau Adjusted by HEW Data	Sum of Day-care Center Receipts from Census plus Direct Provision by Government and Public Purchase per Child under 18
Public Subsidy Variables			
ALLKIDS2	Subsidized Children per 1000 children under 18	HEW	Subsidized Children as a Share of All Children under 18
SUBKIDS2	Subsidized Children per 1000 Children under 18	HEW	Subsidized Children in Day-care Centers as a Share of All Children under 18
Independent Variables			
EMPR	Percentage Points	Labor Department	Employment Rate of Female Labor Force Multiplied by Female Labor Force as a Percentage of Female Population
KIDSP2	Percentage Points	Census Bureau	Number of Children under 18 from Single Parent Families as a Share of All Children
INCOME	Dollars	Census Bureau	Median Income of Families in 1975
URBAN	Percentage Points	Census Bureau	Share of the Population Living in Central Cities in 1970
KIND2	Percentage Points	HEW	Share of Children in Preprimary, Public School Programs

Variable Name	Units	Sources	Definitions
SALPER	Thousands of Dollars per Year	Census Bureau	Annual Payroll for Average Center Divided by Number of Employees
REQRAT	Children per Staff Member	Abt	State Average Required Child/Staff Ratio
INSPEC	Number of Visits	Abt	Inspections per Center
PARFEE	Dollars per Week	Abt	Average Weekly Fee Charged for Unsubsidized Care
KIDPOV2	Percentage Points	Census Bureau	Number of Children under 5 in Poverty Households as Share of All Children
DD	Zero-One Dummy	HEW	Equals One If "Children with Special Needs" Are in Subsidized Day-Care Totals

[a] All variables for 1976–1977 unless otherwise noted. There are 50 observations excluding Alaska and including the District of Columbia.
[b] Children under 18 used as denominator because a finer breakdown is not available for noncensus years.

The only measure of substitutes available on an interstate basis is information on public kindergarten services. This is measured by KIND2.

The actual level of services demanded also depends, of course, on the price charged. If I am correct in assuming that suppliers respond to profitable opportunities on the margin, then the above determinants of demand will influence the price-quantity combination observed in each state, but information on cost conditions in the industry will be important in determining the actual market conditions we observe. For the reasons outlined above, it seems likely that costs vary widely across centers within individual states and that cost and quality differences will be difficult to separate. However, some broad interstate differences can be measured directly. Since personnel costs are a high share of center costs,[15] and since these costs may vary by states, I have included a measure of salary per employee (SALPER) to capture interstate differences in costs.

I also have measures of regulatory policy which may affect costs especially for marginal producers. Presumably, the stringency of the regulations and the strength of the enforcement effort affect entry decisions. A provider may remain in the informal sector or not provide services at all if regulations are very stringent. State licensing requirements differ, but all but two states set child/staff ratios for various ages of children, and these regulations are believed to be among the most important.[16] Thus, as a regulatory proxy, I have used each state's required average child/staff ratio (REQRAT). Although many centers do not find these constraints binding, the requirements may still prevent the entry of other firms and may be a good proxy for regulatory stringency. As a rough measure of enforcement, I used a measure of inspections per center from regulatory agencies (IN-SPEC). Unfortunately, there is no measure of enforcement actions taken, licenses revoked, and so on.

Obviously, my proxies for costs are likely to be imperfect. A regression of these variables on the average weekly fee charged to unsubsidized parents (PARFEE) only explained 20% of the interstate variance, and only REQRAT, the required child/staff ratio was significant.[17] Therefore, I have also studied the impact of the price variable directly even though this measure is only a state average which conceals considerable intrastate variation and which may reflect quality as well as cost differences. The basic idea here is that if profit maximizing producers are important forces in the market, price will be exogenously determined by cost conditions. If price were only weakly related to quantity demanded, that would be evidence that market clearing forces were not very powerful.

The shares of children from parents and minority families (KIDPOV2 and KIDMIN2) are hypothesized to affect the level of subsidized day care but not the overall size of the sector. The dummy DD is included to correct for a measurement error in the data on subsidized children. These variables are included in regressions attempting to explain the level of public subsidy, ALLKIDS2 and SUBKIDS2.

RESULTS

Subsidized Day Care

Before turning to study the organized day-care sector as a whole, I begin by attempting to explain interstate differences in subsidized day care. On the one hand, if places in subsidized day care were allocated on the basis of need, we might suppose that states with more children in single parent families (KIDSP2), more jobs for women (EMPPR), more of the population in urban areas (URBAN), and more children from poverty (KIDPOV2) or minority families (KIDMIN2) would subsidize more children. On the other hand, if ability to pay were an important criterion, high income states (INCOME) might be more willing to subsidize children, and states where costs per child are high (as measured by PARFEE) might subsidize fewer children. If decisions about the stringency of regulations were made independently of the subsidy decision then required child/staff rations (REQRAT) and inspections (INSPEC) could affect choices unless these differences are already reflected in the cost measures.

The regressions did a very poor job of explaining the numbers of subsidized children either overall (ALLKIDS2) or in day-care centers (SUBKIDS2) and are not reported in detail here.[18] The *F* tests indicate that there is a very high probability that no linear relationship exists between the independent variables and the measures of subsidized children. The only significant coefficient is the inspection variable (INSPEC) in SUBKIDS2, and there the direction of causation is not clear. The positive sign may simply mean that states which subsidized many children in day-care centers decide to carry out more stringent inspection programs. Overall measures of demand such as the female employment rate (EMPPR) or the proportion of children in single parent families (KIDSP2) do not affect state behavior. Especially noteworthy is the fact that none of the measures of need has any impact on the results. Neither the proportion of children in poor families nor the proportion in minority families (KIDPOV2, KIDMIN2), affects subsidy levels. Decentralizing the allocation of federal dollars does not appear to produce horizontal equity for poor children.[19] Political and bureaucratic forces, not incorporated into the model and uncorrelated with the independent variables, appear to play a major role in determining the level of day-care subsidies.

Therefore, these results indicate that there is no serious simultaneous equation problem in using SUBKIDS2 to help explain the size of the overall day-care sector. It would be inappropriate to use a two-state least-squares procedure here since it would remove the variation in SUBKIDS2 caused by unknown political variables not formally incorporated into the model.

The Organized Day-Care Sector

In the previous section I used economic measures of demand and "need" to predict the political choices of state governments. The at tempt was unsuccessful, implying that a simple economically based model is an inadequate way to study state political choices. In contrast, when I turn to examine the behavior of the market for organized day-care services, I find that the sector appears to be very responsive to the basic determinants of demand. I estimate linear reduced form regressions that use both the proportion of children in day-care centers (DCKIDS2) and various measures of receipts (RCPTS2, PPDR2, DPR2) as dependent variables. All of the regressions produce consistent results. Table 8.2 presents two sets of regressions. In the first set, labelled (1), (3), (5), (7), measures of costs (SALPER, REQRAT, and INSPEC) are included as independent variables. In the second, labelled (2), (4), (6), and (8), because of multicolinearity between costs and prices, the price estimate (PARFEE) is substituted for the cost estimates.

In both the quantity and revenue regressions the female employment rate (EMPPR) and the proportion of children from single parent families (KIDSP2) are highly significant. A 1% increase in the employment rate of women leads to a 2–3% increase in the share of children in day care, and if the number of children under 18 in single parent families increases by

Table 8.2   The Day-Care Industry—1977

	DCKIDS 2		RCPTS2		PPDPR2		DPR2	
	(1)	(2)	(3)	(4)	(5)	(6)	(7)	(8)
Intercept	−34.13	−2.90	−63.89	−31.17	−69.33	−41.83	−73.50	−42.21
	(2.56)[a,b]	(.29)	(3.56)[b]	(2.00)[b]	(3.39)[b]	(2.41)[b]	(3.82)[b]	(2.53)[b]
EMPPR	.97	.76	1.14	.95	1.24	1.07	1.21	1.03
	(3.95)[b]	(3.42)[b]	(3.42)[b]	(2.76)[b]	(3.33)[b]	(2.94)[b]	(3.48)[b]	(2.94)[b]
KIDSPR2	1.00	1.20	1.97	2.38	2.58	2.88	2.29	2.72
	(4.08)[b]	(6.16)[b]	(5.96)[b]	(7.91)[b]	(6.54)[b]	(8.49)[b]	(6.19)[b]	(8.32)[b]
KIND2	−.86	−1.08	−2.58	−2.76	−2.22	−2.45	−2.30	−2.52
	(1.36)	(1.87)[c]	(3.01)[b]	(3.11)[b]	(2.33)[b]	(2.60)[b]	(2.57)[b]	(2.79)[b]
INCOME	−.0017	−.0001	−.0009	−.0002	−.0006	.0004	−.0004	−.0005
	(3.28)[b]	(.20)	(1.28)	(.23)	(.70)	(.46)	(.55)	(.53)
SUBKIDS2	.48	.74	.77	.89	1.23	1.34	.89	.98
	(1.98)	(3.51)[b]	(2.34)[b]	(2.74)[b]	(3.32)[b]	(3.87)[b]	(2.57)[b]	(2.93)[b]
URBAN	−.006	−.028	−.01	.01	−.11	−.12	−.09	−.09
	(.07)	(.38)	(.09)	(.07)	(.85)	(.95)	(.73)	(.69)
SALPER	.013	—	4.18	—	2.10	—	4.02	—
	(.01)	—	(2.00)[b]	—	(.90)	—	(1.84)[c]	—
REQRAT	1.20	—	.85	—	.95	—	.85	—
	(4.53)[b]	—	(2.37)[b]	—	(2.40)[b]	—	(2.27)[b]	—
INSPEC	.23	—	.23	—	−.27	—	−.12	—
	(.36)	—	(.27)	—	(.28)	—	(.13)	—
PARFEE	—	−1.20	—	−.46	—	−.72	—	−.59
	—	(5.68)[b]	—	(1.41)	—	(2.08)[b]	—	(1.79)[c]
R²	.73	.76	.81	.78	.81	.80	.81	.80
d.f.	40	42	40	38	40	38	39	37

[a]t-statistics in parentheses.
[b]Significant at 95% in a two-tailed test.
[c]Significant at 90% in a two-tailed test.

100 the number of children in day-care centers can be expected to increase by 10 to 12.

The measure of subsidized children (SUBKIDS2) also has explanatory power. The coefficient is between one-half and three-quarters. Multiplying both sides by KIDPOP, this means that an increase of between 13 and 30 full-time subsidized children in day-care centers is needed to increase the total number of children in day-care centers by 10. Either some publicly subsidized children would have been in centers without public subsidy or else some unsubsidized children, formerly cared for in centers run by child care professionals, move to the informal sector, when the number of subsidized children increases. Since most subsidized children are cared for in nonprofit centers, this may be an indication that many nonprofit firms behave as "ideological" suppliers. These results are consistent with the revenue regressions, which also show that SUBKIDS2 is significant especially in those regressions which attempt to include subsidy money in the dependent variable.

In equation (1) in Table 8.2 income (INCOME) has a negative impact on quantity (DCKIDS2)—suggesting that, at least at the aggregate state level, the demand for day-care *center* services falls with prosperity, holding job opportunities for women constant. This may, however, be a statistical artifact. INCOME and PARFEE have a correlation of .55, and when PARFEE is included in equation (2), income becomes insignificant. Neither the measure of density (URBAN) nor the measure of the cost of day-care workers (SALPER) is significant in DCKIDS2. The proportion of children in kindergarten is negatively but weakly linked to enrollment in day-care centers. In contrast, in the revenue regressions (3)–(8) the proportion of children in kindergarten has a significant negative impact, and salary per worker is significant in RCPTS2 and DPR2.

Regulatory stringency is measured by the required child/staff ratio (REQRAT), so that high values imply lax regulations. This measure does have a significant impact on the number of places in centers as well as on revenues: the more lax the regulations, the higher the enrollment in centers. The number of inspections *(INSPEC)* is, however, unimportant. Inspections are apparently a poor measure of enforcement activity.

When PARFEE was substituted for the direct measures of costs in equation (2), it proved to be a highly significant determinant of quantity and a weaker determinant of revenues. The price elasticity in the DCKIDS2 regression is -2.1 calculated at the means. In the revenue regressions the implied price elasticity is between -1.4 and -1.6. Thus demand for day-care center services appears to be quite price elastic.[20] Therefore, regulations which increase costs and hence prices can be expected to reduce the size of the sector. The only exception would be regulations which overcome parents' lack of information about the quality of day care. Parents may be willing to accept higher fees in return for regulations of this type.[21]

CONCLUSIONS

I have shown that the fears of those who believe that there is a large unmet demand for day care are unfounded. Although some centers may provide high quality–low cost services, and so be oversubscribed, other kinds of providers appear willing to fill the gap. The size of the industry is responsive to demand conditions as measured by female employment opportunities and children in single parent families. Thus, there seems to be no reason for pessimism about the willingness of private individuals and organizations to set up centers when demand is strong.

Public subsidies have stimulated the growth of the industry although there may have been some displacement of unsubsidized children by subsidized ones. These subsidies, however, appear to be very inequitably distributed. The level of subsidy payments and the proportion of children who are subsidized bear no relation to measures of the incidence of children in poor, minority, or single parent families or to the female employment rate. At least in this case, federalism appears to permit the allocation of national social service funds in an essentially arbitrary way.

However, a showing that the number of places in organized day-care centers is adequate to meet the demand does not imply that public policymakers can simply ignore the supply side of the market and concentrate only on assuring adequate and equitable subsidies. Quality varies widely across centers, and both nonprofits and for-profits have been found to be substandard.[22] Yet stringent quality control regulations will raise prices and reduce supply and push more children into the unregulated informal sector. Strict regulations accompanying public subsidy will limit the reach of the program and may promote segregation by class and race.[23] Clearly the responsiveness to market cues demonstrated here is only part of a broader set of policy concerns.

NOTES

1. This paper was partially supported by the Yale Program on Non-Profit Organizations (PONPO). A more complete version is available as S. Rose-Ackerman, *The Market for Loving-Kindness: Day-Care Centers and the Demand for Child Care* (New Haven, CT: Yale University, PONPO, 1983). Neil Briskman did the computer work and Arnold Sheetz helped locate sources of data and information on the day-care industry. I am grateful to both of them for their excellent assistance, and to Dov Dublin for generously sharing with me his computer data tape from the day-care supply study performed by Abt Associates. Avner Ben-Nur, Paul DiMaggio, and Richard Murnane made helpful comments on earlier drafts.

2. Estimates differ, but from 45 to 60% of day-care firms were nonprofits in 1977. The higher number is from D. Coelen, F. Glantz and D. Galore, *Day Care Centers in the U.S.* (Final Report of the National Day Care Study), vol. III (Cambridge, Mass.: Abt Associates, 1979), which requires that firms have a capacity of 13 or more children in order to be counted. The smaller percentage is from U.S. Department of Commerce, *1977 Census of Service Industries*, Geographic Area Series, Sc 77-A-53 (Washington, D.C.: U.S. Department of Commerce, 1981), Table 1, pp. 53-1-2, 53-1-3, which includes more very small firms in its tabulation.

3. See, for example, Henry Hansmann, "The Role of Non-Profit Enterprise," *Yale Law Journal* 890 (1980), 835–907, which argues that nonprofits will be more trustworthy than for-profit firms.

4. Gilbert Steiner, *The State of Welfare* (Washington, D.C.: The Brookings Institution, 1981), is very pessimistic about the responsiveness of the private sector to increases in demand for day care.

5. A study by the U.S. Department of Commerce, Bureau of the Census, *Money Income and Poverty Status in 1975 of Families and Persons in the United States,* Current Population Reports, P-60 (Washington, D.C.: U.S. Department of Commerce, 1978), showed that 81% of children aged 3 to 13 years old in the United States in 1974–1975 (or about 33 million children) are usually cared for by a parent when they are not in school.

6. According to Coelen, Glantz and Galore, *Day Care Centers in the U.S.*, p. 83, about 900,000 children were enrolled in day-care centers in 1977–1979. On the basis of this estimate, centers cared for less than 2% of children aged 3 to 13. Other research indicates that in 1977 about 15% of the preschool children of working mothers were in group care centers.

See Marjorie Lueck, Ann Orr and Martin O'Connell, *Trends in Child Care Arrangements of Working Mothers*, Current Population Report, no. 117 (Washington, D.C.: U.S. Department of Commerce, Bureau of the Census, June 1982), p. 23.

7. Emma Jackson, "The present system of publicly supported day care," in D. Young and R. Nelson, *Public Policy for Day Care of Young Children* (Lexington, Mass.: Lexington Books/D. C. Heath, 1973), pp. 21–46, argues that "directors of many supplying agencies, both non-profit and proprietary, are service rather than profit oriented. They are in business to see that children receive wholesome care, not especially for the financial returns. Our impression is that such individuals are generally absorbed with trying to provide programs of good quality for their own clientele, but are less interested in growth, or in responding to demands for additional capacity. Their standards remain high, their waiting lists grow, but their inclination to service these unmet demands is weak. While this is reassuring insofar as the treatment of enrolled children is concerned, it points to the need for some mechanism to stimulate supply to be responsive to outstanding demands for day care services." See also M. D. Keyserling, *Windows on Day Care: A Report on the Findings of Members of the National Council of Jewish Women on Day Care Needs and Services in their Communities* (New York: National Council of Jewish Women, 1972), p. 73, who shows that public and private philanthropic centers are much more likely to have waiting lists than proprietary centers.

8. The largest source of direct subsidy in 1977 was Title XX of the Social Security Act (SSA), which provided social service grants to states but gave them considerable leeway in deciding how to spend the money. In fiscal year 1979 the state and federal governments together spent $803 million under this title plus two smaller SSA programs according to U.S. Department of Health and Human Services, Office of Human Development Services, *Social Services U.S.A. FY '79*, No (HDS) 80-02020 (Washington, D.C.: Department of Health and Human Services, 1981). According to Abt, reported in Coelen, Glantz, and Galore, *Day Care Centers in the U.S.*, p. 44, 25% of the children in day-care centers were subsidized by government in 1977, accounting for 29% of center revenue. Federal subsidies for day care fell when Congress passed the Omnibus Budget Reconciliation Act of 1981, amended Title XX to create the Social Services Block Grant, and in the process cut appropriations by 20%.

9. Obviously, quantity and revenue are not independent: they are simply alternative ways of measuring the size of the industry which would be redundant if one were confident of the accuracy of both the quantity and revenue information.

10. This assumption is plausible given the small size of most centers. In the Abt Associates' study, according to Coelen, Glantz and Galore, *Day Care Centers in the U.S.*, p. 44, 30% of all centers had 25 or fewer children, and only about 0.5% has over 100. John E. Kushman, "A Three-Sector Model of Day Care Center Services," *Journal of Human Resources* 14 (Fall 1979), 543–562, makes this assumption about all day-care centers in his study of the industry in North Carolina.

11. The data merge government information with the results of a detailed survey of day-care supply carried out by Abt Associates under contract with the Department of Health, Education and Welfare. I measure the overall size of the day-care center industry in terms of both number of children served and receipts. All of these variables are expressed in relation to the number of children in the state. I have calculated three measures of day-care center receipts in an attempt to take account of the data's inconsistent treatment of government operated centers.

12. Although some evidence suggests that the expansion of subsidized day care would have little impact on the labor force experience of women with preschool children (see Jack Ditmore and W. R. Prosser, *A Study of Day Care's Effect on the Labor Force Participation of Low-Income Mothers*, Working Paper of the Office of Economic Opportunity, Office of Planning Research and Evaluation [Washington, D.C.: Office of Economic Opportunity, 1973]), one ought not to ignore this difficulty entirely.

13. This variable reflects the fact that women are more concentrated in some occupations and industries than others but that there is no reason to think that mothers with preschool children have a special set of skills.

14. Given detailed data on individual families, I would expect a nonlinear relationship between income and the demand for organized day care. Over some range, an increase in income increases demand, but eventually at higher incomes, parents substitute expensive in-home care for organized care. In a study as aggregated as this one, however, such subtleties are unlikely to be important, so I use per capita personal income alone, but make no prediction about the sign.

15. Over two-thirds, according to Coelen, Glantz, and Galore, *Day Care Centers in the U.S.*, Table 119, p. 149.

16. See Jane Roosevelt Gold, *Administration of the FIDCR: A Description and Analysis of the Federal Day Care Regulatory Role.* (Washington, D.C.: U.S. Department of Health, Education and Welfare, National Center for Educational Statistics, 1977).

17. The Abt data provide a measure of the average weekly fee charged to parents in each state (PARFEE). Regressing the three cost increases on PARFEE yields the following result:

$$PARFEE = 29.10 - .54REQRAT + .064INSPEC + .77SALPER,$$
$$(6.91) \qquad (3.10) \qquad\quad (.16) \qquad\quad (.97)$$
$$R^2 = .20$$

t-statistics in parentheses. Only the required child/staff ratio, REQRAT, a measure of regulatory laxness, is significant.

18. The data include children subsidized under Title XX of the Social Security Act, plus two smaller programs also administered by the Social Security Administration.

19. Kushman, "A Three-Sector Model of Day Care Center Services," made a similar estimate for North Carolina counties in 1973 but only for places in government operated centers. He also found that female labor force participation was unimportant. Only cost related measures had any explanatory power. Kushman, however, did not have a separate measure of the incidence of poverty by county.

20. Compare Kushman's study of North Carolina, "A Three-Sector Model of Day Care Center Services." His results are broadly consistent with mine. He has no measure of children in single parent families, but a measure of women in the labor force with children under six (LABOR) is significantly associated with day-care center places. Unfortunately his LABOR variable is more open to the problem of simultaneity noted in the text than my more inclusive measure. The results are also consistent with estimates of demand based on individual household data. Philip Robins and Robert Spiegelman, "An Econometric Model of the Demand for Child Care," *Economic Inquiry* 16 (January 1978), 83–94, found that the use of "market care" was both price elastic and sensitive to the wage rate of the female parent. Demand for formal market care (centers and licensed homes) was especially sensitive to the price charged.

21. See the discussion of this phenomenon in the PONPO Working Papers version of this paper, Rose-Ackerman, *The Market for Loving-Kindness.*

22. See Keyserling, *Windows on Day Care* and Susan Rose-Ackerman, "Unintended Consequences: Regulating the Quality of Subsidized Day Care," *Journal of Policy Analysis and Management* 3 (Fall 1983), 14–30.

23. Rose-Ackerman, "Unintended Consequences," pp. 17–23.

9

Structure and Process in Community Self-Help Organizations

CARL MILOFSKY

There is once again growing interest in community organizations among policymakers and activists after a period of relative skepticism about the usefulness of these organizations for achieving policy goals. One source of the interest is the national trend to use local nonprofit organizations as funding conduits for a variety of social programs. Another is recognition that in a contracting economy, well organized interest groups will be influential in determining how funding cutbacks will be made. Strong and well financed business and professional lobbies have been growing in number. To counteract their influence, consumer advocates and representatives of ethnic groups, of the poor, and of other populist causes have asserted that grass-roots organizing is needed.

Although the need for more community organizations is perceived by some, there is also recognition that the growth of national funding for community centered organizations has brought profound changes to many local groups. Whereas in the past the emphasis was on encouraging participation and activism to impress local politicians and to build community, the complexities of locating funding opportunities and of selling local programs to national funders has led a new profession to emerge, that of the grantsman.

These people are entrepreneurs in the nonprofit realm. Although they have been responsible for channeling new money into local organizations, there is a price for their representation. In a number of instances reported by observers of small, local nonprofit organizations, the demands of national fund-raising motivate entrepreneurial leaders to insist on changes in their organizations to make them more salable.[1] The changes are needed to make organizational programs more easily described, the uniqueness of programs more apparent, the accountability of officers more demonstrable, and the activities of organizations more relevant to national priorities. One might describe the organizational changes which occur as the result of a variety of market signaling.[2]

The work of Mancur Olson[3] suggests that when, as a consequence of these market signaling changes, community organizations become more professionalized and structured to a greater degree around principles of rationality, formal definition of rules, and construction of bureaucratic roles, then the organizations will become more exclusive and hence less participatory and less democratic. This paper summarizes a review of case studies of small organizations and of community studies[4] to explore the organizational processes by which formalization and the resulting decline of democracy occur in local organizations.

Given the hostility which is expressed in the social science literature toward professionals[5] and toward bureaucracies,[6] perhaps it is no surprise that formalization closes out opportunities for community participation. We are encouraged to believe that professionals and bureaucrats alike are concerned with protecting personal privileges and with preserving and expanding their domains of responsibility and their access to and control over resources. Let professionals and bureaucrats into an organization and it is inevitable, we are told, that the community voice will be driven out.

The case studies I have reviewed suggest a more ambivalent view of the interplay between participatory and bureaucratic forms of organization. If entrepreneurs impose formalization on an organization in response to market signaling pressures, it is not their desire for self-aggrandizement per se which leads to organizational change. Rather, fund-raising demands that entrepreneurs make numerous overtures to people outside their local communities who are deluged with grant applications. Formalization, goal definition, and other bureaucratic processes are important to convincing funding agents that one is responsible and that one's organization performs a distinctive function.[7] Making these demonstrations is necessary to help grant administrators make decisions which are to them and their supervisors convincingly rational. Once a social system moves from supporting community organizations locally to supporting them nationally, Eisenstadt[8] suggests, there must be a profound change in the structure and orientation of the local organizations.

In addition to these systematic arguments about why formalization is likely to undercut community participation, there are a variety of reasons embedded in internal organizational processes that community organizations are easily overtaken by bureaucracy. Voluntaristic organizations are hard to establish and to maintain. They demand great energy of leaders and they are vulnerable to moderate changes in their environments. Issue oriented advocacy or service organizations such as those concerned with school integration[9] or with disaster relief,[10] for example, have trouble maintaining themselves during those periods when their special issues are not matters of public concern. Organizations which require volunteers to contribute skilled advice or labor may have problems attracting such help or terminating participation when it is no longer needed. This can make it difficult to shift from one project to another or to carry on several projects at once.[11]

Bureaucracy provides solutions to these and to other operating problems which we shall return to presently. This is partly because bureaucracies rely on paid staffs and are imperialistic. It also is because different elements of a bureaucratic organization balance and support each other, whereas in participatory organizations different elements often are independent.

As Olson[12] argues, formal, exclusive, bureaucratic organizations resolve in one fell swoop a variety of problems endemic to participatory organizations. By claiming a domain or defining a market niche which is shared with relatively few others, formal organizations attempt to gain exclusive access to those resources available to a community or within a market for performing a particular function.[13] Bureaucratic organizations stabilize relations with an environment in which service demands change by accumulating resources during bullish periods or borrowing to build inventories during slow periods or trying to even out environmental demands so that paid staff can work on specialized problems continuously.[14]

Bureaucracies stabilize relations with their environments in part by establishing their power and by becoming corporate actors, being a single voice in interorganizational affairs.[15] Participatory organizations may have trouble regularizing their activities because they cannot discipline members well. They cannot then assure sponsors that they will have a particular fund of experts to draw upon when needed. These limitations make it difficult for them to become recognized as legitimate providers of specialized services.

This is not to say that every complex organization solves those problems which trouble participatory organizations. Nor is it to say that there are no functions that participatory organizations perform better than bureaucracies. Bureaucracies are bad at community building. The literature is full of examples where large organizations sponsor community movements to solve certain kinds of problems. Grass-roots fund-raising, for example, requires extensive informal contacts and well developed exchange relations within a locality. Organizations such as the Red Cross[16] and the March of Dimes[17] rely heavily on volunteers to tap informal social networks for fund-raising. Service organizations such as the YMCA which are based on an ideology of moral improvement also rely heavily on voluntarism both for fund-raising and for program operations.[18] Though all of these are national, bureaucratic organizations they tolerate disorderly, rebellious local volunteer organizations doing things they cannot do as bureaucracies.

The argument of this chapter is that participatory organizations in different arenas face typical organizing problems. By organizing problems I mean difficulties attracting a public following which identifies with the organization and from whose numbers people can be recruited to carry out necessary work or to make donations of resources. These are the ingredients essential for building and keeping up the momentum necessary for a social movement or an organization to persist through time.

Participatory organizations face organizing problems in the following four areas:

1. Definition of goals and smoothing out inconsistencies in the demand for action or for services;
2. Achieving exclusive control over important areas of decision making;
3. Defining organizational boundaries and relevant constituencies;
4. Maintaining autonomy in interorganizational relations so that they are not taken over when they interact with powerful organizations.

The organizing problems which arise in each of these areas contain traps for leaders which can destroy participatory organizations, or at least destroy open public access to them. A variety of adaptations by which leaders solve these problems and by which certain common organizational mechanisms are produced are reported in the literature.

Whereas these characteristic organizing problems threaten participatory organizations, they are solved naturally in bureaucracies. Establishing a domain or a market niche and employing a permanent, specialized staff regularize goal definition and achievement. The principles of ownership and acceptance of legal authority and responsibility for organizational action provide bases for excluding interested parties from specified areas of decision making. They also allow establishment of an internal hierarchy. Hierarchies by their nature are bounded social systems. Even if a hierarchical system includes everyone, the higher levels are exclusive. Together regular productivity, narrowed loci of decision making, and boundary definition allow bureaucratic systems to function as relatively autonomous social systems. This autonomy allows them to interact with other organizations without losing identity.

The organizational mechanisms of bureaucracy are powerful, seductive, and dangerous to participatory organizations because they are interdependent. Taking on some trappings of bureaucracy makes it easy to take on others. This tends not to be true of organizing mechanisms characteristic of participatory organizations. Adaptations their leaders work out to solve organizing problems do not always make it easy to build in other desirable mechanisms. For example, some of those organizations which address intermittently arising issues bridge fallow periods between crises by forming sectlike, ideological cores. Students for a Democratic Society (SDS), though not a local organization, followed this pattern.[19] A core of committed members, however, may make difficult the return to a broad based participatory form when public interest in the organization is increased. There are a host of problems like this described in the case studies literature which are avoided in bureaucracies by their tendency to become integrated social systems.

The danger the emergence of grantsmen poses to participatory organizations is not just that these new professionals are jealous of privilege and dislike public meddling—if this is commonly true at all. Not only do they strive to make community organizations attractive to outside funders, they also make it easier for community leaders to keep their organizations running smoothly. Since organizing a community is hard, frustrating, often threatening work, finding shortcuts through formal organization is attractive. Bureaucracy offers a way to avoid work where voluntarism is absorbing. As economists tell us, when people are given a choice they usually will take easier, less costly ways to solve problems. Thus they choose bureaucracy.

THE STRUCTURE OF COMMUNITY SELF-HELP ORGANIZATIONS

At this point I would like to define the object of this study more sharply. Because this is a discussion of the fate of voluntarism in local community activist groups, I shall introduce a new term—"community self-help organization"—to distinguish them from the more formal, service providing community organizations usually discussed in the social welfare literature.

Community self-help organizations are a part of a class of organizations receiving increasing attention of late because they do not fit comfortably into familiar schemes for analyzing formal organizations and for interpreting bureaucratic phenomena. Although it is hard to study them, there are suggestions—though little evidence—that such organizations are increasing in number. Public dissatisfaction with centralized government, growing emphasis on providing social services at government expense through small nonprofit organizations, and resurgence of interest in "community" among urban ethnics and among a maturing 1960s college generation all have turned attention to mechanisms by which social problems can be solved locally.

Community self-help organizations represent such attempts to solve social problems through local participation, social action, resource mobilization, and building a sense of community and of geographic identification. Some of these organizations take the form of voluntary associations not unlike those described in classic sociological community studies such as Warner's *Yankee City* series,[20] pluralist studies of local politics such as Dahl's *Who Governs?*[21] or Banfield's *Political Influence*,[22] anthropological studies of urbanization in traditional societies as in Mitchell's[23] collection of Rhodesian network studies and Little's[24] study of voluntary associations in other African countries, or contemporary American studies like those of Kornblum,[25] Hunter,[26] and Suttles.[27] Voluntary associations in each of these studies form webs of cross-cutting affiliations which bind communities together and which provide channels to direct and control conflicts among members.[28]

Other community self-help groups are specifically issue oriented. Some have arisen through the Alinsky inspired[29] community organizing movement, from the programs of local community action agencies,[30] and from the recent growth of federal categorical grants programs on which small local organizations may feed. Most of these organizations have as one of their primary goals the building of feelings of mutual responsibility among local residents. This is a theme in crime prevention, community mental health, housing rehabilitation, education, and issue advocacy programs. While the theme of self-help is important to these organizations, they emphasize the primacy of demanding a fair share of the local government pie. They focus on battles over indivisible public resources, and they sponsor actions or events, sometimes conflict oriented, which increase geographic identification and social integration among residents of an area. The strategy of doing so is often explicitly activist or oriented to decentralized and unconventional service provision programs.

Since the decline of the War on Poverty, these attempts at community building through voluntary organizations have been viewed with skepticism by social scientists and policymakers.[31] Urban society is supposed to be dominated by the mass media, by physical and social mobility, and by communities of interest rather than of contiguity. Janowitz[32] talks about urban, cosmopolitan neighborhoods as "communities of limited liability." Residences are simply places from which to venture out to work or to sample the variety of life-styles and commodities available in the city.[33] For wealthier people, neighborhoods work best if they are fortresses, protected by their architecture and by security devices so that residents can ignore the people who live around them, according to critics like Jane Jacobs[34] and Oscar Newman.[35] Cities, we are told, are alienating and anomic.

To counteract this malaise, an emphasis in many self-help organizations, particularly Alinsky oriented ones, is on providing short run payoffs to participation. Funding consensual issues on which to base organization, stimulating sharp conflicts, or promoting activities to encourage participation for its own sake all are strategies for diminishing the community of limited liability. The task is to convince residents to identify with a local area and to overlook their narrow personal interests in order to build feelings of unity and loyalty to the local collectivity. This also is the theme of Janowitz's[36] analysis of the community press.

Recent opposition to big government together with a shift of popular culture in the direction of taking more responsibility for oneself and for personal improvement provide a stimulus to the growth of these self-help groups. Beyond whatever importance this social movement may have for its own sake in the eyes of social scientists, self-help groups are intriguing because though we think of them as systems that are purposively inspired, semipermanent social inventions, many lack the characteristics of formal, rational organizations. Rothschild-Whitt[37] calls them collectivist organizations. They pose a challenge to organizational analysis because there is little theory to guide our studies of them as *organizations*.

By studying them we also learn more about bureaucracies because we can create natural experiments which relax assumptions upon which conventional organizational theory rests. Some community self-help organizations have extremely fuzzy boundaries, for example. This allows us to study the importance of boundaries for the emergence of centralized authority, formalized role definitions, and a routinized division of labor. Other organizations are structurally discontinuous in that their size, focus, and resource support change radically, suddenly, and often. These organizations help us understand better the importance of organizational arrangements which sometimes are described as irrational or as latent functions. In still other organizations we can witness the construction of a formal organizational structure from a previously informal aggregation. We can compare the relative importance of an infusion of resources and the construction of routinized organizational coalitions as contributors to the establishment of a formal organizational structure.

Research on collectivist organizations thus is not just substantive. It also provides a methodological approach to organizational study which has not been systematically exploited. For the natural experiments to be worthwhile, research must be concrete and sensitive to the complex institutional context in which particular forms appear. At the same time there should be an effort to overcome the particularism to which intensive case studies are prone. This is not always amenable to the presentational style of ethnographic research. Thus, to build a theory of collectivist organizations and to explore the implications of case studies for the theory of complex organizations it is important that there be a tradition of secondary analysis and reinterpretation of studies based on comparative readings.

This paper summarizes such an effort.[38] It is primarily based on a literature review I conducted of community studies in which so-called voluntary associations or secondary organizations played important roles. Focusing on the contemporary community organization movement and initiating empirical research on community self-help organizations, my review was eclectic and went well beyond the community study literature. I sought out studies of organizations which, though not specifically community organizations, shared concerns, commitments, and organizing problems with them. The theme of this not very systematic review is an examination of the consequences of relaxing underlying assumptions in the theory of formal organzations.

The review summarized in the following pages begins by offering a series of contrasts between bureaucratic organizations and collectivist organizations. Contrasts are necessarily dimensional, however, which presents certain dangers. For purposes of comparison, we treat as separate variables such things as the formalization of rules, the mechanisms of and centralization of authority, and the clarity of goals. This breaks up and freezes what actually are many-sided, complex organizational processes. The appeal of comparing case studies, as is done in this paper, is that we see them as part of a single fabric and as part of an unfolding process of organization. At the same time, focusing only on process makes it difficult to find points of comparison. To more sharply define what is distinctive about community self-help organizations, we focus on points of comparison that make this type of organization look most different from those we are used to thinking about.

THE AMBIGUITY OF COMPLEX ORGANIZATIONS

Although contrasts between collectivist and bureaucratic organizations help sharpen our definition of the former, they also carry the danger of making bureaucracies seem too static in structure. In the past few years there has been a trend in organizational theory to reject a long-standing emphasis on rationality and on formal organizational arrangements as keys to explaining administrative behavior and as a basis for planning. Those concerned with administration and with social planning have emphasized the essential uncertainty, ambiguity, and unpredictability of organizational behavior.[39] Organizations are to be understood in historical or incremental terms.[40] If the rationality so often attributed to bureaucracy implies knowledge and a systematic approach to problem solving, we are cautioned to recognize how indirectly and unpredictably data and logical thought feed into social problem solving.[41]

Self-help organizations share with professions, people-processing organizations,[42] and governments qualities which make difficult rational planning and attempts to solve social problems through rational planning rather than through incrementalism. All of these types of organizations are process and issue oriented. Often their organizational form is under continual revision. Their leaders do not gain legitimacy and power simply by the legal authority vested in an office. Leadership must be earned through persuasion and influence. Social action and change tend to involve forces like the mobilization of a social movement rather than the routine application of legally defined roles.

Support for the rational-administrative conception of planning may be eroding, now replaced by a more indeterminate view of the world of social action. This paper suggests that the decline of an ideology of national planning does not mean that the organizational mechanisms its promoters described are now invalid or nonexistent. Community self-help organizations are very different from the picture of organizations we receive from traditional administrative science. At the same time, bureaucratization as a social process interacts with the social basis of participation in community organizations.

We may think of the two as at different ends of several continua of institutionalization. Perhaps administrative theorists have exaggerated the frequency with which important organizations are highly institutionalized, and perhaps they have misunderstood the contribution bureaucratization or formalization makes to social problem solving. However, they also have described social mechanisms which by their contrast to collectivist forms help us to understand better the continua of institutionalization upon which both extremes lie. To understand the character of self-help organizations, we need to see how and why they differ from more formal organizations.

CONTRASTS BETWEEN BUREAUCRATIC AND COLLECTIVIST ORGANIZATIONS

Like the collectivist work organizations Rothschild-Whitt[43] describes, community self-help groups often favor open, democratic decision making procedures over centralized decision making. This is true even in situations where the authority of expertise seems uncessary, as described in Taylor's[44] analysis of a free clinic. Although they often have charismatic leaders and thus follow Michels's[45] "iron law of oligarchy," there is little formal, enduring hierarchy.

One reason for this is that participation is often voluntary. Where this is true, organization leaders have at their disposal only weak instruments for convincing other members to follow their suggestions or orders. Whether or not collectivist organizations can achieve goals depends heavily on whether members are committed to some set of ideals which leads them to submit to the authority of the group[46] and on whether members accept the personal authority of the leaders.[47]

This contrasts sharply with bureaucratic organizations in which leadership becomes routinized by the evolution of a stable structure. Bureaucracies produce enduring systems of roles and statuses which make up their division of labor. Their hierarchical arrangements persist independently of whoever it may be that are the incumbents of particular positions. Many collectivist organizations rely on what Weber[48] would call charismatic leadership. These organizations must continually be reinvented, and they regularly face struggles to establish and to maintain their legitimacy to act in and for their communities.

These tend to be issue and process oriented organizations rather than product oriented ones. Such fluidity makes it difficult for them to develop routinized exchange relations with a clientele or with a network or other organizations. These relationships are a cornerstone of the theory of bureaucracy and of structural-functional analysis. They explain how organizations become legitimated,[49] how social functions are allocated to particular organizations within a broader system,[50] and how internal processes are nurtured and maintained by the flow and the transformation of resources.[51] The importance of exchange relations for organizational survival is used to explain a drive to eliminate uncertainty from the organizational environment[52] and, in turn, the inclination of bureaucrats to try to plan rationally and to justify action in universalistic terms. One finds collectivist organizations continuing along insouciantly ignoring the imperative to routinize and rationalize exchange relations.

Formal rationality is not only central to the evolution of structural features in the theory of bureaucratic organizations, it also is central to the creation of an ideology by which workers, managers, and clients are committed to them.[53] Defining products, roles, and the logic of exchange emphasizes the contractual nature of individual relations to organizations and gives primacy to notions that participation is justified by an expectation that participants will in some manner profit in the economic sense.

In collectivist organizations there often is an expectation of zero profit or even of loss. Collectivist organizations tend to value expressive, communal activities which provide diffuse returns to members. This is not to say that one cannot find specifiable benefits in individual participation, since, to the extent it operates, a community of limited liability demands short run payoffs for members. The cosmopolitan, urban residents visualized by limited liability theory strive to satisfy specialized tastes. They avoid becoming too committed to expressive organizations because they wish to keep open their options to go elsewhere to acquire better or more appropriate products and services.[54] Though they may provide calculable benefits to members, collectivist organizations tend to treat these as necessary evils on the way to creation of stronger commitment to the collectivity among residents of a locale.

In the long run, individual benefits are to be derived from participation in a community. The organization itself may have only an indirect relationship to the ultimate payoffs participants receive. It is valuable because it is part of the community, because it promotes community, and because social processes essential to community building and maintenance go on within collectivist organizations. If participation is intended to contribute to the collective good, the ideology of participation may demand that no individual profit more than others. Some people may earn salaries or otherwise gain special benefits, but this circumstance just reflects their greater contributions of time and effort. As Rothschild-Whitt[55] points out, even when they are incorporated as businesses, collectivist organizations often act as though they were legally nonprofit organizations.

Abandoning formalism, failing to routinize relations, and having a strong community orientation tend to weaken and to confuse efforts to draw boundaries. This outcome causes problems in traditional theory because one of its important assumptions is that bureaucracies are bounded social systems. We treat each organization as a separate hierarchy with an autonomous and often centralized decision making process. This perspective allows us to think of them as corporate actors within interorganizational fields or market systems equivalent to individual rational actors, rather than as collectivities.[56] Boundaries also are essential to rationality and to formal structure. These notions assume some consensus among members about what the nature of the organization is, what its structure of deference is, and how members are mutually dependent upon each other.

Many community self-help organizations, though legally incorporated, lack clear boundaries. When studying a group of them, it is difficult to decide which ones to call organizations. This is a quality community organizations share with professions[57] and professional organizations[58] and lobbying and interest groups which cause all of these kinds of structures to frustrate organizational analysis. New mathematical modeling techniques of network analysis have been most useful when applied to these kinds of amorphous organizations.[59] Such bodies are junctures in broader social systems or settings and arenas in which interaction important to such broader systems may take place. In this they are more like what Weber[60] calls status group organizations than like bureaucratic ones. Network studies like Wheeldon's[61] study of voluntary associations in a Rhodesian colored community and Barnes's[62] study of a Norwegian island parish make the lack of boundaries in such organizations clear.

A consequence of this is that within a particular community system, there are many equivalent junction points. Although community organizations may differ substantially, a number of these can be socially equivalent. They may share members and be a focus of various expressive activities which together help to integrate communities. Any of the organizations may be brought into play to address conflicts among a given set of actors. Because of this possibility, they bring stability to a community for reasons Simmel[63] has recognized: they provide overlapping and cross-cutting social ties which make it possible for members of the community to impose a concern for the well-being of the collectivity on disputes between individuals.

If this is true it may be a mistake to take any *particular* community organization very seriously either as a focus of organizational study or as an instrument of social action. Organizations may come and go without seriously affecting the nature of the whole system and without harming the interests of any particular group of citizens. Similarly, it would be a mistake to be too insistent that community organizations not duplicate each others' functions, something which has been a persistent concern of social workers and community planners.[64]

Table 9.1 summarizes these contrasts between collectivist and bureaucratic organizations. It is not hard to find examples of both formal, complex, business organizations and community organizations which violate the propositions set forth here, and thus it should not be taken as a statement of empirical hypotheses. The table describes two ideal types. Across the range of organizational elements, bureaucracies systematically limit and depersonalize social interaction. This makes the organization relatively static and allows us to think of it as predictable and its processes as susceptible to formal analysis. We know that expectations about the predictability, stability, and orderliness of bureaucratic organizations tend to be optimistic. At the same time, the real exclusivity of ownership, the subordination of interaction to expertise, and other factors do simplify and routinize social relations in a bureaucracy.

The opposite is true in collectivist organizations. No doubt leaders of collectivist organizations are just as blind to hidden status rankings and to concerns about financial solvency as they trumpet the importance of community building as bureaucrats are blind to the uncertainties that exist

Table 9.1 Contrasts between Collectivist and Bureaucratic Organizations

Organizational Elements	Collectivist Organizations	Bureaucratic Organizations
1. Outputs	Social Process Is Often a Product in Itself Successful, Community Building Interactions Are as Important as or More Important than Profitability or Efficiency	Efficient or Profitable Generation of Products Justifies Organizational Existence—Alternative Social Means of Production Often Have No Inherent Value Ordering
2. Organizational Ideology	Tend to Be Informal and Ad Hoc in Terms of Substantive Particulars Based More on Commitment to Social Ideals than Requirements of Economic or Productive Necessity Practical Definitions of Organizational Purposes May Easily Be Changed to Fit Political Necessity	Tend to Be Formal and Rational, Emphasizing Impersonality and Universalistic Interdependence of Productive Processes Social Process and Personal Loyalty Subordinated to Process of Transforming Raw Materials into Output and to Creation of Value
3. Interorganizational Linkages	Frequently Reordered in Response to Local Political or Community Demands and Requirements Organizations Part of and Embedded in Larger Social and Organizational Systems	Strive to Make Linkages Routinized and Economic Exchanges Thought of as between Separate Corporate Actors Even When Organizations Are Parts of Larger Conglomerates
4. Returns to Members or Investors	Often Indirect and May Not Be Provided through the Organization Payoffs May Be Received as Broader Community Is Strengthened	Commitment to Evaluating Returns in a Monetary, Measurable Way Formulas for Reimbursement Often Set Forth in Contracts Binding on Officers
5. Exlusivity a. Boundaries	Boundaries Often Permeable to the Point of Disappearance Origins of Particular Social Events or Actions Often Must Be Sought in a Larger Social or Cultural System	Because They Are Defined, Boundaries Generally Sharply Drawn Organizations Form Autonomous Social Systems and Organizational Cultures
b. Hierarchy	Because They Are Democratic Organizations, Leaders May Have Trouble Limiting Legitimate Access to Decision Making	Tend to Have Centralized Decision Making Derived from Principles of Ownership or the Primacy of Expert Authority

within their administrations. At the same time, valuing social process for its own sake, being committed to the health and well-being of a collectivity which transcends organizational boundaries, and being opposed to privilege and status rankings mean that leaders of community organizations live in a complicated, energy draining, and ever changing world.

If they are living in a closed community or if their organizations have certain convenient qualities such as a technical base which provides a structure to social relations, then the communal form may provide efficiencies not available to bureaucracies. These will tend to be specific to organizations and to situations, however. For them as a class what will tend to be true is that the social complexity which they encourage requires that leaders be charismatic and inventors of social mechanisms which work locally. The exclusivity of bureaucracies creates a pressure for interactional simplification which makes these organizations as a class similar to each other. Collectivist organizations, in contrast, contain a pressure to be idiosyncratic and different from each other.

ORGANIZING PROBLEMS AMONG COLLECTIVIST ORGANIZATIONS

The contrasts between collectivist organizations and bureaucracies highlight what will demand attention in a study of community self-help organizations. One reason organizational theory has progressed as a subfield of sociology is that the stable and regular character of bureaucracies makes them easy to study, to compare, and to isolate from complexities of the broader society. These efficiencies for research are lost when organizations lack identifiable boundaries, when their leadership and decision making arrangements change often, and when the products of activities cannot be easily measured and may not be related to any immediate activities.

This is not to say that there are no important regularities in the organization of community self-help groups. However, the patterns are related to a logic of voluntarism and to processual aspects of organization, and they require a longitudinal view. The conception of social structure adopted in most studies of bureaucracy suggests no reason a snapshot of organizational life should distort description. Structure is stable and related to objective characteristics such as the size of an organization, the extent of its division of labor, the flatness of its authority structure,[65] and the composition of its technology.[66] These all are slow to change and are thought to have specific kinds of effects. Regardless of institutional or historical context, one may hypothesize that large organizations, for example, will be more impersonal and will tend to be more rational and rule governed than are small organizations. The size of a particular organization may change because of unforeseen events, but at any point in time, a constellation of a few organizational characteristics like this one, we are encouraged to believe, can explain a great deal about the behavior of an organization.

Organizational patterns in collectivist organizations tend to change cyclically. Thus, regularities of community self-help groups observed at any point in time may represent only part of a broader organizational pattern. Since unforeseen events are likely to intrude and to upset an orderly progression of cycles, claims that any particular organization is in a given phase do not presuppose that later on some other predictable state will be achieved. Typically, as organizations move from one phase of development to another there is an internal struggle. Members become alienated and there is some risk to the continuation of the organization.

When we speak of organizations being at one or another phase of a typical cycle, this refers to aggregate tendencies for organizational change. When they are applied to a particular organization, it is most useful to use cyclical hypotheses as a way of predicting how and when a present arrangement is likely to become unstable. They point to the kinds of problems leaders may have motivating member participation and either maintaining the organization in a particular form or moving it to a new state.

Much of the writing about collectivist organizational structure focuses on the problems leaders have organizing their members or keeping control as organizations change. To understand what the regularities of collectivist organizations might be, it is useful to begin by talking about common organizing problems reported in the literature and then following with a discussion of what cycles are suggested.

Four factors define the major organization problems of organization.

1. The first is the character of the communities in which organizations are located. The more self-contained a community is, such as ethnic or geographically isolated communities, the more likely it is that community organizations will have permeable boundaries and will act more as part of a broader social system than as a sharply defined organization. This means that leaders will find their organizations often shifting goals and activities to meet broader community purposes and that the salience of the organization to the community as a whole will often change.

2. A second factor is the inclusiveness of the membership. This refers to whether an organization has jurisdiction over an entire community, or an ascribed group within one, or whether it serves a narrower interest group or leadership faction. In general, the more inclusive an organization, the less successful it will be at defining and achieving goals or at winning conflicts with other organizations. Leaders are likely to be concerned about how ineffectual their organizations seem when sharp social action is called for.

3. Third, organizations may vary in terms of whether continuous or intermittent actions typify the projects, programs, or struggle an organization undertakes. Organizations that specialize in intermittent activities must develop organizational mechanisms to bridge periods of inactivity if they are to remain viable. Finding these mechanisms and successfully changing the organization so that it can address its primary problem after a period of inactivity are recurring problems.

4. Finally, organizations vary in terms of the character of their relations to other organizations. The fluid structure of many community organizations makes it difficult for them to carry out routine administrative maintenance functions. To do so, they may ally with bureaucratic or corporate organizations which provide an administrative framework. Doing so, however, can interfere with efforts by collectivist organizations to encourage participation among members because of demands more formal organizations make for accountability and for regularity in decision making.

These four factors are interrelated because each concerns a different aspect of voluntarism. All involve the way a necessary measure of commitment is achieved in organizations which have little power to coerce or to reward members. Let us consider each in detail.

COMMUNITY STRUCTURE AND ORGANIZATIONAL PROCESS

Many of the community studies which discuss community self-help organizations implicitly distinguish between closed and open communities. Closed communities are those which are sharply bounded by members limited economic opportunities, by racial or ethnic prejudice, by a shared history or culture among members, or by geography. The nature of the boundary is not particularly important, nor need boundaries be impermeable. What is essential and what characterizes the type is that people share many different kinds of relationships with a relatively small group of coparticipants. There exist many cross-cutting affiliations, many redundant ties, and a variety of social hierarchies within the population. This gives the community as a whole qualities like those that experimental social psychologists have described for small groups.[67] The communities are so highly structured that individual actions tend to have ramifications throughout the system. It is for this reason that community organizations are not to be analyzed as autonomous organizations. They are settings for interaction within a larger system.

Open communities are in some respects a residual category including everything which is not a closed community. There are, however, a number of analysts who, like Janowitz, make the distinction more sharply. Open communities are ones in which individuals are cosmopolitan.[68] Any individual is likely to have established a large number of relationships with a unique set of partners so that the networks of neighbors are unlikely to overlap. Each individual builds relationships, makes commitments, and gathers information about opportunities in response to idiosyncratic tastes, skills, and career history. People will forge some overlapping local ties as a result of neighboring or child care experiences. But otherwise, they will construct local relationships in such a way that they have minimal commitment to others in the community. This is because the energy involved in building relationships is a finite resource. Local relationships are to be avoided if they demand aimless participation in meetings or collective activities. They are not likely to provide proper returns for the amount of energy invested in them. To use Janowitz's[69] terms, people in open communities set up relationships so that they have few liabilities and can easily break free. The advantages individuals gain from making many idiosyncratic relationships with limited liability are described by Granovetter[70] as "the strength of weak ties" and by Wirth[71] as "urbanism."

Whether one views open communities as communities of limited liability based on weak tie networks or simply as a residual category, the tendency is for community self-help organizations in them to be bounded and autonomous organizations. There are exceptions according to Janowitz and as his view is reflected in the work of Hunter.[72] An important function of small, locality based nonprofit organizations is to enhance a sense of local identification among the populace and to build a network of interconnected local organizations which together promote civic pride. Depending on the success of these efforts and on the nature of the local population, the organization of open communities will vary along a continuum of interconnectedness. Some will be independent, probably seeming to serve the interests of the business community openly. In others these initially self-centered efforts will take off, creating a stronger community.

However successful these community building efforts may be it is unlikely that they will produce a closed community. The essence of a closed community is that members rarely seek help or opportunities outside their locality. They depend upon each other for mutual support, protection, and help in solving different major problems of living. People help each other to find and obtain jobs. People share family and kinship relations. People share religious beliefs and symbolic rituals that are products of shared ethnicity or a common outlook on the nature of society and on their status within it. Because they depend on each other to solve all kinds of problems of living, preservation of the community as a whole becomes more important to individuals than nearly any particular relationship with other members of the community. Kornblum[73] describes this sort of interdependence in a working class steel community where the union, the factory, ethnic groups, and the political structure are closely interlocked and together provide local residents with most of their social and economic opportunities. Wheeldon[74] describes a similar sort of interdependence in a Rhodesian coloured community whose members, having racially mixed parentage, feel superior to Blacks but are not accepted by Whites. Opportunities in both cases are limited, and they are allocated by the community.

The combination of limited opportunity and the difficulty for most people of finding opportunities outside the community as good as those available to them as members of the collectivity make it important to all that the integrity of the social system be maintained. When conflicts erupt between members or factions within such communities or when one individual gains rewards at the expense of another, there exist mechanisms within the community to limit and control the conflict. These controls are lacking in open communities because members are likely to move or to exit[75] rather than submit to discipline, control, and deprivation at the hands of others in the locality.

For closed communities to exist and to prosper it is essential that they solve the problem of how to maintain a social order. This is less of a problem in open communities, where the main community problems are direct and require little in the way of social cohesion to be worked out. They may involve issues of personal safety[76] or child care and socialization.[77] Although both of these are natural by-products of a tightly integrated community, they also can be purchased and obtained even if one chooses to ignore one's neighbors.[78] In an open community the emphasis among residents is on cultivating esoteric tastes and on remaining free to build loose ties and to pursue entrepreneurship outside the local community.

Closed communities do not allow these so readily. There consequently is a limited pool of opportunities and of resources to be distributed among locals. Inevitably this means that decisions will be made about career advancement, local leadership, or resource distribution which favor some members over others. For closed communities to persist it is necessary that members be prevented from looking outside community boundaries for opportunities, or, when there are losers, that they not form splinter communities. Although both happen, the organizational structure of closed communities works to prevent it through a host of indirect social mechanisms, many of which operate in and through community organizations.

It is because community organizations buffer, control, and direct conflict to preserve social order that there often is such a strong emphasis in them on participation and process rather than on products. In Wheeldon's Rhodesian example several mechanisms are described. Because people think of community groups as organizations with their own leadership and their own purposes, however much a part they are of the larger interaction patterns of a community, they provide a means for ambitious people in the same age cohort to demonstrate their competence, to create a following, and to compete with other leaders on issues of much reduced importance and intensity than those which might split the community. In Wheeldon's description, these organizations allow the community to rehearse for later situations when hard and potentially explosive choices must be made. The organizations also bind combatants and force them to interact or to compete on issues which do not justify open hostility or deep disagreement. Being limited and focused on simple, practical matters, leaders who might conflict find themselves cooperating and learn how to do so. The organizations also provide contacts and pathways by which people in competing factions who oppose conflicts may collaborate and block an escalation of hostilities.

A corollary of the proposition that community organizations are instruments of social control and of preservation of order is that when they attempt to achieve goals, they are likely to do so in a roundabout way. To achieve goals, people with talent, knowledge, and local followings must be convinced to invest time and energy in a particular project.[79] To get potential volunteers motivated, leaders may play on the ambitions of community members and draw upon simmering competition between factions.

Seeley et al.,[80] for example, explain that the Red Cross in Indianapolis was a vital fund-raising organization in large part because several local influential people had each taken on the chairmanship of important fund-raising committees. Their personal competition for leadership in the community elite system caused intense competition each year between the different committees to see which could raise the most money. This contrasted with the community leadership of the Community Chest, which primarily recruited business leaders. Seeley reports that these people tend to be transferred often and view their fund-raising activities in terms of their corporate careers. These leaders are inclined to look for a way of producing a quick success to advance their careers. A consequence was that the Community Chest had a record of failing on elaborate, highly publicized campaigns, whereas the Red Cross had a record of consistent fund-raising success.

One consequence of a strategy which plays on the ambitions of local leaders is that the work people invest in completing a project many have more to do with scoring points over the opposition or with advancing careers than with the practical requirements of attaining a given end. In Wheeldon's[81] case study, this problem was managed as a local organization, attempting to build a gymnasium and athletic field, slowly rotated leadership and volunteer help as new phases of the project unfolded. In the early fund-raising stages, leaders who wanted to strengthen their ties to leaders in the outside White community were recruited. Once funding was lined up, younger leaders who were competing to be community spokesmen took over to coordinate planning and development. Once the facility was built, still younger leaders who were in the process of building a personal following were recruited. There was a need for large numbers of volunteers to contribute time, and these leaders found contacting many people a convenient way of getting to know the community and developing new relationships.

One of the things which separates collectivist organizations from bureaucracies is that in the former effectiveness may depend on maintaining the sort of fluidity in structure and purpose which Wheeldon describes. In bureaucracies, there is an emphasis on establishing fixed roles and on developing or recruiting experts who can perform a specialized function for a long time as staff members.

In collectivist organizations where volunteers become local experts on some problem they may come to treat the organization as a personal domain. It is difficult to unseat or to control such people once they become entrenched, because the organization is not likely to have a clear standard such as profitability to use for evaluating their performance. These established leaders may block recruitment of new talent, and the organization can become locked into a particular approach to a narrow problem. Indeed, perhaps one reason there are many organizations and so many seem moribund is that they have been captured in this way and are prevented from turning out old, ineffective leaders. One might draw this conclusion from Dennis Young's research[82] on entrepreneurship in small nonprofits since again and again his case studies report entrepreneurs changing organizations which had ossified around an outmoded purpose under the guiding hand of a long-standing volunteer board.

INCLUSIVE AND EXCLUSIVE ORGANIZATIONS

Whether communities are open or closed, organizations may be divided into those which are participatory democracies and those which are to some extent exclusive in their acceptance of members and in allowance of access to decision making processes. The former are participatory democracies in the sense that a plurality of the membership may at any time influence the outcome of organizational decision making. Although there are likely to be formal positions of leadership and authority in such organizations, officeholders direct decision making only to the extent that there is acquiescence among members of the constituency or to the extent that they are influential with the members.

Some organizations are participatory democracies because of values shared by the membership favoring collective decision making, as in Rothschild-Whitt's[83] worker collectives or Taylor's[84] free clinic. More commonly democracy is imposed or maintained by the character of organizations' constituencies. This is most true of organizations which include as members all individuals who share an ascribed characteristic *whether or not they choose to attend meetings*. These are inclusive organizations. Examples are local civic organizations, ethnic clubs, and organizations such as the PTA which encourage participation by all clients or participants in major institutions.

In such organizations, that leaders claim to represent members a majority of whom probably never attend meetings makes their legitimacy easy to attack. They face essentially the same problems of leadership which Banfield[85] describes for political leaders. Despite the leaders' formal authority, there are many people who could block or veto decisions if they wanted to. Leaders can make some decisions because members of inclusive organizations are usually inactive. With issues on which blocs of constituents are likely to disagree, it may be safer for leaders to avoid taking strong positions. If they were to do so, previously inactive groups might be stimulated to oppose not only the decision outcome but also the representativeness of the leadership. Such challenges can carry extra weight because it is not known whether other hidden or unformed interest groups which share opposition exist in the population.

Allowing decisions to be openly debated helps bring opposition groups into the open. Once this happens it is easier for decisions to be made without the legitimacy of the organization or its leadership as representatives of the community being challenged. As Banfield[86] describes the actions of politicians, leaders may simply block any resolution of an issue until opposing factions have formed coalitions and a consensus is achieved within the constituency. It may also happen that once potential opposition groups have been drawn into the open, leaders will find it easier to calculate whether they can convincingly win a floor fight and whether they can afford to take the lead on an issue. Finally, in a closed community or one

in which actors are in the habit of interacting frequently around a particular issue, bringing potential conflict into the open makes it easier for indirect sources of influence to be located and mobilized.[87] If conflicts have
become public policy, they can be resolved by bringing pressure from the
collective on individual combatants.

A major side effect of these imperatives for democratic decision making
in inclusive organizations is that it is difficult for these organizations to
initiate innovative or conflict oriented actions or those which will serve
only a small part of the constituency. This is not just because leadership
may not wish to alienate supporters. It also is because innovation and
activism may require speed in decision making, disciplined acceptance among
the membership for initiatives begun by leaders, and elaborate delegation
of authority. All of these are possible in inclusive organizations. This is
particularly true if there are covert factions at work, as Selznick points out
in *The Organizational Weapon*,[88] an analysis of the Bolshevist strategy for
capturing mass democratic organizations. These associations more often
act on consensual and expressive issues.

Thus, one of the concerns the national leadership of the PTA has expressed recently,[89] now that consumerism is on the upswing, is that local
chapters are not often aggressive toward and critical of local school systems. Further, when they engage in conflict PTAs seem always to be de-
feated by special interest groups such as the parents of disabled children
or civil rights advocates, the PTA leaders complain. Their inclusiveness
makes them ineffective groups.

Exclusive organizations, in contrast, have available a tremendous number of options in making decisions, delegating authority, and competing
with other organizations, as Olson[90] argues. Indeed, organizational theory
for the most part is the theory of these organizations and these options.
Describing the types of exclusivity is thus itself a complex topic which is
beyond the scope of this paper. Suffice it to say that one of the reasons it
is important to assume that organizations are sharply bounded in most
organizational analysis is that boundaries allow exclusiveness. Although
inclusive organizations may serve sharply defined populations, not knowing who might become active on a particular issue and what kinds of opposition to prepare for means that inclusive organizations cannot draw
boundaries *within* this population. Lacking boundaries it becomes difficult
to establish formal structure and to create the sorts of specialized organizations which occur when membership is exclusive.

CONTINUOUS VERSUS ISSUE-ORIENTED ORGANIZATIONS

When the distinction between closed and open communities was made, I
mentioned that organizations may become ineffective if a group of volunteers comes to consider a community self-help organization their personal
domain. This is most seriously a problem, however, in organizations which

respond to crises or issues which infrequently or intermittently inflame public interest. Organizations such as volunteer fire departments[91] or those with yearly fund-raising efforts such as the Red Cross[92] appear to be more effective if there is little turnover in membership. Members then become experienced at handling a characteristic sort of problem so that they can respond flexibly to new kinds of problems—members of volunteer fire departments are effective helpers during weather disasters. Demanding regular donations of time, members of these organizations work out integration arrangements which commit people to respond to demands of the organization when they face role conflicts. These may be conflicts between organizational responsibilities and family concerns during an emergency.[93]

Organizations which intermittently become a community representative on matters of civic concern or which are called to solve infrequently occurring problems may have difficulties responding. Although such groups may receive great public support during their periods of intense activity, public interest is low during periods of inactivity so it is difficult to motivate volunteer participation. To survive and reactivate themselves these organizations must find ways to bridge periods of inactivity.

Two ways commonly found among community self-help organizations are the adoption of a secondary purpose, which makes regular demands for work and participation on members, and the emergence of an ideological core or sect.

The problem with creating secondary purposes is that the people recruited to volunteer are likely to be most talented at and interested in the secondary projects. As they take over the decision making apparatus and fill membership roles, the supposed primary purpose may decline in importance until the bridging activity becomes the main business of the organization. This was true of the Red Cross in Form and Nosow's[94] account of a tornado disaster. The Red Cross was founded as a disaster relief organization and raised funds for this purpose. Because disasters are infrequent, however, the Red Cross in the town hit by the storm had become a specialized fund-raising organization. Its leadership was made up primarily of local businessmen and community influentials who used the fundraising drives as opportunities to demonstrate community leadership. These people were not prepared to respond when the disaster occurred and the Red Cross was ineffective at responding to community needs. In Barton's[95] terms, the leaders of the Red Cross were incompetent to carry out the mandate of their organization.

Organizations which act as community opinion leaders and mobilizers of local action during periods of high citizen concern over civic, political, and moral issues seem more likely to bridge periods of activity by forming an ideologically committed cadre. The members evolve an elaborate theory of the organization's mission and work to establish a high level of consensus among active members. The Salvation Army and other religious sects do this by absorbing people's entire lives into the church, requiring frequent and regular attendance at services and donations of personal resources and labor to institution building and missionary work.[96] Though with such extreme religious commitment sect members are likely to be rejected by the rest of the community, making leadership during crises unlikely because of their stigmatization, a similar problem of overcoming the prescriptions of an orthodox church is faced by members of less extreme faiths. Campbell and Pettigrew,[97] following a distinction made by Troeltsch,[98] note that ministers in church centered or episcopal religions had more difficulty maintaining their moral leadership during the civil rights crises in Little Rock than did their counterparts in presbyterian or community centered churches. Having a centralized, less flexible doctrine which favored human rights made leadership difficult to maintain in an anti-civil rights community.

A similar level of commitment is achieved in explicitly political organizations in which members meet together often to discuss ideology and to engage in commitment building projects. Although not concerned with a community self-help organization, Sales'[99] description of the Students for a Democratic Society (SDS) fits this mold. What he describes for SDS leaders between periods of campus political upheaval seems to apply as well to some community organizers in the Alinsky tradition. Committed to a particular analysis of the source of social injustice and social problems and being part of a national movement, well-educated and skilled individuals decide to donate time and resources to a cause for virtually no salary. Being martyrs for a cause, these workers invest great energy in organizing projects whose products seem insignificant in comparison to the investment of energy they require and the personal risks they entail for members. What might be called the economic irrationality of their efforts can make possible remarkable achievements of community building and representation as in Alinsky's Back of the Yards Council or The Woodlawn Organization (TWO).

The costs of centering an organization on a leadership sect may be high because when there is a resurgence of popular interest organizational ideology may not meet public approval. In SDS, for example, each time widespread student concern about the Vietnam War was reignited, the membership greatly expanded. The old leadership was swept aside as new, charismatic opinion leaders emerged and took over from those who had preserved the organization through the fallow period.

An alternative outcome is that the sectlike leadership may not be superseded by new charismatic leaders. Rather than allowing new chapters of the organization to be formed and new members accepted, old leaders may close membership, leading a number of similar splinter groups to form. It may also happen that over an extended period, no new issues arise to inflame public interest. Here the sects may become more and more ingrown and exclusive. Where this happens with political groups a result may be that the organizations become more and more radical and perhaps violent, as happened with the Weathermen.

In more structured organizations which perform intermittent functions, a permanent leadership often emerges which creates elaborate means for recruiting and controlling participants during periods of activity. This is most evident in national organizations which stimulate local fund-raising, institutional development, and volunteer service provision. In these organizations, there is usually a professional national office staff which is permanent and highly bureaucratized and a variety of local boards of community influentials. The influentials are called to service infrequently to solve some newly arising organizational problem. Nonetheless, being responsible for substantial resource mobilization these local leaders tend to demand some control over how funds are spent.

The March of Dimes[100] controlled these demands by creating two parallel organizations. The national fund-raising organization was highly professionalized. It recruited a large local fund-raising staff, but the volunteers it used here were assigned tasks that were narrowly defined, were of short duration, and allowed little contact with other workers. They would have little opportunity to organize and to demand control over funding distribution. A board of community influentials would also be recruited on a semipermanent basis to promote the fund drive. They might be given control over a small amount of the money collected locally, but since they were not directly involved in fund-raising, they were discouraged from making demands. The YMCA uses an even more elaborate system of control to prevent its local branch governors' boards from controlling policy.[101]

Though leaders of these national organizations continue to speak about the importance of voluntarism in their activities, the solutions they have worked out to the organizing problems caused by having intermittent projects are bureaucratic. They use many of the devices bureaucratic businesses use to smooth over irregularities in the supply of raw materials or in demand for products. They contract for labor, try to control the flow of raw materials, and build up a backlog of activities or products to carry them through slow periods. All of these are difficult to arrange in voluntaristic organizations where leadership is impermanent, decision making processes are open, and there are no means for accumulating excess profits.

INTERORGANIZATIONAL LINKAGES

If one identifies a set of self-help groups within a community one is likely to have problems deciding which to count as organizations. Some organizations, though incorporated, that have staff and some protected resources, still appear to be administrative fictions. They are created by more established organizations to serve some legal or symbolic purpose which could not be achieved within the legal structure of a corporate, bureaucratic organization. Others, although having a definite constituency of local citizens who can be brought out for meetings or who are concerned about some issue, are difficult to distinguish from a political "coffee" as an organizational form. They do not meet regularly, they have little in the way of standing resources, and they have no agreements about how to make decisions or take actions. To the extent such organizations come to our attention, it usually is the case that some more formally constituted organization provides material and technical support to facilitate meetings.

Although entities like these stand on the margins of what we would call organizations, their insubstantiality is shared with other community self-help groups which depend upon other organizations for continued survival. One way of thinking of such interorganizational relationships is that the self-help groups are institutionally incomplete.[102] They not only lack qualities which are essential for independent survival but also ones which would make them believable as organizations. Sociologists such as Parsons,[103] Mayhew,[104] Collins,[105] and Laumann and Pappi[106] talk about this as the extent to which social systems have and maintain *structure*. Lacking in some elements of structure, organizations fail to become institutionalized, to follow Broom and Selznick's[107] usage. Such organizations may borrow structure from more formalized organizations to survive.

It is well beyond the scope of this chapter to enter the debate about whether categorizing schemes like Parsons's AGIL are either helpful or accurate in describing organizations. The idea that organizations may be institutionally incomplete, however, emphasizes that the interorganizational relationships community self-help organizations have influence the form of their administrative arrangements in important ways. In contrast to bureaucracies which may be units of a conglomerate but nonetheless independent, self-help organizations may seem more like departments of larger organizations than like units which are largely autonomous. Depending on the nature of their relationships to others, we may question not only whether we are looking at examples of the category "organization" but also whether the entities we have noted are independent from more formal organizations and thus whether they are based on participation enough to be considered self-help groups.

Some community self-help organizations are begun to serve explicit purposes of other formal organizations. Organizations which we might initially count as community self-help organizations were never intended to do more than serve these special interests. One can imagine that some self-help organizations are established to take advantage of their nonprofit status.[108] One can also imagine that such organizations might be set up to carry on business "off the books" of sponsoring organizations in various ways.

There also, however, are a group of organizations established by the need or desire of business or nonprofit organizations to stimulate community integration, participation, and mutual support. Janowitz's[109] analysis of the community press and of the need among small local businessmen and leaders of local institutions to stimulate a sense of geographic identification and community concern among residents is a case in point. For the self-interested support of these individuals to be believable to the public it is important that it not appear economic. Hence, though community newspapers survive on advertising support and often are given away free, they are likely to contain a large amount of local news and to promote local civic issues. There are a variety of other local civic betterment institutions and social clubs such as the Rotary, Kiwanis, and businessmen's associations which can be similarly analyzed.

A variation on this theme that some community self-help efforts are products of the self-interest of corporate organizations is the professed commitment certain national social service organizations have to providing opportunities for participation through their local chapters. The commitment to encouraging voluntary action to help others is deeply embedded in the Christian heritage of organizations such as the YMCA.[110] However, participation by local community activists and leaders also has become an essential part of the fund-raising efforts of these organizations.

Although it is easy to see the self-interest in building up a local constituency which will tap friendship networks to raise money not available to more bureaucratized fund-raising efforts such as the United Way, the participation these national organizations stimulate has community building effects. This is especially evident in the YMCA, where local talent is recruited not only to help pay for facilities in the neighborhood but also to provide leadership to youth clubs. A persisting problem for the YMCA is how to control local programming once community influentials have raised the money to pay for a branch, have stimulated enough public interest to build the membership of users, and then have been installed on the local board of directors. This makes it difficult for the national or regional organization to pursue social equity goals which work against the self-interest of wealthy communities.[111]

Another example of external efforts to build community participation which can be construed as self-interested is represented by organizations which promote an ideology of community organization or which attempt to stimulate local movements on particular locally relevant issues. The Community Action Program was the largest effort to promote community organizing for its own sake. It gave way to a widespread mandate that publicly funded institutions provide for public involvement in decision making,[112] which is a much narrower and institution centered goal than that which initially informed community action.[113] There remain a number of organizations and foundations, however, which continue to support community organizing.[114]

An important contemporary movement is the development of intermediate organizations which act as clearinghouses, technical assistance services, and administrative conduits for emergent community movements concerned with specialized issues. There exist, for example, national organizations which support local community arts centers, gang delinquency counseling efforts, self-help groups for the disabled, and housing rehabilitation organizations.

With some of these organizations, local chapters are essentially franchises of a national chain much as are branches of the YMCA. Although these organizations are not-for-profit, extralocal organizations can use locally generated money to support the national organization. The influence of national organizations with large foundations or the federal government is increased if there is a large network of local programs which fit a single model. This is especially true in fields such as housing rehabilitation where there are great technical problems in designing projects and raising funds. Specialized local nonprofits may develop a monopoly on relevant network ties and on expertise and essentially gain a license from an interested area government to be the local provider of the service in question. An appearance of community responsiveness may be important for such organizations but their service monopoly is likely to guarantee continued legitimacy and local support even if there is only token community input.

At the same time, these technical support organizations are playing an increasingly important role in providing an administrative structure to informal community movements which would otherwise fade away. The availability of categorical grant programs at the state and federal levels has increasingly required that small organizations employ professional fund raisers to survive. This is partly because with an increase in public sponsorship, there seems to be a decline in public willingness to contribute money to private, local self-help efforts. It also is because the funding environment has become so complex for both those seeking money and those giving it away that something like a market-signaling system which governs how locals should contact regional or national funding sources and how proposals should be prepared has emerged.[115]

The growth of this sort of funding militates against the amateur leadership which is the essence of community self-help. Not only are amateurs unlikely to know the lay of the land in the funding world, the entrepreneurship required of leaders in order to compete for funds seems to demand that community organizations become more like bureaucracies. In a series of case studies of entrepreneurship collected by Dennis Young,[116] it was often the case that decision making became centralized, goals were redefined to fit more closely with national policy interests, and mechanisms of fiscal and administrative accountability were introduced so that funders who would not know participants in an organization could be assured that their money would be well spent.

Some of this pressure to bureaucratize can be reduced by organizations which provide technical assistance to community movements. Some organizations lend out staff people who provide meeting space, arrange agendas, perform secretarial work, help prepare proposals, and make contacts with representatives of funding agencies. The question remains whether such intermediaries do not also force community movements to become more formalized than they might have been in earlier times when local fundings was more available. At present, however, these technical assistance organizations are an important vehicle for keeping community organizing movements alive without robbing indigenous leadership of decision making authority.

The examples I have given are not intended as a complete catalog of interorganizational arrangements one finds among community self-help organizations. Rather, they are chosen to illustrate the way in which alliances with more structured organizations may be used as a vehicle for carrying out necessary organizational maintenance functions. Community self-help organizations which begin as social movements can be thought of as institutionally incomplete social systems. This makes it difficult for them to mobilize resources, guarantee accountability, and carry out administrative housekeeping chores which make it easier and more attractive for members to continue participating in organizational affairs.

The examples also emphasize that there often is an uncomfortable union between self-help organizations with a participatory orientation and their organizational partners which are more structured. Raising money from nonlocal sources and working out regular patterns of interaction tend to require that organizations take on some of the trappings of rational administration. Being too closely associated with formal organizations or too concerned about obtaining and keeping grant money can threaten the democratic, participatory base of self-help organizations. What may seem to organization leaders as simple, lucrative choices to make it easier to keep a self-help organization together can shortly turn what was a self-help organization into a professionalized service organization.

At the same time, it is important to note that participation does not automatically wither in the face of money and formal administration. Large bureaucracies sometimes go out of their way to create and nurture participatory community organizations because they do things which cannot be done by formal organizations. Here the problem may be viewed as that of the particpatory elements getting out of control.

When self-help organizations mate with formal organizations there may be a genuine exchange between units with different special capacities. This exchange may not be stable or endlessly productive, however. It is likely to be a source of continuing tensions for both the more and the less formalized partners. It may also end as the self-help organizations tip either in the direction of being more formal, and then perhaps more autonomous, or in the direction of having more local control, again becoming critical of their formal organizational sponsors.

THE DANGERS OF BUREAUCRACY TO COLLECTIVIST ORGANIZATIONS

Bureaucracies have played an important role in this paper. The contrast I drew between collectivist and bureaucratic organizations in the early pages suggests that these two kinds of organization are qualitatively different, or that they are on opposite ends of a continuum of organization forms. Bureaucracy was also important in the part of the paper where I discussed a number of common organizing problems leaders of community self-help organizations face. Bureaucratic features can be viewed as solutions to these organizing problems.

The efficiencies of bureaucratic forms of organization are important to recognize because those committed to community organization often speak of actions by leaders to make their organizations more formal as though a moral flaw were being expressed. Bureaucrats may be insensitive to clients or to outsiders, and large organizations may be more committed to expanding and maintaining themselves than in serving the public, as some organizers claim. However, given the difficulty of keeping small community organizations alive, it is likely that many bureaucratic organizations come about as a product of efforts to keep less strucured organizations going. Rather than being a sign of moral turpitude, bureaucratization may in essence be an unintended consequence of systematic efforts by leaders to make their organizations work better.

Thus, although hierarchy may be a source of social inequality and worker alienation, it also reduces the number of people who make legitimate claims to participate in decision making. Making some parts of organizations less democratic may make them less responsive to their constituencies, but it also can make possible effective entrepreneurship or conflict management among leaders. Similarly, sharp boundaries create problems of accountability and are responsible for some of the arbitrariness so often noted in the actions of bureaucrats. At the same time, boundaries make specialization possible, and they facilitate accountability by allowing particular organizational actors to take on specialized functions. With this, people know where to go for services and to whom to direct complaints.

It is because the features of bureaucracies are so reasonable and helpful in solving their problems that they pose dangers for participatory organizations. These organizations are hard to run and they are demanding of leaders. Leaders are easily criticized. After putting in great effort they may soon be ignored by a fickle public, and they have chronic problems mobilizing resources or support for projects. Many of these headaches can be overcome by introducing what seem to be a few bureaucratic conveniences: regularizing meetings, defining goals more sharply, undertaking projects which bring in a steady flow of cash, employing people to raise productivity in the provision of essential services, hiring a professional or two, or seeking new grants from the government or from large foundations.

The problem is that bureaucracies work because they solve many interlocked problems simultaneously, and because of this they tend to take over a participatory organization. Sharp boundaries make possible exclusivity in decision making which enables organizations to move aggressively in areas of specialization, which in turn facilitates development of internal differentiation, hierarchy, and accumulation of excess profits. The efficiencies of bureaucracies are of a piece, and because of this where they take hold they tend to produce a characteristic sort of organization.

This is much less the case in collectivist organizations. Bureaucracies tend to homogeneity, organizational theorists argue.[117] Organizations which depend heavily on participation and collectivism are not so regular. Indeed, after one has read through several hundred accounts of collectivist organization, what is striking is the tremendous number of organizational mechanisms that come into play and the ingenuity of the solutions leaders work out to solve their organizing problems.

Thus when I say that bureaucratic solutions to organizing problems are dangerous to collectivist organization this is a statement about the probability that participatory forms of organization will persist. Bureaucracy is seductive. It also is not usually apparent to organizational leaders how small concessions to convenience can lead to profound changes in the relationship between an organization and its membership.

Accepting a grant from a national funding agency may seem initially innocuous. But along with grants come expectations of accountability, a commitment to particular goals, employment of permanent staff members, careful accounting which distinguishes the funds of one organization from those of another, and so on. All of these demand greater formalization and crystallization of normal operating procedures. They also set before organizational leaders the prospect of greater convenience, future success, and control over an important group of services or activities in a community. What seemed like a small initial step tends to lead to big organizational changes which are hard to reverse once begun.

All of this is not to say that bureaucracy is necessarily and irrevocably bad. There are some things bureaucracies do not do well, however, and community building is one of them. This is partly because the boundaries they erect to outsiders make established bureaucratic organizations resistant to public participation and interference. But more seriously, they cannot build community because bureaucratic mechanisms are so seductive. Community building requires that citizens work hard, that they commit themselves to activities which have few clear payoffs, that they identify with an area and with fellow residents, and that they have experiences running organizations or putting together movements. These are difficult things for people to do. Given an alternative we avoid doing them. The main reason bureaucracies block community organization is that they are so convenient, familiar, and easy to run.

NOTES

1. One example is illustrated by Dennis Young in *If Not For Profit, For What?* (Lexington, Mass.: Lexington Books, 1983) and *Casebook of Management for Non-profit Organizations: Entrepreneurship and Organizational Change in Human Services* (New York: Haworth Press, 1984). He has completed case studies of a large number of entrepreneurial efforts among small nonprofit organizations. His case studies provide numerous examples of the way that funding imperatives cause entrepreneurs to seek organizational changes.

This also has been a concern of a project jointly undertaken by the Department of Housing and Urban Development and the New World Foundation reported in *New World Founda-*

tion, *Initiatives for Community Self-Help: Efforts to Increase Recognition and Support* (New York: New World Foundation, 1980).

2. See A. Michael Spence, *Market Signaling: Informational Transfer in Hiring and Related Screening Processes* (Cambridge, Mass.: Harvard University Press, 1974).

3. Mancur Olson, *The Logic of Collective Action* (Cambridge, Mass.: Harvard University Press, 1965) pp. 33–52.

4. See Carl Milofsky, "Non-Profit Organizations and Community: A Review of the Sociological Literature." Program on Non-Profit Organizations, Institution for Social and Policy Studies, Yale University, PONPO Working Paper no. 6, 1978.

5. For example, Eliot Freidson, *Profession of Medicine: A Study of the Sociology of Applied Knowledge* (New York: Harper and Row, 1970) and Frances Fox Piven and Richard A. Cloward, *Regulating the Poor: The Functions of Public Welfare* (New York: Vintage, 1971).

6. See Michel Crozier, *The Bureaucratic Phenomenon* (Chicago: University of Chicago Press, 1964) and *The World of the Office Worker* (New York: Schocken, 1965).

7. See Philip Selznick, *Leadership in Administration* (New York: Harper and Row, 1957).

8. S. N. Eisenstadt, "The Social Conditions of the Development of Voluntary Association—a Case Study of Israel." *Scripta Hierosolymitana* 3 (1956), 104–125.

9. See Lillian B. Rubin, *Busing and Backlash* (Berkeley and Los Angeles: University of California Press, 1972).

10. See Allen H. Barton, *Communities in Disaster: A Sociological Analysis of Collective Stress Situations* (Garden City, N.Y.: Doubleday, 1969).

11. See P. D. Wheeldon, "The Operation of Voluntary Associations and Personal Networks in the Political Processes of an Inter-Ethnic Community," pp. 128–180, in J. Clyde Mitchell (ed.), *Social Networks in Urban Situations: Analyses of Personal Relationships in Central African Towns* (Manchester: Manchester University Press, 1969).

12. Mancur Olson, *The Logic of Collective Action*.

13. See R. L. Warren, "The Interorganizational Field as a Focus for Investigation." *Administrative Science Quarterly* 12 (December 1967), 396–419.

14. See James D. Thompson, *Organizations in Action* (New York: McGraw-Hill, 1967).

15. See James Samuel Coleman, *Power and the Structure of Society* (New York: W. W. Norton, 1974).

16. See John R. Seeley, B. R. Junker and R. W. Jones, *Community Chest* (Toronto: University of Toronto Press, 1957).

17. See David Sills, *The Volunteers: Means and Ends in a National Organization* (Glencoe, Ill.: The Free Press, 1957).

18. See Mayer H. Zald, *Organizational Change: The Political Economy of the YMCA* (Chicago: University of Chicago Press, 1970).

19. See Kirkpatrick Sale, *SDS* (New York: Random House, 1973).

20. See William Lloyd Warner, *The Living and the Dead: A Study of the Symbolic Life of Americans* (New Haven: Yale University Press, 1959); William Lloyd Warner and Paul G. Lunt, *The Status System of a Modern Community* (New Haven: Yale University Press, 1942); W. Lloyd Warner and Leo Srole, *The Social System of American Ethnic Groups* (New Haven: Yale University Press, 1945); and Maurice R. Stein, *The Eclipse of Community: An Interpretation of American Studies* (Princeton, N.J.: Princeton University Press, 1960).

21. Robert A. Dahl, *Who Governs? Democracy and Power in an American City* (New Haven, Conn.: Yale University Press, 1961).

22. Edward C. Banfield, *Political Influence* (Glencoe, Ill.: Free Press, 1961).

23. J. Clyde Mitchell (ed.), *Social Networks in Urban Situations*.

24. Kenneth Lindsay Little, *West African Urbanization: A Study of Voluntary Association in Social Change* (New York: Cambridge University Press, 1965).

25. William Kornblum, *Blue Collar Community* (Chicago: University of Chicago Press, 1974).

26. Albert Hunter, *Symbolic Communities: The Persistence and Change of Chicago's Local Communities* (Chicago: University of Chicago Press, 1974).

27. Gerald D. Suttles, *The Social Order of the Slum, Ethnicity and Territoriality in the Inner City* (Chicago: University of Chicago Press, 1968).

28. See Lewis A. Coser, *The Functions of Social Conflict* (New York: Free Press, 1956) and Georg Simmel, *Conflict and the Web of Group Affiliations* (Glencoe, Ill.: The Free Press, 1964).

29. Saul D. Alinsky, *Rules for Radicals: A Pragmatic Primer for Realistic Radicals* (New York: Vintage, 1972).

30. See Daniel P. Moynihan, *Maximum Feasible Misunderstanding* (New York: The Free Press, 1969), Stephen M. Rose, *The Betrayal of the Poor: The Transformation of Community Action* (Cambridge, Mass.: Schenkman, 1972) and Roland L. Warren, S. M. Rose and A. F. Bergunder, *Structure of Urban Reform: Community Design, Organization and Stability and Change* (Lexington, Mass.: Lexington Books, 1974).

31. See David Kirp, "Has Organizing Survived the 1960s?" *Social Policy* 3 (1972–1973), 44–49.

32. Morris Janowitz, *The Community Press in an Urban Setting* (Glencoe, Ill.: The Free Press, 1952).

33. See L. Wirth, "Urbanism as a Way of Life," *American Journal of Sociology* 44 (July 1938), 3–24, and Lyn H. Lofland, *A World of Strangers: Order and Action in Urban Public Space* (New York: Basic Books, 1973).

34. Jane Jacobs, *The Death and Life of Great American Cities* (New York: Vintage, 1961).

35. Oscar Newman, *Defensible Space* (New York: Collier, 1973).

36. Morris Janowitz, *The Community Press in an Urban Setting.*

37. Joyce Rothschild-Whitt, "The Collectivist Organization." *American Sociological Review* 44 (August 1979), 509–528.

38. See Carl Milofsky, "Non-Profit Organizations and Community."

39. See James G. March and Johan P. Olsen, *Ambiguity and Choice in Organizations* (Irvington-on-Hudson, New York: Universitetsforlaget, distributed by Columbia University Press, 1976).

40. See C. E. Lindblom, "The Science of Muddling Through." *Public Administration Review* 19 (1959), 79–88, and Aaron Wildavsky, *The Politics of the Budgetary Process.* (Boston: Little, Brown and Co., 1964).

41. Charles E. Lindblom and David K. Cohen, *Usable Knowledge: Social Studies and Social Problem Solving* (New Haven, Conn.: Yale University Press, 1979).

42. David Street, R. Vinter and C. Perrow, *Organizations for Treatment* (New York: Free Press, 1966).

43. Joyce Rothschild-Whitt, "The Collectivist Organization."

44. R. C. R. Taylor, "Free Medicine," pp. 17–48 in John Case and Rosemary C. R. Taylor, *Coops, Communes and Collectives, Experiments in Social Change in the 1960s and 1970s* (New York: Pantheon, 1979).

45. Robert Michels, *Political Parties* (Glencoe, Ill.: The Free Press, 1949).

46. Robert K. Merton, *Sociological Ambivalence and Other Essays* (New York: Free Press, 1976) pp. 73–89.

47. Philip Selznick, *Leadership in Administration.*

48. Max Weber, *The Theory of Social and Economic Organization* (New York: Oxford University Press, 1947) pp. 329–336 and 358–373.

49. Roland Warren, Stephen Rose, and Ann Bergunder, *The Structure of Urban Reform.*

50. Roland L. Warren, "The Interorganization Field as a Focus for Investigation."

51. H. E. Aldrich and J. Pfeffer, "Environments of Organizations." *Annual Review of Sociology* 2 (1976), 79–106.

52. James D. Thompson, *Organizations in Action.*

53. See Chester Barnard, *The Functions of the Executive* (Cambridge, Mass.: Harvard University Press, 1968).

54. See Morris Janowitz, *The Community Press in an Urban Setting;* Albert Hunter, *Symbolic Communities;* and Scott Greer, "Urbanism Reconsidered: A Comparative Study of Local Areas in a Metropolis," *American Sociological Review* 21 (1956), 19–25.

55. Joyce Rothschild-Whitt, "The Collectivist Organization."

56. James Coleman, *Power and the Structure of Society*.

57. See James S. Coleman, Elihu Katz, and Herbert Menzel, *Medical Innovation* (Indianapolis: Bobbs Merrill, 1966).

58. See E. O. Laumann, J. P. Heinz, "Specialization and Prestige in the Legal Profession: The Structure of Deference," *American Bar Foundation Research Journal* 1 (1977), 155–216.

59. See, for example, Edward O. Laumann and Franz U. Pappi, *Networks of Collective Action: A Perspective on Community Influence Systems* (New York: Academic Press, 1976); E. O. Laumann, J. Galaskiewicz and P. V. Marsden, "Community Structure as Interorganizational Linkage," *Annual Review of Sociology* 4 (1978), 455–484, H. C. White, S. A. Boorman, and R. L. Breiger, "Social Structure from Multiple Networks. I. Blockmodels of roles and positions," *American Journal of Sociology* 81 (1976), 730–780, and S. A. Boorman and H. C. White, "Social Structure from Multiple Networks. II. Role Structures," *American Journal of Sociology* 81 (1976), 1384–1446.

60. Max Weber, "Status Groups and Classes," vol. 1, part 1, chapter 4, and "Class, status and party," vol. 2, chapter 9, section 6, in Ross, Guenther, and Wittick, Claus (eds.), *Economy and Society* (New York: Bedminster Press, 1968). See also Paul DiMaggio, "Cultural Capital and School Success: The Impact of Status-Culture Participation on the Grades of U.S. High-School Students," paper presented at the meetings of the American Sociological Association, New York, 1980.

61. Patricia Wheeldon, "The Operation of Voluntary Associations and Personal Networks in the Political Processes of an Inter-Ethnic Community."

62. J. A. Barnes, "Class and Committees in a Norwegian Island Parish," *Human Relations* 7 (1954), 39–58.

63. Georg Simmel, *Conflict and the Web of Group-Affiliations*.

64. See Janet Weiss, "Substance vs. Symbol in Administrative Reform: The Case of Human Services Coordination," Chapter 4 in this volume.

65. See Peter Blau, "A Formal Theory of Differentiation in Organizations," *American Sociological Review* 35 (April 1970), 201–218, P. Blau and W. R. Scott, *Formal Organizations: A Comparative Approach* (San Francisco: Chandler, 1962), Peter M. Blau and R. A. Schoenherr, *The Structure of Organizations* (New York: Basic Books, 1971).

66. Joan Woodward, *Industrial Organization: Theory and Practice* (Oxford: Oxford University Press, 1965) and "Technology, Material Control and Organizational Behavior," in A. R. Negandhi and J. P. Schwitter (eds.), *Organizational Behavior Models* (Kent, Ohio: Kent State University Press, 1970) and Charles Perrow, "A Framework for Comparative Organizational Analysis," *American Sociological Review* 32 (April 1967), 194–208, and "The Effect of Technological Change on the Structure of Business Firms," in *Industrial Relations: Contemporary Issues,* (ed.) B. C. Roberts (London: The Macmillan Co., 1968), pp. 205–219.

67. See George C. Homans, *The Human Group* (New York: Harcourt, Brace and World, 1950), Robert Freed Bales, *Personality and Interpersonal Behavior* (New York: Holt, Rinehart and Winston, 1970).

68. See Arthur L. Stinchcombe, *Creating Efficient Industrial Administrations* (New York: Academic Press, 1974), pp. 45–63.

69. Morris Janowitz, *The Community Press in an Urban Setting*.

70. Mark Granovetter, "The Strength of Weak Ties," *American Journal of Sociology* 78 (May 1973), 1360–1380.

71. L. Wirth, "Urbanism as a Way of Life."

72. Albert Hunter, *Symbolic Communities*.

73. William Kornblum, *Blue Collar Community*.

74. Patricia Wheeldon, "The Operation of Voluntary Associations and Personal Networks in the Political Process of an Inter-Ethnic Community."

75. Albert O. Hirschman, *Exit, Voice and Loyalty: Responses to Decline in Firms, Organizations and States* (Cambridge, Mass.: Harvard University Press, 1970).

76. Oscar Newman, *Defensible Space*.

77. Elizabeth Bott, *Family and Social Network* (New York: Free Press, 1971).

78. Jane Jacobs, *The Death and Life of Great American Cities.*

79. Robert K. Merton, *Sociological Ambivalence,* pp. 90–105.

80. John R. Seeley, et al., *Community Chest.*

81. Patricia Wheeldon, "The Operation of Voluntary Associations and Personal Networks in the Political Process of Inter-Ethnic Community."

82. Dennis Young, *If Not For Profit, For What?* and *Casebook of Management for Nonprofit Organizations: Entrepreneurship and Organizational Change in Human Services.*

83. Joyce Rothschild-Whitt, "The Collectivist Organization."

84. Rosemary C. R. Taylor, "Free Medicine."

85. Edward C. Banfield, *Political Influence.*

86. Edward C. Banfield, *Political Influence.*

87. Patricia Wheeldon, "The Operation of Voluntary Associations."

88. Philip Selznick, *The Organizational Weapon: A Study of Bolshevist Strategy and Tactics* (New York: McGraw-Hill, 1952).

89. Fred Strodtbeck, Personal communication.

90. Mancur Olson, *The Logic of Collective Action.*

91. See William Humbert Form and Sigmund Nosow, *Community in Disaster* (New York: Harper, 1958).

92. John R. Seeley et al., *Community Chest.*

93. Allen H. Barton, *Communities in Disaster.*

94. William Form and Sigmund Nosow, *Community in Disaster.*

95. Allen Barton, *Communities in Disaster.*

96. In addition to William Form and Sigmund Nosow, *Community in Disaster,* see James A. Beckford, *The Trumpet of Prophecy: A Sociological Study of Jehovah's Witnesses* (New York: Halsted Press, 1975), and J. Stillson Judah, *Hare Krishna and the Counterculture* (New York: John Wiley & Sons, 1974), and John Lofland and Rodney Stark, "Becoming a World Saver: A Theory of Conversion to a Deviant Perspective," pp. 28–47 in Glock, Charles Y. (ed.), *Religion in the Sociological Perspective* (Belmont, Calif.: Wadsworth Press, 1973).

97. E. Q. Campbell and T. F. Pettigrew, "Racial and Moral Crisis: The Role of Little Rock Ministers," *American Journal of Sociology* 64 (March 1959), 509–516.

98. Ernst Troeltsch, "The Relationship of Religion to the World," pp. 124–128 in Thomas F. O'Dea and Janet K. O'Dea (eds.), *Readings on the Sociology of Religion* (Englewood Cliffs, N. J.: Prentice-Hall, 1973).

99. Kirkpatrick Sale, *SDS.*

100. David Sills, *The Volunteers.*

101. Mayer Zald, *Organizational Change.*

102. See Carl Milofsky, "Getting the Job Done: Variations in the Modes of Institutionalization and the Effectiveness of Organizational Action in Public Service Organizations," paper presented at the meetings of the Pacific Sociological Association, San Jose, California, 1974.

103. Talcott Parsons, *The Social Systems.* (Glencoe, Ill.: The Free Press, 1951).

104. L. Mayhew, "Ascription in Modern Societies," pp. 308–323 in E. O. Lauman, P. M. Siegel and R. W. Hodge (eds.), *The Logic of Social Hierarchies* (Chicago: Markham, 1970).

105. Randall Collins, "A Conflict Theory of Organizations," *Conflict Sociology: Towards an Explanatory Science* (New York: Academic Press, 1975), chapter 6.

106. Edward Laumann and Franz Pappi, *Networks of Collective Action.*

107. L. Broom and P. Selznick. *Principles of Sociology* (New York: Harper and Row, 1970).

108. Marion R. Fremont-Smith, *Philanthropy and the Business Corporation* (New York: Russell Sage, 1972).

109. Morris Janowitz, *The Community Press in an Urban Setting.*

110. See Mayer Zald, *Organizational Change* and Joseph R. Gusfield, *Symbolic Crusade: Status, Politics and the American Temperance Movement* (Urbana: University of Illinois Press, 1963).

111. Mayer Zald, *Organizational Change*.

112. Roland L. Warren, Stephen M. Rose and Ann Bergunder, *The Structure of Urban Reform*.

113. See Peter Marris and Martin Rein, *The Dilemmas of Social Reform* (New York: Atherton, 1967), Daniel P. Moynihan, *Maximum Feasible Misunderstanding*, and Stephen M. Rose, *Betrayal of the Poor*.

114. New World Foundation, *Initiatives for Community Self-Help*.

115. A. Michael Spence, *Market Signalling*.

116. Dennis Young, *Casebook of Management for Non-profit Organizations*.

117. See Chapter 3 by DiMaggio and Powell in this volume. Also see A. L. Stinchcombe and T. W. Smith, "The Homogenization of the Administrative Structure of American Industries, 1940–1975" (Chicago: National Opinion Research Center, November 1975).

10

The Structure of Funding Arenas for Neighborhood Based Organizations[1]

CARL MILOFSKY and FRANK P. ROMO

Resource exchanges between organizations and their environment are increasingly being seen as important causes of organizational behavior. At first the focus was on the "environment" as a causal factor in explaining the internal structure of organizations.[2] Recently, however, analysts have emphasized "organizational fields"[3] or "organizational ecologies"[4] as the primary unit of analysis. Less attention is focused on particular organizations. Rather we look at the ways that field forces shape organizations, or at how organizations carve out niches as they interact with others.

Appealing as the theoretical debate is, most discussion of how organizations relate to larger systems remains abstract. We are outlining the general rules for defining fields and for examining how they should affect particular organizations. This general discussion leaves unexamined how one might apply the broad concepts to particular industries or to particular types of organizations. This paper explores the importance of external system effects on a particular type of organization, neighborhood based organizations (NBOs). In particular, we will explore (1) whether NBOs have routinized resource exchange relationships with other organizations and (2) what impact such relationships have on the structure of NBOs.

For the sake of simplicity, we will treat money income and in-kind donations of material and manpower as the resources we shall study. We also will look primarily at the relationships between NBOs and the agents that provide them with these necessary operating resources. Thus, when we ask whether NBOs have routinized exchange relationships we in fact ask whether NBOs generally receive their resources from particular funding sources or whether they are eclectic. As a group they may draw from many rather than few sources and any particular organization may draw from either many or few sources. If the resource exchange perspective is accurate, we should find that organizations obtain resources from few rather than many sources.

NBOs are an appropriate target for research of this kind because it is likely that organizations like them will be especially vulnerable to dependency relationships with other organizations that provide resources. NBOs are nonprofit organizations[5] that serve or are affiliated with a particular geographic community. Often they are committed to democratic participation of community residents in decision making, program planning, and program administration. Participation is important in part because these organizations often represent the interests of the community before those of outside organizations and institutions. Participation also provides a way for low income communities to substitute labor for cash in undertaking community betterment projects. Because they are community based and often serve low income communities, NBOs tend to be small and loosely structured, and they often report a chronic cash flow shortage. NBOs tend to have simple rather than highly differentiated administrative structures and relatively open decision making mechanisms.

Being structurally simple and resource poor, NBOs ought to find it difficult to buffer themselves from constraints imposed by resource providers. Larger organizations that have more sharply defined structures of authority and a more complex division of labor may find it easier to pursue resources from several sources at once. The YMCA,[6] for example, simultaneously raises funds from local communities, solicits grants from local United Ways, submits grants to the federal government, and operates a variety of businesses (hotels, laundries, restaurants) to raise funds. Efforts to mobilize and use resources from each of these sources must be distinct. Consequently, it is likely to be difficult for any one source of funds to dominate such a multifaceted organization. The YMCA is shaped by the rigors of fund-raising in local communities. But, as Zald points out, its complexity allows if to be sufficiently autonomous that it can resist efforts from those local organizations to direct its activities.[7]

NBOs lack structural means for buffering their activities from funders' demands. They also have fewer resources available for seeking alternative sources of funds should they be rejected by a primary resource provider. Thus, small, loosely structured organizations like these should provide a good test of resource exchange theory. If the theory is correct, they should be limited to particular funders. The distinctive demands different kinds of funding sources make upon recipient organizations also should shape NBOs in characteristic ways. Organizations that receive funds from the federal government should be different from those that earn them by providing services, that hold bake sales, or that raise funds from foundations, churches, or corporations. If we cannot find these sharp contrasts, then perhaps the resource exchange perspective lacks power to explain variations in organizational behavior.

FUNDING ARENAS

To test the resource exchange theory, we begin by suggesting an array of funding sources from which NBOs might obtain their resources. These sources are aggregations of organizations rather than particular funding entities. NBOs are not captives of particular federal offices or particular foundations any more than a small business is a captive of a particular bank. Rather, "funding sources" represent several distinct institutional systems or *funding arenas* with norms that may or may not be clearly articulated about why their members distribute funds, what rules should govern the distribution of grants, and what characteristics "responsible" or "appropriate" recipient organizations possess.

These shared norms coupled with their similar resource bases give funding arenas cohesiveness and boundaries. They also present leaders of NBOs with a set of "fund-raising rules" that are specific to each funding arena. For each arena, there are a set of unwritten rules or strategies recognized by those who successfully obtain funds that tell how to approach funders, how to make one's case, and what kinds of projects have the greatest chances of success. These rules go beyond things successful grantsmen should know. They also define organizational characteristics that make one sort of organization seem acceptable to one sort of funding agent, although those same characteristics may make it appear to be an inappropriate recipient of funds to an agent in another arena. Organizations seeking funds from the United Way for the first time are most likely to succeed if previous funding has come from local businesses rather than from the federal government, for example.[8] The organization which has received federal funds in the past may be better equipped, however, to obtain new grants from the federal government than organizations that have only received business funding in the past.

In an earlier paper[9] we suggested a list of arenas from which NBOs might obtain funds. That list was compiled in part from conventional wisdom and in part from a reading of the literature on community organizations. We also have assembled a list of nineteen funding sources generated as we developed a survey instrument for the New World Foundation (see the Appendix). Combining similar funding sources (three kinds of foundations are listed along with three kinds of corporate sources) also yields a list. The seven arenas which theoretically ought to shape NBOs are the following.

The Federal Government

The federal government provides resources to communities in many ways. However, where NBOs are concerned the most important direct source of funds from the federal government over the past quarter century has been categorial grants programs. Categorical grants are funds allocated by Congress to address narrow problems. These funds are distributed and their use is overseen by a large number of technically specialized offices in Washington to which NBOs must submit proposals if they wish to obtain grants. All of these offices follow similar general rules for seeking and evaluating proposals. However, each of them also identifies its own set of priorities, its own technical standards, and the constituencies it most needs to serve. Since those who give out grants receive many applications from NBOs they know little about around the country, some of the most important dynamics in the grant evaluation and decision making process revolve around how granting agencies decide what makes a proposal a strong one and what makes an NBO an appropriate recipient of fund. Generally the technical competence of proposals, the closeness of suggested programs to the priorities of the granting program, and the ability of NBO leaders to build political, personal, or professional contacts with the staff of an agency are important.[10]

From the standpoint of an NBO, federal fund-raising places a premium on grant writing skills and on learning about the priorities of particular federal agencies. Both of these requirements can be expensive and may militate against heavily participatory organizations' being successful at fundraising. Residents of low income neighborhoods are less likely to have the literacy skills and the experience with writing grants required for success than are staff members of large social service agencies who have college degrees and years of grant writing experience. Gathering information about the priorities of federal programs often requires visiting Washington and cultivating professional networks with others who seek grant money and who hear gossip about what certain federal officers are looking for in proposals. Money for travel and the leisure to exchange shoptalk with other professionals in far-flung locations are expensive for small, voluntaristic organizations. These are more easily afforded by large organizations with many administrators and an established budget for project development.

We should expect, then, that successful federal fund-raisers will be organizations that have large staffs and budgets and are old enough for staff members to have had some experience with the granting agencies. Federal grants, once received, tend to be large. This means that although obtaining the first grant may be difficult, organizations become large after receiving that grant and henceforth have the resources available and the connections needed to continue writing grants successfully.

State Governments

Historically, state governments have not played any consistent role in funding NBOs. Some states, notably New York, have traditionally funded NBOs through a variety of their own categorical grants programs. Most states provided little support to neighborhood organizations or, if they did so, provided resources through intermediaries such as local governments or large social welfare institutions such as the United Way.

In the last decade, however, block grants to states have increasingly replaced categorical grants as the federal government's favored means to distribute social service money intended for community use. Since block grants have been accompanied by drastic funding cuts, state funding still plays a small role in funding for NBOs. Nonetheless, many state governments are experimenting with new ways of distributing resources so that they will be available to NBOs. Increasingly, states should be an important if diverse funding arena for NBOs.

Local Governments

Decision making in categorical grants programs is characterized by an "open systems rationality"[11]—that is, by the need for program officers to make allocation decisions when they know very little about the people to whom they are giving money. Studies of local government suggest that decision making within "small" political jurisdictions—a city like Chicago is a small jurisdiction in this discussion[12]—is sharply different. Where categorical grant programs require bureaucrats to give money to strangers, localities generally divide up funds among competing local constituencies whose members are known to those that govern. The system is closed rather than open and explicit trade-offs of favors, constituency support, and resources are important in decision making.[13]

Where local government funding is concerned, elegantly written grant proposals are less important than are political contacts and an ability to mobilize a geographical constituency. Local leaders are, of course, still accountable to the public so proposals usually must have face validity. But fund-raising success most requires that leaders become participants in the local political culture, that they recruit supporters within that culture who have influence, and that they demonstrate an ability to deliver support to politicians from among members of their constituency. These elements of success emphasize the social and political skills of NBO leaders rather than attributes of their programs or administrative structure. Local government fund-raising should encourage organizations to define and nurture a strong neighborhood constituency and close ties to local political leaders.

Businesses

Federal program cutbacks have been accompanied by repeated assertions that private sector funding should make up for the decline in public support for social programs. It has been hoped that business contributions would become an important source of funds for local organizations. These contributions might come in the form of grants from corporations or their foundations, or joint ventures and coparticipation in programs. At the time of this study there was relatively little business support of NBOs, although there has been widespread support from business for cultural and artistic enterprises such as museums, symphony orchestras, and the public media.[14]

Businesses tend to be idiosyncratic in their funding practices. Some give grants to promote ideological or philosophic interests of their owners.[15] Others give to improve their image in the community and with employees. Some industries invest in local organizations hoping that by improving their hometown it will be easier to attract professional employees. Some cities have strong traditions of corporate philanthropy that make corporate leaders feel obliged to support local causes.[16]

Obtaining business funding is partly a matter of luck for NBOs. They must have corporate neighbors that want to help solve local social problems. At the same time, there is an art to corporate fund-raising. In confronting Kodak in Rochester, New York, Saul Alinsky demonstrated that local organizations can sometimes force corporations to accept more responsibility than they otherwise would.[17] This strategy seems most likely to succeed if an NBO argues that the lives of company employees would be improved if their services were supported. Confrontation is not the most common NBO fund-raising strategy. More often, leaders have contacts with business representatives or manage to recruit to their boards members of the business community who will represent them to other members of the business class. In some cities there exist intermediary organizations whose explicit goal is to build bridges between NBOs and local corporations.[18] Thus, to raise funds successfully with businesses, NBOs generally must show that support is in the interests of the corporation whose help is being solicited, and local leaders must find ways to bridge the social and cultural gap between low income people and the economic elite which exists in most communities.

Foundations

Large national foundations share with the federal government the problem that they receive applications from strangers whose requests and competence are difficult to evaluate. Consequently grant writing skills often are an important part of fund-raising success. At the same time, however, foundations are not accountable to the public as is government, and they are not vulnerable to the sort of political pressure which can be brought to bear on federal agencies. Foundations also prefer to provide seed funding for new projects rather than to accept a continuing responsibility to fund a project. Local foundations will often fund a fledgling organization and accept a sponsorship role. Since professional and institutional connections tie together national and local foundations in an information exchange system, NBOs often enter the foundation funding arena by first raising funds through foundations committed to supporting activities within a particular city. When they then apply for funding from a national source, local foundation leaders can act as intermediaries, commenting to outside foundation officers on the quality of NBO programs.[19]

Foundations tend to be less universalistic than the government in evaluating proposals.[20] Personal contacts with foundation officers can have an important impact on grant decisions. In contrast to the network ties that help fund-raising with local governments or with business leaders, NBO leaders are most successful with foundations if they become known within the national foundation circle.[21] One not only learns which foundations are most likely to be receptive to particular kinds of program proposals;

foundation leaders also become more interested in certain organizations or projects if their peers within the foundation network seem excited by particular kinds of projects. Foundation fund-raising, thus, is similar to federal fund-raising in that NBO leaders must often cultivate contacts outside their communities and learn what fads are sweeping the foundation community. This sort of fund-raising is similar to that with business and local government in that personal contacts and a capacity to participate in a specialized culture are important. However, in contrast to the local political arena and the business arena, success seems to depend less on an appeal to the self-interest of the funder than on an ability to seem like an informed insider.

Religious Organizations

Churches are consistently among the most important sponsors of grassroots community movements. Many churches are themselves community organizations.[22] The clergy is also a unique occupation because members are explicitly charged with being moral leaders for their communities. Consequently, among the prime initiators of the community organization movement have been ministers and priests who have devoted themselves to politically mobilizing residents against social, political, and economic repression.[23] Churches, consequently, are often key actors in the earliest developmental stages of NBOs. Church leaders not only provide moral support and encouragement to local activists; they also supply all manner of in-kind resources—space, secretarial services, administrative support—to emergent local organizations, which allow those groups to mobilize a constituency, write proposals, and launch projects. Support for community efforts is often easy to obtain from local churches as long as the project is heavily voluntaristic and committed to idealistic goals.

Churches also are important as providers of seed money for community betterment projects. Housing development programs especially require large infusions of cash to purchase property and build buildings. Usually this money is provided by some governmental authority. But often that money takes years to be allocated and carryover funding is required to pay for the staff of a neighborhood development organization and to provide emergency funding to purchase property and to undertake other activities. This initial funding may be reimbursed at a later time when full government funding becomes available. But without stopgap funding the project will fail, and churches often become sponsors of such projects.

We include with churches large, denomination-specific fund-raising programs such as Catholic Charities or the United Jewish Appeal although there has been little academic research exploring how these organizations distribute their funds.

Earned Income

If NBOs are constrained in their organizational structure by dependency relationships with large funding organizations, then means of fund-raising which do not require submission of grant applications or any relationship with another organization should be an important way to escape dependency. NBOs may autonomously raise funds by charging a membership fee to users, by having fund-raising events, by obtaining gifts and creating an endowment fund, or by collecting fees for carrying out some project or service.

Successful autonomous fund-raising can allow an organization great freedom to experiment with new organizational forms or with unusual ideological missions.[24] It also can provide means for attracting resources to a community. Local organizations can help businesses invest in the community and can earn profits through collaboration in a for-profit enterprise.[25] Autonomous fund-raising has the advantage that organizations do not need to seek approval for their internal administrative arrangements. It has the disadvantage, however, that it often is very difficult to raise operating funds sufficient to launch or carry out a project. That problem, of course, is why NBOs so often seek outside funding. NBOs that are successful autonomous fund-raising organizations are often either represented by an energetic, and probably independent, entrepreneur[26] or composed of an unusually cohesive and ideologically committed membership body, prepared to donate labor and to endure hardship for the organization's cause.[27]

The literature on NBOs suggests that these seven arenas ought to be important supporters of community organizations. The remainder of this paper explores whether in fact NBOs draw resources from particular arenas, whether they draw resources from these particular arenas, and whether drawing resources from one or another arena has any impact on their organizational structure.

FUNDING CLUSTERS

In the first step of our analysis we will see whether NBOs are eclectic in their fund-raising or whether they draw primarily from particular sources. If they draw from specific sources, are those sources the ones we have specified theoretically? We used two methods to examine funding clusters within the New World Foundation survey data. First, we inspected the raw questionnaire data and rearranged the cases by hand (using a computer text editor) so that organizations were grouped together if they drew heavily from the same sources. We then applied to the same data the FAST-CLUS clustering procedure from the SAS statistical package.[28]

Both methods show clearly that our NBOs draw primarily from single sources and that those sources correspond to those we predicted theoretically, as the results from the hand clustering given in Table 10.1 show. Although the fit is remarkably close to the theoretical prediction, a reader can see by referring to the Working Paper version of this chapter that the theoretical model preceded this clustering effort.[29]

Table 10.1 Neighborhood Based Organizations Receiving More Than 70%, 60–69%, and 50–59% of Their Funding from One of Seven Funding Arenas

% of Funding	Federal Govt.	Local Govt.	Federal + State + Local Funding	Private Sources				Total
				Large Business	Founda-tions	Mass Funds + Church	Internal	
>70%	37	17	32	2	11	8	33	
	26%	12%	23%	1%	8%	6%	24%	140
	100%	100%	67%	50%	69%	67%	87%	70%
60–69%			7	0	4	3	3	
			41%	0%	24%	18%	18%	17
			15%	0%	33%	25%	8%	9%
50–59%			9	2	1	1	2	
			60%	13%	7%	7%	13%	15
			19%	50%	6%	8%	5%	7%
<50%								28
								14%
Total	37	17	48	4	16	12	38	200
	18%	9%	24%	2%	8%	6%	19%	100%

SOURCE: New World Foundation Survey of Community Self-Help Organization, 1978 (See New World Foundation 1980).

We see in Table 10.1 that 70% of the 200 organizations in the sample received 70% or more of their funding from a single one of the seven funding sources described in the last section. Over 85% received at least 50% of their funding from one source, and only 14% received their funding in small portions from many sources. We also see in Table 10.1 that most NBO resources come from only certain arenas. Federal and local governments are large contributors. About one-fifth of the organizations survive primarily on earned income, with foundations and churches contributing smaller amounts. Businesses make few contributions.

The FASTCLUS procedure is useful in two ways. First, it helps us explore which number of clusters best explains the data. Second, it allows us to see better whether the clusters are "pure" or heterogeneous. When one applies a clustering procedure to these sorts of data, the procedure only looks for groups of similar cases. Cases included in a cluster may draw resources from one or many sources. If there were organizations that collectively drew from diverse sources, they would show up as a separate cluster.

Table 10.2 shows how well different numbers of clusters explain the data using the "cubic clustering criterion." In the FASTCLUS procedure, one selects the number of clusters one wishes to generate. With successive iterations, one can seek the number of clusters that best fit the data. The score of 6.615 that we obtained at the three-cluster level would, under

Table 10.2 Changes in the Goodness
of Fit Measure (the Cubic Clustering
Criterion) as the Number of
Clusters Increases

Number of Clusters	Value of the Cubic Clustering Criterion
3	6.635
4	9.573
5	32.081
6	42.054
7	48.079
8	50.418
9	49.867
10	53.859
11	48.535
12	49.085
13	48.609

normal circumstances, demonstrate that these data are clustered to a statistically significant extent. The pattern we wish to examine in this table, however, is the number of clusters required before gains in the cubic clustering criterion begin to flatten out. One can see that the criterion increases substantially with each additional cluster until we select seven clusters. The criterion increases only slightly with higher numbers of clusters. Parsimony suggests we should use the smallest number of clusters possible. Thus, seven—the number we suggested theoretically—is the best number of clusters.

In Table 10.3 we see the seven clusters produced by FASTCLUS arrayed against eight funding sources from the New World questionnaire. Consistent with the data presented in Table 10.1, organizations in most of the clusters draw heavily from one source. In clusters 1, 2, 3, and 7, more

Table 10.3 For NBOs within Clusters Identified by FASTCLUS Program, Mean Percentage of Total Income Taken from Each of Eight Funding Sources

Cluster	No.	Federal Govt.	State Govt.	Local Govt.	Church	Founda- tions	Business	Earned Income	Other
1	59	.75	.07	.03	.02	.05	.01	.05	.01
2	28	.11	.03	.74	.01	.05	.03	.04	.00
3	12	.06	.03	.00	.74	.03	.01	.10	.03
4	22	.10	.57	.08	.08	.05	.02	.11	.00
5	28	.06	.03	.03	.02	.67	.03	.15	.01
6	6	.11	.02	.03	.02	.15	.60	.10	.00
7	42	.04	.01	.01	.02	.03	.01	.87	.01
	197[a]								

[a]Two organizations received no money income—all of their resources were in kind. They were omitted from this analysis.

than 70% of the income of member organizations comes from one source. In the other clusters we see minor funding sources linked to primary funders. Cluster 4 combines three types of government funding, with state funding predominating. Cluster 5 combines foundation income with earned income. Cluster 6 combines business income with foundation income. Each of these combinations makes sense. There are many government programs that pass funding from one level of government to another so that determining exactly where money originated is difficult.

It is instructive that foundation income is most strongly linked to business and earned income. Foundations generally are launched by the wealthy or by corporations, and it should therefore be no surprise that when businesses sponsor projects they bring along foundation funding. The linkage to earned income may also reflect connections to the business community since an important source of earned income among certain organizations is interest from investments. This linkage between earned and foundation income may also reflect the policy interest in entrepreneurial community ventures that has been so often voiced by political and business leaders since the late 1970s. It is noteworthy that earned income made a substantial contribution to funding in every single arena.

FUNDING ARENAS AND ORGANIZATIONAL STRUCTURE: A THEORETICAL MODEL

Clearly NBOs do draw their funding primarily from single sources. We cannot tell from the data so far presented what, if any, organizational consequences this concentration of funding has. Having established that clusters exist we can now treat membership in a cluster as a variable and examine whether funding arenas act as the coercive forces resource dependency theories expect them to be.

How would arena membership affect organizational structure? Some organizational variables will be less influenced than others. For example, *neighborhood* based organizations will not usually change their neighborhoods to satisfy a funder (although it is not hard to find examples of ones that do). Generally, the population base of an organization will be fixed and independent of whatever coercive force funding arenas may exert. We may find a selection effect—that certain funders will not serve Black people or rural populations or some other specific group. This could produce a strong correlation between community characteristics and funding agents, but we should treat community type as causally prior to funding arenas.

There also are variables concerned with organizational structure that ought to be causally prior to funding arenas. The first is the age of an organization. Again, we may expect an association between funding arenas and organizational age. Older organizations are likely to be larger and thus more capable of mounting fund-raising campaigns to distant sources or particularly balky funders such as the United Way.[30]

The second structural variable is the function performed by an organization. Most of our NBOs perform specific functions rather than many at once. Those that build houses have radically different funding needs than do those that promote cultural affairs, and we consequently should expect an association between functional areas and funding types. Housing organizations, for example, will often draw heavily on funds from the federal Department of Housing and Urban Development. Since construction projects demand large amounts of money, federal funding will tend to dwarf smaller grants such organizations might receive from churches or foundations to cover administrative expenses.

What organizational qualities may be affected by funding arenas? First, we should expect them to be related to what we might call the bureaucracy/participation dimension. A central concern in the literature on democratic organizations, of which NBOs and other community organizations are a subcategory, is the observation that as organizations become older and larger they become more structurally complex,[31] gradually adding levels of hierarchy and building a larger and more formalized division of labor. As this happens, we expect decision making and power to become more concentrated in the hands of a few decision makers, limiting the extent of democratic participation in planning and agenda setting.

This is in part a consequence of organizational aging. With time, organizations will make connections to more and more community institutions or they will pick up activities as members help address issues of local concern. This proliferation will tend to produce a multicentered organization which may need coordination from some single administrative unit that can oversee the whole operation. It is hard to see why this source of complexity would have any specific relationship to funding sources.

Other aspects of the formalization of structure and centralization of decision making are likely to be strongly affected by funding sources. We know that some kinds of fund-raising—federal fund-raising especially— require an elaborate grant writing process, complex administrative arrangements to ensure accountability and the competent use of resources, and ability to demonstrate technical sophistication. Some kinds of funding also produce large organizational budgets that must be serviced by an army of administrative personnel. We might expect decision makers in other funding arenas to reject explicitly those organizations that seem bureaucratic and highly professionalized, preferring instead to support grass-roots community movements. Church funding may work this way, as may grass-roots fund-raising (earned income). In other words, we should expect a relationship between funding arenas and measures of size, on one hand, and measures of participation on the other.

The second factor that we may expect funding arenas to affect is the long term survivability of an organization. Given the number of our organizations that depended heavily on federal funding in 1978 one would expect a bloodbath with many organizations dying in the aftermath of the massive recent federal funding cuts for social programs. This effect may be softened by certain advantages of size, however. Being more complex and institutionalized, large old organizations would be better equipped to weather a sudden change in funding practices in a major arena than would small, young organizations. Since small organizations are less often supported by the federal government, the advantages of size should be counterbalanced by mortality caused by federal budget cuts.

Figure 10.1 summarizes this system of relationships. Funding arena membership has "organizational function" and "community variables" as causal antecedents. Structural complexity and community participation are affected by arena membership, and these variables intervene between arena membership and long term survival potential.

Figure 10.1 shows that organizational age is independent of funding arena membership and that it is linked to "structural diversity," a factor also not linked to funding arenas. In fact, there is a connection between age and membership in some arenas. Organizations that earn their own income are younger than organizations that draw from other arenas. Older organizations are likely to have a variety of funding connections, however, so they are less likely to depend exclusively on one arena. For them, arenas will be less coercive. Structural diversity includes the number of functions an organization performs, the number of funding sources upon which it depends, and the number of administrative departments it contains. It thus includes those variables that liberate organizations from dependence on single resource providers. Naturally, diversity is strongly related to measures of "structural complexity" such as budget size, number of staff and volunteer members, and levels of hierarchy. It also will have a strong effect on survival since diverse organizations may pursue more options when funding from one sources dries up.

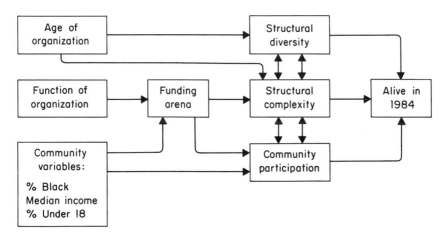

Figure 10.1 Causal Model Predicting Survival of Community Organizations between 1978 and 1984.

TESTING THE MODEL

Table 10.4 is a correlation matrix showing relationships between funding sources and the antecedent variables "organizational function" and "community composition." FUNCTION is a continuous variable in which activities that are more project focused and cash intensive (economic development, physical development) are given low values and activities that are less specific and require more public participation (education, arts, and culture) are given high values (see Appendix, Table 1). Values were assigned on the basis of what "primary function" respondents reported for their organizations.

Funding arena membership is represented in two ways in Table 10.4. FUNDBLOC is a continuous variable based on the seven funding clusters identified earlier. Federal funding is at the low end of the continuum, and earned income is at the high end. Values are based on the clusters to which organizations were assigned by FASTCLUS. We also have provided data on the percentage of organizational income drawn from each of the seven arenas.

The two summary variables, FUNCTION and FUNDBLOC, have a significant positive relationship. This is accounted for by a sharp split in the preferences of different funders. Organizations funded heavily by local government or by several levels of government at once or by businesses are sharply different from those funded by foundations or churches. This mostly reflects a difference in support for advocacy activities, with the first group avoiding them and the second strongly supporting them. The first group also shows a preference for building projects. It is instructive that the two sources of funds that were most important to organizations in the sample, the federal government and earned income, show only a weak association with organizational function. The variety of categorical grants provided by the federal government causes it to support every kind of community activity. Similarly, independent fund-raising is likely to be used for every sort of purpose.

Of the community variables, %UND18 is easier to interpret in structural terms than the race and income variables. Government seems most strongly to support communities with many children in them, as one would expect since there will be more dependent people there. Organizations in such communities do not manage to used earned income—perhaps because parents do not have a lot of time for grass-roots fund-raising. The race and class variables are not so clear. It is surprising to see such heavy business support of organizations in Black communities and that whereas Black organizations receive little federal support, organizations in low income communities receive high federal support. Black communities ought to be poor communities. In Chapter 11 of this volume, Hunter and Staggenborg analyze the relationship between community and organizational variables more closely. They argue that one must incorporate a well articulated theory of neighborhood politics to understand the relationship of community

Table 10.4 Correlation Matrix of Community, Technical Function, and Funding Variables[a]

	FUNCTION	EC. DEVEL.	EDUC.	ADVOCACY	MINCOME	%BLACK	%UND18
FUNDBLOC	.16[b]	-.08	-.02	.15[b]	.11	.02	-.15[b]
	(200)	(200)	(200)	(200)	(151)	(159)	(136)
PCFED	.02	.09	.06	.00	-.10	-.21[b]	.11
PCLOGGOV	-.15[b]	-.06	-.05	-.14[b]	.18[b]	.09	.09
ALLGOV	-.17[b]	.05	-.04	-.13[b]	-.01	-.11	.15[b]
BUSINESS	-.13[b]	.14[b]	-.06	-.07	-.07	.26[b]	.02
FOUNDATIONS	.21[b]	-.04	.14[b]	.21[b]	-.06	.02	.02
CHURCHES	.10	-.01	-.06	.14[b]	-.13	-.06	.02
OWN FUNDING	.04	-.05	.01	-.04	.17	.09	-.20

[a]Variables:
FUNDBLOC   Funding arena: 1 = federal, 7 = own fund-raising.
PCFED   Percentage of total budget from federal sources.
PCLOGGOV   Percentage of total budget from local government sources.
ALLGOV   Percentage of total budget from all government sources combined.
BUSINESS   Percentage of total budget from corporation, financial institutions, and local businesses.
FOUNDATIONS   Percentage of total budget from foundations and the United Way.
CHURCHES   Percentage of total budget from churches and religious fund drives such as United Jewish Appeal.
OWN FUNDING   Percentage of total budget raised by organizataion alone.
FUNCTION   Technical function of organization: 1 = technical assistance, 6 = art and culture.
EC. DEVEL.   Extent of involvement in economic development (3 = hi).
EDUC.   Extent of involvement in educational programs (3 = hi).
ADVOCACY   Extent of involvement in advocacy programs (3 = hi).
MINCOME   Median income of the community.
%BLACK   Percentage of residents who are Black.
%UND18   Percentage of residents who are under 18 years of age.
[b]$p < .05$.

variables to the structure of NBOs properly. This discussion is beyond the scope of this paper. Suffice it to say that the community variables as a group relate to organization structure variables in an ambiguous way.

Although the antecedent variables do not tell us much about the reasons organizations enter particular funding arenas, Table 10.5 and 10.6 show us that funding arenas have a strong influence on organizational structure. As Figure 10.1 anticipated, organizational size is best explained by the source of funding and by the age of an organization. Nearly one-quarter of the variance in SIZE is explained by the source of an organization's funding. As we expected, government funded organizations are much more likely than privately funded organizations to be large, as are old organizations. SIZE is also strongly correlated with an organization's function, but most of that association is eliminated when we enter into the equation the source of funding.

Organizational diversity is also strongly affected by the source of funding. Funding source is a slightly stronger explanatory variable than is the age of an organization. Organizational function is also a significant factor. The relationship of FUNDBLOC to diversity measures is really a proxy for

Table 10.5 Regression of Organizational Age, Funding Arena, Organizational Function, and Community Variables on Organizational Size

Variables in the Equation	Mean	Std. Dev.	N of Cases
Organizational Age (ORGAGE)	3.15	1.16	197
Funding Arena (FUNDBLOC)	3.91	2.35	200
Primary Function (FUNCTION)	3.50	1.41	200
Percentage Black (%BLACK)	22.06	28.07	159
Percentage Under 18 (%UND18)	25.60	13.79	136
Median Income (MINCOME)	9132.45	5037.10	151
Dependent Variable:			
Organizational Size (SIZE)	15.90	4.14	200

Variable	B	Beta	Std. Error B	F
ORGAGE	.7477698	.20940	.28660	6.808
FUNDBLOC	−.6969132	−.39512	.14278	23.825
FUNCTION	−.3492931	−.11932	.24046	2.110
%BLACK	−.1863639$E-01$	−.12634	.01226	2.310
%UND18	.3035545$E-02$	.01011	.02422	.016
MINCOME	−.5352760$E-04$	−.06513	.00007	.678
(CONSTANT)	18.31181			

Variable	Simple r	Multiple r	r^2	Δr^2
ORGAGE	.19	.19	.04	
FUNDBLOC	−.43	.47	.22	.18
FUNCTION	−.16	.48	.23	.01
%BLACK	−.06	.49	.24	.01
%UND18	.08	.49	.24	.00
MINCOME	−.10	.49	.24	.00

Table 10.6 Regression of Organizational Age, Funding Arena, Primary Function, and Community Variables on Organizational Diversity

Variables in the Equation	Mean	Std. Dev.	N of Cases
Organizational Age (ORGAGE)	3.15	1.16	197
Funding Arena (FUNDBLOC)	3.91	2.35	200
Primary Function (FUNCTION)	3.50	1.41	200
Percentage Black (%BLACK)	22.06	28.07	159
Percentage Under 18 (%UND18)	25.60	13.79	136
Median Income (MINCOME)	9132.45	5037.10	151
Dependent Variable: Diversity of Organization			
(DIVERSE)	10.75	4.51	200

Variable	B	Beta	Std. Error B	F
ORGAGE	.6839962	.17570	.33997	4.048
FUNDBLOC	−.3840681	−.19974	.16937	5.142
FUNCTION	.5335976	.16720	.28524	3.500
%BLACK	$-.3327471E-02$	−.02069	.01454	.052
%UND18	$.3636623E-01$	.11111	.02873	1.602
MINCOME	$-.1977230E-04$	−.02207	.00008	.066
(CONSTANT)	7.550865			

Variable	Simple r	Multiple r	r^2	Δr^2
ORGAGE	.18	.18	.03	
FUNDBLOC	−.19	.26	.07	.04
FUNCTION	.12	.30	.09	.02
%BLACK	−.01	.30	.09	.00
%UND18	.12	.32	.10	.01
MINCOME	−.04	.32	.10	.00

the relationship of size with complexity. Naturally size and complexity are mutually reinforcing. Given the strong effect of funding arenas on size, that effect is reflected in the interaction between size and complexity. In short, the structural variables demonstrate the relationships we anticipated.

This is not true where measures of participation are concerned. Table 10.7 is a correlation matrix showing relationships between the structural variables we have thus far discussed and five measures of participation. One can readily see that participation as measured by our questionnaire is, like community, a complex matter. We cannot relate participation to organizational structure in any straightforward way.

This is mainly because "participation" can mean many things. It may be a measure of the number of people involved in participatory activities or the number who volunteer their time in some organizational project. However, organizations with large membership lists are likely to have many passive or inactive members. A different definition of participation would

Table 10.7   Correlation Matrix with Participation Variables and Antecedent
Structural Variables

	NOPARTIC	VALINKIN	NOHEARNG	%ACTIVE	PCVOL
ORGAGE	.16*	−.14*	−.04	.09	.06
	(197)	(191)	(173)	(197)	(197)
FUNCTION	.16*	.13*	.12	.09	.06
	(200)	(194)	(176)	(200)	(200)
FUNDBLOC	−.05	.11	.10	−.05	.34*
PCFED	.14*	−.07	−.04	.02	−.25*
PCLOGOV	−.13*	−.05	−.02	.07	−.04
ALLGOV	.02	−.12*	−.05	.05	−.32*
BUSINESS	−.08	.17*	−.09	−.03	.14*
FOUNDATION	.01	.04	.05	.03	.12
CHURCH	−.05	−.02	.18*	.18*	.04
OWN FUNDING	.03	.04	−.07	−.17*	.22*
%BLACK	−.10	.05	−.15*	−.05	.14*
	(159)	(154)	(157)	(159)	(200)
%UND18	−.07	−.05	−.08	−.01	−.07
	(136)	(130)	(135)	(136)	(136)
MINCOME	.10	.07	.05	−.15*	.12
	(151)	(146)	(150)	(151)	(151)

*p less than .05
NOTE: Variables:

FUNDBLOC	Funding arena: 1 = federal, 7 = own fund-raising.
PCFED	Percentage of total budget from federal sources.
PCLOGOV	Percentage of total budget from local government sources.
ALLGOV	Percentage of total budget from all government sources combined.
FOUNDATIONS	Percentage of total budget from foundations and the United Way.
BUSINESS	Percentage of total budget from corporations, financial institutions, and other businesses.
CHURCH	Percentage of total budget from churches and religious fund drives such as United Jewish Appeal.
OWN FUNDING	Percentage of total budget raised by organization alone.
FUNCTION	Technical function of organization: 1 = technical.
MINCOME	Median income of the community.
%BLACK	Percentage of residents who are Black.
%UND18	Percentage of residents who are under 18 years of age.
NOPARTIC	Total number of participants.
VALINKIN	In-kind resource income compared to total budget.
NOHEARNG	Number of public meeting held by organization last year.
%ACTIVE	Percentage of members active in the last six months.
PCVOL	Percentage of staff members who are volunteers.

ask how many of these members have been recently active in organizational affairs. A different approach to participation asks how many members have made contributions of time or have donated in-kind resources. Such donations suggest the organization has a public constituency familiar with its ongoing affairs and socially involved with its leading activists. We may ask what fraction of the staff is composed of volunteers or what fraction of an organization's total resources come from donations of in-kind resources.

These measures of participation imply different sorts of involvement from the public. Active involvement may be most important when an organization is pursuing advocacy goals. Voluntarism seems most important to service organizations. A high volume of in-kind contributions involves members as sponsors. None of these forms of participation is better or more intense than any other. They simply are different, and they consequently are not highly intercorrelated.

A few of the associations reported in Table 10.7 are worth noting. As one would expect, organizations that have many participants (large size) are strongly associated with federal funding. Local governments, however, prefer funding organizations with few participants. This probably is related to local government's preference for funding economic and physical development projects that involve few people. It is not very surprising to see that organizations using a high volume of in-kind resources depend heavily on business funding. Businesses may find it easier than other funders to lend meeting space and secretarial help to organizations they are helping. Since reliance on in-kind resources is most common in young organizations, given the negative correlation with organizational age, donated resources appear to be important to the launching of organizations. This association with age may account for the negative correlation with government funding since it seems likely that governments will generally support only more established NBOs.

The number of hearings or public meetings an organization holds per year and the percentage of members who have been active in the last six months both are measures of the political activism of an organization. It should, therefore, be no surprise that these variables are related to church funding since, as we saw in Table 10.4, churches tend to fund advocacy activities. It is striking that autonomous fund-raising is so negatively associated with the percentage of members who are active while being *positively* associated with the percentage of staff members who are volunteers. Whatever participation means, having community people involved has no automatic effect on what an organization will be doing. Volunteer work, in particular, represents an ethos of service that is not politically oriented. We see this ethos represented in organizations supported by businesses and foundations, and it is strongly rejected in organizations supported by government. This is reminiscent of a pattern discussed by Seeley in his 1957 study of the Indianapolis Community Chest.[32]

There is a lot to say about the relationships between funding and participation in NBOs, but there seem to be few simple structural lessons to be taken from these data. This negative finding is important because it tells us that federal funding and the supposed administrative effects that follow from obtaining large grants from categorical programs do not squelch democracy. This is demonstrated in Table 10.8. Size and diversity are nega-

Table 10.8 Correlation Matrix of Structural Variables:
Size, Diversity, and Participation Measures

	SIZE	DIVERSE	NOPARTIC	NOHEARNG	%ACTIVE	PCVOL
SIZE	1.00	.44 *	.31 *	.15 *	.01	−.17 *
	(200)	(200)	(200)	(176)	(200)	(200)
DIVERSE		1.00	.28 *	.16 *	−.03	−.12 *
NOPARTIC			1.00	.18 *	−.19 *	−.03
NOHEARNG				1.00	.05	−.11
				(176)	(176)	(176)
%ACTIVE					1.00	−.02
					(200)	(200)
PCVOL						1.00

* p less than .05
NOTE: Variables:

SIZE	Size of organization.
DIVERSE	Diversity of organizational functions.
NOPARTIC	Total number of participants.
VALINKIN	In-kind resource income compared to total budget.
NOHEARNG	Number of public meetings held by organization last year.
%ACTIVE	Perecentage of members active in the last six months.
PCVOL	Percentage of staff members who are volunteers.

tively related only to the percentage of staff who are volunteers. We noted previously that this probably has more to do with the ethos of voluntarism than to structural effects. Large organizations have many participants and many hearings. Size has no relationship to the percentage of members who are active.

In Table 10.9 all of the variables described in Figure 10.1 are used to explain survival of sample organizations between 1978 and 1984 when we resurveyed them. Two-thirds of the organizations overall survived. This is a strikingly high number when compared to the survival rates of small businesses.[33] Most of the variables with explanatory power are structural: the age of organizations, the size of organizations, the diversity of organizations, and the source of their funding. As we suggested earlier, large, old organizations have a substantial advantage over small, young organizations. *FUNDBLOC* does not correlate very highly with long term survival, but its contribution to explaining survival is nonetheless significant. Importantly, organizations that received government funding were *more* rather than less likely to survive.

The most surprising result is that *%ACTIVE* is the strongest explanatory variable. The more active members an organization possessed in 1978, the less likely it was to have survived until 1984. This is consistent with the ideas of social movement theorists following Michels[34] who argue that people lose interest in participatory organizations over time. One tendency this produces is for oligarchic leadership to emerge, reducing the democracy of such organizations and making them more centralized. One might

Table 10.9 Regression of All Variables in the Model on Survival in 1984

Variables in the Equation	Mean	Std. Dev.	N of Cases
Age of Organization (ORGAGE)	3.15	1.16	197
Primary Function (FUNCTION)	3.50	1.41	200
Percentage of Black (%BLACK)	22.06	28.07	159
Percentage Under 18 (%UND18)	25.60	13.79	136
Median Income (MINCOME)	9132.45	5037.10	151
Funding Arena (FUNDBLOC)	3.91	2.35	200
Diversity (DIVERSE)	10.75	4.51	200
Size (SIZE)	15.90	4.14	200
No. of Participants (NOPARTIC)	4.95	2.16	200
No. of Meetings (NOHEARNG)	15.62	24.82	176
Percentage Active (%ACTIVE)	58.00	32.54	200
Percentage Staff Volunteers (PCVOL)	3.09	2.23	200
Dependent Variable:			
Alive in 1984 (ALIVE84)	1.35	.48	179

Variable	B	Beta	Std. Error B	F
ORGAGE	$-.6129781E-01$	$-.14838$	.03866	2.514
FUNCTION	$.1663693E-01$	.04913	.03281	.257
%BLACK	$.1031083E-02$	.06043	.00161	.411
%UND18	$.3437133E-02$	.09896	.00319	1.163
MINCOME	$-.5733305E-05$	$-.06030$	.00001	.438
FUNDBLOC	$-.3279795E-01$	$-.16075$	.02099	2.442
DIVERSE	$-.2089911E-01$	$-.19695$	.01092	3.661
SIZE	$-.2388634E-01$	$-.20649$	.01343	3.162
NOPARTIC	$.2002417E-01$	.09021	.02243	.797
NOHEARNG	$.0480985E-02$	.07676	.00180	.675
%ACTIVE	$.2777992E-02$	.18876	.00134	4.272
PCVOL	$-.1166410E-01$	$-.05439$	.01989	.344
(CONSTANT)	1.914025			

ALIVE84: 1 = YES, 2 = NO

Variable	Simple r	Multiple r	r^2	Δr^2
ORGAGE	$-.18$	.18	.03	
FUNCTION	.02	.19	.03	.00
%BLACK	.12	.20	.04	.01
%UND18	.06	.21	.04	.00
MINCOME	$-.07$	.22	.05	.01
FUNDBLOC	$-.06$	.23	.05	.00
DIVERSE	$-.22$	.32	.10	.05
SIZE	$-.20$	.35	.12	.02
NOPARTIC	$-.08$	.35	.12	.00
NOHEARNG	.02	.36	.13	.01
%ACTIVE	.18	.41	.17	.04
PCVOL	$-.07$	.41	.17	.00

expect some organizations to resist oligarchic control by simply ceasing to exist.

DISCUSSION

One part of the funding arena theory is correct. NBOs generally draw funding from single funding arenas. They are not eclectic in their fund-raising. There must be good reasons that such a dominant pattern prevails with these organizations. At the same time, our analysis of the New World Foundation survey data shows that the organizational effects of member-ship in one or another arena are ambiguous. We began this paper specu-lating that the "culture" that predominates in an arena would coerce or-ganizations to adapt their structure to certain norms or expectations imposed by funders. Thus, we thought we might find in the survey data evidence of sharply different types of organizations associated with arena membership.

Whatever reason there is for NBOs to concentrate their fund-raising ef-fort in single arenas, other established explanations for variations in or-ganizational style and structure remain powerful. What function an orga-nization carries out has an effect on where organizations go for money as well as on whether they are diverse in their structure. This is consistent with technology focused organizational theories[35] and with institutional theory.[36] Measures of organizational size, complexity, and diversity are related to organizational age and contribute to long term organizational survival independently of funding arenas. These results are consistent with structural organizational theories[37] that downplay the importance of the historical context in which an organization operates as well as the idiosyn-cratic structural effects of different modes of technical organization.

Finally, funding arenas have no single effect on democratic governance in NBOs. One sees this most clearly in the relationship between member activism, a variable seemingly unrelated to organizational structure, and long term survival. This is not to say, however, that funding sources have no association with our measures of democracy. Federally funded organi-zations are probably encouraged by procedural requirements for commu-nity involvement in planning to hold many meetings or hearings each year. Also, because these organizations are large they attract many members. Similarly, an ethos of voluntarism seems to be associated with receiving funding from private institutions such as foundations and churches.

All of these effects area related to the specific historical and cultural context in which funders operate. They do not reflect the translation of requirements imposed by funders into structural proclivities that discour-age or encourage democracy. This is important because we started by spec-ulating that alterations in NBOs caused by arena membership would have functional causes. Federally funded organizations would be nondemocratic because the grant process would make them large and burdened with ad-ministrative requirements. It is sharply different to say that federally funded organizations do not use volunteers because an ethos of voluntarism has not been required by federal policy as it is by the policies of churches and foundations. Presumably the style of democracy practiced in federally funded NBOs could be changed simply by changing federal participation requirements.

CONCLUSION

The problem with the theory of funding arenas we articulated at the beginning of this paper is that it too heavily emphasizes structure as a determinant of NBO behavior. We looked at three aspects of structure in this chapter: the major technical function of organizations, variables related to the size and age of organizations, and affiliation with a particular funding arena. We expected that understanding how these three factors interact would give us important information about whether NBOs are bureaucratic or democratic, whether they will survive the tests of time and of challenging events, and how participation in funding arenas alters administrative structure. All of these factors have proved important in explaining organizational structure. Measures of size, age, and complexity are especially so.

Although these factors exert powerful influences on the characteristics of particular NBOs, historical context, politics, and cultural styles seem more important in explaining how NBOs evolve and respond to adversity. Because these organizations are small they are profoundly affected by the people who happen to participate in them. As Dennis Young has shown,[38] previously moribund organizations can be infused with dynamism when entrepreneurial leaders join. Similarly, an NBO's evolutionary development is profoundly affected by the kind of community it is associated with. A variety of observers have suggested that upper middle class people from the 1960s generation of college students bring to voluntary organizations a special commitment to community and democracy.[39] NBOs that serve their communities have access to a pool of enthusiastic leaders who can replace veterans who burn out from the rigors of managing a democratic organization. Participants also insist on remaining involved in decision making so that the oligarchic processes Michels[40] anticipated are held at bay. Because NBOs are so affected by the accidents of who participates, what communities they serve, and when issues arise that excite participation, structural variables do not predict their long term development very well.

Thus, although funding arenas are related in certain strong, consistent ways to structural variables it is hard to find a distinctive signature for any arena. Whatever it is that causes NBOs to rely so heavily on single arenas does not seem rooted in structure. More likely, funding arenas embody certain institutionalized practices, norms, and sets of network connections that make it convenient for fund-raisers to continue relying on similar sources. It is expensive for small organizations to forge new contacts and learn new ways to write grant applications. But faced with necessity caused by the decline of funding in a favored arena, the high long term survival rate among our sample organizations shows NBO leaders have little difficulty shifting their attention to new sources of funding. Consequently, contrary to our earlier expectations, NBOs are quite capable of surviving a sharp cutback like that we have recently seen in federal funding.

This is, of course, an assertion made with few qualitative data on what life is like in the NBOs we studied in 1978. Survival does not mean that organizations are prospering, that they are effective at solving community problems, or that they are highly democratic. At the same time, the data we did obtain show that most organizations have prospered. Asked about changes in program size between 1978 and 1984, 58% (62) of those surviving organizations that provided data claimed their programs were larger and 21% (22) claimed their programs were about the same size.

The results of this study give some clear indications about how those who would like to increase the chances of survival for their organization ought to proceed. Although organizations can shift their funding sources, this is easiest when they carry on diverse activities and gain support from many sources. Diversity is a benefit provided by size and age. But since NBOs are by nature fluid and loosely structured, there are few barriers preventing leaders at any stage of organizational development from seeking out a diversified base of support. Doing so is likely to increase chances of long term survival.

NOTES

1. An earlier version of this paper was titled "The Structure of Funding Arenas for Community Self-Help Organizations" and appeared as PONPO Working Paper no. 42 (New Haven: Yale University, Program on Non-Profit Organizations, 1981). This earlier draft was prepared for the American Sociological Association Conference on Problems of the Discipline titled "Survey Approaches to Community Organization Research." The conference was co-sponsored by PONPO and was held May 2–3, 1981.

2. See James D. Thompson, *Organizations in Action* (New York: McGraw-Hill, 1967).

3. See Paul W. DiMaggio and Walter W. Powell, "The Iron Cage Revisited: Institutional Isomorphism and Collective Rationality in Organizational Fields," *American Sociological Review* 48 (1983), 147–160. That paper is also Chapter 3 in this volume. For an early discussion of organizational fields see Roland L. Warren, "The Interorganizational Field as a Focus for Investigation," *Administrative Science Quarterly,* 12 (1967), 396–419.

4. See Howard Aldrich, *Organizations and Environments* (Engelwood Cliffs, NJ: Prentice-Hall, 1979); Michael T. Hannan and John H. Freeman, "The Population Ecology of Organizations," *American Journal of Sociology* 82 (1977), 929–964, and "Structural Inertia and Organizational Change," *American Sociological Review* 49 (1984), 149–164, and J. Miller McPherson, "A Theory of Voluntary Organization," Chapter 2 in this volume.

5. For a fuller definitional discussion of NBOs see Carl Milofsky, "Neighborhood Based Organizations: A Market Analogy," pp. 277–295 in *The Nonprofit Sector. A Research Handbook,* ed. Walter W. Powell (New Haven: Yale University Press 1987).

6. See Mayer Zald, *Organizational Change: The Political Economy of the YMCA* (Chicago: University of Chicago Press, 1970).

7. Mayer Zald, *Organizational Change.*

8. See Deborah Kaplan Policy, "The United Way: Understanding How It Works Is the First Step to Effecting Change," Chapter 7 in this volume.

9. Carl Milofsky and Frank Romo, "The Structure of Funding Arenas for Community Self-Help Organizations."

10. See Neil S. Mayer and Jennifer L. Blake, *Keys to the Growth of Neighborhood Development Organizations* (Washington, D.C.: The Urban Institute Press, 1981) and Sue A. Marshall and Neil S. Mayer, "Neighborhood Organizations and Community Development" (Washington, D.C.: The Urban Institute, 1983).

11. See James D. Thompson, *Organizations in Action.*

12. We mention Chicago as a "small" jurisdiction because an early study that articulated this theory of political pluralism examined several case studies of political decision making in Chicago. The book is Edward C. Banfield, *Political Influence* (Glencoe, Ill.: The Free Press, 1961). Although Chicago is a city with millions of people, it is a closed and relatively stable political system in which the power of political leaders is based on their ability to mobilize votes and support in neighborhoods. This contrasts with large political systems such as the federal government where the most important resource distribution mechanisms for NBOs are usually based more on universalistic competition than on the effective use of political support networks.

13. In addition to Banfield's *Political Influence,* see Robert A. Dahl, *Who Governs? Democracy and Power in an American City* (New Haven: Conn.: Yale University Press, 1961).

14. See Paul W. DiMaggio, "Nonprofit Organizations in the Production and Distribution of Culture," pp. 195–220 in *The Nonprofit Sector A Research Handbook,* ed. Walter W. Powell (New Haven: Yale University Press, 1987).

15. See Michael Useem, "Corporate Philanthropy," in Walter W. Powell, *Between Public and Private: The Non-Profit Sector* (New Haven, Conn.: Yale University Press, 1987), chapter 20.

16. In addition to Joseph Galaskiewicz and Barbara Rauschenbach, "The Corporation Culture Connection," see John R. Seeley, B. R. Junker, and R. W. James, *Community Chest* (Toronto: University of Toronto Press, 1957).

17. In addition to Saul Alinsky, *Reveille for Radicals* (New York: Random House, 1969), see Joan E. Lancourt, *Confront or Concede: The Alinsky Citizen Action Organizations* (Lexington, Mass., Lexington Books, 1979).

18. One such organization is Greater Hartford Process described in New World Foundation, *Initiatives for Community Self-Help: Efforts to Increase Recognition and Support* (New York: The New World Foundation, 1980).

19. See New World Foundation, *Initiatives for Community Self-Help.*

20. See Paul N. Ylvisaker, "Foundations and Nonprofit Organizations," pp. 360–379 in *The Nonprofit Sector. A Research Handbook,* ed. Walter W. Powell (New Haven: Yale University Press, 1987).

21. See Scott A. Boorman and Paul R. Levitt, "Network Matching: Nonprofit Structure and Public Policy, chapter 1: Cultural Conflicts and the Roots of Non-Profit Social Structure" (New Haven, Conn.: Department of Sociology, 1981).

22. See, for example, Joseph Fichter, *Social Relations in the Urban Parish* (Chicago: University of Chicago Press, 1954) and W. Lloyd Warner, *The Living and the Dead: A Study of the Symbolic Life of Americans* (New Haven, Conn.: Yale University Press, 1959).

23. See E. Q. Campbell and T. F. Pettigrew, "Racial and Moral Crisis: The Role of Little Rock Ministers," *American Journal of Sociology* 64: (March 1959), 509–516, and *Christians in Racial Crisis: A Study of Little Rock's Ministry* (Washington, D.C.: Public Affairs Press, 1959).

24. A variety of religious communes grew and prospered because they were able to develop a unique product for sale. This allowed them to pursue a unique life-style without being subject to outside economic interference. See, for example, Benjamin Zablocki, *The Joyful Community* (Chicago: University of Chicago Press, 1980). The free clinic described by Rosemary Taylor in "Free Medicine," pp. 17–48 in *Coops, Communes and Collectives: Ex-*

periments in Social Change in the 1960s and 1970s ed. John Case and Rosemary C. R. Taylor (New York: Pantheon, 1979) is another example.

25. See William McDonough, "Neighborhood Fiscal Empowerment Analytic Paper," prepared for Division of Community Planning and Neighborhood Studies, Office of Policy Development and Research, HUD (Hartford, Conn.: McDonough, Bond and Associates, 1983). Also see Bruce Boyd and Hans Spiegel, "Financing Community Organizations: The Business Option," *Journal of Community Action* 1, 5 (1983), 9–13.

26. See Dennis Young, *If Not For Profit, For What?* (Lexington, Mass.: Lexington Books, 1983) and *Casebook of Management for Non-Profit Organizations: Entrepreneurship and Organizational Change in Human Services* (New York: Haworth Press, 1984).

27. A good example is provided in Rosemary Taylor, "Free Medicine."

28. W. S. Sarle, "FASTCLUS," pp. 433–449 in *SAS User's Guide: Statistics*, 1982 ed. (Cary, N.C.: SAS Institute, 1982).

29. Our earlier effort used the CONCOR block modeling technique described by Harrison White, Scott Boorman and Ronald Breiger in "Social Structure from Multiple Networks. I. Blockmodels of Roles and Positions," *American Journal of Sociology* 81, 4 (1976), 730–780, and did not achieve such striking results. The results are different because in the earlier effort the magnitude of funding had to be reduced to a code of "1" or "0" to conform to the requirements of CONCOR. When we entered a "1" when an organization received funding from any source we exaggerated the eclecticism of NBO funding. In this analysis we used actual funding dollars received from each source, expressed as a percentage of the total funding an organization received.

30. See Carl Milofsky, "Structure and Process in Community Self-Help Organizations," Chapter 9 in this volume.

31. This is Robert Michels's hypothesis in *Political Parties* (Glencoe, Ill: The Free Press, 1949), which is echoed in Philip Selznick, *The Organizational Weapon: A Study of Bolshevist Strategy and Tactics* (New York: McGraw-Hill, 1952). They argue that as democratic organizations age, members lose interest in participation and there is a tendency for a small leadership cadre to emerge, dominating organizational policy-making. In this way mass organizations become oligarchic and lose their democratic orientation.

32. John R. Seeley, et al. *Community Chest.*

33. Howard Aldrich, *Organizations and Environments*, pp. 39–51.

34. Robert Michels, *Political Parties.*

35. See Joan Woodward, *Industrial Organization: Theory and Practice* (Oxford: Oxford University Press, 1965) and "Technology, material control and organizational behavior" in A. R. Negandhi and J. P. Schwitter (eds.) *Organizational Behavior Models* (Kent, Ohio: Kent State University Press, 1970), and Charles Perrow, "A Framework for Comparative Organizational Analysis," *American Sociological Review* 32 (April 1967), and 194–208, "The effect of Technological Change on the Structure of Business Firms," in ed. B. C. Roberts (London: The Macmillan Co., 1968), pp. 205–219.

36. See Charles Perrow, *Complex Organizations: A Critical Essay* (Glenview, Ill.: Scott, Foresman, 1972).

37. See Peter Blau, "A Formal Theory of Differentiation in Organizations," *American Sociological Review* 35 (April 1970), 201–218, Peter Blau and W. Richard Scott, *Formal Organizations: A Comparative Approach* (San Francisco: Chandler, 1962), and Peter M. Blau and Richard A. Schoenherr, *The Structure of Organizations* (New York: Basic Books, 1971).

38. Dennis Young, *If Not for Profit, for What?* and *Casebook of Management for Non-Profit Organizations.*

39. See Joyce Rothschild and J. Allen Whitt, *The Cooperative Workplace. Potentials and Dilemmas of Organizational Democracy and Participation* (Cambridge: Cambridge University Press, 1986).

40. Robert Michels, *Political Parties.*

11

Local Communities and Organized Action[1]

ALBERT HUNTER and SUZANNE STAGGENBORG

Why do local communities persist as bases of collective sentiment and collective action? Like Mark Twain's reported death, their demise has been exaggerated by various versions of mass society theory. Some of the major works capture this thesis in their very title, such as Maurice Stein's *The Eclipse of Community*[2] and Robert Nisbet's *The Quest for Community*[3] Most of these mass society theories of the mid–twentieth century simply projected outward the theses put forward in the earlier classics of Durkheim, Marx, and Weber, among others.[4] Though different, to be sure, a common thesis of these theorists was that the parochial solidarity and sentiments of place would be superseded or displaced in the modern urban world by associations of interest based on occupations, classes, and more general political interests or parties, respectively (for a notable exception see Shils's alternative view of "mass society"[5]). Within urban sociology, Louis Wirth in his seminal article on "Urbanism as a Way of Life"[6] (following Simmel's earlier lead in "The Metropolis and Mental Life"[7]) pointed to the decline of ascriptive ties of heart and heath (blood and land), and the rise of rational individualism as the basis of association in the modern urban world of strangers. These theories attribute what Polanyi calls "the great transformation"[8] to major structural shifts from a feudal to a capitalist market system, or from agricultural to industrial modes of production.

A parallel set of arguments has also been advanced in recent theories centering around the rise of the modern world system of nation-states in the work of Wallerstein,[9] and more specifically, the modern welfare state as analyzed by Janowitz.[10] These theories, again with varying emphases, in general propose that the prevailing and preeminent identifications and interests of individuals are based on the assertion of the rights of citizenship in the nation-state, which have expanded from more narrow political rights to include economic rights as well and, finally, a broad range of social rights and entitlements such as education, health, and housing. The concerns and claims of citizenship in the nation-state, though often based on a variety of collective groupings such as gender, race, ethnicity, religion, or region, are seen to be more central than those based on the more parochial and more trivial day-to-day concerns of people in their local communities.

However, recent events have called these varying theories into question by pointing to the persistent role played by local communities acting collectively through voluntary local community organizations of various kinds. This phenomenon has been empirically well documented in detailed studies of the emergence, structure, and activities of local community organizations in recent decades (see, for example, the work of Castells,[11] Crenson,[12] Hunter,[13] Knoke and Wood,[14] and Warren[15]). Only through torturous reasoning may these organized activities be reduced to direct manifestations of narrow economic and class interests, or to limited political interests of political parties. Rather, they are often status rather than class based, noneconomic, nonprofit, and avowedly disconnected from more formally established political structures. Several different explanations have been offered for the emergence (or persistence) of parochial sentiments and locally organized collective action, explanations which may be classified into two broad categories: the ecologically based organization (disorganization) of social networks, and the differential distribution of resources to facilitate the mobilization and organization of social networks. The former is rooted in the classic tradition of the Chicago School, which emphasized the disorganizing impact of size and heterogeneity of urban populations on the tight networks of primordial solidarities. More recent extensions of this school, however, have pointed to a selective and variable persistence and emergence of local community solidarity in the modern metropolis.

The second approach, drawn from the social movements literature and the currently dominant "resource mobilization" perspective of Tilly and Zald,[16] in particular, has emphasized in turn the varying capacity of local communities to organize to engage in collective action. This varying capacity to create enduring and powerful organizations is seen to directly depend upon the preexisting distribution of resources, and upon organizations' ability to establish links with other organizations and institutions that may provide critical external resources. Whether these are money and other material resources, or the skills and talents of people, or political resources such as legitimacy, they are critical in providing the organizational capacity to engage in effective and sustained collective action.

The model to be developed here combines these two perspectives by focusing on the ecological basis of the distribution of resources, the structure of social networks internal to local communities that may aid in this mobilization, and the external organizational linkages that may lead to sustained action and activities by these organized local community interests. It is, in short, a model focused on the networks of mobilization at two distinct levels, that of the local community itself and that of the interorganizational linkages of the local community to its wider society. Ultimately, the type and amount of resources mobilized are hypothesized to affect the very structure of these organizations and the types of actions and activities in which they engage.

TWO PERSPECTIVES ON LOCALLY ORGANIZED ACTION

There are a number of general, and a few more specific, theories that have been advanced to explain the emergence and persistence of local community organization as a basis of collective action. For heuristic purposes we will divide these into two: the Chicago School of urban sociology which in both its traditional form as in the work of Robert Park and Ernest Burgess and in its more modern manifestation as in the work of Gerald Suttles and Albert Hunter focuses upon the ecological characteristics of local communities themselves as a point of departure[17]; and second, the more organizationally based perspective of collective action which in current theories is variously concerned with resource mobilization by organized groups (see the work of Mayer Zald and his students[18]), and their varying repertoires of collective action (on this point see the work of Charles Tilly[19] and William Gamson[20]). We will briefly review each of these in turn and then suggest a synthetic model that combines critical elements from each.

The Local Community in the Chicago School

The ambivalence expressed about the fate of local communities from the early research and writing of the Chicago School is perhaps most clearly evidenced in the empirical work of Harvey Zorbaugh in his classic *The Gold Coast and the Slum* published in 1929.[21] Zorbaugh is repetitively adamant in his analysis in decrying the disintegration and loss of community in the different neighborhoods of Chicago's Near North Side including the Gold Coast of the elite, the bohemian Towertown of artists, and the slum of Little Sicily, the home of recent Italian immigrants. This theoretical conclusion about the loss of local solidarity and integration among these diverse populations sharing a common geographical area is based upon an explicit comparison to the idealized (though empirically unstudied) rural village of an earlier era (more recently Laslett has addressed this very point in his historical analysis of *The World We Have Lost*[22]). Such conclusions were later elaborated by Louis Wirth in his seminal article, "Urbanism as a Way of Life,"[23] which is often seen as a summary of much of this perspective. The picture portrayed by Wirth was of the isolated individual urbanite, operating on a rational cost/benefit calculus in both market and personal transactions, removed (liberated) from the primordial social control of disintegrating ties of neighbors and kin. Hence, the theoretical label often associated with the Chicago School is "social disorganization." This label, however, fails to reflect the empirical reality of what was found in these studies and ignores an entire line of research, primarily the work of Ernest Burgess and his students, on the persisting role of the neighborhood in urban life. Where others saw an endemic disorganization, Brugess saw not only the need, but, more prophetically, the ability to construct consciously meaningful forms of neighborhood social organization. For example, in his article "Can Neighborhood Work Have a Scientific Basis?"[24] he maintained that the local urban neighborhood could, in today's parlance, be mobilized and organized to deal with diverse urban ills ranging from substandard housing, to family disorganization, to crime and delinquency. Furthermore, a close reading of the numerous empirical studies of the diverse populations in these urban neighborhoods, seen especially in Zorbaugh's work, depicted what today would be called "dense networks" of self-help and mutual assistance. Ironically, in more contemporary research such as that by Claude Fischer, Carol Stack, and Barry Wellman,[25] these same networks are seen as evidence of the persistence of community in modern urban life which refutes the disorganization perspective of the Chicago School. It is not so much that community was lost then, and has now been rediscovered, since the empirical descriptions are themselves identical; rather, the concept of community itself has undergone a critical redefinition. The early Chicago School depicted community as an institutionally structured entity, whereas today community is often relegated to a more social-psychological ego centered system of dyadic interactions ramifying through networks. The question of the relationship between such networks and the more enduring institutions of the local urban community are often ignored in this more recent research.

Zorbaugh[26] observed a number of dense social networks of prestige, provision, and protection, respectively: what today are defined as naturally occurring self-help networks. But Zorbaugh also looked to other institutions in the Near North Side, specifically the local community council and the settlement house, that could conceivably be the basis of integration among these diverse social groups. It was here that Zorbaugh failed to find enduring structures that served to integrate these populations into a single cohesive community of identification and action. Instead he saw their rising and falling episodically to meet specific needs of specific groups, but failing as unifying institutions. Networks of proximate neighbors, yes; enduring institutions of community, no.

On the basis of Zorbaugh's and others' work, Wirth advanced his central thesis about the erosion of primary community sentiments and collective action. He linked these outcomes of social disorganization to three basic demographic and ecological variables of urban populations—namely, their size, density, and heterogeneity. Each of these, at its zenith in the large metropolis, would produce the nadir of human personal and social disorganization. Though much of this research described the poor of the city (as did Wirth's earlier work on *The Ghetto*[27]), left implicit in his argument was the simple, but powerful idea that such social disorganization might be the result of poverty itself. However, as Zorbaugh's spot maps indicated, no social class was free of these disorganizing effects; it was simply the case that deviance and disorganization would take different forms among the different classes. For example, serious crime was highest among the Sicilians, suicides among the dwellers in "the world of furnished rooms," whereas those arrested in a raid on a speakeasy were from Chicago's middle and upper classes. Reversing the sign of this negative causal explanation, one could advance the corollary that the types of social *organization* and *collective action* among different classes would also take different forms and have different foci of activity. For example, family life was pictured as a relatively stable feature among both the Sicilians of the Slum and the elite of the Gold Coast, whereas it was in disarray if not absent among the bohemian artists of Towertown. Therefore, according to these early ecological explanations, variations in the ecological and institutional complexity of urban life explained the prevailing social disorder, whereas variations in social class merely explained the more specific variation in form that such disorders might take. It was to this specific variation resulting from basic inequalities that later theorists turned to explicate differences in social organization and disorganization in local communities.

Resources and Organization

The War on Poverty with its related Model Cities Program was a milestone in the application of a theory of community construction, and local institution building for it emphasized that social disorganization was intimately related to poverty itself. To be sure the causal relation was seen to work both ways: poverty leading to various forms of disorganization and disorganization, in turn, trapping people in poverty. Whether framed from a cultural or a structural perspective (culture of poverty versus unemployment, discrimination), community organization, both in the narrow and broader senses of that term, was seen to require resources; and once organized, resources could be more readily acquired. Earlier, Saul Alinsky had reversed the prevailing view of local voluntary organizations by suggesting that the benign hand of voluntarism generally did not operate in communities that need it most, and that the prevailing benign neglect of such communities could only be overcome through political mobilization of people to engage in conflict, protest, and demonstration in airing their grievances to the powerful who controlled the distribution of those resources. The "success" of a number of Alinsky-formed local community organizations in cities throughout the nation (for example, TWO, The Woodlawn Organization in Chicago, and FIGHT in Rochester, New York.)[28] suggested that indeed poor people could be mobilized.

Analysts such as Piven and Cloward, Moynihan, Warren, and Gittell[29] soon came to realize that poor people's movements at both the national and local levels depended on resources that were controlled by the very people, institutions, and centers of power that were the targets of their attacks. The "Catch 22" was that those funds would be cut off if the organization of collective action were proving too successful in its challenges, or the organization would alter its demands, programs, or goals so as not to threaten the very resource flows on which it depended. The resulting organizational dilemma led to a theory of "resource dependency" which saw the very structure and activities of organizations determined by the amount and sources of their resources.

This line of argument within the local community organizations literature was supported by and contributed to a more general perspective in both theories of social movements and of formal organizations. In the former it is referred to as "resource mobilization," and in the latter as the "ecology of organizations." Both perspectives emphasize that the capacity of local communities to organize for collective action is dependent upon resources, primarily of personnel and funds but also including moral and legitimizing support (on this point see the seminal work of Jenkins and Perrow)[30] to form relatively enduring structures that will be the basis of collective community action. Most often these resources are seen to derive from sources external to the local community, whether they be private, nonprofit, or public funds to support particular activities and programs. The capacity to tap into these external funding sources was in turn seen to depend on the linkages which a local community, or more specifically the local community organization, was able to establish with other organizations external to the local community. From this perspective the emphasis shifted from a more general "institutional" approach to community to the more specific "organization" of the community. The major analytical problem of this research is determining how to combine the key elements of both the institutional "community perspective" and the organized "social movement perspective" in understanding under what conditions local communities are likely to mobilize for collective action, and the form that action will take.

A Synthetic Model

The synthetic model that we will outline here and elaborate more fully later draws from these distinct literatures on urban communities, social movements, and formal organizations and integrates the key concepts and propositions from each. From the local community literature we focus on the patterns of ecological segregation in cities that produce distinct clusters of populations selected by choice and constraint into varyingly homogeneous local neighborhoods based on race, class, ethnicity, and family composition among other social characteristics. We hypothesize that these social characteristics result in different types of local networks that vary in their density, or the degree to which they are open or closed network structures. These local networks are critical in mobilizing resources to support locally organized collective action. From the organizational and social movements literature we draw on the critical role of external networks of organizations within an organizational field (ecologically considered an "environment," or from the social movements literature a social movement "industry"). The quality and quantity of resources that a local organization can muster depends on its ability to establish these dense external networks with potential resource providers. Finally, both the structure and the activities of local organizations, for example, their degree of professionalism and formalization and their degree of cooperation or conflict, depend on the nature of these internal and external networks and the quality and quantity of the resources they have mobilized. This synthetic model is depicted in simplified form in Figure 11.1. In the more detailed discussion which follows we will focus in turn upon each of the major components of this model—internal networks, external networks, the mobilization and organization of resources, and briefly, types of organized collective action. Finally, we will offer an empirical test of the model in an analysis of several hundred local community organizations.

INTERNAL NETWORKS AND NEIGHBORHOOD RESOURCES

From their earliest entry into the maze of the modern metropolis sociologists have searched for meaningful patterns in cities' baffling babble of people, activities, sights, and smells. Recognition of the fact that, in Louis Wirth's[31] expression, cities are a "mosaic of little worlds" led many in Western thought to conclude that they are also a "quilt of disquietude" (see, for example, White and White's analysis of America's *Intellectuals Versus the City*).[32] Dante's epic entry into hell, which he called The City of Dis, fittingly implied that disobedience led to dislocation or disorder, and in turn to disease and disorganization. However, the continuing search for patterns to this seeming disorganization produced a degree of pattern recognition, though often patterns of change rather than of stability.

First attempts to find the order in the urban mosaic focused on patterns of spatial distribution of people, buildings, institutions, and activities. One of the earliest and still most cited is Ernest Burgess's now classic pattern of concentric zones which summarized a vast number of spot maps and case studies of particular populations, institutions, and local communities.[33] Like a nuclear fireball at ground zero, the zonal model begins with a central business district expanding into the surrounding zone of light industry, which in turn engulfs the surrounding slums of "zone in transition." This zone then expands into areas of working class apartments, then into the single family homes of the middle class. Finally, the outwardly expanding fringe of suburban development creates a banal wasteland of the nearby countryside. This concentric zonal arrangement was later overlaid by Homer Hoyt's[34] pie shaped "sector theory," a pattern which was empirically based on variations in land values and rents. To complete the trilogy, Harris and Ullman[35] then posited a more spatially varying theory of "multiple nuclei" in which dominant institutions (businesses, hospitals, universities, and so on) selected primary locations best suited to their needs, and around which residential populations would sift and sort themselves through competitive processes of attraction and repulsion.

All of these theories posited sharp variations in the distribution of people and institutions that were linked to the critical resource of advantageous economic location. Those able to afford the best locations for either production or consumption purposes reaped the benefits of prime locations, and those with fewer resources in turn suffered the costs of less advantageous places. What was a functional inequality both reflected and resulted in a continuing inequality in wealth, status, and life chances. Though a number of critiques of the theoretical explanations of these patterns were raised (for earlier critiques see the works of Form, Alihan, and Firey, and more recently those of Molotch, Harvey, and Castells),[36] these patterns were empirically demonstrated in numerous quantitative studies of class segregation[37] (Duncan and Duncan), racial segregation[38] (Taeuber and Taeuber), and family and life-style segregation (Mowrer, Rossi, and Greer[39]). On the basis of these findings and their theoretical critiques Eshrev Shevky and Wendell Bell[40] developed a newer perspective that focused on the social bases of these patterns of segregation rather than their spatial pattern. This "social area analysis" was later expanded into "factorial ecology" by Brian J. L. Berry and his colleagues.[41] They found repeatedly that the three primary dimensions or factors of residential segregation in American cities were socioeconomic status, racial/ethnic status, and family life cycle or lifestyle status.

Subsequently, Anderson and Egeland[42] showed in an ingenious synthesis of the older spatial ecology with the newer social ecology that socioeconomic status varied most by sectors, family or life cycle status varied by concentric zones, and racial/ethnic status was ghettoized into multiple nuclei. By overlaying all three of these dimensions on the spatial grid of American cities distinctive local areas or neighborhoods are defined that are *relatively* homogeneous on each of the three dimensions. The ecological base had been established for more sociological intepretations of the varying social and spatial patterns in populations, institutions, and behaviors that make up the urban mosaic. The two key questions of communally based identification and collective action that remain from this research are, to what degree is homogeneity versus heterogeneity significant in affecting the viability of local communities, and which of these three dimensions is most important as a basis for forming these local solidarities?

Social-Spatial Homogeneity and Shared Interests

From Louis Wirth's article "Urbanism as a Way of Life"[43] a central proposition can be extracted that the size, density, and heterogeneity of cities are responsible for the decline of community, the rise of rational impersonality, and the prevalent personal and social disorganization. What is true of cities as a whole, however, can be generalized to communities at all levels from the largest (the nation-state) to the smallest (the neighbor-hood). The hypothesis is, namely, that a communal social order is more likely the smaller and the more homogeneous the community. This is, of course, a direct extension of Durkheim's thesis that the smaller, segmental communities of an earlier era had a minimal division of labor and there-fore a solidarity based on shared social positions and emphatetic under-standing or shared interests (mechanical solidarity). With larger and more heterogeneous communities in which there is a greater division of labor, solidarity is based on the interdependence among different peoples (or-ganic solidarity).[44] The communal solidarity of gemeinschaft, in short, is based upon these two ecological factors of small size and homogeneity. The solidarity of gesellschaft, by contrast, is not to be found in the modern residential community comprising diverse individuals, but rather, exists in the relatively homogeneous positions (occupations) people occupy in the currently complex division of labor. Shared interests are positional or oc-cupational, not spatial or communal.

However, local territorial interests empirically exist in modern society (for notable recent analyses see Castells and Crenson[45]). They have not disappeared but have taken on a somewhat new form. (In the absence of widespread empirical research on their historical condition we cannot be sure that the hypothesized gemeinschaft solidarity of an earlier day was as "solid" as many assert. On this point see Laslett's *The World We Have Lost*).[46] There are three critical characteristics of the new local community that recent researchers have documented. First, local community solidarity is "limited," meaning it is neither comprehensive of a person's life space nor of his or her total interest and sentiment. This "community of limited liability" is partial and calculated against other competing institutions and interests (for the development of the concept of "the community of limited-liability" see Janowitz, Greer, and Hunter and Suttles).[47] Second, the new communal solidarity is seen to be spatially "liberated" for most people who choose to operate in metropolitanwide networks, whereas those lack-ing resources are more likely to be constrained to the parochial community of the local neighborhood (see here the recent work of Fischer and Well-man).[48] And third, the new communal solidarity is not a presumed pri-mordial given, but rather is more often socially constructed in interaction with other communities and institutions external to the local community (on this point see Suttles, Taub and assoociates, and Davidson).[49] Because of these three characteristics of modern local community solidarity—lim-ited, liberated, and constructed—it is not seen as dependent as the older conception of solidarity based on the ecological characteristics of small size and homogeneity. The differential distribution of scarce resources rather than the ecological composition of the population is seen to be critical in explaining local solidarity. And, reflexively, local solidarity itself may have implications for a community's ability to mobilize resources. The next log-ical question must therefore be how the differential distribution of re-sources is related to differences in local community solidarity.

Local Resources and Mechanisms of Mobilization

Two general categories of substantive resources may be defined: (1) economic resources of wealth (income, property, and so on) that can be used to further one's goals and (2) human resources of talents, skills, and labor that can also be expended to further one's goals. Following Becker's[50] seminal work, these may be labeled economic capital and human capital. The two are often correlated in the same individuals and in the same communities; that is, those with greater wealth are also likely to have more talents and skills at their dispoals. However, where wealth is absent, human capital is not necessarily absent; as Piven and Cloward[51] among others note, the poor still have the human capital no matter how undeveloped it may be. The one thing the poor still have, in short, is their numbers, and their labors may be organized into collective action. To a certain extent both financial and human resources are needed to create organized collective action. However, the two are substitutable, within limits, and the more economic resources a community has, the fewer human resources it need expend to achieve collective ends. Similarly, the fewer economic resources a community has, the more reliant it must be upon human capital to achieve its ends. In short, in the realm of collective goals, the rich can buy what they want, while the poor must work for it. As a simple case in point, to achieve public safety in urban neighborhoods, the rich may purchase additional police services in the form of doormen and private police patrols, while the poor may have to organize to pool their labors in a citizen patrol or "neighborhood watch" program. Therefore, depending upon a community's social class composition, collective wealth, size, and the number of people it can draw upon for either economic or human capital, the resources available to create an organizaiton to pursue collective goals will vary. Furthermore, the nature of the organization created and the specific goals and activities pursued are also likely to vary depending upon the different proportions of the two types of resources that are mobilized. For example, an organization with economic capital may be able to hire professionals to direct and administer the activities of the organization and may be more likely to engage in legitimate institutionalized activities to achieve collective goals, whereas an organization with few economic resources may have to rely upon the labors of a larger number of volunteers and engage in more episodic "direct action" tactics, such as rallies, demonstrations, sit-ins, and the like.

Given these two different types of resources, their correlated nature, and the fact that they are inequitably distributed in local communities throughout a metropolitan area, we must still consider the specific mechanisms that are required to mobilize them. The local communities and neighborhoods with which we are concerned are by and large nongovernmental entities; that is, they lack the power of the state to use coercion to mobilize either economic capital (taxes) or human capital (conscription). Instead they must rely upon voluntary, informal mechanisms of resource mobili-

zation. We suggest that there are two critical components to such voluntary mobilization: (1) the nature of social networks within a community
and (2) the strength of symbolic sentiments of collective identity within a
community. The first is a structural, the second a cultural expression of
solidarity.

Social Networks

The rediscovery of strong and significant social ties in the seemingly anomic neighborhoods of modern cities has come about through several lines
of research. Most important perhaps have been the case studies of poorer,
working class ethnic communities that have either retained or re-created
the strong interpersonal ties that many social thinkers had projected into
the dustbin of history. Herbert Gans's "peer group" society among the
Italians of Boston's West End,[52] Gerald Suttles's "dyadic bonds of interpersonal trust in the "segmental social order" of Chicago's Addams Area,[53]
and Carol Stack's "networks of sustenance" existing among the women of
a black slum community all point to the important role played by dense
interpersonal networks in the lives of the urban poor.[54] These results are
generally supported by the survey research of Wellman and of Fischer,
who explore the friendship and support networks of individuals and find
that for middle class residents such networks are scattered throughout a
metropolitan area, while for the poor they are limited to the parochial
confines of the local community and neighborhood.[55] The middle class are
"liberated" into metropolitanwide networks of choice, whereas the poor
are constrained to local networks of necessity. One would expect, therefore, that poorer local communities would be more likely to have a dense
network of local ties that could be mobilized into action by local community organizations.

There is, however, a set of findings that would reverse this hypothesized
relationship between social class and local networks and their capacity to
be mobilized into collective action, namely, the research which reports uniformly that the higher the social class the greater the rates of participation
in voluntary associations of all kinds, and local community organizations
in particular.[56] From this research one might expect that though local networks might be dense within poorer and working class communities, they
may be relatively nonoverlapping, resulting in small and noncooperating
friendship and kin cliques. In short, the form of the networks, not simply
their density, must be taken into consideration.

There is a second major set of ecological considerations that strongly
influences the density of local networks that can be mobilized for collective
action, and these are based on the family composition of the community.
Beginning with the early Chicago School, both theory and empirical studies have emphasized that the primary denizens of local neighborhoods and
local communities are children. For example, the local neighborhood was
seen by Charles Horton Cooley to be one of the central "primary groups"
of socialization and social control,[57] and William H. Whyte, Jr., went so

far as to call the local neighborhoods of suburban Park Forest "filiar-chies," territorial domains ruled by children.[58] More recent survey re-search has also documented that residents with children at home are more likely to be knowledgable of, concerned about, and involved in the social life of the local community (see, for example, Hunter's research on Chi-cago's communities and Fischer's work on the Bay Area of San Fran-cisco).[59] Furthermore, many of the major institutions of the local commu-nity, such as schools, churches, and local organizations of various kinds, have activities expressly geared to the socialization and social control of children. Through such institutional linkages parents are more likely to come into contact with one another and are therefore more readily avail-able for organized collective action at the local community level. There-fore, the demographic and ecological composition of local communities may have a direct effect on the nature of local networks found in the communities that can be activated to mobilize for collective action.

Symbolic Sentiments
The existence of a social network as a structural precondition for local community mobilization and action is paralleled on the cultural level by the symbolic sentiment of community. The spirit, sense, or identification of and with a community is a complex psychological and cultural process that both forms and merges individual and collective identities. The mech-anisms that create such identifications and identities are perhaps best understood from the perspective of symbolic interaction and the social construction of community. Such mechanisms involve first the ability to demarcate a clear and relatively unambiguous collective whole—one that appears "natural," as in the older conception of "natural areas" with their "natural boundaries." Socially, such unambiguous and natural collectives are perhaps most clearly constructed in the area of race relations with seemingly natural ascriptive categories of race and ethnicity. Certainly, such identifications and identities appear to be as much less ambiguous than those of social class. Therefore, it is not surprising to find race and ethnic-ity as one of the central bases for defining a symbolic identity.

The second major component of the symbolic construction perspective is that the process of creating community occurs between a given collectiv-ity or community and other outside actors and institutions. In short, local communities are not simply created internally from the grass roots out-ward, but the very idea of community may be sown and cultivated by actors external to the local community interacting with it. (On this critical point see Davidson, Hunter, Hunter and Suttles, and Taub.[60]) These exter-nal actors may be economic institutions such as banks, political and gov-ernmental institutions such as political parties and school districts, or so-cial institutions ranging from churches to youth organizations. The identifications and identities so constructed may be formal or informal, legally defined or merely carried on in the rich connotative local culture of a city. However defined, such identities are crucial for forming a disparate set of individuals who may merely share the same space into an organized set of actors willing to engage in collective community action. The ability to draw upon a preexisting set of local community symbols and sentiments greatly facilitates the mobilization of local resources for collective action.

EXTERNAL NETWORKS AND NEIGHBORHOOD RESOURCES

The significance of internal networks and the collective sentiment of community is paralleled by that of the external linkages and networks of local communities and their organizations to the outside world. To the degree that local community organizations are seen as instruments for social change, their activities are often oriented toward altering or influencing forces and factors that lie beyond the boundaries of their locale. As Crenson[61] has phrased it, researchers must be concerned with the "foreign relations" of these local community organizations. Just as with the internal networks, there is both a structural and cultural component to these foreign affairs, the former dealing with very real material linkages in terms of substantive resources such as financial and human capital, and the latter concerned more with symbolic resources of legitimacy and prestige.

Substantive Resources and External Links

The central dilemma in the resource dependency thesis of recent social movement literature centers upon movement organizations' external linkages to larger, often state, structures of resource distribution. Given that these larger structures have the power to decide the distribution of resources and are also, simultaneously, often the primary adversaries in conflict with the smaller movement organizations, the dilemma is apparent: one can either bite the hand that feeds one, or, fearing retaliation and the withdrawal of sustenance, one can lick the hand one would otherwise want to bite. This basic dilemma has been advanced earlier under a variety of rubrics—goal displacement, selling out or buying in (depending upon one's positional view), cooptation, social control, and maintenance and enhancement needs of organizations. All of these concepts communicate three points: (1) that the organization itself requires resources to maintain its structure and functioning, (2) that these resources are often provided by agencies and actors outside of the organization, and (3) that the goals, actions, and activities of the organization are significant in determining the degree to which these other actors in the environment will withhold or provide resources to the organization. In a nutshell, this is the dilemma of dependency.

From the general perspective of the local community, the local organization is often seen as a resource conduit to these external funding agencies. These substantive resources are by and large monetary in the form of grants and donations, but they may include other material resources, such as office space, advertising space, or transportation and communication facilities. Over the years local community organizations have tapped into a variety of sources for these external material resources. First historically have been private philanthropic groups at either the local level (Community Chest, United Way, and so on) or the national level (Rockefeller and Ford Foundations, for example). These private philanthropic groups have often been concerned with very specific agendas and issues of social amelioration, and in deciding the recipients of these grants they have turned to a variety of local organizations in different cities throughout the country to administer the specific programs. The better-organized local groups have been able to shift their organizations' activities and actions when needed (goal displacement) to match the foundations' stated objectives in order to obtain the necessary funds to support the organization. These organizations may be seen therefore as the creatures or products of specific national foundations that have brought them into existence.

Over the more recent decades, however, these local organizations have increasingly responded to the varied programs and agendas of government agencies ranging from specific programs in housing, to crime, to economic development. The rise of the national welfare state and the shifting policy priorities with different administrations have produced a varyingly astute grantsmanship by local groups that have simultaneously attempted to influence the definition of these national agendas and to take advantage of these programs as they have been implemented. Just as local groups have eagerly sought the appropriate sources to maintain their organizational activities, so the funding sources, faced with limited information and heightened local demand, have sought assurance that the groups and programs which they do fund will be able to carry out effectively the programs they wish to be implemented. It is at this point that the two-pronged question of "legitimacy" becomes salient.

Symbolic Resources of Legitimacy and External Links

The sheer number and proliferation of local community organizations leaves potential funding agencies in information overload, unable to evaluate the adequacy of all potential local groups to carry out the mandate or agenda of specific policies and programs they wish to implement. Therefore, they search for satisficing rather than optimal solutions to their funding decisions; namely, they support organizations that are "known" to have a track record in their area of interest. Failing this, they are willing to anoint certain local organizations as carriers of their programs and to provide them with the necessary funds and expertise. As Richard Taub has found in his research, in the extreme they will even create the necessary organizations to provide a formal conduit into previously underorganized local communities.[62] From the local organization's perspective the central question becomes how to become known or how to achieve visibility and credibility.

Recent research from the social movement literature suggests that not only are external organizations important for providing substantive resources, but they are also politically important in providing alliances that legitimize an organization. Zald and Ash refer to these allied groups as "conscience constituents"[63]; Jenkins and Perrow also point out that they are important in neutralizing potential opponents of a movement organization.[64] When translated to the level of the local community, the sheer number of local organizations requires a special degree of external networking for recognition and legitimacy to stand out even slightly from other organizations competing for funds. In Chicago, to use one city as an example, several institutions have developed simply to provide this critical information link between local organizations and potential funding agencies and foundations, the Donor's Forum and the Center for Economic Development Organizations. These organizations themselves do not provide funds but act as clearinghouses as much for agencies and foundations as for local organizations.

Finally, on the question of symbolic legitimacy for visibility and credibility we should note that one of the easiest fallback positions is to rely on local organizations that are relatively widely known within the local culture of a city. This strategy favors, ipso facto, older organizations that have been around long enough to have established a track record with potential funding sources. Not only can their capacity to implement programs be assessed by looking at their previous activities, but, perhaps as important, their political style and tactics can be assessed too. For these combined reasons, older local organizations are likely to be more readily funded than newer organizations, contributing to what Stinchcombe has called the "liability of newness."[65]

In summary, local community organizations, like the neighborhoods in which they develop, cannot be viewed apart from the larger social structure of the city in which they exist, not from the state and federal agencies and national foundations that so often support that development. These external linkages are significant first and foremost for providing a flow of funds into the local community that can be used to support local organizations, but also for providing legitimacy, heightened visibility, and credibility through their support of local organizations' activities and goals.

THE ORGANIZATION AND MOBILIZATION OF RESOURCES

Given the general resource dependency perspective being developed in our model it is important to explore in more detail the variable nature of the resources themselves. Specifically, we focus on three characteristics or variables of these resources: the source, the type, and the amount of resources. These are of course but three among numerous other characteristics that could be identified, but they are critically important in allowing us to link the structure and activities of local organizations to the structural charac-

teristics of their local communities. After exploring these three characteristics of resources we will then elaborate the impact resources have upon
the structure of the organizations themselves. Here, we will explore three
characteristics of organizational structure: the degree of formalization or
bureaucratization of an organization, the degree to which a local voluntary
organization relies upon a professional paid staff, and the degree to which
it relies upon community volunteers.

Variable Resources

One of the first distinctions about resources that is particularly important
to make is the degree to which local community organizations rely upon
resources generated internally from members and local institutions itself
versus their reliance upon resources from actors external to the local community. Other distinctions could also be made about such sources, such as
whether they are private (foundations) or public (governmental agencies).
But, if autonomy and dependency of action are our principal concerns, it
is important to establish the degree to which a local community and its
organization are resource-dependent. A discussion of resource autonomy
or dependency upon the external setting must of course take into consideration the previous discussion of the differential ecological distribution of
socioeconomic status among local communities in metropolitan areas
throughout the country. The recognition that there are richer and poorer
local communities would seemingly suggest that organizations in richer
communities are less likely to depend upon external resources than are
poorer communities. However, it is also likely that residents of communities with higher socioeconomic status have both greater organizational skills
and more external contacts that permit them to mobilize more funds from
external sources. As Hunter has suggested with respect to suburban communities,[66] the interdependency of local communities with their larger setting may mean simultaneously that richer communities garner more external resources while retaining a high degree of autonomy of action. In short,
interdependency and dependency are distinct dimensions, and the degree
of autonomy of action may be distinct from the degree of resource dependency.

   The major argument of the resource dependency proposition is, however, that poorer communities are more dependent upon external resources
and are therefore more likely to enagage in local organized activities that
do not challenge or threaten the source of their continued existence. Whether
framed more narrowly, as in the organizational literature, or more generally, as in the social movements literature, this proposition suggests that
the allocation of resources by external actors works as a mechanism of
social control to channel the activities of local organizations. The less the
external funding, the less the control, while the greater the external funding, the greater the control over locally organized activities.

   A second critical distinction to be made about resources is that between financial capital and human capital. This distinction becomes especially important when referring to local community organizations, in that they are often seen to be the bulwark of volunteerism, where people give of their time and energy as much as they give of their pocketbook to achieve their collective goals. Again, this distinction may be seen to be critically linked to the ecological segregation of class and status among local communities. In wealthier communities one could expect that financial capital may be used to "buy" the services needed, including the creation of well funded and professionally run local community organizations. In poorer communities, where residents lack financial capital, they rely more upon the human capital and establish local organizations with larger volunteer memberships that provide the necessary labor and "work" to carry out the organization's activities and goals. For example, will the crossing guard at the corner be a neighbor who volunteers, or someone paid by the local organization; or, will local residents organize to demonstrate for a given legislative decision to benefit the local community, or will a paid professioanl lobbyist be hired to argue for a given piece of legislation. As Piven and Cloward have most powerfully argued,[67] poor people's movements are more reliant upon human capital and large memberships, whereas, as Hunter and Staggenborg[68] have empirically shown, the more money local organizations have, the less likely they are to engage in political action. Given, then, the distribution of these two different types of resources in local community organizations, one may expect different structures and different activities to follow.

Finally, any consideration of resources must take account of the sheer quantity of resources that a local organization is able to mobilize. Whether this be human capital (large or small memberships) or financial capital (large or small budgets) the amount of these resources will constrain the types of structures that organizations can develop and the nature of the activities in which they can engage. The ability to hire professional staff, rent office space, or publish a local newsletter depends upon financial resources; and the ability to mount petition drives, influence local political leaders, or stage demonstrations is dictated by the number of members that can be mobilized.

Organizational Structure

Previously we have suggested that the sources, types, and amounts of resources that local organizations can mobilize are critically important in limiting or determining the types of activities in which they will engage. The central link between resources and activities is the very nature or structure of the organization itself. Borrowing extensively from the organizational literature, we can advance the simple but powerful proposition that the greater the resources of an organization the larger its size and the more formal or bureaucratic its structure. To keep this proposition from becoming a mere tautology, it is important that size be considered apart from membership itself, and that the focus instead be placed on size as a structural feature of the administration of the organization. A central feature of organizations that is directly linked to their efficiency and effectiveness in carrying out tasks is their degree of formalization or bureaucratization. The presence of distinct levels of authority and communication and of distinct departments or committees suggests a formal division of labor designed to heighten rationality and efficiency. This formalization may or may not conflict with democratic procedures of organization and decision making so often thought to be a defining characteristic of local voluntary community organizations. However important this question, it is not our principal concern here. Rather, we are more interested in the degree to which different types and amounts of resources enable organizations to become more formally structured and more enduring local community institutions. Furthermore, we suggest that the degree of formalization is likely to affect the types of activities local organizations engage in. For example, we suggest that more formal organizations are more likely to provide routine services and to monitor activities, in that they are linked to other organized actors both internal and external to the local community. Less formal local community organizations are by contrast more likely to engage in episodic political actions and protest.

A closely related feature of the degree of formalization is the degree of professionalization of the staff. Again, the ability to hire trained professionals, either generalists at "organizing" or specialists at some particular activity such as housing, counseling, or health care, is likely to be highly dependent upon the amount of resources the organization has mobilized. In turn, the presence of paid professionals is likely to influence the organization's activities. For example, a paid staff, concerned about maintaining and enhancing the organization, may be expected to engage in activities that are generally seen as service oriented rather than political so as not to threaten the basis of their livelihood. Furthermore, they may be expected to provide the organization with a greater continuity in interests and actions through their routinized activities, and also to link the organization personally through contacts with fellow professionals in other agencies and organizations. In short, the greater the amount of resources, the greater the number of professional staff; and, in turn, the greater the degree of enduring, routinized activities that the organization engages in.

The final characteristic of the structure of local community organizations to be considered is the volunteer labor local residents perform. The amount of volunteer staff is not necessarily inversely proportional to the amount of professional staff; in fact, the two may be highly correlated or may simply be unrelated to one another. However, volunteer staff is by definition much less dependent upon the local organization's financial resources than is the professional staff, who depend on such resources for their pay. Furthermore, volunteer staff may be more problematic in their continuity of participation, involved in less routinized activities, or in short less "disciplined" in their "work" than are paid staff. The character of such volunteer staff may therefore be expected to affect the kinds of activities and actions the organization engages in.

In summary, the nature and amount of resources that can be mobilized by the local community to establish a local organization are likely to affect the type of organization that is established. These in turn are likely to constrain the types of collective action and activities the organization can engage in. We now turn to a consideration of the differing types of collective behavior, or, in short, the ultimate question of this research, how they act.

ORGANIZED ACTIVITIES AND COLLECTIVE ACTION

Ultimately we are interested in explaining how and why social actors, individual or collective, do what they do; consequently, accounting for the variability of behavior engaged in by local community organizations is the final step in developing our theoretical model. The two somewhat related sets of behaviors we will consider are organized activities and collective action. Whereas the former is more often the concern of theory and research from the organizational literature, the latter is the more recent concern expressed by researchers in the social movement literature. As that literature has increasingly focused on organizations as central actors within social movements, the actions of these organizations have moved to center stage.

One way of conceptualizing the distinction between activities and actions is to consider the former as more routinized behaviors connected with relatively well defined, longer term specific programs and the latter as more episodic, shorter term, and politically oriented behaviors directed toward existing authorities. Tilly, for example, speaks to the different "repertoires" or types of collective action,[69] and Gamson distinguishes more specifically between violent and nonviolent types of protest engaged in by organized groups.[70] Local community organizations have themselves displayed the full range of behaviors between routinized delivery of services connected with specific programs to political advocacy and protest. In fact, different theories or philosophies of community organizing have often debated this critical point, with Saul Alinsky representing a more politically oriented conflict and protest approach[71] and others, such as Howard Hallman, representing a more routinized service orientation as the basis of organizing.[72] The critical link to resource dependency theories also often is expressed in terms of existing authorities' desires to transform actual or potential organized protest groups into more compliant and complacent agencies engaged in the routinized delivery of local services. From this social control perspective routine organized activities represent goal displacement or the cooptation of groups that might otherwise be engaged in political advocacy. Groups that "sell out" by disengaging from political action may be considered to "buy in" to the more legitimate system of exiting programs with their routinized activities.

A second major distinction when looking at organized activities and collective action is to determine whether they are need driven, that is, generated from a demand side by local communities, or whether they are initiated by higher authorities and external agencies and therefore represent supply side programs. Of course, elements of both are likely to be present in any given organization's repertoire of action and activities. However, the relative emphasis placed on the demand or the supply side is likely to make a critical difference in the influence local community characteristics versus external resources have on the types of actions pursued by local organizations. For example, poorer communities may have specific needs which may or may not be met by existing externally funded programs, and organizations in these communities may therefore engage in similar activities independent of whether or not external funds are available to implement them. Alternatively, if the supply side is dominant, than the availability of funds for specific programs may generate similar activities independent of the variable characteristics or different types of communities in which the organizations operate. In short, it is important to determine the degree to which local organizational activities are ecologically determined by the demands and needs of different communities, or the degree to which these activities are determined by the availability of external resources for specific programs designed to generate these specific activities.

A final consideration in understanding organizational activities and actions is the need for a more dynamic model to explore the likelihood that organizations may change their activities and actions over time. For example, new organizations may begin as political advocates and protest groups, and as they age (if they do in fact survive) they may shift gradually to more formalized structures engaged in more routinized activities. This is of course the transition that would be predicted by the social control, resource dependency perspective. However, it is also likely that, given "the liability of newness" hypothesis proposed by Stinchcombe, unless new organizations acquire sufficient resources quickly they are likely to disappear. Therefore, the same outcome might be predicted, but for different reasons, namely, that organizations acquiring greater external resources that require them to engage in more routinized activities are more likely to survive. Either way, newer organizations would be less likely to engage in routine activities compared to older organizations. Older organizations would become a formalized part of the local community's social landscape, a landscape riddled with dead organizations that were either squashed to death by authorities because of their unpopular political action or starved to death by their inability to acquire the necessary material sustenance for sustained action.

TESTING THE MODEL

The discursive synthetic theory we have developed incorporates a large number of diverse concepts and variables gleaned from research in differ-

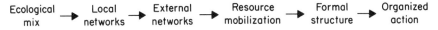

Figure 11.1 Synthetic Model of Resource Mobilization by Local Communities for Organized Action.

ent subdisciplines and literatures within sociology. In order to subject the numerous explicit and implicit propositions of this theory to even a partial test it is necessary to make a number of assumptions and simplifications to yield a more wieldy model. We have expanded our previous model of global concepts outlined in Figure 11.1 to a more discrete set of variables that will ideally tap critical components of these concepts. The expanded model with its discrete variables is presented in Figure 11.2. The specific variables were selected or constructed from a mail questionnaire survey of

Figure 11.2 Local Communities and Collective Action: A Resource Mobilization Model.

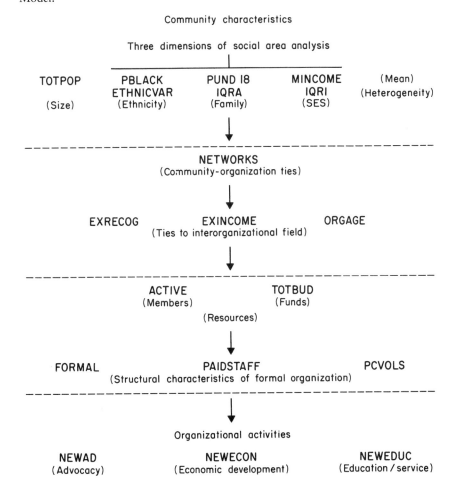

199 local community and neighborhood organizations conducted by the New World Foundation in 1981.[73] Here we will present the operationlization of the key variables that we were able to extract for our secondary analysis from this survey, recognizing that there are inherent limits to the data in both form and content as to the variables we were able to use to test our model. We have broken these into discrete "variable clusters" that are the major components of the synthetic model.

Ecological Characteristics of Communities

Seven variables were constructed to tap the ecological characteristics of the local communities and neighborhoods in which these organizations operate. The ideal was to construct variables that tapped several of the theoretical concepts contained in previous research stemming from the ecological theory of community. First and foremost was community size, and second was the issue of the homogeneity or heterogeneity of a community. Social characteristics were selected which approximated as closely as possible the three dimensions of social area analysis and factorial ecology, namely, socioeconomic status, racial-ethnic status, and family or life cycle status. On these latter three we measured both the absolute standing of the community (average or mean, median, and so on) and its degree of variability or heterogeneity (range, variance, and so on). The specific variables are as follows:

TOTPOP = population size of the local community. This variable is simply an estimate by the respondent of the population size of the local community or neighborhood.

PBLACK = percentage of the local community which is Black. This variable is simply an estimate by the respondent of the percentage of local community residents who are Black.

ETHNICVAR = degree of ethnic heterogeneity of the community. This variable was constructed by asking respondents to estimate the percentage of local residents who belonged to various racial and ethnic groups. The variable was computed by assigning low values if a single group was preponderant within a community to high values where a number of different groups comprised roughly equal percentages of the local population.

MINCOME = median income of residents of the local community. This variable was computed from a question asking respondents the percentage of local residents estimated to belong to a series of income categories. The median point was calculated proportionately within the category where the cumulative percentage was 50%.

IQRI = interquartile range in income of residents of the local community. This variable was computed from a question asking respondents the percentage of residents estimated to belong to a series of income categories. The upper and lower quartiles were calculated proportionately within appropriate categories and their difference is the interquartile range.

PUND 18 = percentage of the population under 18 years of age. This variable was constructed from a question asking respondents to estimate the percentage of the local population that fell into a series of age categories, the lowest one being percentage under 18 years of age. This provides a measure of the degree of family and child oriented life-style within the local community.

IRIA = interquartile range in age of local residents. This variable was constructed from an item that asked respondents to estimate the percentage of local residents falling into a series of age categories. The upper and lower quartiles were calculated proportionately for their appropriate age categories, and their difference was the interquartile range in age.

Networks of Organizations

In our model we posit that the ecological characteristics of local communities will affect the nature of their local networks and, more specifically, the degree to which the community organization is tied into the local networks. In addition, we suggest that these ecological characteristics and the local networks will also determine the degree to which a local organization is or is not linked to agencies and organizations that are external to the local community, in short, the degree to which it is networked with outside actors.

Therefore, we were concerned with measuring both the degree to which the community organization was tied into networks of local community residents, what we refer to as internal networks, and the degree to which the organization was linked to organizations outside the local community, external networks. Four variables were selected to measure internal and external networks:

NETWORKS = percentage of staff of the local organization who were residents of the local community. This was a direct question asked of respondents of the local organization.

EXRECOG = degree to which the local organization considers external recognition by outside agencies and actors important to the organization. This variable is a simple additive index of three items asking respondents the degree to which such external recognition was important for political legitimacy, for donors' giving money, and for building networks to locate and gather resources of all kinds.

EXINCOME = percentage of the organization's budget from sources external to the local community. This was constructed from a series of questions which asked respondents to give dollar figures from income derived from various sources. Those that were identified as extralocal (e.g., federal and state governments, nonlocal foundations, nonlocal corporations) were added together and divided by the total income of the organization.

ORGAGE = age of the organization. This variable was simply constructed from a question which asked respondents when their organization was founded. Though it is not a direct measure of internal and external organizational networks, we posit that the age of a local organization is an additional measure of the degree to which it has become a part of both the local community social structure and of the larger environment external to the local community and its residents. Therefore, we have incorporated this important variable at this point in our model.

Resource Mobilization and Organizational Structure

The ecological characteristics of local communities and the nature of the internal and external networks of their local organizations are posited as critical determinants of the nature and amount of resources local community organizations can mobilize. In turn, these prior characteristics and these resources are likely to determine the degree to which the local organization becomes formalized, bureaucratized, and professionalized in order to carry out its activities and actions. Therefore, we have selected or constructed two critical measures of resource mobilization, and three of organizational structure:

ACTIVE = number of active members of the organization. This was simply the respondents' answer to a question asking for the number of active members of the organization. This is considered a measure of "human capital" in our model.

TOTBUD = total budget of the organization. This is simply the respondent's answer to a question asking for the total budget of the organization in dollars. This is considered our measure of "financial capital."

FORMAL = degree of formalization or bureaucratization of the organization. This variable is an additive index constructed from three items on the questionnaire, and respondents' answers to each were dichotomized into no or yes. The first was whether or not the organization was divided into distinct departments or committees; the second was whether or not it had three or more levels of hierarchy in the organization; the third was whether or not there was an executive director or administrator of the organization.

PAIDSTAFF = number of paid staff in the organization. This variable was simply a question that asked respondents for the number of both full-time and part-time paid staff members in the organization.

PCYOLS = number of volunteer staff members. This variable was simply a question that asked respondents for the number of volunteer staff in the organization.

Organized Activities and Collective Action

The final "dependent variables" to be considered in our model are the collective actions and activities of local community organizations. Although we are interested in how ecological characteristics of local communities and the networks, resources, and structures of these organizations are interrelated, we also want to assess the degree to which they all influence the nature of these organizations' activities. Fortunately, there was a series of questions about "the major services, functions, or activities" engaged in by their organization. They were presented with a list of eight broad categories ranging from physical development to law and justice. Respondents were first asked to indicate which one of these activities was the primary function of their organization. They were then asked to circle any of the other functions they might also perform. We selected three of the most frequently mentioned categories of functions for our analysis. These were defined as follows:

NEWECON = economic development—the utilization of the production, distribution, and consumption of goods and income to increase opportunities, options, and satisfaction for community members.

NEWDUC = education—the process of teaching particular skills and developing mental, aesthetic, physical, and moral qualities of community members.

NEWAD = advocacy—acting as a spokesman or pressure group for a particular subgroup or interest group of the community, seeking attention, resources, support, and legitimacy to act from governmental or private institutions.

Each variable was coded trichotomously, with the highest value going to groups that mentioned a particular activity as their primary function, the intermediate value going to groups that mentioned it as one of their secondary activities, and the lowest value going to groups that did not mention that activity.

MODE OF ANALYSIS

We decided to test our model with a series of unfolding standardized regression equations. We present the full regression equations, not simply their reduced forms, preferring in this initial test of the model to show clearly the insignificant as well as significant relationships among variables in the model. The first set of equations, presented in Table 11.1, treats the ecological characteristics of communities as independent variables on which

Table 11.1 Networks of Organizations (Regression Equations)

Independent Variables	Dependent Variables			
	Local Ties	External Income	External Recognition	Organization Age
Total Population of Community	−.01	−.14	−.11	.07
Percentage Black	−.18[b]	−.13	.10	.21[b]
Ethnic Heterogeneity	.00	.04	−.09	.01
Percentage Under 18	.14	.01	−.05	.04
Interquartile Range Age	−.05	.12	.08	−.14
Median Income	.16[a]	.00	.08	.05
Interquartile Range Income	−.05	.12	−.04	−.14
Local Ties		.00	.03	−.05

[a] $p \leq .10$; [b] $p \leq .05$; [c] $p \leq .01$.

are regressed the network variables of these organizations. The second set of equations, presented in Table 11.2, regresses the dependent variables of resource mobilization on both the ecological characteristics of the communities and the networks of the organizations. Also presented are the structural characteristics of the organizations as dependent variables regressed on the ecological variables, the network variables, and the resource mobilization variables. The final set of regressions presented in Table 11.3 regress the three activities on all of the preceding variables—ecology, networks, resources, and structure.

RESULTS

We present the regression results in the sequence of our model by first looking at (1) the effects of local community ecological variables on inter-

Table 11.2   Resource Mobilization and Organizational Structure (Regression Equations)

Independent Variables	Dependent Variables				
	Active Members	Budget	Paid Staff	Percentage Volunteers	Formal Structure
Total Population of Community	−.10	.06	−.01	.05	−.07
Percentage Black	−.09	.12	−.23^c	.16^a	−.03
Ethnic Heterogeneity	.11	.01	−.08	−.03	−.07
Percentage Under 18	.13	.09	.23^c	.02	.01
Interquartile Range Age	−.07	.10	−.23^c	−.11	.12
Median Income	.04	−.09	−.10	.10	−.09
Interquartile Range Income	.21^b	.08	.05	−.05	−.15^a
Local Ties	−.09	.02	.06	−.02	−.02
External Income	.12	.36^c	.03	−.17^a	.30^c
External Recognition	−.05	.08	.16^b	.06	−.13
Organizational Age	.13	.15	.21^c	.09	.19
Active Members			.13^a	−.01	.13
Budget			.39^c	−.34^c	.34^c

$^a p \leq .10$; $^b p \leq .05$; $^c p \leq .01$.

Table 11.3 Collective Actions and Activities of Organizations
(Regression Equations)

Independent Variables	Dependent Variables		
	Advocacy	Service	Economic Development
Total Population of Community	$-.19^b$	$-.07$	$-.04$
Percentage Black	$-.27^b$	$-.15$	$.16$
Ethnic Heterogeneity	$.13$	$.07$	$-.03$
Percentage Under 18	$-.05$	$.00$	$-.05$
Interquartile Range Age	$.05$	$.02$	$.11$
Median Income	$-.10$	$-.02$	$-.21^b$
Interquartile Range Income	$-.08$	$.11$	$.12$
Local Ties	$.08$	$-.10$	$.01$
External Income	$.04$	$.01$	$.11$
External Recognition	$.07$	$-.15$	$-.02$
Organization Age	$.04$	$.19^a$	$-.13$
Active Members	$.11$	$-.02$	$-.01$
Budget	$-.03$	$-.01$	$.13$
Paid Staff	$-.02$	$.02$	$.02$
Percentage Volunteers	$.15$	$.14$	$.10$
Formal Structure	$.04$	$.05$	$.11$

$^a p \leq .10;\ ^b p \leq .05;\ ^c p \leq .01.$

nal and external networks, (2) the effects of both on resource mobilization, (3) the effects of these three variable sets upon the structure of local organizations, and (4) how all of the preceding affect the activities and actions of the organizations. We will highlight the statistically significant variables and also discuss those that may be substantively important though not statistically significant.

Internal and External Networks

Only two of the community ecological variables—percentage Black and median income—have any statistically significant effect on the nature of local community networks (see Table 11.1). Specifically, the greater the percentage of Blacks in a community and the lower the median income of the community, the fewer local community residents who serve as staff of the local organization. This suggests that in poor and Black communities the staff of local organizations are more likely to come from outside the local community, whereas in wealthy and White communities the staff of local organizations are more likely to be drawn from among residents of the local community itself. Of the three variables measuring the external networks of the local organizations, neither the percentage of external income nor the degree of external recognition is significantly affected by any of the ecological characteristics of the local community. However, organizational age is also positively affected by percentage Black, with Black communities' having older organizations than White communities. In short, these results suggest that in Black communities local organizations are more likely to be older and that in poorer Black communities, especially, they are more likely to be staffed by external nonresidents. Conversely, in White communities organizations are newer, and in wealthier White communities their staffs are more likely to be local community residents.

Resource Mobilization

Only two variables have statistically significant effects on our two measures of resource mobilization (number of active members and size of budget). These are the interquartile range of income of local community residents and the amount of external income received by the local organization, respectively (Table 11.2). Simply stated, the greater the income heterogeneity of a community, the greater the number of active members in the local organization; and the greater the amount of external income, the larger the organizational budget. The latter finding is not particularly surprising, but it does emphasize the degree to which local organizations' budgets appear to be driven by funding sources that are external to the local community, rather than internal. Also, we should note that though they are not quite statistically significant, both the age and ethnic heterogeneity measures have effects on organizational membership that are relatively large and in the same direction as the income heterogeneity measure. Therefore, these results strongly suggest that the greater the heterogeneity of local communities, the larger the number of active members in local organizations, and that more homogeneous communities have organizations with fewer active members.

Organizational Structure

Though to this point in the analysis the model we have sketched appears to have had limited payoffs in terms of the number of statistically significant results, when we turn to the model's hypothesized effects on organizational structure its utility is readily apparent. There are thirteen significant relationships of our antecedent variables on our three measures of organizational structure—the number of paid staff, the percentage of staff who are volunteers, and the degree of formalization of the organizational bureaucracy. Turning first to community ecological characteristics, we see that organizations with a greater number of paid staff are more likely to be found in local communities that are White, have many children, and are relatively homogeneous with respect to income. Stated conversely, organizations with little or no paid staff are more likely to be found in Black communities with few children and greater income heterogeneity.

Of the antecedent network and resource mobilization variables we see that the size of budget, the number of active members, the age of the organization, and the amount of external recognition of the organization are all positively related to the size of the paid staff. That is, older organizations with larger budgets, more members, and greater external visibility are more likely to have paid staff, whereas newer, poorer, smaller, and more isolated organizations are likely to have few if any paid staff members.

When we turn to the percentage of volunteers among the staff a different picture emerges, one that suggests that paid staff and volunteer staff are two distinct organizational strategies from different types of communities. The staff of local organizations is likely to have a greater percentage of volunteers in communities that are Black, where there is little external income, and where the organization has a small budget. Again, stated conversely, staffs are less likely to be volunteers in organizations in White communities that have greater external income and larger budgets. In short, organizations with paid staff are found in White communities with larger organizational budgets, and organizations with a greater percentage of volunteer staff are found in Black communities with smaller organizational budgets.

Finally, when we turn to our index of bureaucratization measuring the degree to which these local community organizations are formalized into levels, departments, and so forth, we see that in income homogeneous communities they are more formalized, whereas in communities with greater income heterogeneity they are less formal or bureaucratic. Also, we see that the greater the amount of external income and the larger the organizational budget, the more formal and bureaucratic the local community organization. In short, links to external funding sources and larger organizational budgets are positively related to the degree of bureaucratization of local community organizations, while organizations without such external links and smaller budgets are less formal.

Collective Activities and Actions

Few of the variables in our model have a statistically significant direct impact on the three different types of collective activities and actions we have identified for analysis—advocacy, service, and economic development (see Table 11.3). However, the picture that emerges suggest that communities ecological characteristics are more important in defining which of these actions an organization will undertake than are the network, resources, or structural variables in our model. We find, first, that organizations which engage in advocacy are more likely to be found in smaller and white communities; or, conversely, larger and Black communities are less likely to engage in advocacy. The only other variable having any relative though not statistically significant effect is the percentage of volunteers on the staff; organizations with a greater proportion of volunteer staff are perhaps more likely to engage in advocacy than those with fewer volunteers.

When we look at organizations that engage in service activities, none of the ecological variables is statistically significant, though again percent Black is somewhat inversely related (organizations in White communities are slightly more likely to be service oriented). The only variable that significantly affects service activities is the age of the organization, with older organizations being more service oriented, and newer organizations less likely to be service oriented.

Finally, when we turn to economic development activities we see that only one variable is statistically significant and it again is a community ecological variable. The higher the median income of the community the less likely is the organization to be oriented to economic development; or, perhaps more to the point, the poorer the local community the more likely is the local community organization to be engaged in economic development activities. When we look at other variables having a modest but not statistically significant effect, we see that local organizations engaged in economic development activities are slightly more likely to be found in Black communities, to be newer organizations, and to have somewhat larger budgets.

CONCLUSION

The model we have outlined and the results of our test of that model clearly suggest that theories about the structure and activities of local community organizations that fail to consider the variable ecological characteristics of the local communities themselves can provide only a limited understanding of variations in the form and functioning of these local groups. It is also clear that the resource mobilization perspective, which we have incorporated in our model, is extremely powerful in predicting the variable structure of these local organizations, though it is somewhat less powerful in directly predicting the particular collective activities and actions in which these organizations are likely to engage. However, by extending the resource mobilization perspective and looking at the ecological composition and social structure of local communities as resources themselves, the perspective gains even greater power in accounting for variation in resources and the mechanisms of mobilization by locally organized groups.

We of course recognize that the model we have proposed is but a starting synthesis and that further investigation is in order. First, the chains of causation—the specific ordering among the variables in the linear model we have outlined—undoubtedly could be recast at strategic points and treated as nonrecursive with mutual cause and effect relationships. Perhaps this is most important to consider in the relationship we posit suggesting that variations in external networks and the mobilization of resources affect the formal structures of local organizations. One could as readily posit that the structure of the organization, especially the presence of paid staff, affects the extent of external linkages and the amount of external funding that the local organization is able to mobilize. Our model does not capture the subtleties of timing and the dynamics of organizing that this mutual cause and effect relationship probably exhibits in the real life of these organizations.

The preceding suggests a second major course for future research, modeling the dynamics of these organizations from birth through mobilization, formalization, and periodic inflation and deflation to ultimate collapse or death. Recent research in the organizational literature is seriously beginning to explore these dynamics at various stages in the organizational life cycle for large populations of organizations. With but a few exceptions,[74] these analyses have not extended to not-for-profit organizations in general, and local community organizations in particular, where the dynamics may be expected to differ or to be occurring at a faster rate. It is as if these little local organizations were the perfect analogues to the fruit flies used in biological experiments, for given their notoriously short life spans, dynamic models of organizational genesis and morphological variation through successive generations could readily be explored. However, getting the over-time data is particularly difficult given their seemingly ephemeral existence.

Finally, we suggest that our general synthetic model could benefit from the input and scrutiny of researchers from a number of different disciplines and subdisciplines. The methods and models of urban sociologists, social movement researchers, and organizational theorists could all be brought to bear upon this particular model, but, more important, should be brought together to study the real life phenomenon itself which the model is attempting to depict. The study of the real life activities of local residents attempting to fashion a day-to-day world that enables them to act in concert upon the larger economic, political, and social scene should not be categorized into distinct disciplines, singular theories, traditions, or schools. Neither should the phenomenon itself be ignored because of the seeming smallness of its scale. Many bothersome insects have, it seems, adapted quite well and survive by flying in very large swarms of countless numbers.

NOTES

1. This chapter is in large part the outcome of a leave granted by Northwestern University to the senior author which enabled me to spend a fruitful and fateful semester in the Sociology Department at Yale and as a Fellow of the Program on Non-Profit Organizations of the Institution for Social and Policy Studies at Yale University in the fall of 1981. Thanks are due to John Simon, then Director of the Program, and Paul DiMaggio, current Director and to Carl Milofsky for both the professional and personal stimulation they introduced me to. Special thanks are due to Carl Milofsky, who made his data available to us, assisted in the computer analysis, and, as editor, commented profusely and cajoled patiently on various drafts. In the all too fleeting networks of knowledge, we acknowledge their more enduring commitments to friendship and scholarship; and beyond customary genuflections, we hold

only ourselves accountable for any errors of judgment made during the course of this collaboration.

2. Maurice Stein, *The Eclipse of Community: An Interpretation of American Studies* (Princeton, NJ: Princeton University Press, 1960).

3. Robert Nisbet, *The Quest for Community* (New York: Oxford University Press, 1953).

4. See Emile Durkheim, *The Division of Labor in Society,* trans. George Simpson (New York: The Free Press, 1949); Karl Marx, *Capital,* vol. 1 (New York: Vintage, 1977); and Max Weber, *Economy and Society* (Berkeley: University of California Press, 1978). For a brief summary of many of these classic themes, see Richard Sennett (ed.), *Classic Essays on the Culture of Cities* (New York: Appleton-Century-Crofts, 1969).

5. Edward Shils, *Center and Periphery* (Chicago: University of Chicago Press, 1975).

6. Louis Wirth, "Urbanism as a Way of Life," *American Journal of Sociology,* 44 (1938), 3–24.

7. See the essay originally published in 1905 by Georg Simmel, "The Metropolis and Mental Life," pp. 635–646 in *Cities and Society* ed. Paul K. Hatt and Albert J. Reiss, Jr. (New York: Free Press, 1957).

8. Karl Polanyi, *The Great Transformation* (New York: Farrar and Rinehart, 1944).

9. Immanuel Wallerstein, *The Politics of the World Economy: The States, the Movements and the Civilizations* (New York: Cambridge University Press, 1984).

10. Morris Janowitz, *The Last Half Century: Societal Change and Politics in America* (Chicago: University of Chicago Press, 1978).

11. Manuel Castells, *The City and the Grass Roots* (Berkeley, University of California Press, 1983).

12. Matthew A. Crenson, *Neighborhod Politics* (Cambridge, Mass.: Harvard University Press, 1983).

13. Albert Hunter, *Symbolic Communities* (Chicago: University of Chicago Press, 1974).

14. David Knoke and James R. Wood, *Organized for Action: Commitment in Voluntary Associations* (New Brunswick, NJ: Rutgers University Press, 1981).

15. Donald Warren, *Black Neighborhoods: An Assessment of Community Power* (Ann Arbor: University of Michigan Press, 1979).

16. See Charles Tilly, *From Mobilization to Revolution* (Reading, Mass.: Addison-Wesley, 1978), and "Do Communities Act?" in Marcia Effret (ed.), *The Community,* pp. 209–240. Also see Mayer N. Zald and John D. McCarthy, "Social Movement Industries: Competition and Cooperation among Movement Organizations," *Research in Social Movements and Change* 3 (1980), 1–20 and John McCarthy and Mayer Zald, "Resource Mobilization and Social Movements: A Partial Theory," *American Journal of Sociology,* 82 (1977), 1212–1241.

17. For exemplary statements of the early Chicago School, see Robert E. Park, Ernest W. Burgess, and Roderick D. McKenzie (eds.), *The City* (Chicago: University of Chicago Press, 1967).

18. See Zald and McCarthy, "Social Movement Industries" and McCarthy and Zald, "Resource Mobilization and Social Movements," and Mayer Zald and Roberta Ash, "Social Movement Organizations: Growth, Decay and Change," *Social Forces* 44 (1966), 327–340. See also Roberta Ash Garner, *Social Movements in America* (Chicago: Markham, 1972).

19. Tilly, *From Mobilization to Revolution* and "Do Communities Act?"

20. William Gamson, *The Strategy of Social Protest* (Homewood, Ill: Dorsey Press, 1975).

21. Harvey Zorbaugh, *Gold Coast and Slum: A Sociological Study of Chicago's Near North Side* (Chicago: University of Chicago Press, 1929).

22. Peter Laslett, *The World We Have Lost,* 3rd ed. (New York: Charles Scribner's Sons, 1984).

23. Wirth, "Urbanism as a Way of Life."

24. Ernest Burgess, "Can Neighborhood Work Have a Scientific Basis?" pp. 142–155 in Robert Park et al. (eds.), *The City.*

25. See Claude S. Fischer, *Networks and Places: Social Relations in the Urban Setting* (New York: Free Press, 1977) and *To Dwell among Friends: Personal Networks in Town and City* (Chicago: University of Chicago Press, 1982); Carol Stack, *All Our Kin: Strategies*

for Survival in a Black Community (New York: Harper and Row, 1975), and Barry Wellman, "The Community Question: The Intimate Networks of East Yorkers," *American Journal of Sociology* 84 (1979), 1201–1231.

26. Zorbaugh, *Gold Coast and Slum.*

27. Louis Wirth, *The Ghetto* (Chicago: University of Chicago Press, 1982).

28. See Saul Alinsky, *Rules for Radicals* (New York: Vintage, 1971) and Joan Lancourt, *Confront or Concede: The Alinsky Citizen Action Organizations* (Lexington, Mass.: Lexington Books, 1979).

29. Frances Fox Piven and Richard A. Cloward, *Poor People's Movements* (New York: Random House, 1977); Daniel Moynihan, *Maximum Feasible Misunderstanding* (New York: The Free Press, 1969); Roland Warren, Stephen Rose and Ann Bergunder, *The Structure of Urban Reform: Community Design, Organization, Stability and Change* (Lexington, Mass.: Lexington Books, 1974); and Marilyn Gittell, *Limits of Citizen Participation: The Decline of Community Organization* (Beverly Hills, Calif.: Sage, 1980).

30. J. Craig Jenkins and Charles Perrow, "Insurgency of the Powerless: Farm Workers' Movements 1947–1972," *American Sociological Review,* 39 (1977), 249–258, and J. Craig Jenkins, *The Politics of Insurgency: The Farm Worker Movement in the 1960s* (New York: Columbia University Press, 1985).

31. Louis Wirth, "Urbanism as a Way of Life," in Hatt and Reiss, *Cities and Society,* pp. 46–63.

32. Morton White and Lucia White, *The Intellectual Versus the City: From Thomas Jefferson to Frank Lloyd Wright* (New York: Oxford University Press, 1977).

33. Ernest W. Burgess, "The Growth of The City," in Park, et al. *The City,* pp. 47–62.

34. Homer Hoyt, *The Structure and Growth of Residential Neighborhoods in American Cities* (Washington, DC: U.S. Government, Federal Housing Administration, 1939).

35. Chauncy D. Harris and Edward L. Ullman, "The Nature of Cities," *Annals* 242 (1945), 7–17.

36. William H. Form, "The Place of Social Structure in the Determination of Land Use," *Social Forces* 32 (1954), 317–323, Milla Alihan, *Social Ecology* (New York: Columbia University Press, 1938); Walter T. Firey, "Sentiment and Symbolism as Ecological Variables," *American Sociological Review* 10 (1945), 140–148; Harvey Molotch, "Capital and Neighborhood in the United States: Some Conceptual Links," *Urban Affairs Quarterly* 14 (1979), 289–312; David Harvey, *Social Justice and the City* (Baltimore: Johns Hopkins University Press, 1973); and Manuel Castells, *The Urban Question.*

37. Otis D. Duncan and Beverly Duncan, "Residential Distribution and Occupational Stratification," in Hatt and Reiss, *Cities and Society,* pp. 283–296.

38. Karl E. Taeuber and Alma F. Taeuber, *Negroes in Cities* (Chicago: Aldine, 1965).

39. Ernest R. Mowrer, *Family Disorgainzation* (Chicago: University of Chicago Press, 1927); Peter H. Rossi, *Why Families Move* (New York: Free Press, 1955); and Scott Greer, *The Emerging City* (New York: Free Press, 1962).

40. Eshref Shevky and Wendell Bell, *Social Area Analysis* (Stanford, Calif.: Stanford University Press, 1955).

41. Brian J. L. Berry and John D. Kasarda, *Contemporary Urban Ecology* (New York: Macmillan Publishing Company, 1977).

42. Theodore R. Anderson and Janice A. Egeland, "Spatial Aspects of Social Area Analysis," *American Sociological Review* 26 (1961), 392–398.

43. Wirth, "Urbanism as a Way of Life."

44. Emile Durkheim, *The Division of Labor in Society,* trans. George Simpson (New York: The Free Press, 1933).

45. Castells, *The City and the Grassroots;* Crenson, *Neighborhood Politics.*

46. Laslett, *The World We Have Lost.*

47. Morris Janowitz, *The Community Press in an Urban Setting,* 2nd ed. (Chicago: University of Chicago Press, 1967); Scott Greer, *The Emerging City* (Glencoe, Ill.: The Free Press, 1962); Albert Hunter and Gerald D. Suttles, "The Expanding Community of Limited-Liability," in Suttles, *The Social Construction of Community.*

48. Fischer, *To Dwell Among Friends* and *Networks and Places* and Wellman, "The Community Question."

49. Suttles, *The Social Construction of Community;* Richard Taub, George Surgeon, Sara Lindholm, Phyllis Betts Otti, and Amy Bridges, "Urban Voluntary Associations: Locality Based and Externally Induced," *American Journal of Sociology,* 83 (1977), 425–442, and Jeffrey Davidson, *Political Partnerships* (Beverly Hills, Calif.: Sage Publications, 1979).

50. Gary S. Becker, *Human Capital; A Theoretical and Empirical Analysis, With Special Reference to Education,* 2nd ed. (New York: National Bureau of Economic Research, distributed through Columbia University Press, 1975).

51. Piven and Cloward, *Poor People's Movements.*

52. Herbert Gans, *Urban Villagers: Group and Class in the Life of Italian Americans* (New York: Free Press, 1962).

53. Gerald Suttles, *Social Order of the Slum: Ethnicity and Territoriality in the Inner City* (Chicago: University of Chicago Press, 1968).

54. Stack, *All Our Kin.*

55. Claude Fischer, *To Dwell among Friends* and *Networks and Places* and Barry Wellman, "The Community Question."

56. See Herbert H. Hyman and Charles R. Wright, "Trends in Voluntary Association Memberships of American Adults," *American Sociological Review,* 36 (1971), 191–206, and J. Miller McPherson, "A Dynamic Model of Voluntary Affiliation," *Social Forces* 59 (1981), 705–728.

57. Charles Horton Cooley, *Social Organization: A Study of the Larger Mind,* pp. 23–31 (New York: Schocken, 1962).

58. William H. Whyte, Jr., *The Organizaiton Man* (Garden City, N.Y.: Anchor, 1957).

59. Hunter, *Symbolic Communities* and Fischer, *Networks and Places* and *To Dwell among Friends.*

60. Davidson, *Political Partnerships;* Hunter, *Symbolic Communities;* Hunter and Suttles, "The Expanding Community of Limited-Liability," and Taub, et al., "Urban Voluntary Associations."

61. Crenson, *Neighborhood Politics.*

62. Taub et al., "Urban Voluntary Associations."

63. Zald and Ash, "Social Movement Organizations."

64. Jenkins and Perrow, "Insurgency of the Powerless."

65. Arthur L. Stinchcombe, "Social Structure and Organizations," in *Handbook of Organizations* ed. James G. March (Chicago: Rand McNally, 1965), pp. 142–193.

66. Albert Hunter, "Suburban Autonomy/Dependency: Elite Perceptions," *Social Science Quarterly* 65 (1984), 181–189.

67. Piven and Cloward, *Poor People's Movements.*

68. Albert Hunter and Suzanne Staggenborg, "Communities Do Act: Communal Characteristics, Resource Mobilization and Political Action by Local Community Organizations," *The Social Science Journal* 23 (1986), 169–180.

69. Tilly, *From Mobilization to Revolution.*

70. Gamson, *The Strategy of Protest.*

71. Alinsky, *Rules for Radicals.*

72. Howard W. Hallman, *Neighborhood Control of Public Programs: Case Studies of Community Corporations and Neighborhood Boards* (New York: Praeger, 1970) and *Neighborhood Government in a Metropolitan Setting* (Beverly Hills, Calif.: Sage, 1974).

73. For a fuller description of the New World Foundation Survey of Community Self Help Groups, see the Appendix.

74. Wim Wiewel and Albert Hunter, "The Interorganizational Network as a Resource: A Comparative Case Study of Organizational Genesis," *Administrative Science Quarterly* 30 (1985), 482–496.

Appendix

The New World Survey of Community Self-Help Organizations

CARL MILOFSKY

The New World Survey of Community Self-Help Groups whose results are reported in this book was undertaken as a beginning step to rectify the lack of theory and comparative data that exists on community organizations. Since an adequate structural theory of these small organizations was lacking, the goal of the survey was exploratory. The patchwork quilt of research which referred to these organizations suggested a number of theoretical propositions, but they were largely untested in any systematic way. This study would be primarily exploratory and directed at theoretical development rather than systematic description or the use of probability theory to test specific propositions about the nature of the population of community organizations.[1] Lacking either a rigorous set of theoretical propositions or a clear notion of what it means to talk about a population of community organizations, conventional survey research was not practical. Our goal was rather to conduct something like a large-scale case study—a case study with two hundred focal organizations.

When the New World Foundation approached us to help them conduct a national survey of community self-help organizations, the opportunity was a good one, even though the study would be carried out with fewer resources than are normally required to conduct a systematic survey research project.[2] We collected names of community organizations from across the United States carrying on as many different kinds of activities as possible. We then mailed out 2000 questionnaires to directors of community self-help organizations. The instrument sought detailed answers on six aspects of organizational structure: (1) the technical functions organizations performed, (2) the demography of the communities they served, (3) the extent to which achieving democratic governance was an organizational concern, (4) the extent of differentiation and hierarchy within the organization, (5) the nature of interorganizational contacts possessed by organizations, and (6) sources of resources for the organization. Ultimately we received 256 returns. Fifty-six of these were removed from the study because data were incomplete or because the organizations served national or regional rather than local constituencies. In addition to questionnnaires, we received annual reports and information describing programs from many of the organizations.

Under normal survey research conditions, a 10% response rate would be disappointing because it would make it difficult to generalize our findings and to make assertions about the population. In this case the response rate is what one would expect and, given the goals of this project, it is acceptable. We went out of our way to find community organizations that were highly participatory, informal, and neighborhood based. However, these organizations are unstable and difficult to survey in a national study such as ours. Old lists of organizations (and in this case one year is old) often do not have the names of currently active members. Furthermore, these organizations are so diverse that it is difficult to construct a questionnaire which seems equally relevant to everyone. Our questionnaire worked well where organizations had paid staffs and definite programs, but it was difficult to complete for leaders of block clubs whose organizaitons lacked budgets and formal structure. Despite problems surveying small, participatory organizations our data contain responses from such organizations. More than 10% of our respondents have no paid staff and 12% have annual budgets below $10,000.

For our purposes it was more important to achieve diversity among our respondents than to gain a high response rate. We might have sought a sampling frame which would have given our sample a more defined character. In 1981, for example, we obtained files on 2000 organizations from the Neighborhood Information Sharing Exchange (NISE), which until 1980 had provided networking services to neighborhood organizations under a contract from the Department of Housing and Urban Development. The NISE organizations are similar to those in the New World (NW) study although the data we have on them are too fragmentary to use for research purposes and they became available too late to use as a sampling frame for the New World Survey.

Even had the NISE data been available earlier, we probably would not have have used this file as a sampling frame because it would not have included a diverse enough collection of organizations for study. Comparing the NISE and NW organizations, we find that 65% of the former are engaged in building construction, or economic development activities (major activities of HUD) whereas only 32% of NW are so occupied.[3] NISE organizations also obtain the preponderance of their funding either from the federal government or from local government sources. NW organizations although relying on government funds draw as well from foundations, state governments, private fund-raising organizations, and their own earned income. Being heavily sponsored by government agencies, NISE organizations have larger budgets than do NW organizations, and they tend to have more employees than NW organizations even when they carry out the same activities. That means we probably have many more small, voluntaristic organizations in the NW sample than in the NISE file.

The greater diversity of the NW file is critical for the exploratory and explanatory research we have undertaken here. A central question organizational research on community organizations must address is how government funding affects the participatory character of community based organizations. On one hand, many argue that government funding means neighborhood groups will have large budgets, that they will be hampered by having to adhere to numerous regulations, and that ultimately the groups will become formal, bureaucratic, and distant from community residents. On the other hand, the community literature emphasizes the value of organizations created and run by volunteers, relying heavily on donated resources.

A sampling frame like the NISE data base would have weighted our sample with large organizations dependent on government. We know very little about small participatory organizations. How many are there? What do they do? Do they persist over time? How does one obtain lists of them? At what point do groups cease being organizations and become instead aggregations of neighbors? There are no answers for these questions at present. We need them to try seriously to construct a sampling frame that would include the array of organizations contained within the category of community organizations. Lacking these answers, we instead sought only to produce examples of many different kinds of community groups. We are not providing a sample from a population. Rather, we are trying to generate theories about the structure of community organizations which as much as possible encompasses the diversity which exists among them. Theory about these organizations has up to now been fragmentary. We seek explanatory theories which can be tested in more systematic surveys.

To enrich our data, in 1983–1984 we conducted a follow-up survey of the 200 organizations whose responses are included in the chapters of this book. After a preliminary analysis of the 1978 data, we selected five items which were printed and sent out on self-return postcards. We then conducted a telephone follow-up of organizations which did not return cards or whose cards were not returned by the post office. We achieved an 89.5% response by using these methods and consequently can use the 1978 data to explore the causes of long term survival and of organizational death.

THE ORGANIZATIONS

What are the sample organizations like? When asked what "major function" they perform, respondents were most heavily concentrated in the three general areas of community development, social service, and advocacy as Appendix Table 1 shows. Community development groups are evenly divided between those that undertake physical development projects and those that engage in economic development. Both sorts of organizations tend to have small staffs, large budgets, and heavy dependence on government funding, especially local government funding. Social service organizations are primarily composed of those that provide educational services

Appendix Table 1 Major Functions Performed by Sample
Organizations

Major Function of Organization	Number	Percentage
Technical Assistance		
1. Technical Assistance	6	3
Community Development		
2. Economic Development	32	16
3. Physical Development	32	16
Social Services		
4. Education	13	7
5. Health	4	2
6. Law	2	1
7. Social Services	20	10
Governance		
8. Federations of organizations	3	1
9. Governance	10	5
Advocacy		
10. Advocacy	71	35
Culture		
11. Arts and Culture	7	4
Total	200	100

NOTE: Functions are arrayed from those that are more project oriented, and presumably more administratively intensive, to those that require more community involvement and thus probably produce a more participatory organization. This array corresponds to the variable FUNCTION reported in Chapter 10.

or those that supply a variety of social services. There is little representation among either health or law and justice organizations. Social service organizations tend to be more eclectic in their fund-raising than other organizations drawing income from fees, from federal sponsorship, and from private funders such as the United Way. The largest group of organizations describe themselves as advocacy organizations. These organizations tend to draw funding heavily from the private sector, especially from churches and foundations.

Most of the organizations claim to represent a specific geographic area, although as we see in Appendix Table 2 about 10% do not and another 16.5% do not identify with any local political jurisdiction. Included among those organizations that serve no specific areas are some providing technical assistance and some federations. Among those that could not find the type of area they serve in our list are organizations that serve states or other large areas—rural farmworkers' organizations, for example—and others that serve very small groups outside of cities—a block club in a small city might enter "none of the above". We have reviewed each of these organizations and decided that they are concerned with neighborhood and community development at the local level even though they do not identify with the kinds of areas we listed in the questionnaire. Orga-

Appendix Table 2 Type of Area Served by Organizations

	Number	Percentage
Part of a Major City	59	29.5
All of a Major City	20	10.0
Suburb	4	2.0
Satellite City	5	2.5
Small City	7	3.5
Rural Area	43	21.5
None of the Above	33	16.5
Serve No Single Area	25	12.5
No Response on This Item	4	2.0
Total	200	100.0

nizations that did not fit this standard—national organizations, narrowly technical organizations, and special interest lobbies are examples—were among the 56 organizations removed from the file. Thus, whether or not organizations report serving a specific area we judged all 200 "neighborhood based organizations."

Among the remaining organizations, most work in or near large cities. About one-third of the organizations work in parts of large cities—presumably neighborhoods. About 12% serve all of some large city, addressing the needs either of some particular interest or ethnic group or being the sole provider of some service. A small number of organizations work nonurban settlements (suburbs, satellite cities, or small cities away from major urban areas). About one-quarter of the organizations serve specific rural areas. Taking all of these numbers together, about two-thirds of the organizations are clearly neighborhood based. Others serve special interest groups and are not so clearly focused on a particular geographic area.

The communities served are predominantly low and moderate income as we see in Appendix Table 3. Twenty percent served communities whose mean income in 1978 was about $2500, and another 42% served communites with mean incomes of about $7500. These would have been poverty communities. Another 30% had mean incomes of about $13,000, and the remaining 6% represented wealthier communites. Forty-nine organizations provided no data, presumably because they either serve no area (25) or they serve areas not usefully described as having an average income (the 20 that served all of major cities, for example).

The communities are ethnically diverse. Thirty-eight percent of them are less than 50% White, whereas 25% are more than 90% White. One-quarter of the communities have more than 35% Blacks, and 10% have more than 60% Blacks. One-quarter have 10% or more Hispanics, and 10% have 30% or more Hispanics. This means that within the sample we have some communities that are quite homogeneous in terms of ethnicity and others that are mixed. We also have communities with substantial non-White ethnic minorities.

Appendix Table 3 Approximate Median Income of the Community
Organizations Serve

Mean Income Level	Number	Percentage	Cumulative Percentage
$ 2,500	30	15	15
$ 7,500	64	32	47
$13,000	48	24	71
$20,000	5	3	74
$25,000	4	2	76
Serve No Area or Area Cannot Be Described as Having Average Income	49	24	100
Total	200	—	—

When we look at structural characteristics of the organizations we also
find substantial variation. Our organizations tended to be quite young—
nearly two-thirds were less than eight years old and one-third were less
than four years old. Only 9% were more than sixteen years old. This corresponds with a widely held perception that the sixties and seventies were
a time that spawned new community organizations more rapidly than had
earlier periods. Since 65% of our 1978 respondents had survived in 1984,
it seems likely that we would have found older organizations had they
been there in 1978.

Despite being young, some of our organizations were quite large. As
Appendix Table 4 shows, the median budget size was $136,000 and 10%
had budgets over $1,000,000. At the other extreme, 12% had budgets
under $10,000. Ten percent of the organizations employed more than 45
people, whereas at the other extreme more than one-third employed 3 or
fewer and thirty-two organizations employed no one. The median number
of employees was 6. About 20% of the organizations claimed they had
between 1000 and 5000 members who had been active in the past six
months. Twelve percent reported they had fewer than twenty active members with the median being between 100 and 200 active members.

Most organizations carried on activities in several of the functional areas
listed in Appendix Table 1.1 with 58% carrying on programs in four or
more areas. This did not necessarily translate into administrative complexity. Nearly half of the organizations claimed to have no formal internal
divisions into departments. At the same time, among those organizations
that did create a formal administrative structure they tended to be quite
differentiated with more than a third reporting four or more departments.
Despite this differentiation, organizations tended to be flat in terms of hierarchy. About one-third claimed to have no hierarchy at all, and more
than 80% claimed to have two or fewer levels (a director and one layer of
subordinates would be two levels).

These data suggest that our sample included organizations that operated

Appendix Table 4   Size of Annual Budget for Sample Organizations

Size of Annual Budget	Number	Percentage	Cumulative Percentage
$10,000 or less	20	10	10
$10,001 to $50,000	35	18	28
$50,001 to $100,000	26	13	41
$100,001 to $200,000	32	16	57
$200,001 to $300,000	16	8	65
$300,001 to $400,000	10	5	70
$400,001 to $500,000	13	6	76
$500,001 to $600,000	4	2	80
$600,001 to $700,000	8	4	84
$700,001 to $800,000	5	3	87
$800,001 to $900,000	3	1	88
$900,001 to $1,000,000	3	1	89
$1,000,001 to $2,000,000	18	9	98
Over $2,000,000	3	1	99
Total	200		

Mean Income = $343,548   Median Income = $135,710

as professionalized, administratively formal social service agencies as well as ones that were highly participatory and democratic. One indication of this is the in-kind resources organizations collected, measured as a fraction of the value of their dollar budget. Forty-six percent of the organizations received few in-kind resources, their total value being less than 10% of the dollar budget. Fifteen percent of the organizations received more than one-quarter of their resources in the form of in-kind contributions. This corresponds to the findings of Chapter 10 that substantial numbers of these organizations did not depend on conventional grant making organizations for their funding resources.

In summary, these organizations are generally small and young. Many of them draw heavily on support from a lower income community, and most provide a variety of services. Organizations are primarily located either in large cities or in rural areas, and they serve a variety of ethnic groups. Some of the organizations are quite formal in their administrative structure, but others are quite participatory. The latter have many active members and receive substantial donated, in-kind resources that they must raise from their host community. These are all qualities we would expect to find among neighborhood based organizations.

NOTES

1. Earl Babbie, *Survey Research Methods* (Belmont, Calif.: Wadsowrth Publishing Company, 1973), pp. 58–59, discusses this rationale for survey research. Some surveys are used for exploratory purposes to develop the theoretical basis for later investigations. Lacking a

developed theoretical perspective, it may be difficult to identify an appropriate sampling frame. Without such a frame, it is impossible to generate a systematic random sample. Under such circumstances the best strategy is to seek a diverse set of respondents so that one's theory encompasses the range of variation likely to exist in the population. This was our approach.

2. For a report on the project see New World Foundation, *Initiatives for Community Self-Help* (New York: New World Foundation, 1980).

3. The New World Foundation survey was also funded in part by HUD. However, HUD's funds were more than matched by the New World Foundation, which ran the project. The New World Foundation had two goals for the project. First, it wished to publicize the importance of community self-help projects around the nation. It also wished to provide some pragmatic suggestions to decision makers in other foundations about how to evaluate proposals from neighborhood organizations in hopes that other foundations would provide more funding to neighborhood groups. Whereas NISE organizations included ones which were seeking funding from HUD, and some of which presumably had had success in raising such funds in the past, the organizations in the New World sample were not selected from a pool of organizations seeking funding. This no doubt contributed to the greater diversity of the NW sample.

Index

Allocation procedures, 138, 141, 161–162
Ambiguity, 88–90

Blacks, 229–230
Board
   of directors, 120
   members, 126
Bureaucratic constraints on coordination, 105
Bureaucratization, 77–78, 184–211
   efficiency of, 210

CAP, 31
Careers, 23
Career paths, 86
Carrying capacity, 48–49, 51, 73n
Cartel, 143
Categorical grants programs, 32–35, 40–41n, 219–220, 230
Charities, 136–139, 145, 146, 148
Charity market, 147
Chicago School, 244–247
Church-related organizations, 56–57, 223
Citizen participation, 30
Civic associations, 56–60
Closed systems, 21–24
   opinion formation, 27
Collective action, 261–262, 266–267, 271
Community, 20, 197
   as a background factor, 4
   boundaries, 22
   building, 185, 188, 198
   closed, 20–24, 195, 197–200, 201
   conflict, 29
   decision organizations, 29
   distributional structure, 20–24, 28
   erosion, 27
   level of distribution of resources, 63
   of limited liability, 10, 188, 192, 197
   open, 197

   organizing, 187, 248
   scarcity and, 21–24
Community Action Program, 207
Community Chest, 200
Community organizations, 193, 244, 257, 261. See also neighborhood based organizations; voluntary associations
   distribution of public resources, 31
   entrepreneurship, 36
   as an independent variable, 4
   resource dependency, 30
   self-help organizations, 187–191, 277–283
   task completion vs. solidarity, 16–17
   typology of, 5–12
Conceptual conflict, 102
Connectedness, 79, 95n
Coordination, 100, 102, 161
   defined, 101
   outcomes of, 108–110
   political contexts, 108–110
   symbolic value, 110–113
Corporations, 125
Cultural communities, 9
Cultural elites, 123
Cultural organizations, 119, 123–127

Day care, 170–180
   industry, 171
   subsidized, 176
Donors, 136–137, 146

Elderly-serving associations, 56–57
Entrepreneurs, 170, 183, 200
Exchange theory, 119–121

Filiarchy, 254
Formalization, 260
Foundations, 222–223, 257
Fraternal associations, 56–57
Free rider problem, 150

Funding
  arenas, 37–38, 217–240
  sources, 208
Fund-raising, 136, 184, 185

Gift relationship, 4
Governmental services, duplication of, 147
Grants, 32–33, 147, 148, 184, 211
Grantsmen, 183

Health appeals, combined, 146
Housing and Urban Development, Department of, 228, 278

In-kind donations, 217
Institutional perspective, 121–123, 248
Institutionalization, 190
Interorganizational
  distribution of resources, 63
  relations, 119–123, 185, 194
Isomorphism, 80
  and change, 87–89
  coercive, 81–82
  mimetic, 81–83, 88
  normative, 81, 84–87

Legitimacy, 122
Log linear, 127–129

March of Dimes, 185, 205
Market
  defined, 7
  signals, 25
Mass society, 20, 243
  community erosion in, 27–31
  decline of, 31–35
  distributional structure of, 24–27
  information problem, 25–27
Minneapolis-St. Paul, 124–125

Natural areas, 254
Nebraska Annual Social Indicators Survey, 52–53
Neighborhood, 246, 249
  resources, 255–256
Neighborhood based organizations. See also community organizations; voluntary associations
  defined, 3
  and markets, 8
  resource dependency, 30, 217–240
Neighborhood Information Sharing Exchange, 278

Networks, 246, 248–250, 253–257, 263, 269–271
  defined, 6
  of organizations, 265
New World Foundation, 225, 277–283
Niche, 43–48, 71n
  breadth, 45, 47, 55
  dimension, 44–45, 64
  overlap, 55–56
  volume, 47
Nonprofit, organizations, 170, 218

OEO, 31–35
Open systems, 21–, 24–27
Organizational
  boundaries, 189, 196
  change, 95n
  demography, 63
  field, 78–79, 89–91, 217
  legitimacy, 122
  mechanisms, 186
  myths, 122
  rationality, 190, 191
  size, 71n
  structure, 259–261, 270
  theory, 78, 164–165, 217
Organizations, 248
  collectivist, 188, 191–197
  competition for members, 49, 64
  complex, 190
  ecological competition, 49–50, 67–68
  equilibrium distribution, 62
  homogenization of, 80–82
  inclusive, 201
  loosely coupled, 88–89
  participatory, 185–211
  specialist vs. generalist, 56–57, 62, 66–67, 78
  survival, 228–240
Organizing, 185
  problems, 186, 195

Participation, 24, 30
  multidimensional, 28
Patronage, 119
Payroll deductions, 145, 146, 157
Population ecology model of organizations, 42–43
  difficulty of testing, 58
Prestige, 126–127, 132–133
Primary groups, 254
Priority planning, 140, 141
Professional associations, 56–57, 192

Professional resistance to coordination, 103–105
Professionalism, 84–87, 91, 184, 228, 260
PTA, 202
Public funding priorities, 147

Red Cross, 185, 199–200, 203
Resources, 88, 90, 258–259
 allocation, 139, 140
 dependency, 255, 258, 261
 economic vs human, 252, 259
 in interorganizational relations, 119–121
 mobilization, 244, 248, 257, 263, 270
 in organizational ecology, 43, 217

Salvation Army, 203
SDS, 186, 204
Secondary functions, 203
Self-help organizations, 30
 and resource dependency, 30
Social movement perspective, 248, 257
Social services, 137, 146, 156
Social system, crystalized vs. interactive, 4
Spatial ecology, 249–250
Sports associations, 56–57
Status groups, 193
Structural equivalence, 79
Symbolic
 construction perspective, 254
 issues, 100
 resources, 256–257
 sentiments, 254–255

Technical assistance organizations, 208
Transactions of exchange, 132

United Funds, 136–150, 157–168, 219–220, 227
 admission, 159–160, 167–168
 decision processes, 164–167
 membership practices, 145, 158–159
 monopoly power of, 143, 146, 157
 organizational structure, 160–164
 responsiveness to community, 159–160
 as a substitute government, 149

Voluntarism, 187
Voluntary associations, 44–70, 187, 239, 258. See also community organizations; neighborhood based organizations
 community conflict and, 29
 critical variables, 4
 markets and, 8
 networks and, 6
 niche breadths, 54–55
 as social building blocks, 17–18, 28
 typology of, 5
Volunteers, 140, 184, 200, 235, 236, 260

War on Poverty, 188, 247
Welfare state, 147

YMCA, 185, 205, 207, 208, 218
Youth-serving associations, 56–57